THE COMPLETE
BOOK OF VEGETABLES

THE COMPLETE BOOK OF
VEGETABLES

THE ULTIMATE GUIDE TO GROWING, COOKING AND EATING VEGETABLES

MATTHEW BIGGS

REVISED EDITION WITH A FOREWORD BY
JEAN-CHRISTOPHE NOVELLI

FIREFLY BOOKS

To Gill, Jessica, Henry, and Chloe

A FIREFLY BOOK

Published by Firefly Books Ltd. 2010

First printing

Publisher Cataloging-in-Publication Data (U.S.)

Biggs, Matthew.
   The complete book of vegetables : the ultimate guide to growing, cooking and eating vegetables / Matthew Biggs.
[280] p. : ill. (chiefly col.), photos. (chiefly col.) ; cm.
Includes bibliographical resources and index.
Summary: Advice on planting, growing, harvesting, preserving and eating vegetables; includes lists of gardening suppliers and sources for further information.
ISBN-13: 978-1-55407-581-2 (pbk.)
ISBN-10: 1-55407-581-5 (pbk.)
1. Vegetable gardening. 2. Vegetables. I. Title.
635 dc22   SB320.9B544 2009

Library and Archives Canada Cataloguing in Publication

Biggs, Matthew
   The complete book of vegetables : the ultimate guide to growing, cooking and eating vegetables /
Matthew Biggs.
Includes bibliographical references and index.
ISBN-13: 978-1-55407-581-2
ISBN-10: 1-55407-581-5
1. Vegetable gardening. 2. Cookery (Vegetables). I. Title.
SB320.9.B53 2009   635   C2009-903558-8

Published in the United States by
Firefly Books (U.S.) Inc.
P.O. Box 1338, Ellicott Station
Buffalo, New York 14205

Published in Canada by
Firefly Books Ltd.
66 Leek Crescent
Richmond Hill, Ontario L4B 1H1

Acknowledgments

With thanks to Kyle Cathie for taking a chance, and to Candida Hall and Penny David for their expertise, patience and encouragement. To Suzanna de Jong for her skill, enthusiasm and constant cheerfulness, Jean-Christophe Novelli for allowing us to use his recipes and Tina Carter for her persistence. Also to Marilyn Ward and Jill Cowley at the Royal Botanic Gardens, Kew; Charles Grace for information on tamarillo; Karen Box and Peter Lipsham in New Zealand; Mike Darcy and the late Robert Fleming in the U.S.; Simon Hickmott for his willingness to experiment; and Anita Bean, Consultant Nutritionist to the Fresh Fruit and Vegetable Information Bureau. Finally, thanks to Ray Desmond and my wife Gill for her support and administrative skills.

Publisher's note

An asterisk (*) beside a variety name indicates a vegetable that has received an award from the Royal Horticultural Society (see page 268).

Author's note on organic vs. chemical

Since writing the original edition, organic gardening has become mainstream and the choice of available chemicals is being reduced. I am delighted to say that this book is based on organic techniques for pest control. However, if you would prefer to use synthetic chemicals, it is your right to continue to do so — but I won't be coming around for dinner!

Printed in China

CONTENTS

FOREWORD BY JEAN-CHRISTOPHE NOVELLI

As a Frenchman with Italian ancestors, the food traditions of these two beautiful countries run deep in my veins. Both in France and in Italy, cooking with fresh, local ingredients is a given, a part of everyday life, and when I was a child the vegetable garden was at the center of many family activities. That, and the kitchen, of course! Even now, freshly dug up vegetables conjure up pleasant childhood memories — of time spent together tending and nurturing our plants into bearing produce, and cooking with the results of our labor.

In the kitchen, no one, from Michelin-starred chefs to maman Novelli, can fully demonstrate their skills without the finest, freshest ingredients to work with. In my kind of cooking, meat and fish are often the heroes of a dish, but they would be nothing without a supporting cast of vegetables to provide color, flavor and texture.

There is no question that homegrown vegetables taste better than anything store-bought — you only have to savor the aroma of a freshly-picked tomato to realize the difference. Grow them in your garden and you minimize the time between harvesting and cooking; you take away the need to chill them, handle them excessively and haul them over long distances. It is easy to see why they taste so amazing.

Matt and I started working together when he joined the Novelli Academy, sharing his expertise on vegetable gardening with my students and bringing it into practice in the Academy's kitchen garden. It's very important to me that my students learn to appreciate the finesse and flavor that homegrown vegetables add to a dish — my beet gazpacho always tastes best when I use beets from my own vegetable patch!

The Complete Book of Vegetables shows the incredible range of vegetable varieties available from seed catalogs these days — more than you will ever find in stores. Grow your own and you have a world of culinary experiences in your garden; a crop of sweet peppers, for example, could take you on a culinary journey from France's delicious pipérade, past the indulgent pimientos fritos (fried peppers) of Spain to a hearty goulash in Hungary. And that's just one vegetable...

I am very pleased that it's becoming more and more popular to grow your own vegetables, and with *The Complete Book of Vegetables* anyone can try it. Matt's brilliant instructions show you how easy it can be, whether you have a tiny windowsill or a large garden to work with. Thanks to Matt, you'll know exactly what to do and when; even when a family of slugs comes to visit your patch, you will have a green and friendly solution on hand. Follow his advice and not only will you be eating your own produce in no time — and believe me, there is nothing quite like it — but it will also become a pleasure to eat your "five a day."

Bon appétit!
Jean-Christophe Novelli

INTRODUCTION

We all have to eat to survive, and there is nothing like homegrown vegetables to increase that pleasure. To some people eating was, and still is, a rather functional process, while the more privileged have developed it into a cultural experience and a pastime to be enjoyed. Plants are the basis of the food chain — even for meat eaters — and vegetables make a meal more delicious. They are visually attractive, nutritious and essential for a balanced diet, adding a range of flavors and interest to a meal. The greater the choice of vegetables we have, the more exciting our culinary experience will be.

For centuries, vegetable gardens throughout the world have been the focal point of family and community survival. From the Middle Ages onward in rural Europe, vegetables were grown of necessity and villagers cultivated turnips, leeks, kales and cabbages as part of their simple diet. Later, cottage gardens contained a mixture of vegetables, herbs and flowers for providing food, medicine, flavoring, ornament and a nectar supply for bees. Where every plant had a part to play, flowers grown only for their ornamental value were considered a luxury.

This philosophy still prevails in France, where vegetable gardening has been refined to create the "potager" or ornamental vegetable garden, satisfying an artistic and practical need. The finest example exists at the chateau garden at Villandry in the Loire Valley, where formal borders are embellished with a magnificent array of vegetables. Why not try this on a smaller scale at home? There is a wholesome beauty in a display of vegetables — a row of vibrantly colored ruby chard, 'January King' cabbages dusted with snow, the aristocratic foliage of globe artichokes — all have a unique yet distinctive charm. I hope this book encourages you to experiment further.

The French also revolutionized eating, changing it into an artistic experience in which every meal was considered an important occasion. After the French Revolution and the fall of the aristocracy, many chefs — finding themselves unemployed — opened restaurants and, in time, social eating became widespread. For the wealthy, fine food had always provided an opportunity to indulge in pleasures both sensual and cultural; a meal was the ideal occasion to savor the exquisite flavors of fresh vegetables, meat, fish, good wine and fruit as well as a time for conviviality and friendship. The social aspect of eating is still an essential part of the pleasure, and a satisfying meal in good company should last for many hours. It is, of course, also an opportunity for the chef to show his or her skill in the preparation and presentation of food.

But what would a meal be without vegetables? They add finesse to a dish that meat alone cannot provide. And where would a cook be without recipes? Where the gardener's skill finishes, culinary creativity takes over. While researching this book I became aware of exciting developments in cooking with vegetables, stimulated by the increasing popularity of vegetarianism. Such new ideas elevate even the most basic crops to tantalizing heights: I hope you will find the recipes given here tempting.

Too many people treat the ubiquitous vegetable with indifference rather than appreciation. Yet these loyal servants not only provide our daily food, but also help maintain health and cure ills. It is believed that Henry VIII of England (1491–1547) died from malnutrition due to a predominantly carnivorous diet! Some vegetables have an ancient and fascinating past, having been developed over many centuries, while others have even influenced social and political history — most notably our good friend, the common potato.

During the Industrial Revolution many people were uprooted from their rural heritage as they turned to the cities. Now many of those working in cities are seeking their rural past, creating community gardens. There is certainly a resurgence of interest in vegetable growing. What's more, an increasing number of people are determined to grow vegetables organically, free from health-damaging chemicals, taking the opportunity to be "in touch with the soil" while enjoying fresh air and exercise. Vegetable growing is more uplifting and undoubtedly more productive that a visit to the gym — what can be a better reward for your efforts that a tasty meal with fine homegrown vegetables?

The Vegetable Garden, Coombe by Paul Riley, 1988

I heartily recommend that everyone tries their hand at growing vegetables. You only have a balcony? Use buckets, boxes, windowboxes or pots — almost any container will do. Grow mini vegetables or dot them among your flowers. Are you uninspired by the same old veg? Experiment with lesser known varieties, oriental vegetables or exotics such as okra; enliven your salads with white cucumbers, bicolored beets, red spring onions and red-fleshed radishes.

With careful planning, your vegetable garden can be productive for much of the year, providing an endless supply of fresh vegetables and enabling you to fill your freezer. And who can argue that a commercially produced vegetable, jaded after its journey from field to supermarket, is comparable with those eaten straight from the garden, bursting with vitality and packed with goodness and flavor?

Vegetable growing is tremendously fulfilling and should not be seen as the exclusive domain of gruff old men in baggy jeans and baseball caps, wandering around their yards. Nor are vegetables inferior to flowers, as so many people erroneously seem to think. To neglect them would be a great loss. Not only are they part of our history, they greatly enrich the present and are vital to sustain our future. Don't just take my word for it. This book is intended to help, inspire and encourage you to get out into the garden. Go on, try it, enjoy yourself, and discover the pleasures of good eating!

HISTORY OF VEGETABLES

The selection of food crops is believed to have been a process of trial and error. Plants were sampled and remembered for being either pleasant tasting, or unpleasant and to be avoided. This same process must have also led to the selection of medicinal plants. There would have been times of considerable hardship and even fatalities as people gradually found out what could be eaten and how it should be prepared — as with the discovery that cassava was edible only after washing several times to remove the injurious calcium oxalate crystals.

Early humans collected food from the surrounding countryside and followed migrating animals. The first settlements were established in areas where food was plentiful all year round; one of the earliest, found in Tehuacan in southern central Mexico, dates from 5000 BCE. Later came the discovery that seeds could be planted and nurtured to ensure easily accessible food supplies.

Cereals and peas were the first crops to be domesticated. Cultivated wheat and barley have been found dating from 8000 BCE to 7000 BCE and peas from 6500 BCE, while rice was recorded as a staple in China by 2800 BCE. Later crops such as oats, which have been in cultivation only since 2000 BCE, may well have originated as weeds among cultivated crops.

The most productive areas were along great rivers, where the vast flood plains were ideal for constructing dwellings and growing crops. Here civilizations developed like those in the "Fertile Crescent" of Mesopotamia, in the flood plains of the Euphrates and Tigris, and in Egypt, along the Nile and its delta. Annual flooding brought deposits of rich, fertile alluvial soil, and the rivers together with their gods were respected and revered for their bounty. Agriculture became highly developed and complex irrigation systems were established. The sophistication of these societies seems to indicate that once a regular, plentiful food supply was guaranteed, other parts of their culture were developed — in Egypt many cultivated vegetables were an integral part of the system of medicine.

With domestication came early selection of plants for beneficial characteristics such as yield, disease resistance and ease of germination. These were the first cultivated varieties, or "cultivars."

This has continued extensively and by the 18th century in Europe, seed selection became a fine art in the hands of skilled gardeners. Gregor Mendel's work with peas in 1855–64 in his monastery garden at Brno in Moravia was one of the most significant discoveries, leading to the development of hybrids and scientific selection. This has evolved to the extent that plant breeders are now able to change the genetic makeup of plants using x-rays and colchicine, a chemical extracted from the autumn crocus or *Colchicum*. Most development has centered on the major food crops. Minor crops like sea kale have changed very little, apart from the selection of a few cultivars. Others, like most carrots, are similar to their wild relatives, but the roots are larger and more tender.

A Russian botanist, Nikolai Vavilov, concluded there were up to 12 main centers of origin, including North Africa, the Mediterranean and Asia. Food crops traveled from one central point with expanding populations and invading armies. Migrating peoples took maize from the Andes to Central and later North America, while the Romans (who were certainly cultivating beets, cabbage, kale and asparagus) took vegetables, including peas, to distant parts of their empire. In later years settlers took their crops to new lands. Polynesians took the sweet potato to New Zealand, where it became a staple, and Europeans took their crops to Australia, where, prior to their arrival in 1788, the Aborigines were "hunter-gatherers" and had no domesticated crops.

The greatest exchange of foods began in 1492 with the discovery of the "New World." Columbus returned with maize and took European crops to the new lands. Less than one hundred years later potatoes were being sold in Spain; by the end of the 17th century, maize was a staple crop in the Iberian peninsula and chilies were being added to the curries in India.

There are estimated to be between 250 and 350 plant families, yet our main food crops are derived from just 10. From one single species, *Brassica oleracea*, comes a diverse variety of vegetables: kale and cabbage are grown for the leaves, cauliflower and broccoli for the immature flower heads, and kohlrabi for the swollen stem bases. *Leguminosae* provide us

Large kitchen gardens were formerly attached to great houses: *Vegetable Garden at Charlton Park* by Thomas Robins, c. 1745

In the past, varieties were maintained by saving seeds after harvest for sowing the following year. Many were local or regional cultivars that had been bred or selected specifically to flourish in the soil, climate and other growing conditions of the area. Staple crops like the potato were widely developed and there are many regional varieties, like 'Edzell Blue' from Edzell near Forfar in Scotland. Others were developed by enthusiasts such as Donald Mackelvie on the Isle of Arran in Scotland, who sold his general store and became a full-time potato breeder. He introduced about 20 different varieties, the most famous of these being 'Arran Pilot'.

Yet the existence of such diversity and genetic richness is under threat. If varieties are lost, material for breeding new cultivars will disappear. Many old types have fallen from favor, displaced by modern, standardized cultivars in bright, glossy packages. This valuable resource is protected by enthusiasts and societies such as Seed Savers in the United States and Seed Savers International. The future of crop breeding is in their hands and they deserve our support.

Another exchange of vegetables took place with the fall of the Berlin Wall, opening up another "new world" with invaluable new varieties, such as cold-resistant tomatoes, emerging from the former Eastern bloc. This — and the advent of refrigeration and air transport, allowing even the most perishable of vegetables to travel — has introduced new cultivars and "exotic" vegetables to the West. Chinese, West Indian and Asian immigrants have contributed their culinary heritage to North America, enriching the diet of those around them. Many grow their own crops which, I am certain, will gradually become more widely accepted — the potato and tomato were once "exotics." For vegetable growers and lovers of good food, the future looks tasty indeed!

St Paul de Vence **by Margaret Loxton**

with peas and many kinds of beans, *Gramineae* with cereals like wheat and barley, plus corn and rice, and *Solanaceae* contribute potatoes, tomatoes, sweet peppers and chilies.

FADS & FASHIONS

While some vegetables have remained universally popular, others have waxed and waned, remained peripheral or become regional specialities. Consistently high yields over a long harvesting season — particularly when few other vegetables are available — coupled with versatility, have guaranteed the establishment of many vegetables. Winter brassicas are a good example of this.

Regional popularity can be attributed to several factors, one of which is climatic suitability. Hamburg parsley, for instance, has been widely grown in Central Europe (notably Germany) for centuries because of its robust nature and ability to crop successfully in such a climate. Yet it never achieved the same status in other countries, even if the conditions were equally favorable. Why not? It could be argued that a taste for it was never "acquired." When it was introduced to Great Britain, similar, better quality vegetables such as parsnip with its larger roots and the more refined curled parsley were already well established. The level of popularity enjoyed by Hamburg parsley was never enough to persuade those who cultivated it to save and distribute widely. And so it simply remained a peripheral vegetable which never gained a footing in Great Britain.

Trends are set by commercial producers seeking marketing opportunities or by innovative, wealthy or famous people whose opinions are valued and actions mimicked because they are considered to be "arbiters of taste." This applies to trends in clothes, fine wines and many forms of entertainment, and extends to the adoption of another country's cuisine. The cuisine of France and Italy, for instance, is regarded as the height of good taste and so many seek to imitate it. Endive, arugula and chicory are perfect illustrations of current "trendy" salad crops from continental Europe. Fads and fashions have always been part of vegetable gardening, be they varieties or techniques. The spotlight is currently on microgreens, seed sprouts that are eaten before the first true leaves appear. But will they establish themselves as "mainstream" or fade away? Only time will tell.

VEGETABLES
A–Z

MUSHROOMS, EDIBLE FUNGI

Simple organisms growing on decaying substrate or symbiotically with living plants, some with edible fruiting bodies. Half hardy/tender. Value: low in calories, moderate potassium, linoleic and folic acid, carbohydrates, iron, niacin and B vitamins.

Fungi are extraordinary organisms: lacking both chlorophyll and root systems, they are more akin to molds and yeasts than to traditional vegetable plants. The fleshy mushroom that you eat is a fruiting body, dispersing spores in order to reproduce in the same way that plant fruits disperse seeds. Instead of drawing nutrients through roots, however, a fungus is sustained by a network of fine — often microscopic — threads (known collectively as the *mycelium*). This can extend over vast distances into rotting wood, soil or some other preferred medium. To help identify a fungus it is important to know the particular substrate on which it depends, or the higher plant species with which it lives in symbiosis (certain fungi, for example, grow only in the vicinity of specific trees such as birch or oak); when attempting to cultivate any kind of mushroom, you must provide similarly congenial conditions.

However, few of the many thousand fungus genera are amenable to cultivation. Even in nature, fruiting is wildly unpredictable: the organism depends on precise moisture and temperature variables to produce fruiting bodies, and more generally is sensitive to environmental changes such as recent air pollution and high nitrate levels.

Their erratic behavior and mysterious origins — allied with the deadly toxins some contain — have given rise to a love-hate attitude toward fungi. Some have been collected as "wild food" since ancient times. The Romans esteemed them as a delicacy and the rich employed collectors to find the most desirable species. However, Gerard, writing in his *Herball*, remained unimpressed: "few…are good to be eaten and most of them do suffocate and strangle the eater." John Evelyn advised that all types of mushrooms should be kept well out of the kitchen.

By the late 17th century, varieties of *Agaricus* began to be grown in underground caves in the Paris region, in which giant heaps of manure were impregnated with soil taken from areas where field and horse mushrooms grew naturally. For many centuries cultivated mushrooms were a delicacy enjoyed only by the wealthy, and from the 18th century most stableyards had a shady corner where there was a mushroom bed. Some garden owners had outhouses converted to provide ideal growing conditions: George IV had a large mushroom house at Kensington Palace in London. In seasons when wild or cultivated crops were plentiful, surplus mushrooms were conserved in the form of sauces and ketchups, and only recently has the role of mushroom sauce in the kitchen been usurped by tomato sauce.

Cultivated *Agaricus* species have remained popular in North America and the English-speaking world, yet elsewhere they are eclipsed by other mushrooms. In Japan, velvet shank, nameko, oyster and shiitake mushrooms are established as the cultivated varieties, and some of them are slowly becoming popular in other countries.

A number of species is commercially available, some of them to amateur growers, and usually work by inoculating the growing medium with *mycelium* or "spawn." Home growing of many fungus species is in its infancy, but gaining ground each year. As adventurous gardeners and mushroom eaters increasingly experiment, advances in mushroom cultivation will also help to conserve wild species.

Ensure fungi are correctly identified before eating

 species

The following lists include several of the more common and better known edible fungi.

Commonly available for home cultivation

These fungi are grown commercially and can occasionally be bought from specialized suppliers as kits, "spawn" or impregnated dowels for inoculating logs. A notable advantage of buying mushrooms in this form is that you are assured of their identity. You should follow suppliers' detailed cultivation instructions carefully to increase the chances of success. Some producers have their own selected strains of these fungi.

Agaricus bisporus (cultivated mushroom, button mushroom) has a smooth white to brownish cap and white stem and flesh. Excellent flavor raw and cooked. This accounts for 60% of the world's mushroom production. Available as kits or spawn (see "Cultivation" below). Commercial growers are developing new races with color variation in the cap: watch out for them in the future as kits.

Flammulina velutipes (enokitake, velvet shank, velvet foot, winter mushroom) occurs naturally on dead wood and is grown commercially on sawdust, particularly in Japan. Small tan-yellow caps on dark brown stems. Do not eat stems and wipe or peel off any stickiness from the caps before cooking.

Hericium erinaceus (lion's mane, bearded tooth, hedgehog, pom pom, monkey head) produces large, rounded clusters of icicle-like growths that taste like lobster — delicious fried with butter and onions. Grows in the wild from wounds on living hardwoods such as beech, and can be cultivated on stumps or logs.

Cultivated mushrooms are easy to grow

Lentinula edodes (shiitake) is a small to medium sized mushroom with light brown stem and pale to dark reddish brown cap. Documents record this strongly flavored gourmet mushroom being eaten in 199 CE and it is the second most important cultivated fungus. In Japan it is grown commercially on logs of chestnut, oak or hornbeam. Different forms tolerate warmer or colder conditions, and include **'Snowcap'**, a thick-fleshed form with a long fruiting season, grown on large logs, and **'West Wind'**, which is ideal for inexperienced growers, yielding well over a long period.

Pholiota nameko (nameko, viscid mushroom) is among the four most important fungi cultivated in Japan. Grows in clusters on tree trunks or wood chips. Orange-brown caps atop paler stems are 2–2½ inches in diameter. It is pleasantly aromatic.

Pleurotus (or oyster mushroom) is a genus with a number of distinct species and strains. Popular in Japan and Central Europe, they are increasingly available in kit form, or can be grown from plugs of spawn. Eat when small, discarding the tough stem. Sauté in butter until tender, season, then add cream or yogurt. The first two are fairly common in the wild and are also offered in seed catalogs.

Pleurotus ostreatus (oyster mushroom) has large fan-shaped caps, slate-blue to white in color and with white or pale straw-colored gills; used coffee grounds (sterilized as the coffee is brewed) are becoming a popular medium for inoculating with the spawn.

P. cornucopiae (golden oyster) has a white stem with a cream cap turning to ocher-brown. Grows on the cut stumps of deciduous trees, usually elm or oak. Other species may be harder to find, and some need warmth to fruit.

P. ergyngii (king trumpet, king oyster, french horn) has a concave cap, whitish becoming gray-brown. It tastes sweet and meaty and grows in clusters on the decaying roots of plants in the carrot family. It can be grown on chopped straw.

P. flabellatus is an oyster mushroom with pink caps.
P. pulmonarius has brown or gray caps.
P. samoneus-tramineus from Asia is pink-capped.
P. sajor-caju has brown caps.

Stropharia rugosoannulata (king stropharia, wine

Chanterelles

cap, burgundy) is a brown-capped, violet-gilled fungus commonly cultivated in eastern Europe; it is claimed to be capable of growing in vegetable gardens. It requires a substrate of humus containing rotting hardwood or sawdust. Grow spawn from reputable sources: lookalikes include the deadly *Cortinarius* species.

Volvariella volvaceae (Chinese or straw mushroom, paddy straw, padi-straw) has a gray-brown cap, often marked with black, and a dull-brown stem. Grown on composted rice straw, it is regarded as an expensive delicacy in China and other Asian countries. Needs high temperatures and humidity to grow well. Harvest when it is immature.

Naturally occurring edible fungi
Many edible species of fungi may be found growing in your garden if it happens to provide the host trees or other conditions that form their natural habitat. In Continental Europe, fungi collected in the wild are often sold in markets; but local pharmacists or health inspectors are on hand to verify that those on sale are edible species.

NEVER EAT WILD FUNGI UNLESS YOU HAVE FIRST HAD THEIR IDENTITY CONFIRMED BY AN EXPERT

Agaricus arvensis (horse mushroom) and
A. campestris (field mushroom) are cousins of the cultivated mushroom, found in clusters or rings in grazed or mowned grassland. Dome-shaped white "buttons" open to wide caps. Horse mushrooms can grow to soup-plate size with thick, firm flesh smelling of aniseed; the gills are pale grayish pink darkening to chocolate brown. Field mushrooms are smaller and rather more delicate in stature, with a "mushroomy" smell; their deep-pink gills go from dark brown to black.

Boletus edulis (porcini, cep, penny bun) grows on the ground near trees, favoring pine, beech, oak and birch woodlands. The rounded, bunlike brown cap (often covered with a white bloom when young) sits on a bulbous whitish stem — also edible. Tubelike pores (rather than gills) beneath the cap are white, turning dull yellow at maturity. This delicious, fleshy fungus is highly prized and can be eaten fresh, pickled or dried. Related species of *Boletus* are also edible.

Cantharellus cibarius (chanterelle, golden chanterelle) is funnel-shaped; egg yolk–yellow caps, fading with age, are thick and fleshy with gill-like wrinkles running down from the cap underside into the stem. Has a mild peppery aftertaste when eaten raw and an excellent flavor when cooked. True chanterelles grow on soil in broadleaf forests: similar-looking species are highly toxic.

Hirneola auricula judae, syn. ***Auricularia auricula-judae*** (wood-ear) looks like a human ear and is date-brown, drying to become small and hard. Found on living and dead elder, beech and sycamore. Can be dried and reconstituted with water. Popular in Taiwan and China.

Wild — and free!

Hypholoma capnoides, syn. ***Nematoloma capnoides***, is a gilled fungus found growing in clusters on conifer stumps. Caps 3/4–2 1/2 inches diameter are pale ocher with a buff-colored margin. Check identity carefully: other *Hypholoma* species are suspect.

If you can't grow your own, try shopping for a wide range of varieties

Oyster mushrooms

harbor dirt and insects — rinsing in water is advised.) Found on well-drained soils under deciduous trees, particularly in ash and elm woods, in gardens and near old hedges. Other edible species include **M. rotunda**, found on heavier soil, and **M. vulgaris**, on richer soil. Some similar-looking mushroom species are highly toxic.

Sparassis crispa (cauliflower mushroom, brain fungus) has a folded, rounded fruiting body, creamy white when young, which looks more like a cauliflower than a mushroom. It tastes nutty, with a spicy fragrance. Found at the base of pines and other conifers. As with morels, rinse to remove any debris.

Tuber melanosporum (the Périgord or black truffle), often found in oak woods, is highly desirable and the most valuable truffle. Pigs and trained dogs are used to sniff them out. Truffle-inoculated trees and hazel are now available to amateur gardeners but need specific growing conditions to flourish.

Pick fungi at their prime

Laetiporus sulphureus, syn. **Polyporus sulphureus** (chicken of the woods, sulfer shelf) is a bracket fungus found on many hardwoods and softwoods, often on sweet chestnut, oak and beech. Has the flavor of chicken breast and is an orange to sulfur-yellow color. Eat young, but only try a little the first time: it can cause nausea and dizziness in some people. The largest ever found weighed 100 pounds.

Langermannia gigantea (giant puffball) can be enormous: large and round with white skin, it sits on the ground like a giant soccer ball. The biggest ever recorded, according to the *Guinness Book of Records*, was 8⅔ feet in circumference and weighed 49 pounds! It is found on soil in fields, hedgerows, forests and gardens, often near nettles. Eat when young, while the flesh is pure white; it tastes good sliced, dipped in breadcrumbs and fried. Other related (and smaller) species of puffball are also edible while they remain white all through.

Lepista nuda (blewit, wood blewit, blue-stalk) is medium to large with a light cinnamon-brown to tan cap; the gills and stems are violet to lavender. It is found in forests, parks and hedges. It can be grown in leaf debris around compost heaps. Better eaten young, it is well flavored and particularly good in stews or fried. Never eat raw: cook thoroughly to remove traces of cyanic acid.

Marasmius oreades (fairy ring mushroom) is found on lawns in a "ring" of dark green grass with dying grass in the center. Small with a bell-shaped light tan-colored cap, matching gills and similar stem. Good in omelettes. Beware: similar looking species are toxic.

Morchella esculenta (common morel) is a delicious fungus that emerges annually in spring, earlier than most autumn-fruiters. The hollow cap has a surface covered in honeycomblike pits and varies from round to conical in shape. (The many crevices of the cap often

Boletus edulis — delicious

 ## cultivation

Propagation

Nameko mushrooms favor moist toilet paper rolls or arrive with packs of clean straw that the fungi grow on. It is also possible to cultivate mushrooms in the garden; the spawn of field mushrooms grows in rich soil and is an ideal candidate for cultivating around the compost heap, while blewit mushrooms thrive in a mixture of well-rotted leaf mold and pine needles. They are also grown using kits or on heaps of rotted horse manure.

It is also possible to buy mushroom growing kits or "logs" supplied with dowels inoculated with spores of fungi like shiitake, which are hammered into holes drilled in the logs, or to buy the dowels and use logs of beech, birch, oak or similar wood that have been harvested at home. Put them in the shed, cellar or a shady corner of the garden, in conditions similar to those enjoyed by shade-loving plants and cover them with damp sacking.

Mushroom logs take six months to a year to become productive; flushes of growth appear when temperatures drop in autumn, though shiitake logs can be shocked into production in summer by plunging them into cold water.

Each log crops for about three years.

Growing

Humidity is essential for success, along with a plentiful supply of organic matter. Choose a shady position and, on a moist day in spring or autumn, "plant" blocks of spawn, about the size of a golfball, 2 inches below the soil and 12 inches apart. A good crop of mushrooms often appears when spent mushroom compost is used as a mulch around other crops.

Maintenance

Indoor crops can be planted any time of the year. Plant spawn outdoors in spring or autumn.

Protected Cropping

Indoor crops grow well in an airy shed, cellar, greenhouse or cold frame. They do not need to be grown in the dark.

Container Growing

See "Propagation."

Harvesting and Storing

The first "button" mushrooms are ready for harvesting 4–6 weeks after "casing;" there may be another 2 weeks before the next "flush."

Harvesting lasts for about 6 weeks. To harvest, twist and pull mushrooms upward, disturbing the compost as little as possible, removing broken stalks and filling holes with "casing."

Mushrooms last in a ventilated plastic bag in the salad drawer of a refrigerator for up to 3 days. Most species can be dried. Thread them on to a string and hang them over a radiator or in an airing cupboard, then store in a cool dry place. Reconstitute with water or wine.

After the final harvest, you can use the spent mixture as a mulch; you should never try to respawn for a second crop.

Pests and Diseases

Mushroom fly can be a problem; pick mushrooms when young.

 ## medicinal

Edible fungi lower blood cholesterol, stimulate the immune system and deactivate viruses. Shiitake mushrooms are particularly effective. Wood-ear has been used in herbal medicine for treating sore throats.

 ## warning

If you gather wild mushrooms, be certain of their identity before eating. Best of all, collect with an expert. Those that are highly toxic are often similar to edible species. Mistakes can be fatal.

Feeling hungry yet?

culinary

Fungi should always be eaten fresh as the flavor is soon lost and the quality deteriorates. Avoid washing: the fruit bodies absorb water, spoiling the texture and flavor. Simply clean the surface by wiping with a damp cloth or brushing off any dirt. Peel only when necessary.

Both caps and stems of *Agaricus* species can be eaten. With some other fungi, stems may be discarded as inedibly tough. Check for any special instructions on preparation: some fungi, for instance, are toxic unless cooked.

Harvested cultivated mushrooms at the "button" stage can be eaten raw, added to salads; more mature caps can be baked, grilled or fried whole, or sliced and stir-fried, made into soups, pies or stuffings, added to stews or the stockpot, or used as a garnish. Other fungi can be prepared in many similar ways. Large fruit bodies can be stuffed.

Try frying in butter and a little lemon juice for 3–5 minutes. Brush with oil and seasoning and grill each side for 2–3 minutes. Add yogurt or cream before serving, or dip in breadcrumbs and fry. Garlic mushrooms are especially delicious.

Mushroom Soup
Serves 4

Open-capped cultivated mushrooms make a good alternative to the wild variety.

5 tablespoons butter
4 shallots, finely chopped
1 clove garlic, crushed
1 pound field mushrooms, cleaned
  and sliced
4 cups chicken stock
1 tablespoon plain flour
Dash soy sauce
A little thick cream
Salt and freshly ground black pepper

Heat 3 tablespoons of the butter in a heavy-bottomed pan and sauté the shallots until softened; add the garlic and cook for 1 minute more. Add the mushrooms and stir to coat well. Pour in the stock

Mushroom Mélange

and bring to a boil. Season and cover, simmering for 10–15 minutes, until the mushrooms are cooked. Remove from heat.

In a separate pan, heat the remaining butter and stir in the flour to make a roux. Cook for 2 minutes and remove from the stove. Use a blender to mix the roux with the soup (this may need to be done in batches). Add soy sauce, check seasoning and serve with cream.

Grilled Shiitake Mushrooms
Serves 4

Allow 2 mushrooms per person for a first course to be served with Italian bread.

8–12 shiitake mushrooms
6 tablespoons olive oil
1 sprig fresh rosemary
1 tablespoon fresh thyme leaves
2 tablespoons balsamic vinegar
2 tablespoons Barolo wine
1 small onion, finely chopped
4 slices Italian bread, toasted
1 tablespoon butter
1 clove garlic, crushed
Salt and freshly ground black pepper

Wash the shiitakes, ensuring the gills are free from dirt. Discard the stems and add to a stockpot. Dry the caps. Leave the mushrooms in a marinade of oil, rosemary, thyme, vinegar, wine, onion and seasoning for 30–45 minutes, turning them occasionally.

Grill the marinated caps under a preheated grill for 5 minutes each side, brushing with the marinade juices. Serve on slices of toasted Italian bread, buttered and rubbed with garlic. Pour over a little of the juices on each helping.

Mushroom Mélange
Serves 4

1 pound oyster mushrooms
1 pound shiitake mushrooms
4 tablespoons butter
2 cloves garlic, crushed
2 shallots, finely chopped
4 tablespoons white wine
½ cup heavy cream
4 tablespoons grated Parmesan
Salt and freshly ground black pepper

Wash the mushrooms well and chop them, including the stalks. Melt the butter in a heavy saucepan, add the garlic and shallots and allow them to soften over a gentle heat. Add the mushrooms and stir well. Pour in the wine and the cream and bring the mixture to the simmering point. Then cover and leave to stew for 15 minutes.

Pour into a greased sauté pan, season with salt and pepper and sprinkle over the Parmesan. Put under a preheated grill on the highest setting for 3–5 minutes until the cheese is melted.

Serve immediately.

ONION

Allium cepa. Alliaceae

Biennial; grown as annual for swollen bulbs. Half hardy. Value: small amounts of most vitamins and minerals.

A vegetable of antiquity, the onion was cultivated by the Egyptians not only as food, but also to place in the thorax, pelvis or near the eyes during mummification. Pliny recorded six varieties in ancient Rome. The onion was highly regarded for its antiseptic properties, but many other legends became attached to it. In parts of Ireland it was said to cure baldness: "Rub the sap mixed with honey into a bald patch, keep on rubbing until the spot gets red. This concoction if properly applied would grow hair on a duck's egg." Many varieties have been bred over the centuries; some, like 'The Kelsae', are famous for their size, while newer varieties have incorporated hardiness, disease resistance and color.

 varieties

Varieties of *Allium cepa* fall into several different groups according to their color, shape and use. The bulb or common onion has brown, yellow or red skin and is round, elongated or spindle-shaped, or flattened. (Grouped with these are Japanese onions, a type of the perennial *Allium fistulosum*, which are grown as an annual for overwintering.) Spring or bunching onions are harvested small for salads, and pickling varieties (also known as "silverskin," "mini" or "button" onions) are allowed to grow larger before harvesting.

Bulb or Common Onions
'Ailsa Craig', an old favorite, is a large variety; round and straw-colored with a mild flavor. 'Albion' is a round white bulb and ideal in salads or stir-fries. 'Buffalo'* is high-yielding and good for sowing in summer and harvesting the following year. The round, firm bulbs are well flavored. 'Express Yellow O-X' is a Japanese onion for sowing in summer and harvesting the following year. 'Marshalls Giant Fen Globe' is an old, heavy-cropping variety with a mild flavor. 'Red Baron'* is a gorgeous dark, red-skinned onion with a strong flavor and red outer flesh to each ring. Good for storing. 'Rijnsburger'* is large, pale yellow and round, and an excellent keeper. 'Senshyu Yellow' is a Japanese onion with a deep yellow skin and good taste. 'Sturon'*, an old, high-yielding variety, has straw-colored skin and an excellent resistance to running to seed. 'Stuttgarter Giant' is a reliable variety with flattened bulbs and a mild flavor. A good keeper and slow to bolt. 'The Kelsae', a large, round

onion with mild flesh, does not store well. **'Long Red Florence'** is spindle-shaped, sweet and mild-flavored.

Green, Spring or Salad Onions, Scallions

'Beltsville Bunching'* is a vigorous, mild-tasting variety, tolerant of both winter cold and hot, dry weather. **'Ishikura'***, a cross between a leek and coarse chives, is prolific, tender and a rapid grower with upright, white stems and dark green leaves. It can be left in the ground to thicken and still retains its taste. **'Kyoto Market'** is mild, easy to germinate and excellent for early sowings. **'Redmate'** is a colorful variety with a red base, and ideal for livening up salads. It can be thinned to 3 inches apart for mild bulb onions. **'Santa Claus'**, another red variety, is ready from about 6 weeks, keeps its taste well and can be harvested until the size of a leek. The color is stronger during cold weather and when they are earthed up. **'White Lisbon'*** is a tasty, popular and reliable variety. It is fast-growing and very hardy. **'Winter-Over'*** is a well-flavored, extremely hardy variety for sowing in autumn. **'Winter White Bunching'** has slim stalks, stiff leaves and a mild flavor. It is hardy and overwinters well.

Pickling Onions

'Brown Pickling SY300' is a pale brown-skinned early variety. It stores well and remains firm when pickled. **'Crystal White Wax'** grows to a consistent size and shape and produces perfect cocktail onions. **'Paris Silverskin'** is a popular, excellent "cocktail" onion, which grows rapidly and thrives in poor soil. Sow from mid-spring and lift when the size of your thumbnail.

 cultivation

Onions require an open, sunny site, fertile soil and free drainage. "Sets" (immature bulbs that have been specifically grown for planting) are more tolerant than seedlings and do not need a fine soil or such high levels of fertility. Pickling onions tolerate poorer soil than other types. Rotate crops annually.

Propagation

For a constant supply, two or three plantings are needed, one in spring and another in summer when Japanese varieties are planted, or autumn when old, hardy types are used.

Onion sets have several advantages over seed. They are quick to mature, are better in cooler areas with shorter growing seasons, they grow well in poorer soils and are not attacked by onion fly or mildew. They are easy to grow and mature earlier, but are more expensive and prone to run to seed. (Buying modern varieties and heat-treated sets about 1 inch in diameter reduces that risk.) There is a greater choice of varieties when growing from seed. If planting is delayed, spread out sets in a cool, well-lit place to prevent premature sprouting. It is possible to save your own sets from bulbs grown the previous year. Plant onion sets when the soil warms from late winter to mid-spring. Sets that have been heat-treated should not be planted until late spring. Plant in shallow drills or push them gently into the soil until only the tips are above the surface. For medium-sized onions, plant 2 inches apart in rows 10 inches apart; for larger onions space sets 4 inches apart in rows.

Sow seed indoors in late winter at 50–60°F (10–16°C) in seed trays, pots or modules (about 6 seeds in each module). Harden off the seedlings carefully by gradually increasing ventilation, then plant out in early spring when the seedlings have 2 true leaves. When transplanting those raised in modules and pots, ensure that the roots fall down into the planting hole and that the base of the bulb is about ½ inch below the surface.

Onions can be sown outdoors in a seedbed in early to mid-spring in cool temperate zones. Use cloches or polyethylene to ensure the soil is warm, as cold, wet soil leads to poor germination and disease. Use treated seed to protect against fungal disease.

Spring onions add bite to salads

Onion flowers are beautifully ornamental

When the soil is moist and crumbly, rake in a general fertilizer about 2 weeks before sowing and walk over the plot to create a firm seedbed, then sow onions about ½ inch deep in rows 12 inches apart. Once they germinate, thin to 1½ inches apart for medium-sized onions and 3–4 inches for large onions. Thin when the soil is moist to deter onion fly. Plant multisown blocks 10–12 inches apart. Plant firmly.

Sowing times for Japanese onions are critical; sown too early, they run to seed; sown too late, they are too weak to survive the winter. To cover for losses over winter, sow seeds about 1 inch apart in rows 12 inches apart. Top-dress with nitrogen in midwinter. Sow pickling onions in spring, either broadcast or in drills the width of a hoe and about 4 inches apart. Thin according to the size of onions required and harvest them when the leaves have died back.

Sow salad or bunching onions thinly, watering the drills before sowing in dry weather. Rows should be 4 inches apart; thin to a final spacing of ½–1 inch, when the seedlings are large enough to handle, for good-sized onions. For a regular supply sow at 2 to 3 week intervals through late spring and early summer, watering thoroughly during dry weather.

Growing

Dig thoroughly during early winter, incorporating liberal quantities of well-rotted manure or compost if needed. Do not grow on freshly manured ground. Lime acid soils. Before planting, rake the surface level, removing any debris and adding a general granular fertilizer to it at 4 ounces/sq yd. In summer pull back the earth or mulch from around the bulb to expose it to the sun.

Maintenance

Spring Plant sets or seeds. Keep weed-free, particularly in the early stages of growth.
Summer Mulch to reduce water loss and weeds. Watering is only vital during drought.
Autumn Lift early autumn.
Winter Push back any sets that have been lifted by frost or birds.

Protected Cropping

Onions do not need protection, although early sowings in cold weather and overwintering onions benefit from cloching or from horticultural fleece in exceptionally cold or wet weather.

Early sowings of salad or bunching onions can be made in late summer or early autumn and protected with cloches during severe weather for harvesting the following spring.

Onions drying on a metal rack

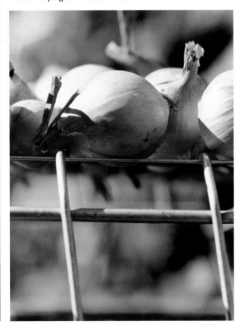

Rows of onion plants growing on a U.S. farm

Harvesting and Storing

Harvesting commences when the tops bend over naturally and the leaves begin to dry out. Do not bend the leaves over. Allow the bulbs and leaves to dry out while still in the ground during fine weather; wait until the dried foliage rustles before lifting. In adverse weather, spread out the bulbs on sacking or in trays in cold frames, cloches or a shed, turning them regularly. Handle bulbs carefully to avoid damage and disease. Before storing, be sure to remove any damaged, soft, spotted or thick-necked onions and use them immediately. Onions can be stored in trays, net bags or nylons, or tied to a length of cord as onion ropes in a cool place.

Harvest salad or bunching onions before the bases swell. During dry weather, water before harvesting to make pulling easier.

Making an Onion Rope

Storing onions on a rope enables the air to circulate, reducing the possibility of diseases. It is attractive and a convenient method of storage. You can plait the stems to form a rope, as with garlic, but they are usually too short and are better tied to raffia or strong string. Firmly tie in 2 onions at the base, then wind the leaves of each onion firmly around the string, with each bulb just resting on the onions below. When you reach the top of the string, tie a firm knot around the bulbs at the top, then hang them up to dry. Cut onions from the rope as they are needed.

Pests and Diseases

If birds are a nuisance, protect plants with black thread or netting. The larvae of onion fly tunnel into bulbs, causing the stems to wilt and become yellow. Seedlings and small plants may die (August-sown crops are most vulnerable). Cultivate the ground thoroughly over winter. Remove and destroy affected plants, rotate crops, sow under mesh. White rot can be a problem, particularly on salad onions. White mold like cotton-wool, dotted with tiny, black spots, appears around the base. Leaves turn yellow and die. It is almost impossible to eradicate. Remove affected onions with as much of the soil around them as possible, dispose of plants and any debris — do not put them on the compost heap. Avoid spreading contaminated soil on tools or boots. Grow on a new site and from seed.

When attacked by stem eelworm, bulbs become distorted, crack, soften, then die. Grow plants from seed; rotate crops; in severe cases do not grow in the same place again. Dispose of plant debris thoroughly and remove any affected plants.

 companion planting

Parsley sown with onions is said to keep onion fly away.

 container growing

Bulb onions can be grown in containers, but yields will be small and not really worth the trouble.

 medicinal

Used as an antiseptic and diuretic, the juice is good for coughs and colds. The bulbs and stems were formerly applied as poultices to carbuncles.

culinary

So indispensable are onions for flavoring sauces, stocks, stews and casseroles that there is hardly a recipe that does not start with some variant of "fry (or sauté or sweat) the onion in oil or butter until soft…" They also make a delicious vegetable or garnish in their own right: roasted or boiled whole, cut into rings, battered and deep-fried, or sliced and slowly softened into a meltingly sweet "marmalade." Finely chopped raw onion adds zing to dishes like rice salad; you can also use the thinnings to flavor salads.

Bunching onions are perfect for salads, pastas, soups and tarts. In France they are chopped, sautéed in butter and added to chicken consommé with vermicelli. Pickled onions are an excellent accompaniment to bread, strong cheese and pickled beets — the traditional "Plowman's Lunch." Besides being pickled, pickling varieties can be used fresh in salads and stir-fries, added to stews or else threaded on to kebab skewers for barbecuing.

Onion Tart
Serves 4

This dish is full of flavor and very filling. Enjoy it with a simple fresh green salad.

½ cup lard or olive oil
2 pounds onions, sliced into rings
¼ pound smoked bacon, diced
1 cup cream
3 eggs, lightly beaten
Salt and freshly ground black pepper
Shortcrust pastry to line a 8–9-inch pie plate

In a heavy pan, heat the lard or oil and sauté the onions until soft but not browned. Drain well on paper towel. Add the bacon to the pan and cook briskly for a couple of minutes, then drain off the fat. Next, mix the cream and the eggs and season well. Then stir in the onions and the bacon and fill the pastry shell.

Preheat the oven to 425°F (220°C) and bake for 10–15 minutes, turning the heat down to 375°F (190°C) for a further 15 minutes, or until the filling is set. Serve warm.

Onion and Walnut Muffins
Makes 20

This wonderful recipe comes from chef Wally Malouf's *Hudson Valley Cookbook*.

1 large onion, peeled and quartered
½ pound unsalted butter, melted
2 large eggs
6 tablespoons sugar
1 teaspoon sea salt
1 teaspoon baking powder
⅔ pound shelled walnuts, coarsely crushed
3½ cups all-purpose flour

Preheat the oven to 220°C (425°F). Purée the onion finely in a food processor and measure it to achieve ½ pound. Beat together the butter, eggs and sugar and add the onion purée. Stir in the remaining ingredients one by one and mix thoroughly. Fill the muffin tins almost full. Bake them for 20 minutes, or until they are puffed and well browned. Serve warm.

Allium cepa (Aggregatum Group). *Alliaceae*

SHALLOT

Small onion, grown as an annual, forming several new bulbs. Hardy. Value: small amounts of most vitamins and minerals.

Shallots are hardy, mature rapidly, are good for colder climates, tolerate heat and will grow on poorer soils than common onions. Sets are more expensive than seed and are inclined to bolt unless they are heat-treated; buy virus-free stock which is higher yielding and vigorous, or save healthy bulbs of your own for the following year.

Shallots are mild enough to be added whole to dishes

varieties

'Atlantic'* can be sown early and produces heavy yields of moderate to large bulbs which are crisp, tasty and store well. **'Creation F1'**, a seed-grown variety, is delicious, highly resistant to bolting and stores well. **'Longor'*** is a French variety with elongated bulbs and mild flesh. **'Giant Yellow Improved'*** is well worth considering. The bulbs have yellow-brown skins and are consistently large and high-yielding. **'Golden Gourmet'*** is a mild-tasting shallot for casseroles and salads. It is reliable and high-yielding, stores well and produces good edible shoots. **'Hative de Niort'** is an extremely attractive variety with elongated, pear-shaped bulbs, dark brown skins and white flesh. **'Pikant'*** is prolific and resistant to bolting. Its skin is dark reddish brown, the flesh strongly flavored and firm. **'Mikor'** has large elliptical bulbs, crisp white flesh and a superb taste. **'Sante'*** is large and round with brown skin and pinkish white flesh, packed with flavor. Yields are high and it stores well. However, it is inclined to bolt and should only be planted from mid- to late spring when conditions improve. **'Red Sun'** is red with firm skin and a crisp and mild flavor that is ideal for salads.

cultivation

Propagation
The ideal size for sets is about 1 inch in diameter, which will result in a high yield of good-sized shallots; larger sets will produce a greater number of smaller shallots. Plant from late winter or early spring, as soon as

soil conditions are suitable. Shallots can also be planted from late autumn to mid-winter for early crops. Cover the soil with cloches, fleece or polythene 2 weeks before planting to warm the soil.

If the weather is unfavorable, bulbs can be planted in 4-inch pots of compost and transplanted when conditions improve.

Space sets 9 inches apart with 12–15 inches between the rows. Make small holes with a trowel rather than pushing bulbs into the ground (the compaction this causes, particularly in heavier soils, can act as a barrier to young roots). Leave the tips of the bulbs just above the soil. Alternatively, plant in drills, ½ inch deep, 7 inches apart, then cover with soil.

F1 hybrids that are grown from seed produce one bulb, rather than several. From early to mid-spring, as soon as soil conditions allow, sow seed thinly ½ inch deep in broad drills, the width of a hoe, thinning until there is 1–2 inches around each plant. If spaced farther apart, clusters of bulbs are more likely to form.

Unlike onions, shallots develop in small clusters

Undersized shallots can be grown for their leaves, or you can pick a few leaves from those being grown for bulbs. Plant from autumn to spring under cloches for earlier crops, in seed trays or pots of compost under cover and outdoors when the soil becomes workable. Each bulb should be about 1 inch apart.

Growing
Shallots flourish in a sheltered, sunny position on moist, free-draining soil, preferably one that has been manured for the previous crop.

Alternatively, double dig the area in early autumn, incorporating plenty of well-rotted organic matter.

Before planting, level the soil and rake in a general fertilizer at 7 ounces/sq yd. If you are sowing sets, a rough tilth will suffice, but seeds require a seedbed of a finer texture.

Water during dry periods and keep crops weed-free, particularly while becoming established. Use an onion hoe with care, as damaged bulbs cannot be stored.

Maintenance
Spring Plant sets when soil conditions allow. Sow seed when the soil warms up.
Summer Keep crops weed-free. Water during dry periods.
Autumn Dig in well-rotted organic matter if needed. Plant sets for early crops.
Winter Plant sets from late winter onward.

Protected Cropping
Shallots are extremely hardy, but benefit from temporary protection under cloches or fleece in periods of severe winter weather, particularly if the soil is poorly drained.

Harvesting and Storing
From midsummer onward, as the leaves die back, carefully lift the bulbs and in dry weather leave them on the surface for about a week to dry out; otherwise dry them as onions. Do not cut off the green foliage as this may cause fungal infection, spoiling the bulbs for storage. Break up the bulbs in each clump, remove any soil and loose leaves, then store them in a dry, cool, well-ventilated place. Store on slatted trays, in net bags or in a pair of old nylons. Harvest shallots grown for their foliage when the leaves are about 4 inches high.

Pests and Diseases
Shallots are usually free of pests and diseases. Bolting may be a problem in early plantings or if temperatures fluctuate. Use resistant varieties for early plantings. Bulbs infected with viruses are stunted and yields are poor. Use disease-free stock. If mildew is a problem, treat as for onions.

Birds can be a nuisance, pulling sets from the ground. Sprinkling a layer of fine soil over the tips can help; otherwise protect the crop with humming wire or similar bird deterrents.

Bulbs lifted by frost should be carefully replanted immediately.

Eelworms and onion fly should be treated in the same way as for onions.

 ## companion planting

Shallots make good companions for apples and strawberry plants; storing sulfur, they are believed to have a fungicidal effect.

 ## container growing

Shallots will grow in large pots or containers of soil-based compost. Add slow-release fertilizer to the mix and put a good layer of gravel or polystyrene in the bottom of the pot, for drainage. Keep plants well watered in dry periods.

 ## culinary

Shallots have a milder taste than onions; generally, the yellow-skinned varieties are larger and keep better, while red types are smaller and have the best flavor. The bulbs can be eaten raw or pickled and the leaves used like spring onions.

Shallots can be finely chopped and added to fried steak just before serving. Do not brown them, as it makes them bitter. Béarnaise sauce is made by reducing shallots and herbs in wine vinegar before thickening with egg and butter.

LEEK

Biennial grown as annual for blanched leaf bases. Hardy. Value: good source of potassium and iron, smaller amounts of beta carotene and vitamin C, particularly in green leaves.

The Bible mentions "the cucumbers, and the melons, and the leeks, and the onions and the garlic" that grew in Egypt, where the leek was held as a sacred plant, and to swear by the leek was the equivalent to swearing by one of the gods.

Giant leek contests have been held in pubs and clubs throughout northeast England since the mid-1880s. At one show in 1895, W. Robson was awarded a second prize of £1 and a sheep's heart; now the world championship has a first prize of over £1,300 (about $1,800 USD).

 varieties

Older varieties are divided into two main groups, long thin and short stout types. In many modern cultivars, such differences are less obvious. There are also early, mid-season and late varieties.

'Autumn Mammoth — Cobra' is a mid- to late harvest, medium-length variety with good bolting resistance. **'Autumn Mammoth 2 — Argenta'** and the similar **'Goliath'** mature in late autumn and can be harvested until mid-spring. A high-yielding leek with a medium shank length and thick stems. **'Bleu de Solaise'**, a French winter variety, can be harvested until spring. **'Bulgarian Giant'** is long, thin and of excellent quality for autumn harvest. **'King Richard'*** is a high-yielding, mild-tasting, early variety with a long shank. Good for growing at close spacing for "mini leeks." **'Prelina'*** is harvested in early autumn and has a moderate-length shank.

 cultivation

Leeks flourish in a sunny, sheltered site on well-drained, neutral to slightly acidic soil.

Propagation
Leeks need a minimum soil or compost temperature of at least 45°F (7°C) to germinate, so you will achieve more consistent results, particularly with early crops, when they are sown under cover. For rapid germination, sow early varieties indoors during late winter at 55–60°F (13–16°C) in trays, pots or modules of seed compost. Pot on those grown in trays or pots, spacing them about 2 inches apart, when 2 true leaves are produced or when they begin to bend over. Harden off gradually before planting out in late spring.

Leeks can also be sown in unheated greenhouses, in cold frames or under cloches. Sow seeds from late winter to early spring, pot on, harden off and transplant in late spring.

Although all varieties are suitable, later sowings of mid-season and later types are particularly successful in seedbeds. Warm the soil using cloches, black polyethylene or horticultural fleece and rake the seedbed to a fine tilth. Sow thinly in rows 6 inches apart and 1 inch deep, providing protection during cold spells. They can also be sown directly in the vegetable plot, 1 inch deep in rows 12 inches apart, thinning when seedlings have 2 or 3 leaves. Sowing seeds in modules — either in pairs or singly — keeping the most vigorous of the two, and multisowing 3 to 5 per cell, avoids the necessity of "pricking out" or thinning.

Growing
Fertile, moisture-retentive soil is essential, so dig in plenty of organic matter the winter before planting, particularly on light soils. On heavy soils, add organic matter and horticultural sand to improve drainage as crops are poor on heavy or waterlogged soil. Rake, level and firm the soil before planting in spring. As they are a long-term, high-nitrogen crop, apply a general fertilizer, fish, blood and bone or ammonium sulfate at 4–6 ounces/sq yd 1 or 2 weeks before planting.

Transplant leeks when they are 6–10 inches tall. Trim the leaf tips back if they drag on the ground, but not the roots, as is often recommended. If the soil is dry, water the area thoroughly before planting. Planting 6 inches apart in rows 12 inches apart provides a high yield of moderately sized leeks. Planting them 3–4 inches apart in rows gives a high yield of slim leeks. A spacing of 6–7 inches each way provides a reasonable crop of medium-sized leeks. Leeks grown in modules should be planted 9 inches apart each way.

Leeks growing in a vegetable bed

There are two methods of planting to ensure well-blanched stems. I find the first method better, as deeply planted leeks are more drought-resistant and soil is less likely to fall down between the leaves. Make a hole 6–8 inches deep with a dibble, drop the plant into it and fill the hole with water (this washes some soil into the bottom of the hole), but do not fill any further.

Alternatively, plant leeks 3 inches deep, and several times through the season pull the earth up around the stems, 2–3 inches at a time, with a draw hoe. Stop earthing up when the plants reach maturity and make sure that the soil does not fall down between the leaves. Earthing up is easier on light soil.

Whichever method you use, after planting, water gently with a seaweed-based fertilizer. If there is a dry period after planting, water leeks daily until the plants are well established and thereafter only during drought conditions. Hand-weed or hoe carefully to keep down weeds, using an onion hoe around younger plants to avoid any damage. In poorer soils, feed weekly in summer with a liquid seaweed or comfrey fertilizer.

Maintenance

Spring Pot on leeks grown under glass; sow seed outdoors.
Summer Transplant seedlings, water and feed. Keep crops weed-free by hoeing or mulching.
Autumn Harvest crops as required.
Winter Harvest mid- and late-season crops. Sow seed under glass in late winter.

Protected Cropping

Apart from early sowings in the greenhouse or cold frame or under cloches and horticultural fleece, leeks are an extremely hardy outdoor crop.

Harvesting and Storing

Early varieties are ready for lifting from early to mid-autumn, mid-season types from early to midwinter and lates from early to mid-spring. Lift leeks carefully with a garden fork and dispose of any leaf debris to reduce the risk of disease in the future. Late varieties taking up space in the vegetable garden that is needed for spring planting can be stored for several weeks in a shallow, angled trench 6–8 inches deep; cover them lightly with soil and leave the tops exposed. If inclement weather is likely to hinder harvest, they can be lifted and packed closely together in a cold frame. The top should be raised to provide ventilation on warmer days.

Pests and Diseases

Leeks share many diseases with their close relatives, onions. Leek rust appears as orange pustules on the leaves during summer and is worse in wet seasons. Foliage developing later in the season is healthy. Feed with high-potassium fertilizer, remove infected plants and debris. Improve drainage; do not plant leeks on the site for 4–5 years; grow partially resistant varieties like 'Autumn Mammoth', **'Titan'** or **'Gennevilliers-Splendid'**. Slugs can be damaging. Collect them at night, use biological control, set traps or use ferric phosphate. Mature leeks usually survive slug damage. Stem eelworm causes swelling at the base and distorted leaves. Destroy affected plants immediately and rotate crops. Leek moth — leaves develop whitish brown patches and tunnels are present in stems and bulbs where caterpillars have burrowed through. Squash caterpillars in leaves. Grow under fleece.

 ## companion planting

Leeks grow well with celery. When planted with onions and carrots they discourage onion and carrot fly. Grow leeks in your rotation program alongside garlic, onions and shallots. Leeks are a useful crop after early potatoes and if they are grown at a 12-inch spacing; their upright growth makes them ideal for intercropping with lettuces like **'Tom Thumb'**, with land cress or winter purslane.

 ## culinary

Leeks can be boiled or steamed, made into terrines, cooked in casseroles, added to pasta dishes, wrapped in pastry and baked. They are a useful addition to soups and an important ingredient in "cock-a-leekie" soup and in French vichyssoise. Braise in stock with a little wine added and bake in a moderate oven. Partially cook trimmed leeks in boiling water, drain well and roll in slices of good country ham and lay them in a dish; cover with a well-flavored cheese sauce and bake in a hot oven until well browned. Slice or chop young leeks and use raw as a spring onion substitute in salads.

Leek and Ricotta Pie
Serves 4

4 large leeks, trimmed and roughly chopped
2 tablespoons olive oil
2 cloves garlic, finely chopped
1 cup ricotta
2 tablespoons pine nuts
3 tablespoons raisins, softened in warm water
1 egg
Salt and freshly ground black pepper

For the pastry:
6 tablespoons butter
1¾ cup all-purpose flour
3 tablespoons water
Pinch salt

Make the pastry by crumbling the butter into the flour and then adding water to make a dough. Add the salt and sprinkle with flour. Wrap in plastic wrap and chill in the fridge for 30 minutes.

Steam the leeks gently for about 10 minutes and drain.

Preheat the oven to 375°F (190°C). In a heavy frying pan heat the oil and gently fry the garlic. Then add the leeks and stir to coat well with oil; allow them to cook for about 5 minutes, stirring occasionally.

Remove from heat. In a bowl mix the ricotta with the pine nuts and raisins, and blend in the egg. Add the leeks, mix well and season.

Gently roll out the pastry to fit an 8-inch pie plate. Prick the base and bake blind for 10–15 minutes. Fill the pastry shell with the leek and ricotta mixture and continue cooking for 30 minutes. Serve with a green salad.

Allium sativum. Alliaceae

GARLIC

Perennial grown as annual for strongly aromatic bulbs. Half hardy. Value: contains small quantities of vitamins and minerals.

Prized throughout the world for its culinary and medicinal properties, garlic, now known only as a cultivated plant, is thought to have originated in western Asia. It has been grown since Egyptian times and for centuries in China and India. Its reputation as a "cure all" has been endorsed by modern science. The Egyptians placed it in their tombs and gave it to the slaves who built the pyramids to ward off infection, while Hippocrates prescribed it for uterine tumors. In medieval Europe it was hung outside doors to deter witches. Today about 3 million tons are produced globally each year.

A garlic field in Aomori, Japan

In areas with heavy soil, cloves can be planted any time over winter in pots or modules containing loam-based compost with added horticultural sand, and can be planted out as soon as soil conditions are favorable. Plant cloves vertically with the flattened base plate at the bottom, twice the depth of the clove with at least 1 inch of soil above the tip. On good soils, planting up to 4 inches deep increases the yield. When planting, you should handle the cloves lightly: do not press them into the soil as this reduces root development. The amount of leaf growth dictates the size of the mature bulb that develops during long summer days.

Growing
Garlic favors an open, sunny position on light, well-drained soil. On heavier soil, grow in ridges or improve the drainage by working horticultural sand or grit in to the topsoil.

Garlic is less successful in areas of heavy rainfall. On poor soils, it is beneficial to rake in a general fertilizer about 10 days before planting. Garlic can be grown on soil manured for the previous crop as well as limed acidic soils.

Rotate the crop and do not grow in sites where onions have been planted the previous year. Keep the bulbs weed-free throughout the growing season.

Maintenance
Spring Mulch to suppress weeds. Water if necessary.
Summer Keep weed-free.
Autumn Plant cloves.
Winter Plant cloves in containers for planting out in the spring.

Protected Cropping
Garlic can be grown in an unheated greenhouse for an early crop.

 ## varieties

There are two main categories of garlic; softnecks, which don't produce a flower stalk, and hardnecks, which do. Hardnecks, also known as "gourmet" garlics, have a greater color range and taste but don't store well.

Softneck
'Germidor'* crops early, producing large cloves and purple bulbs. **'Inchelium Red'** is a regular winner in taste tests. **'Long Keeper'** is well adapted to a cool, temperate climate. The bulbs are white-skinned and firm. **'Solent Wight'***, producing large cloves with a mild flavor, is heavy-cropping with an appealing bouquet.

Hardneck
'Chesnok Red' is robustly flavored, **'Brown Tempest'** and **'Purple Moldovan'** are renowned for their taste and **'Spanish Rioja'** is sought after by enthusiasts.

 ## cultivation

Propagation
Garlic is usually grown from healthy, plump bulb segments (cloves) saved from a previous crop. Where possible, buy nematode and virus-resistant stock.

Plant cloves, a minimum of ½ inch in diameter, in late autumn or early spring, at a depth of 1 inch and 4 inches apart, with the rows 4–6 inches apart.

Garlic is surprisingly hardy and needs a cold, dormant period of 1 or 2 months when temperatures are 32–50°F (0–10°C) to yield decent-sized bulbs; for this reason it is generally better planted in late autumn. A long growing period is also beneficial for the ripening process.

variety with crisp stems. **'Tall Utah Triumph'** has long, succulent, tender green stems. It crops from late summer to early autumn but the season can be extended by growing under cloches.

Leaf, cutting or soup celery
This produces leaves and stems over a long period and is very hardy. It is usually sold as seed mixes, but cultivars are available: **'French Dinant'** is excellent for drying and full of flavor. **'Soup Celery d'Amsterdam'** is aromatic and prolific, producing thin stems and lots of leaves. **'Thai Bai Khuen Chai'** is spicy and leafy with thin stems. Its strong flavor is good in Thai soup, salads, curries and stir-fries.

cultivation

Celery is a crop for cool temperate conditions, flourishing at 59–70°F (15–21°C) on an open site. It requires rich, fertile soil which is constantly moist yet well drained and a pH of 6.5–7.5. Lime acidic soils before planting if needed.

Propagation
Sow celery from mid- to late spring, in trays of moist seed compost, scattering the seed thinly over the surface; do not cover it with compost, as light is needed for germination. Keep the tray in a propagator or in a greenhouse at 55–60°F (13–16°C); germination can take several weeks, so be as patient as possible. When two true leaves appear, transplant the seedlings into trays of moist seed compost about 2½ inches apart or individually into 3-inch pots and allow them to establish. Harden off before planting outdoors from late spring to early summer when they have 5 to 7 true leaves.

Low temperatures after germination sometimes cause bolting later in life; temperatures should not fall below 50°F (10°C) for longer than 12 hours until the seedlings have become established. They are particularly sensitive at transplanting size, so cover them with cloches and do not try to slow down the growth of advanced seedlings by putting them outdoors. It is much better to trim plants back to about 3 inches with sharp scissors and keep them in the warm until outdoor temperatures are satisfactory. Cutting back also seems to lead to more successful transplanting. Planting in modules of seed compost lessens transplanting shock, which can also result in bolting. If you are unable to

provide the necessary conditions, small plants can always be bought.

Celery can also be sown *in situ* but germination is usually erratic and it is not worth the trouble. Celery's low germination rate can be improved by "fluid sowing." If possible, use treated seed to control celery leaf spot. Several sowings at 3-week intervals lengthens the harvesting season.

Sow cutting celery in trays of seed compost from late spring to late summer before hardening off and planting 6 inches apart each way. Alternatively, multisow in modules, about 6–8 seeds in each, and plant each module group 8 inches apart. Leave a few plants to run to seed the following year, then transplant self-sown seedlings at the recommended spacing.

Growing
The planting method is different for "trench celery" and self-blanching types. For the first, dig a trench 15–20 inches wide and 12 inches deep in late autumn or early spring and incorporate as much well-rotted manure or compost as you can find. If more than one trench is needed, their centers should be 4 feet apart. Trench celery can also be grown by filling in the trench to a depth of about 3–4 inches and leaving the

remaining soil alongside for earthing up. A week or 10 days before planting, rake a balanced general fertilizer at rate of 4–6 ounces/sq yd into the bottom of the trench. Celery is easier to manage when planted in single rows with plants 12–18 inches apart. If you plant in double rows, set the plants 9 inches apart in pairs, rather than staggered. This makes blanching easier. Water thoroughly after planting.

Blanch by earthing up plants when they are about 12 inches high. Before you start, tie the stems loosely, just below the leaves, using soft string and make sure the soil is moist, watering if necessary (or earth up after rain). Draw soil up the stems about 3 inches at a time, repeating this two or three times at 3-week intervals until only the tops of plants are exposed. Do not earth up higher than the leaves, nor should you let soil fall into the heart of the plant. If heavy frosts are forecast in winter, place straw or other protective material over plants to keep in good condition for as long as possible.

Plants can also be blanched with "collars." Use 9–10-inch strips of thick paper like newspaper, corrugated cardboard, brown wrapping paper or thick black polyethylene. (Ideally this should be lined with paper to prevent sweating.) I have also seen drainpipes and plastic gutters being used to good effect.

Celery being grown on a commercial scale

Celery blanched by wrapping cardboard around the stem

Begin blanching when plants are about 12 inches high, tying the collar quite loosely around the plant to give it room to expand and leaving about one-third of the plant exposed. Further collars can be added every 2 to 3 weeks as the plants grow.

Remember to unwrap them periodically to remove any slugs hiding beneath. If collars are used in exposed sites, support them by staking with a cane. Cover the top of the cane with a flower pot, film case or ping-pong ball to avoid inflicting any eye damage.

Labor-saving self-blanching types do not need earthing up. They also tolerate a wider range of soils, and are particularly good where the ground is heavy and trenching or waterlogging would be a problem. They are, however, shallow-rooted and should be fed and watered regularly throughout the growing season. Self-blanching celery is planted at ground level. Dig in generous amounts of well-rotted organic matter in spring before planting. The spacing varies according to your requirements and plants should be arranged in a square pattern, not staggered rows. Spacing about 6 inches apart gives a high yield of very tender, small-stemmed sticks; 11 inches apart each way, the optimum spacing, gives high yields of longer, well-blanched sticks and 9 inches apart each way gives moderate stem growth. Plant with the crown at soil level and put straw around the outer plants when they mature to help blanching.

For good-quality crops celery must be watered copiously throughout the growing season and the soil should not be allowed to dry out. Apply up to 6 gallons/sq yd per week during dry periods. Mulching with straw or compost once plants have established conserves moisture and suppresses weeds. Feed with a granular or liquid general fertilizer about 4 to 6 weeks after transplanting. Rotate crops, but do not plant next to parsnips, as both are attacked by celery fly. Avoid anything that checks plant growth throughout the season as this can cause bolting, so transplant the seedlings when the soil is warm, water and feed them regularly, and always mulch or hoe around the plants very carefully.

Maintenance

Spring Prepare the ground for planting. Sow seed and plant earlier crops out under cloches.
Summer Plant out in early summer, keep soil moist and weed regularly. Check for pests and diseases.
Autumn Harvest with care using a garden fork.
Winter Cover with straw or similar materials to allow harvest to continue during heavy frosts.

Protected Cropping

Protect newly transplanted small plants with cloches or horticultural fleece for several weeks after planting, until they become established. This is particularly necessary in cooler conditions.

Harvesting and Storing

Lift celery carefully with a garden fork, easing the roots from the ground. Straw or other protective material placed over trenches assists lifting in frosty weather. Self-blanching celery can be harvested from midsummer to early autumn. Before the first frosts, lift and store any remaining plants and put them in a cool, frost-free shed. They will keep for several weeks. Harvest cutting celery regularly from about 5 weeks after planting.

Pests and Diseases

Celery leaf miner or celery fly larvae tunnel through the leaves leaving brown blisters. Severe attacks check growth. Grow under horticultural fleece or protective mesh, pinch out affected leaves, do not plant seedlings that have affected leaves. Check plants in late spring and late summer. Do not plant near to parsnips as they can be affected.

Slugs are a major problem, particularly on heavy soil. Use biological control, traps, hand pick or use ferric phosphate-based slug pellets. Carrot fly attack the roots and stem bases, stunting growth. Grow under fleece until harvest or put fine mesh netting barriers 18–30 inches high around the crop before or straight after transplanting.

Celery leaf spot shows as brown spots on older leaves, spreading to younger ones. Severe attacks can stunt growth; use treated seed, rotate crops or use copper-based fungicide.

Celery pale leaf spot (early blight) appears as tiny yellow spots on the leaf surfaces with accompanying grey mold in damp conditions. This disease spreads rapidly. Spray with Bordeaux mixture, be vigilant and destroy all plant debris at the end of the season.

 companion planting

Celery helps brassicas by deterring damaging butterflies. It grows well with beans, tomatoes and particularly leeks. If left to flower, celery attracts beneficial insects.

 medicinal

Cultivated varieties are said to be beneficial in the treatment of rheumatism and as a diuretic.

culinary

Usually eaten raw rather than cooked, celery adds welcome crunchiness to salads, particularly in winter months. It is a key ingredient of the famous Waldorf Salad, made with equal quantities of chopped red-skinned apples and celery, combined with walnuts and bound with mayonnaise.

Celery goes well with cheese — sticks filled with cream cheese or pâté are an appetizing "snack." The "heart" is particularly tasty. Cook celery in soups and stews, or stir-fry. Braise hearts by simmering in boiling water for 10 minutes, then cook in a covered dish for 45 minutes in a low oven to accompany roasts.

Add leaves to meat dishes, like parsley. Fresh or dried leaves flavor soups and stuffings. Cutting celery is a flavoring for salads, soups and stews; the seeds can also be used.

Celery will stay fresh in a plastic bag in the refrigerator for up to 3 days. Do not stand in water for long periods, or the freshness is lost.

Freeze celery by washing and cutting the sticks into 1-inch lengths, blanch for 3 minutes, cool, drain and pack into plastic freezer bags. Use frozen celery only in cooked dishes.

Celery and Zucchini with Blue Cheese Dip
Serves 4

4 stalks celery, cut into 3-inch lengths
2 tablespoons olive oil
1 teaspoon chili powder
½ teaspoon paprika
1 clove garlic, crushed
4 fresh basil leaves, roughly chopped
4 zucchini, sliced lengthwise into quarters
Fresh chives, to garnish

For the dip:
4 tablespoons cottage cheese
2 tablespoons crumbled Roquefort cheese
50g yogurt
Salt and freshly ground pepper

In a heavy frying pan over low heat, mix the oil with the chili powder, paprika, garlic and basil. Turn up the heat and fry the zucchini slices, cut side down, until browned and turn them to brown the second side. In a small bowl mix together all the dip ingredients. On 4 small plates, arrange a fan of alternating zucchini and celery sticks and fill the center with the dip. Garnish with finely chopped chives and serve.

Apium graveolens var. rapaceum. Umbelliferae

CELERIAC

Also known as Celery Root. Biennial usually grown as annual for edible root. Hardy. Value: rich in potassium; moderate amounts of vitamin C.

This swollen-stemmed relative of celery has long been popular in Europe. It was introduced to Britain in the early 18th century by the writer and seedsman Stephen Switzer, who brought seed from Alexandria and wrote about the vegetable in his book, *Growing Foreign Kitchen Vegetables*. It is an excellent, versatile winter vegetable, hardier and more disease-resistant than celery, but with similar flavor and aroma.

encourage them to run to seed later in the season. Maintain the temperature and cut off the tops of the plants with sharp scissors to 3 inches — the ideal size for transplanting.

Growing

Celeriac needs rich, fertile, moisture-retentive soil and is ideal for damper parts of the garden. In autumn, incorporate as much well-rotted manure or compost as possible. Space plants 12–15 inches apart each way. Do not bury the crowns; they should be planted at ground level. Plant firmly and water thoroughly and continually. In midsummer remove the outer leaves to expose the crown and encourage the bulb to develop, and remove side shoots if they appear.

Maintenance

Spring Plant out seedlings — harden off. Keep weed-free.
Summer Water in dry weather. Mulch to conserve moisture; feed weekly with a liquid manure, particularly in poorer soils.
Autumn Begin harvesting. Cover with straw.
Winter Prepare ground. Sow seeds under glass.

Protected Cropping

Celeriac only benefits from protection when it is at the seedling stage.

Harvesting and Storing

Celeriac can be harvested through the winter. Harvest when the plants are 3–5 inches in diameter, though they can be lifted when larger with no loss of flavor. Ideally they should remain in the ground until required. Before the onset of severe winter weather, protect plants with a layer of straw or with horticultural fleece to prevent the ground from freezing. If the soil is heavy, the site exposed or needed for another crop, lift and remove the outer leaves, keeping the central tuft attached; cut off the roots and store in a cool shed in boxes of damp peat substitute or sand.

Alternatively, lift and "heel in" or transplant the crop in another part of the garden, laying them close together in a trench and covering the bulbs with soil. They last for several weeks when stored in this manner.

Bulbs can be frozen; cut into cubes, blanch for 3 minutes, dry, store in plastic bags and put in the freezer. They will keep for a week in the salad drawer of the refrigerator.

 ## varieties

The lowest part of the stem, known as the "bulb," is eaten; the roots that grow below are removed. **'Alabaster'** is high-yielding with upright foliage, round bulbs and has good resistance to running to seed. **'Balder'** has round, medium-sized roots, which have excellent flavor when eaten cooked and raw. The "bulb" of **'Brilliant'** is smooth with white flesh and does not discolor. **'Iram'** is a medium-sized "bulb" with few side shoots. It stores well and the flesh remains white when cooked. **'Marble Ball'**, a well-known variety, is medium-sized, globular and strongly flavored. It also stores well. **'Monarch'*** is a popular variety with smooth skin and succulent flesh. **'Prinz'*** has white-fleshed roots with an aromatic flavor and is also resistant to leaf disease and bolting. **'Tellus'** grows quickly and remains white after boiling. It has firm flesh and a smoother skin than many varieties.

 ## cultivation

Propagation

Celeriac needs a long growing season. Sow in late winter to early spring in a propagator at 65°F (18°C) or in mid- to late spring in a cold greenhouse, under cloches or in a cold frame. Plant seeds in peat substitute-based compost either several to a pot or in seed boxes or modules.

Germination is notoriously erratic. Pot strong seedlings when they are about ½ inch tall and large enough to handle. Plant them into single 3-inch pots, modules or in seed trays at 2½-inch intervals, keeping the temperature at 55–60°F (13–16°C). Harden off when the weather becomes warm in late spring and plant outdoors once there is no danger of frost.

Celeriac is sensitive to cold at the transplanting stage; do not try to slow the growth of fast-growing seedlings by lowering the temperature, as this will

Pests and Diseases

Celeriac has the same problems as celery. Protect against slugs; use ferric phosphate-based slug pellets, pick off slugs at night and encourage natural predators. Slugs congregate under lettuce leaves or wet paper; pick off and destroy. Carrot fly is often a pest when established on carrots. Grow under fleece or place a barrier 30 inches high of fine netting or polyethylene, erected before or just after sowing. Keep it in place until harvesting time. Celery fly is less of a problem than on celery. Pick off any brown, blistered leaflets or grow under horticultural fleece.

companion planting

Celeriac grows well where legumes have been planted the previous year and benefits from being placed alongside beans, brassicas, leeks, tomatoes and onions.

medicinal

Celeriac oil has a calming effect and is a traditional remedy for skin complaints and rheumatism. It is also said to restore sexual potency after illness! Celeriac is rich in calcium, phosphorus and vitamin C.

warning

Celeriac is a diuretic. Pregnant women and people with kidney disorders should avoid eating it in large quantities.

Prinz

culinary

Containing only 14 calories per 100g, celeriac is excellent for anyone on a diet.

Scrub the bulb well to remove dirt before peeling. It discolors rapidly when cut; put immediately into acidulated water. Grated celeriac can be added raw to winter salads. Alternatively, blanch the slices or cubes in boiling water for a few seconds beforehand. In France it is cut into cubes and mixed with mayonnaise and Dijon mustard to make *céleri-rave rémoulade*.

The bulb adds flavor to soups or stews and is good with lamb or beef, puréed or seasoned with pepper, salt and butter, it is an ideal accompaniment for stronger-flavored game.

The leaves are strongly flavored and can be used sparingly to garnish salads or dried for use in cooking. The stems can be cooked and eaten like sea kale. Celeriac can be made into delicious fries: boil a whole, peeled root in salted water until just tender and then cut into wedges and fry in a mixture of butter and oil until lightly browned. These fries make an excellent accompaniment to game or plain grilled steaks.

Boiled and sliced, celeriac can be covered with a cheese sauce well flavored with French mustard. It also makes an excellent soup.

Monkfish with Celeriac
Serves 4

¼ cup celeriac, cut into julienne strips
1½ pounds monkfish, cut into chunks
1 large onion, finely sliced
1 carrot, peeled and cut into julienne strips
⅓ cup butter
1 tablespoon flour
2 teaspoons French mustard
2 tablespoons Greek yogurt
1 tablespoon heavy cream
Salt and freshly ground black pepper

Season the monkfish and prepare the vegetables. Heat half the butter in a heavy frying pan and cook the monkfish gently for about 7–8 minutes, turning it until just tender. Remove from the pan and keep warm. Using the rest of the butter, add the vegetables to the pan and sauté until soft. Stir in the flour and cook for a couple of minutes; then add the mustard, yogurt and cream. Stir well and heat through gently. Put the fish pieces in, stir to coat well and serve piping hot.

Arctium lappa. Compositae
BURDOCK

Also known as Edible Burdock, Gobo. Hardy biennial, grown as an annual. Value: moderate levels of dietary fiber plus vitamin B, potassium, calcium and inulin.

After walking his dog one day in the early 1940s, inventor George de Mestral noticed that burdock seeds had attached themselves to his woolen clothes and the fur of his dog. When analyzing them under a microscope, he discovered that the sharply hooked "burrs" were firmly linked to the loops of fur and material. After much research, he devised the famous fastening system "Velcro," which is widely used today. Burdock is naturalized throughout the world; the Chinese introduced it to Japan and neatly packed boxes are a feature of Japanese food markets. The famous French seedsmen Vilmorin-Andrieux, in their book, *The Vegetable Garden*, noted that, "although it cannot be termed delicious, it is certainly not a bad vegetable and is, therefore, deserving of serious consideration." It has an unusual but rather pleasing flavor — perhaps you should give it a try!

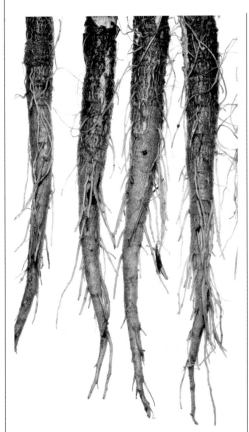

Burdock roots close up

 varieties

Arctium lappa is a large biennial up to 4 feet tall, notable for its large, rough, heart-shaped leaves. Roots can be up to 8 feet long and 1 inch thick. The small, thistle-like flower heads are followed by prickly burrs. However, avoid cultivating wild burdock as a crop as the roots are comparatively small. **'Mitoya Shirohada'** has roots that are white and smooth with a tender texture and just over 3¼ feet long. **'Takinogawa Long'** has small leaves and large roots. **'Watanabe Early'** is ideal for spring sowing, matures rapidly and has roots around 3 feet long.

 cultivation

Propagation
Soak seeds overnight or "scarify" before sowing and place them on the surface as they need light to germinate. Sow in autumn but not too early in the season; smaller plants are more resistant to winter weather and larger overwintering plants usually bolt in spring. Alternatively, sow in spring when temperatures are at a minimum of 68°F (20°C), placing three seeds 16 inches apart, with 20 inches between rows, then thin in late winter, leaving the strongest seedling. Another option is to germinate seeds under glass and transplant before a "taproot" starts to form; modules are ideal for this.

Growing
Burdock grows well in temperate and warm, humid climates at temperatures from 68–77°F (20–25°C) and is most successful on moisture-retentive, free-draining, light or sandy soils for increased rooting depth and easy lifting of the roots. It is less successful on heavier soils, though it can be grown successfully in raised beds or ridges. Clear the site before planting, incorporating copious amounts of well-rotted organic matter as deeply as possible and adding bone-meal to encourage root growth. Keep young plants weed-free until the foliage is large enough to prevent them from germinating. Water plants well during drought.

Burdock is vigorous and spreading, demanding high levels of nutrients and water and should be sited well away from other plants.

Maintenance
Spring Sow seeds under glass or outdoors if soil is warm.
Summer Water well and keep weed-free.
Autumn Lift roots.
Winter Protect overwintering seedlings under cloches.

Protected cropping
Plants can be started off under glass before transplanting them outdoors.

Harvesting and Storing

Plants sown in autumn or spring are ready for harvest the following autumn. Lift the first roots when the foliage dies back after the first frosts; it may not be possible to dig out whole roots because of their length, but those that remain in the ground will not become a problem. Lifting roots when they are immature, up to 18 inches long, ensures they are tender. Cover plants with bracken, straw or similar materials in winter; the roots can then still be lifted when the surrounding soil is frozen. Alternatively, lift all roots after the first frosts and store in boxes of damp sand or wrapped in paper in the salad drawer of a fridge.

Pests and Diseases

Burdock is pest- and disease-free.

 ## container growing

Burdock is not suitable for most containers because of the size of the plant above and below ground, but raised beds should provide adequate space.

 ## medicinal

Burdock contains a chemical that encourages lactation and is also used as a hair and scalp conditioner, blood purifier, diuretic and for the treatment of skin conditions.

Burdock growing in a field

 ## culinary

Burdock is a major ingredient in root beer. Young roots, which are of a better quality, can be eaten raw or stir-fried, whereas older roots are boiled until soft or added to casseroles. One seed catalog even suggests it can be fried with red peppers and makes a good accompaniment to baked beans! The young leaves and stem can be lightly cooked; immature flower stems can also be harvested and eaten before flowering.

In Japan, the roots are pickled and served with sweet sauce, or shredded and braised with several ingredients, including carrot, sake and sesame oil, in a dish called *kinpira gobo*. Burdock *makizushi* is sushi filled with pickled burdock root instead of fish. Soak older roots in water for an hour before use, to purge any bitterness, adding a dash of vinegar to prevent discoloration. Older roots taste earthy and become woody and less palatable with age. Buy burdock in Asian or health food stores — or get it for free when out in the countryside. This dish comes from southern Italy.

Bucatini with Burdock, Artichokes and Peas
Serves 4

1 burdock root, about 10 inches long
1 pound bucatini pasta
Balsamic vinegar
1 tablespoon olive oil
1 shallot, finely chopped
1 small onion, finely chopped
3–4 cloves garlic, crushed
Zest of 1 lemon
4–6 marinated artichoke hearts
½ pound peas
1 large handful basil leaves
½ cup chicken or vegetable stock
2 tablespoons butter
Salt and freshly ground black pepper
Freshly grated pecorino cheese, to serve

Peel the burdock root if you prefer, but remember the vitamins are right under the skin and it has more flavor with the skin left on. Cut into matchstick-sized pieces, cover with water, stir in a couple of teaspoons of balsamic vinegar and leave to soak for 30 minutes.

Cook the pasta in boiling, salted water until al dente, then drain.

Meanwhile, strain the burdock. Heat a large, heavy-bottomed frying pan over a medium heat and pour in the olive oil. Sauté the shallot and onion for 2–3 minutes, then add the garlic, lemon zest and burdock root and cook until the vegetables are softened and lightly colored. Add the artichoke hearts, peas, basil and the butter, and sauté for a further 5 minutes.

HORSERADISH

Perennial herb sometimes grown as annual for its strong-flavored fleshy roots. Hardy. Value: rich in vitamin C and calcium, moderate in carbohydrates.

Thought to be native of southern Russia and the eastern Ukraine, horseradish is now found throughout the temperate zones of the world. Cultivated since classical times, horseradish was probably carried round Europe by the Romans, who used it as a medicine and flavoring. Parkinson noted in 1640, "it is too strong for tender and gentle stomaches," yet it was extensively eaten by country folk in Germany; it is known in France as *moutarde des Allemands*. Its hardiness and ability to regenerate from the smallest particle of root have ensured its success — and sometimes makes it a pernicious weed both in and outside the garden. The common name "horseradish" distinguishes it from the salad radish, "horse" signifying coarse.

damp sand in a cool, frost-free shed. In mid-spring, make holes with a dibber 2 feet apart, deep enough for the top of the root cutting to be covered with soil to a depth of 2–3 inches; insert a piece of root into each hole with the thickest end up and fill with soil.

Growing

Horseradish dislikes heavy shade but grows on any soil with reasonable drainage; roots flourish in deep, rich, well-drained soils. Dig in well-rotted organic matter the winter before planting; where crops are rotated, horseradish should follow a heavily manured crop like beans. After planting, apply a general fertilizer, water as needed, particularly during drought. Keep weed-free.

 ## varieties

The species **Armoracia rusticana** grows up to 3 feet tall; the broad, oblong, dark green leaves have serrated margins. The thick tapering roots penetrate 2 feet or more into the soil. **Armoracia rusticana 'Variegata'** has leaves splashed with cream and is of ornamental merit, though its flavor is not as good as the species.

 ## cultivation

As horseradish is difficult to eradicate once established, lift all plants from late autumn to early winter, keeping some side roots for propagation the following spring. Alternatively, let it grow as a perennial for some years and divide in spring.

Propagation

Grow from root cuttings or young plants. In late autumn or winter lift crowns, remove side shoots of pencil thickness about 6–8 inches long and store them in

Roots are at their hottest when eaten fresh

Maintenance

Spring Plant root cuttings.
Summer Feed, water and keep the crop weed-free.
Autumn Lift whole crowns, keep large roots for use in the kitchen, use others for propagation.
Winter Prepare the ground for replanting.

Harvesting and Storing

Lift and harvest the crowns in autumn when the flavor is strongest and use stored roots over winter and spring. As exposure to light causes greening, store roots in the cool and dark. In summer, lift roots as required.

Pests and Diseases

Do not plant in soil affected by clubroot. Horseradish pale leaf spot — near-white spots with dark margins on the leaves — does not affect the roots and no treatment is needed.

 companion planting

It is said to improve the disease resistance of potatoes.

 container growing

Restrict the growth of horseradish as a perennial by planting in a bucket or garbage can (with drainage holes in the base) sunk into the ground. Use soil with plenty of rotted organic matter or a loam-based compost with a moderate fertilizer content. Water well. Divide in autumn and winter as necessary.

 medicinal

Horseradish is a diaphoretic, digestive, diuretic and stimulant. Modern research has indicated antimicrobial activity against some microorganisms. It is also said to staunch bleeding, prevent scarring and cure stomach cramps. In folk medicine the vapor from grated roots was inhaled to treat colds. It is rich in vitamin C, sulfur, potassium and calcium.

 warning

Grate horseradish using the shredder attachment of a food processor to prevent your eyes from watering.

 culinary

The root stays fresh for about 2 weeks in the salad drawer of a refrigerator, but it is better to freeze grated root in plastic bags and use as required. Trim off the rootlets, scrub or scrape under cold water to remove soil. Finely grate or use a food processor, discarding the central core. Or store by grating into white vinegar (red wine or cider vinegar discolors the root).

Horseradish sauce, made with milk or oil and vinegar, is the traditional accompaniment for roast beef, asparagus and smoked fish like mackerel. Fold into whipping cream, yogurt or sour cream and season with salt, sugar and a little vinegar to make horseradish cream. Don't grate until just before serving or it will lose its flavor. My father made his horseradish sauce just before the roast beef was carved: a teaspoon was absolutely lethal and sent us running for a glass of cold water! Serve with ham, on baked potatoes or cold meats. Grated horseradish can be used in steak tartare, or added to coleslaw, dips and sauces. Blended with butter and chilled it is an alternative to garlic butter to accompany grilled steak.

Apricot and Horseradish Sauce

Serve this more delicate sauce to accompany roast chicken. To serve it with fish, use fennel rather than tarragon.

1–2 tablespoons freshly grated horseradish
1 pound apricots, pits removed
Juice of ½ a lemon
Superfine sugar
1 tablespoon fresh tarragon, chopped
Salt and freshly ground white pepper

Soften the apricots in a little water and purée. To the purée, add the lemon juice, sugar to taste, horseradish and tarragon. Season to taste.

Asparagus officinalis. Asparagaceae

ASPARAGUS

Long-lived perennial grown for slender young shoots and ornamental foliage. Half hardy. Value: high in potassium and folic acid, moderate source of beta carotene and vitamin E.

The genus *Asparagus* provides us with a range of robust foliage houseplants and one of the world's most desirable vegetables. The delicious taste, succulent texture and suggestive shape of the emergent shoots combine to create an eating experience verging on the decadent which has been celebrated for over 2,000 years. Pliny the Elder describes cultivation methods used by the Romans for producing plants with blanched stems, and mentions a cultivar of which three "spears" weighed a pound. These spears were once believed to arise from rams' horns buried in the soil. Wild asparagus grows in Europe, Asia and northwest Africa, in habitats including dry meadows, sand dunes, limestone cliffs and volcanic hillsides.

sow indoors in late winter at 55–61°F (13–16°C) directly into modules, pots or trays. Pot, harden off and plant outdoors in early summer. Male plants are the more productive, so the following year, remove any females (identifiable by their fruits) before they shed their fruits. Transplant the remaining male crowns into their permanent position in mid-spring the following year.

Growing
The autumn or winter before planting, dig in plenty of well-rotted organic matter; lime acid soil to create a pH of 6.5–7.5. It is vital to remove perennial weeds. Fork over the soil 1 or 2 weeks before planting and rake in a general fertilizer at approximately 6 ounces/sq yd.

One-year-old crowns establish quickly; 2- and 3-year-old crowns tend to suffer from a growth check after transplanting. Plant in mid-spring, once the soil is warm. The roots desiccate quickly and are easily damaged, so cover with sacking until ready to plant, then handle with care.

Either plant in single rows with the crowns 12–18 inches apart or in beds with 2 or 3 rows 12 inches apart. For several beds, set them 3 feet apart. Before planting dig a trench 8 inches by 12 inches and make a 1½ inch mound of soil in the base; plant crowns along the top, spreading out the roots, and cover them with 2 inches of sifted soil. As the stems grow, gradually cover with soil; by autumn, the trench should be filled with soil. Keep beds weed-free by hand-weeding or hoeing carefully to avoid damaging the shallow roots. On more exposed sites, support the "ferns" when windy to avoid damage to the crown, and water during dry weather.

After harvesting, apply a general fertilizer to nurture stem growth and build up the plants for the following year. In autumn, when stems have turned yellow, cut

The autumn fruits of Cannover's Collosal

---

 varieties

'Connover's Colossal'*, an early, heavy-cropping, old variety producing large, tasty spears, is suitable for light soils and freezes well. **'Lucullus'*** crops heavily, and has long, slim, straight spears. **'Martha Washington'**, an established favorite in the U.S., crops heavily, has long spears and is rust-resistant. The dark purple spears of **'Purple Jumbo'** seem almost black if temperatures are cold. Tender spikes become green with boiling and makes delicious soup. **'Purple Passion'** also turns green when cooked, is vigorous and excellent for salads.

 cultivation

Asparagus thrives in an open, sheltered position on well-drained soil. As a bed can be productive for up to 20 years, thorough preparation is essential.

Propagation
Asparagus can be grown from seed, though it is easier and less time-consuming to plant crowns. Soak seed for 2 days before sowing in mid-spring, 1 inch deep in drills 18 inches apart. Thin seedlings when they are 3 inches tall until they are 6 inches apart. Alternatively,

back to within 1–2 inches of the surface and tidy up the bed. Ferns can be shredded and composted. Each spring apply a general fertilizer as growth begins. Mulching with manure has little value beyond suppressing weeds and conserving moisture.

Maintenance

Spring Sow seed and plant crowns. Harvest late spring.
Summer Keep weed-free and water as necessary. Stop harvesting by midsummer.
Autumn Cut back yellowing ferns and tidy beds.
Winter Prepare new beds: mix in organic matter and remove perennial weeds.

Protected Cropping

Protect the crowns from late frosts with horticultural fleece or cloches.

Harvesting and Storing

However tempting, do not cut spears until the third year after planting (except possibly with **'Franklim'**). Harvesting lasts for 6 weeks in the first year and 8 weeks in subsequent years. Do not harvest after midsummer: it can result in thin spears the following year. When spears are 4–7 inches long, cut them obliquely about 1–2 inches below the surface with a sharp knife or a serrated asparagus knife.

Pests and Diseases

The black and yellow adults and small grayish larvae of asparagus beetles appear from late summer, stripping stems and foliage. Control by removing dying foliage.

 ## companion planting

Where growing conditions allow, asparagus is compatible with tomatoes, parsley and basil.

 ## medicinal

Asparagus is used to treat rheumatism, gout and cystitis. Anyone who lacks the enzyme to break down asparagine produces urine with a strong odor — a disconcerting but harmless phenomenon.

 ## warning

The berries are poisonous.

 ## culinary

Asparagus spears should be used as fresh as possible, preferably within an hour of harvesting. They can be refrigerated in a plastic bag for up to 3 days. To freeze, tie into bundles and blanch thick spears for 4 minutes, thin for 2. Freeze in a plastic container.

Asparagus is best eaten steamed or boiled and served hot with butter. Also good cold with vinaigrette, Parmesan or mayonnaise. Asparagus tips can be added to salads and pizza toppings.

To boil, wash spears, peel away the skin below the tips, and soak in cold water until all have been prepared. Sort into stalks of even length (perhaps 20 stalks if thin varieties and 6–8 if thicker-stemmed), and tie with soft string, one close to the base and another just below the tip. Stand bundles upright in boiling salted water, with the tips above water level. Cover and boil gently for 10–15 minutes until al dente, then drain and serve. Don't overcook: the tips should be firm, and the spears should not bend when held at the base. The water can be used in soup.

Jean-Christophe Novelli's Steamed Asparagus
Serves 4

20 asparagus spears
4 egg yolks
1 tablespoon white wine vinegar
1 vanilla pod, split and seeds scraped out
1 pound butter, melted
Salt and freshly ground black pepper
Toasted almonds

To make a hollandaise sauce, melt the butter and keep warm. Place a bowl over a pan of boiling water. Put the egg yolks, vinegar and vanilla seeds in the bowl and whisk until the mix is light and fluffy. Take off the heat and slowly whisk in the butter, a little at a time, until all is incorporated. Season to taste.

Steam the asparagus until still slightly crunchy, spoon a generous spoonful of hollandaise on top and garnish with some toasted almonds.

LAND CRESS

Barbarea verna. Brassicaceae

Also known as American cress, Early Yellowrocket. Biennial or short-lived perennial grown as annual for young leaves. Hardy. Value: low in calories, good source of iron, calcium, beta carotene and vitamin C.

The genus *Barbarea* was known as *herba Sanctae Barbarae*, the "herb of St. Barbara," patron saint of miners and artillerymen and protectress from thunderstorms! Land cress is a fast-growing, hardy biennial with a rosette of deeply lobed, shiny leaves and yellow flowers. Native to southwestern Europe, it has been grown as a salad crop since the 17th century; by the 18th century, extensive cultivation had died out in England, though plants became naturalized and are still common in the wild.

above ground. Do not harvest heavily until the plant is established. Soak in water to loosen dirt, then wash it off.

Pests and Diseases
Flea beetle may affect plants; grow under crop covers.

 ## companion planting

Makes a good edging plant for borders. Can be grown between taller crops, like sweetcorn and brassicas.

 ## container growing

Grow in moisture-retentive, peat-substitute compost, water well and feed with a diluted general liquid fertilizer every 3 weeks.

 ## culinary

Use its peppery-tasting leaves as a watercress substitute — as a garnish, in salads and sandwiches. Or cook them like spinach and make into soup. Good in rice, pasta salads and stir-fries.

Cress, Anchovy and Barley Salad
Serves 4

¾ pound cress, washed and dried
1½ cups pearl barley
4 tablespoons virgin olive oil
2 tablespoons white wine vinegar
2 tablespoons finely chopped fresh dill
4 anchovy fillets, roughly chopped
1 cucumber, diced
Salt and freshly ground pepper

Cook the barley in boiling water until tender and drain. Set aside. Make the dressing: mix the oil and vinegar with the dill and seasoning. In a separate bowl, mix the barley with the anchovy, add the cress and cucumber, and pour over the dressing. Toss well.

cultivation

Land cress grows in wet, shady conditions, but is best in moist fertile soil; in summer plant in light shade, under deciduous trees.

Propagation
Sow as soon as the soil becomes workable, in early spring to early summer for a summer crop, and in mid- to late summer for autumn to spring crops. Sow in seed trays or modules for transplanting when large enough to handle, or in drills ½ inch deep, thinning the seedlings to 6–8 inches. Germination takes about 3 weeks in spring but half that time in midsummer. If a few plants are left to run to seed in late spring, the following year they will seed freely; transplant seedlings into rows and water well.

Growing
Before sowing, dig in well-rotted manure or compost.

Transplant seedlings sown in late summer under glass. In heat and drought they run to seed, so water often. Pick flower stalks as they appear.

Maintenance
Spring Sow seed, water well.
Summer Water as necessary so plants do not run to seed.
Autumn Sow winter crops and transplant plantlets under glass.
Winter Prepare beds for spring sowing; harvest protected crops.

Protected Cropping
Improve the quality of autumn and winter crops by growing in an unheated greenhouse or cold frame, or under cloches.

Harvesting
Harvest after 7 weeks when plants are 3–4 inches long. Pick or cut the tender young leaves about 1 inch

Beta vulgaris subsp. *cicla. Chenopodiaceae*
SWISS CHARD

Also known as Silver Chard, Silver Beet, Sea Kale Beet. Biennial grown as annual for leaves and midribs. Hardy. Value: high in sodium, potassium, iron, and exceptional source of beta carotene, the precursor of vitamin A.

The umbrella name "leaf beet" includes Swiss chard and also encompasses perpetual spinach or spinach beet. (The "true" spinach and New Zealand spinach both belong to other genera.) A close relative of the beet, leaf beet is an ancient vegetable cultivated for its attractive, tasty leaves. Native to the Mediterranean, it was well known to the Greeks, who also ate its roots with mustard, lentils and beans. Aristotle wrote of red chard in the fourth century BCE, and Theophrastus recorded both light and dark green varieties. The Romans introduced it to central and northern Europe and from there it slowly spread, reaching the Far East in the Middle Ages and China in the 17th century. The name "chard" comes from the French *carde* and derives from the resemblance of the leaf stalks to those of globe artichokes and cardoons. In 1597 John Gerard wrote in his *Herball*, "… it grew with me to the height of eight cubits and did bring forth his rough seeds very plentifully." If the measurement is correct, his Swiss chard would be approximately 13 feet tall. I wonder where that variety is today, was his yardstick wrongly calibrated, or had it simply bolted?

Fordhook Giant

Both leaves and stems are tasty

 ## varieties

Swiss chard has broad red or white leaf stems and midribs. **'Bright Yellow'*** has golden yellow leaf stems and a mid-green puckered leaf. Delicious! **'Erbette'**, an Italian variety, is well flavored and has an excellent texture. It is good as a "cut and come again" crop. **'Fordhook Giant'*** has huge, glossy green leaves with white veins and stems. It is tasty and high-yielding, producing bumper crops even at high temperatures. **'Lucullus'*** is vigorous and crops heavily, producing pale yellow-green leaves with succulent midribs. Tolerant of high temperatures, it does not bolt.

'Perpetual Spinach'*, or spinach beet, is smaller, with narrower stems and dark, fleshy leaves, and is very resistant to bolting. Good for autumn and winter cropping. **'Rhubarb Chard'*** (**'Ruby Chard'**) is noted for its magnificent bright crimson leaf stalks and dark green puckered leaves. Ideal for the ornamental border or "potager," it needs growing with care, as it is prone to bolting.

 ## cultivation

Though they tolerate a wide range of soils, the best growing conditions are sunny or lightly shaded positions in rich, moisture-retentive, free-draining soil. In poor soil, bolting can be a problem, so dig in plenty of well-rotted organic matter the winter before planting. The ideal pH is 6.5–7.5 and acid soils should be limed.

The ideal growing temperature is 61–65°F (16–18°C), though the range of tolerance is remarkably broad. They survive in winter temperatures down to about 7°F (-14°C) and are more tolerant of higher summer temperatures than true spinach, which is inclined to bolt.

Propagation

For a constant supply throughout the year, make two sowings, one in mid-spring for a summer harvest and another in mid- to late summer. The later crop is usually lower-yielding.

Sow 3–4 seeds in "stations" 9 inches apart, in drills about ½ inch deep. Swiss chard needs 18 inches between the rows, and perpetual spinach 17 inches. Thin seedlings when large enough to handle to leave

SWISS CHARD

the strongest seedling. Alternatively, sow in modules or trays and transplant to their final spacing when they are large enough to handle. Swiss chard is particularly successful as a "cut and come again" crop. Prepare the seedbed thoroughly and broadcast or sow seed in drills the width of a hoe.

Growing
Keep crops weed-free by hoeing or, preferably, mulching with well-rotted organic matter and keep the soil continually moist. In dry conditions, plants will need 2½–3½ gallons per week, but are surprisingly drought-tolerant. A dressing of general granular or liquid fertilizer can be given to plants needing a boost.

Maintenance
Spring Sow the first crop in mid-spring in "stations"; thin, leaving a strong seedling.
Summer Weed, water and feed as necessary. Sow a second crop in mid- to late summer. Harvest as needed.
Autumn Protect with cloches or fleece in late autumn for good-quality growth.
Winter Dig over the area where the following year's crop is to be planted. Harvest overwintering crops.

Protected Cropping
Though they are hardy enough to withstand winters outdoors, plants protected in cloches, cold frames, plastic tunnels or fleece produce better crops of higher-quality leaves.

Harvesting and Storing
Seeds sown in mid-spring are ready to harvest from early to midsummer. Harvest the outer leaves first, working toward the center of the plant and cutting at the base of each stem: snapping them off is likely to disturb the roots. Choose firm leaves and discard any that are damaged or wilted. Pick regularly to ensure a constant supply of tender regrowth, so harvest even if you are unable to use them — they are certain to be welcomed by friends.

They can also be grown as "cut and come again" crops from seedling stage through to maturity. Cut seedlings when about 2 inches tall. After 2–3 crops have been harvested, allow them to regrow to about 3 inches.

Semi-mature plants are harvested leaf by leaf and mature plants can be cut about 1 inch above the ground; from this, new growth appears.

Swiss chard and perpetual spinach are best eaten straight from the plant. Leaves (minus the stalks) keep in a refrigerator in the salad compartment or in plastic bags for 2–3 days.

Pests and Diseases
They are relatively trouble-free, though beware of downy mildew when dense patches of seedlings are sown for "cut and come again" crops. It appears as brown patches on leaves. Birds sometimes attack seedlings, so protect crops; growing plants under brassicas or beans also gives them some protection.

 ## companion planting

They grow well with all beans except runners, and flourish alongside brassicas, onions and lettuce. Herbs like sage, thyme, mint, dill, hyssop, rosemary and garlic are also compatible.

 ## container growing

Swiss chard can be grown in containers and makes a fine ornamental feature. Either transplant seedlings or sow directly into loam-based compost or garden soil, with added organic matter.

 ## medicinal

Leaves are vitamin- and mineral-rich with high levels of iron and magnesium. In folk medicine the juice is used as a decongestant; the leaves are said to neutralize acid and have a purgative effect. Beware of eating it in large quantities!

 ## culinary

Perpetual spinach can be lightly boiled, steamed or eaten raw. Swiss chard takes longer to cook: try it steamed and served with butter. Soup can be made from the leaves and its midribs cooked and served like asparagus, or added to pork pies. 'Rhubarb Chard' tastes milder than white-stemmed varieties.

Spinach Beet Fritters
Serves 4

These robust fritters go well with salmon or cod.

1½ pounds perpetual spinach, well washed
Pat of butter
2 large eggs, separated
1 tablespoon grated Parmesan
1 teaspoon grated lemon zest
Olive oil, for frying
Salt and freshly ground black pepper
Pinch of nutmeg

Prepare the leaves, removing the midribs, and chop roughly. Cook in the water that clings to the leaves until wilted — 2–3 minutes — and drain well. Chop finely and return to the pan with the butter, cooking

until all the liquid evaporates. Leave to cool for 5 minutes and stir in the egg yolks, Parmesan and lemon peel. When almost cold, fold in the stiffly beaten egg whites and season with salt, pepper and nutmeg to taste.

Drop spoonfuls into hot fat, heated in a heavy frying pan, and cook for a minute or two, turning halfway.

Drain well and serve hot.

Beta vulgaris subsp. *vulgaris. Chenopodiaceae*

BEET

Also known as Beetroot. Biennial grown as annual for swollen root and young leaves. Hardy. Value: slightly higher in carbohydrates than most vegetables, good source of folic acid and potassium.

Beetroot is a form of the maritime sea beet that has been selected over many centuries for its edible roots. From the same origin come mangold (a cattle fodder), the beet used for commercial sugar production and Swiss chard. Grown since Assyrian times, the vegetable was highly esteemed by the ancient Greeks and was used in offerings to Apollo. There were many Roman recipes for beet, which they regarded more highly than the greatly revered cabbage. It appeared in 14th-century English recipes and was first described as the beetroot we know today in Germany in 1558, though it was a rarity at that time in northern Europe. The typical red coloration comes from its cell sap, but there are also varieties in other colors.

Beets come in beautiful colors

 varieties

Beets are grouped according to shape — round or globe-shaped, tapered or long, and flat or oval. To reduce the amount of thinning needed, breeders have introduced "monogerm" varieties.

Globe
'Boltardy'* is a delicious, well-textured, smooth-skinned variety and an excellent early cropper as it is very resistant to bolting. Good in containers. **'Bonel'*** has deep red, succulent, tasty roots and is high-yielding. It crops over a long period and is resistant to bolting. **'Detroit 2 Little Ball'** produces deep red, smooth-skinned "baby beet," which are ideal for pickling, bottling or freezing. A good crop for late sowing and for storing. **'Monogram'*** is dark red, well-flavored and vigorous, with smooth skin and rich red flesh. It is a "monogerm" variety. **'Monopoly'** is also a "monogerm" and is resistant to bolting, with a good color and rough skin. **'Pablo'*** is a tasty early with uniform roots and smooth skin. Also bolting resistant. **'Regala'*** has very dark roots and is quite small, even at maturity. An excellent variety for containers, and resistant to bolting.

Tapered
'Cheltenham Green Top'* is a tasty, old variety with rough skin and long roots. It stores well. **'Cheltenham Mono'** is a tasty, medium-sized "monogerm" which is resistant to bolting, good for slicing and stores well.

Others
'Albina Vereduna' (**'Snowhite'**) is a wonderful globe-shaped white variety, with smooth skin and

BEET

sweet flesh. It also has the advantage that it does not stain. The curly leaves can be used as "greens" and are full of vitamins. It does not store well and is prone to bolting. **'Barbabietola di Chioggia'** is a mild, traditional Italian variety. Sliced, it reveals unusual white internal "rings" and gives an exotic look to salads. When cooked, it becomes pale pink. Sow from mid-spring. **'Burpees Golden'** has beautiful orange skin and tasty yellow flesh. It looks great in salads, keeps its color when cooked, does not bleed when cut and the leaves can be used as "greens." It stores well, has good bolting resistance and is better harvested when small. **'Cylindrica'** has sweet-tasting, dark, oval roots that have excellent keeping qualities and good flavor. Because of its shape, it is perfect for slicing and cooks well. Harvest when young. **'Egyptian Turnip Rooted'** (**'D'Egypte'**, **'Egyptian Flat'**) has smooth roots with deep red, delicious flesh. An American introduction, it was first grown around Boston about 1869. **'Forono'*** is very tasty with large, cylindrical roots, smooth skin and good color. Slow to go woody, it is ideal for summer salads and stores well. Susceptible to bolting, it should be sown from mid-spring.

Varieties of "mini vegetables" include **'Pronto'***, **'Action'** and **'Monaco'**.

 ## cultivation

Propagation

In most varieties, each "seed" is a corky fruit containing 2 or 3 seeds, so a considerable amount of thinning is required. "Monogerm" varieties, each containing a single seed, reduce the workload. They also contain a natural inhibitor that slows or even prevents germination. Remove this by soaking seeds or washing them in running water for 30–60 minutes before sowing. At soil temperatures below 45°F (7°C) germination is slow and erratic. To overcome this, sow early crops in modules, "fluid sow" or sow in drills or stations after warming the soil with cloches. These can be left in place after sowing until the weather warms up. Use bolting-resistant varieties until mid-spring; after that, any variety can be used.

Sow the first crops under cloches from late winter to early spring ½–1 inch deep and 1 inch apart with 9 inches between rows. Thin to a final spacing of 4 inches between plants. Alternatively, sow 2–3

seeds at "stations" 4 inches apart, thinning to leave the strongest seedling when the first true leaf appears. Round varieties can be "multisown" in a cool greenhouse planting three seeds per module, thinning to 4–5 seedlings, then planting the modules 4 inches apart when about 2 inches high. Early crops can also be sown thinly in broad flat drills ½–1 inch deep, in a similar way to peas.

Thin as soon as seedlings are touching and keep thinning as plants grow: those large enough can be used whole. If you grow beets under horticultural fleece or a similar cover (put in place once the seedlings have established), yields can be increased by up to 50%. Remove protection 4–6 weeks after sowing. From mid-spring, if the weather is warm seeds can be sown without the protection of cloches, thinning to 3–4 inches apart.

Beets grown for pickling need to be about 2 inches in diameter. Sowing in rows 3 inches apart and thinning plants to 2½ inches apart will give you the correct size.

From late spring to early summer sow the main crop, using any round or long variety. Harvest throughout the summer and for winter storing. Sow in drills or at "stations," thinning to leave a final spacing of 3 inches apart in rows 8 inches apart or 5–6 inches in and between the rows.

For a constant supply of beets, sow round cultivars under glass from late winter at 4-week intervals for mid-spring crops; and for a late autumn crop sow from early to midsummer in mild areas (for lifting during winter thin to 4 inches). For winter storage sow in late May, early June.

Growing

Beet needs an open site with fertile, well-drained light soil that has been manured for the previous crop. The pH should be 6.5–7.5, so acidic soils will need liming. Autumn-maturing varieties tolerate heavier conditions and long-rooted varieties require a deeper soil. The best quality roots grow in moderate temperatures around 61°F (16°C).

Scatter a slow-release general fertilizer at 2–3 weeks before sowing, raking the seedbed to a fine tilth. For good-quality beets, it is important to avoid any check in growth; at the onset of drought, water at a rate of 3 gallons/sq yd every 2 weeks. Do not overwater as this results in excessive leaf growth and small roots.

If watering is neglected, yields are low, roots become woody and when it rains or you water suddenly, the roots will split. Keep weed-free and hoe with care as damage causes the roots to bleed: use an onion hoe or mulch around the plants. Mulching with a 2-inch layer of well-rotted compost or spent mushroom compost will conserve moisture.

Maintenance

Spring Sow early crops under glass or cloches. Mid-spring crops can be sown without protection.
Summer Sow successively every month, harvest earlier crops, keep the plot weed-free and water as required. Sow main crops.
Autumn Lift later crops and those for storage.
Winter In mild areas leave overwintering crops outdoors and protect with straw or similar materials. Alternatively, lift and store indoors.

Protected Cropping

Grow early crops under glass in modules and transplant under cloches. Alternatively, grow under cloches or crop covers and remove these about 6 weeks after sowing.

Harvesting and Storing

Beet takes 60–90 days to mature. It must always be harvested before it becomes woody and inedible. Harvest salad beets from late spring to mid-autumn and maincrop varieties from midsummer onwards.

Boltardy

Early varieties are best harvested when the size of a golf ball; when later crops reach that size, lift every other plant and use for cooking, leaving the rest for lifting when they reach baseball-size.

Lift roots carefully with a fork, shake off soil and twist off the leaves. Do not cut off the leaves: it causes bleeding and makes a terrible mess! Use any damaged roots immediately. Lift beet for storage by mid-autumn and put in strong boxes of moist peat substitute, sand or sawdust, leaving a gap between each root. Store in a cool, frost-free shed or garage. Roots should keep until mid-spring the following year but check regularly and remove any that deteriorate. The long-rooted types are traditionally grown for storage, although most varieties store successfully.

In mild areas and on well-drained soil, they can be left over winter, but need a dense protective covering of straw or similar material before the frosts. This also makes lifting easier.

Pests and Diseases
Beets are generally trouble-free but may suffer from the following problems:

Black bean aphid forms dense colonies on the leaves. Yellow blotches between the veins, the symptom of manganese deficiency, appear on older leaves first and can be a problem on extremely alkaline soil.

Rough patches on the surface of the root and waterlogged brown patches and rings at its center are a sign of boron deficiency. There may also be corky "growths" on the shoots and leaf stalks.

Make sure that beet seedlings are protected against birds. Slugs make holes in leaves. The problem is worse in damp conditions.

 ## companion planting

Beets flourish in the company of kohlrabi, carrots, cucumber, lettuce, onions, brassicas and most beans (not runners). Dill or Florence fennel planted nearby attracts predators. Because they combine well with so many other crops and small roots mature within 9–13 weeks, beets are good for intercropping and useful catch-crops.

 ## culinary

The roots are eaten raw — try them grated as a crudité — or cooked and served fresh or pickled. Young "tops" can be cooked like spinach and used as "greens." They add color and flavor to salads, particularly the red, yellow, white and bicolored varieties. Bean and beet salad is particularly tasty. Wash in cold water, keeping root and stems intact: do not damage the skin, as bleeding causes loss of flavor and color. Boil for up to 2 hours in saltwater, depending on the size, then carefully rub off the skin. It is delicious served hot as a vegetable, otherwise cool for pickling or for a fresh salad.

Beet can also be baked, and is the basis for borscht soup when cooked with white stock. It also makes excellent chutney and wine.

Freeze small beets that are no more than 2 inches across. Wash and boil, skin and cool, then cut roots into slices or cubes and freeze in a rigid container. You should use within 6 months.

In a plastic bag or salad compartment of the fridge, they stay fresh for up to 2 weeks.

Spicy Beetroot Salad
Serves 4

1½ pounds beets, washed and trimmed
Juice of ½ a lemon
½ teaspoon ground cumin
½ teaspoon ground cinnamon
½ teaspoon paprika
1 tablespoon orange flower water
2 tablespoons olive oil
Salt and freshly ground black pepper
2 tablespoons chopped fresh parsley
Lettuce (colored varieties mixed with green leaves
    such as lamb's lettuce)

Cook the beets in a steamer for 20 or 30 minutes until tender. Peel and slice them when cool, reserving the liquid that accumulates on the plate.

Toss them in lemon juice and coat with the spices, orange-flower water and olive oil, together with the liquid. Season, cover and chill. To serve, toss with the parsley and arrange on individual plates on a bed of lettuce leaves.

 ## container growing

Unless growing for exhibition, grow only globe varieties in containers — about 8 inches deep — or troughs or growbags. Sow seed thinly about ½–1 inch deep from mid-spring to midsummer, thinning to 4–5 inches apart. Water regularly, harvest when the size of a tennis ball and keep weed-free.

 ## other uses

The foliage is attractive and ideal for inclusion in an ornamental border or "potager," particularly varieties like **'Bull's Blood'**. The leaf mineral content is 25% magnesium, making it useful on the compost heap.

 ## medicinal

Used in folk medicine as a blood tonic for gastritis, piles and constipation; mildly cardio-tonic. Recent research has shown that taking at least one glass of raw beet juice a day helps control cancer. It is regarded as a "superfood."

 ## warning

The sap stains clothes. To remove, rub the stain with a slice of pear and wash as usual.

MUSTARD GREENS

Brassica juncea. Brassicaceae

Also known as Oriental Mustard. Hardy annual or biennial. Value: rich in vitamin A and C, moderate calcium, iron, potassium and phosphorous.

Commonly grown in Europe for mustard seed, mustard greens have their greatest diversity of shape and form in central Asia and the Himalayas which, along with the warm, central-Chinese province of Sichuan, India and the Caucasus, are thought to be one of the ancient areas of domestication. Sanskrit records show that mustard greens have been cultivated since 3000 BCE and there have been an astonishing range of selections for their desirable characteristics. Among them are forms with tumescent swellings on the leaf stems, fleshy tap roots, large stems, multi-shoots, green stems and curled leaves plus heading varieties both large and small. This selection process is set to continue long into the future, as mustard greens strengthen their position as an indispensable crop for Asian cuisine.

 varieties

Commonly grown groups include:

Giant-leaved Mustard
This is very hardy. **'Green Chirimen'** has green, blistered leaves, while **'Miike Giant'** is broad-leaved and vigorous with mildly-flavored, crinkled leaves and purple veins. **'Osaka Purple'** is fast growing, the large green leaves becoming purple in cold weather. It is easy to grow and cold-hardy.

Wrapped heart
These varieties grow better when there are high temperatures immediately after sowing. **'Amsoi'** produces tender greens with a mustard tang that are often used for pickling. **'Chicken heart'** is a semi-heading variety and well flavored. **'Kekkyu Takana'** forms a small head and the mild flavor becomes stronger as it matures.

Leaf Mustard
Sow in summer and autumn. **'South Wind'** has purple-tinted, undulating leaves and is heat tolerant and good for stir-fries.

Green in the snow
This is fast growing and cold-tolerant with frilly leaves. Young leaves are moderately spicy, older leaves should be cooked. Sow in autumn, can be grown as a "cut and come again" crop.

Curled mustard
These are hardy but also tolerant of high temperatures. **'Green Wave'** is an All American Seed selection; it grows to 2 feet tall with dark green, frilly-margined leaves. It is highly productive, slow to bolt and the flavor is hot.

Swollen stem mustard
These have unusually shaped or formed stems or leaf stems. **'Horned Mustard'** has bright green, frilly leaves with a distinct "horn" in the center of the stem. The leaf buds are also delicious. **'Tsa Tsai Round'** is unusual in that it forms thick, rounded, tumescent-like stems that are up to 6 inches diameter and ½ pound in weight below the leaves. It is a cool season crop.

MUSTARD GREENS

Osaka Purple

 cultivation

Propagation

Sow seeds thinly in situ and thin to the required spacing; summer and autumn sowings can also be made in modules for planting out. Sow according to the ultimate size of the variety or the stage of growth at harvest. Young plants should be 4–6 inches apart; mature at 12 inches apart in and between rows. Large varieties with spreading heads being grown to maturity should be 18 inches apart.

Growing

Grow in an open, sheltered site in fertile soil of any kind, add well-rotted organic matter if necessary; they need plenty of moisture when in growth as they "bolt" in dry conditions. All of the mustard varieties are cool season crops, though the resistance to cold and heat varies according to the variety. Sow from mid- to late summer for growing to maturity outdoors, or under cover, or in spring, for harvesting as "cut and come again" crops. Sow successively to extend the harvesting season.

Maintenance

Spring Sow outdoors when the soil is warm and friable.
Summer Sow crops for harvesting at maturity from midsummer where frosts occur and late summer where frost free. Harvest "curly leaved" and "headed" types or "cut and come again."
Autumn Harvest.
Winter Harvest crops outdoors or under glass.

Protected Cropping

Mustard greens make good autumn sown crops for unheated greenhouses or polyethylene tunnels.

Harvesting and Storing

Cut and use fresh as required.

Pests and Diseases

They suffer from most of the usual brassica problems including flea beetle, cabbage root fly and slugs.

 container growing

Some varieties can be grown as "cut and come again" seedling crops in growing bags or large containers. They tend to be slow growing and are not as productive as other types of Asian vegetables using this method.

 culinary

Mustard greens are renowned for their spicy and peppery flavor which varies according to the plant's age and variety. They can be used raw or cooked in stir-fries and soups, combine well with crab, can be made into pickles and the leaves and shoots can be dried for winter eating. The inner leaves are milder and used in salads; the outer leaves are stronger flavored and usually cooked.

Brassica napus (Napobrassica Group). Brassicaceae
RUTABAGA

Also known as Swede, Swedish turnip, Yellow turnip. Biennial grown as annual for swollen root and young leaves. Hardy. Value: small amounts of niacin (vitamin B) and vitamin C, low in calories and carbohydrates.

Rutabaga is one of the hardiest of all root crops and is the perfect winter vegetable for cool temperate climates. Swede is an abbreviation of "Swedish turnip," indicating its origins. Eaten in France and southern Europe in the 16th century, it came to Britain from Holland in 1755 and rapidly became popular as the "turnip-rooted cabbage." Along with the turnip, it was first used as winter fodder for sheep and cattle, improving milk production during a traditionally lean period. During times of famine, rutabagas were eaten by country folk and still have the reputation among many as peasant food.

To despise them is your loss; they are robust, undemanding and one of the easiest vegetables to grow. New varieties are disease-resistant, tasty and a wonderful accompaniment to sprouts as a winter vegetable — particularly when mashed with butter, cream and spices.

varieties

'Acme' has round roots with pale purple skin but its tops are prone to powdery mildew. 'Angela' produces purple roots and is resistant to powdery mildew. 'Lizzy' is a round variety with purple tops and yellow flesh, a soft texture and sweet, nutty flavor. 'Marian' is purple with yellow flesh and is very tasty and quick-growing. 'Magres'* has deliciously flavored yellow flesh and is mildew resistant. 'Virtue' has red skin and sweet flesh.

cultivation

Propagation

Rutabagas need a long growing season and should be sown from early spring in cooler climates to early summer where temperatures are warmer and germination and growth are rapid. Sow in drills 1 inch deep and 16–18 inches apart, thinning seedlings to 9–12 inches. Thin when they are no more than 1 inch high, when the first true leaves appear, to ensure that the roots develop properly. Firm the soil after thinning.

Growing

Rutabagas prefer a sheltered and open site in fertile, well-drained but moisture-retentive soil. Good drainage is essential. Summer sowings can be made in moderate shade, provided they receive sufficient moisture. Rutabagas prefer a pH of 5.5–7.0, so very acidic soil will need liming. If the ground has not been manured for the previous crop, double dig in autumn, incorporate plenty of well-rotted organic matter and allow the soil to "weather" over winter.

About a week prior to sowing, remove any weeds or debris and rake general fertilizer into the soil at 3 ounces/sq yd. In common with other brassicas, rutabagas grow poorly on loose soil, so rake the soil to a fine tilth and firm it with the head of a rake or by carefully treading. If the soil is dry, water thoroughly before sowing and stand on a planting board to avoid compacting the soil. Mark each row with canes or twigs, and label and date the crop.

Keep crops weed-free by hand weeding and careful hoeing. Rutabagas need a constant supply of water throughout the growing season, otherwise they tend to run to seed or produce small, woody roots. Sudden watering or rain after a period of drought causes the roots

Brassica oleracea (Capitata Group). *Brassicaceae.*

CABBAGE

Biennial grown as annual for leaves and hearts. Half hardy/hardy. Value: rich in beta carotene and vitamin C — especially green varieties and outer leaves; outer leaves contain vitamin E.

The Latin *brassica* comes from *bresic*, the Celtic word for cabbage, a plant cultivated for centuries in the eastern Mediterranean and Asia Minor. The Romans believed that cabbages rose from Jupiter's sweat as he labored to explain two contradicting oracles — esteeming wild and cultivated cabbages as a cure-all as well as recommending them to prevent unseemly drunkenness.

Many varieties have been developed over the centuries. Heat-tolerant types were bred in southern Europe, while many hard-headed varieties were introduced by the Celts and Scandinavians. White cabbages appeared after 814 CE and German literature records the cultivation of red cabbages in 1150; in the 16th century Estienne and Liébault believed these were made by watering cabbages with red wine or by growing them in hot places. By the 13th century "headed cabbage" was well known, and three kinds of 'Savoy' were mentioned in a German herbal of 1543.

January King

 varieties

Cabbages are usually grouped according to the season when they are harvested. They range from fairly loose-leaved heads of pointed or conical shape to rounded "ball" shapes with varying degrees of densely packed leaves.

Spring

Spring cabbages traditionally have pointed heads, but there are now round-headed types. For "spring greens," use their immature leaves or choose a leafy variety bred for this purpose.

'Duncan'* is high yielding so grow for leaves or small solid heads in June. **'Offenham 1 Myatts Offenham Compacta'** is a tasty, very early spring cabbage and has dark green leaves. **'Pixie'** is another very early spring variety that has tight, compact hearts; ideal for small gardens.

Early summer/summer

'Derby Day'* is an excellent "ball-head" cabbage for harvesting from early summer. **'Hispi'*** is reliable, with pointed heads of good quality and taste. It matures rapidly and is ideal for close spacing. **'First of June'*** is a dark-leaved variety with a compact head, good for successional sowing in summer. **'Ruby Ball'*** is an ornamental and colorful red cabbage, very reliable and particularly excellent for use in salads. **'Kalibos'**, also red, is slug-resistant and good for small gardens.

A heart is forming

Late summer/autumn
'Golden Acre', a ball-headed variety, is compact and sweet-tasting and ready in 12 weeks. It tolerates close spacing, is high-yielding and grows well on poorer soils. **'Kilaton'** is delicious, good quality and club root-resistant. **'Kilaxy'** produces compact, tasty heads, stands well and is also club root-resistant. **'Stonehead'*** has a tightly packed head and is early maturing. It is resistant to yellow and black rot.

Winter/winter storage
Winter cabbages are usually ball- or drum-headed. The white-leaved Dutch cabbage (used primarily for coleslaw) matures from mid- to late autumn and can be cut for storage or left to stand in mild conditions. The extremely hardy, tasty and attractive Savoy types with puckered green leaves mature from mid-autumn to late winter.

'January King 3' is an excellent drum-head Savoy type, which is extremely hardy and frost-resistant, maturing in mid-autumn to early winter. **'Multiton'** is a winter-storage cabbage and **'Savoy Express'** is small, sweet and ideal where space is limited.

 cultivation

Propagation
Seeds sown in trays, modules or seedbeds will be ready for transplanting about 5 weeks after sowing. Spacings can be modified according to the size of "head" required. Closer spacing means a smaller head while wider spacing produces slightly larger heads. Sow spring cabbage from mid- to late summer; transplant from early to mid-autumn. Space 10–12 inches apart

in and between the rows. Protect with cloches or crop covers over winter to encourage earlier cropping. For "spring greens," grow suitable varieties with 10 inches in and between the plants, or space spring cabbage plants 4–6 inches apart and harvest when immature.

Sow cabbages for summer and autumn harvest successionally, with "earlies" and "lates" for an extended cropping season (see "Varieties"). You should make the first sowings in a propagator or heated greenhouse at 55–61°F (13–16°C) from late winter to early spring, pot and transplant in mid- to late spring. Follow these with sowings in cold frames or a seedbed under cloches or crop covers. Make further sowings without protection until late spring.

Transplant from early to midsummer, spacing plants 14–20 inches apart depending on the size of head you are after.

Sow winter-maturing varieties successionally from mid- to late spring under cover or outdoors for transplanting from early to midsummer. Space about 18 inches apart.

Growing
Cabbages flourish at around 59–68°F (15–20°C) and should not be transplanted at temperatures above 77°F (25°C), while some overwintering varieties survive temperatures down to 14°F (-10°C).

Cabbage plants in a vegetable patch

They flourish in a rich, fertile, moisture-retentive soil with a pH of 5.5–7.0. Dig in plenty of well-rotted organic matter several weeks before planting and lime the soil if necessary. Rake the soil level before planting and ensure that it is firm but not compacted.

Do not fertilize spring cabbages after planting, as this encourages soft growth and the nutrients are washed away by winter rains. Wait until early to mid-spring and scatter a general granular fertilizer round the plants, or liquid feed.

Summer, autumn and winter cabbages need a dressing of fertilizer after transplanting and will benefit from a further granular or liquid feed in the growing season. To increase stability, earth up spring and winter cabbages as they grow.

Provided growing conditions are good and plants healthy, you can produce a second harvest from spring or early summer varieties. After cutting the head, cut a cross shape ½ inch deep in the stump, which will sprout a cluster of smaller cabbages.

Keep cabbages moist and weed-free with regular hoeing, hand weeding or mulching. Rotate cabbages with other brassicas.

Maintenance
Spring Sow and transplant summer, autumn and winter cabbage. Harvest.
Summer Sow spring cabbage. Harvest.
Autumn Transplant spring cabbage. Harvest.
Winter Sow summer cabbages. Harvest.

Harvesting and Storing
Spring cabbages are ready to harvest from mid- to late spring. Summer and autumn varieties are ready to harvest from midsummer to mid-autumn. Winter types can be harvested from late autumn to mid-spring. Spring and summer varieties are eaten immediately after harvest.

Dutch winter white cabbages and some red cabbages can be lifted for storing indoors. Choose those that are healthy and undamaged and dig them up before the first frosts for storage in a cool, slightly humid, frost-free place.

Remove the loose outer leaves and stand the heads on a slatted shelf or a layer of straw on the shed floor. Alternatively, suspend them in nets. They can also be

CABBAGE

stored in a spare cold frame if it is well ventilated to discourage rotting. They should store for up to 5 months.

Freeze only the best quality fresh crisp heads. Wash, shred coarsely, blanch for about 1 minute and pack into freezer bags or rigid plastic containers.

Wrapped in plastic wrap in a refrigerator, cabbages stay fresh for about a week.

Pests and Diseases
Cabbages suffer from the common brassica problems, including cabbage root fly, clubroot, aphids and birds.

 companion planting

Cabbages thrive in the company of herbs like dill, mint, rosemary, sage, thyme and chamomile. They also grow well with many other vegetables including onions, garlic, peas, celery, potatoes, broad beans and beets.

Like all brassicas, they benefit from the nitrogen left in the soil after legumes have been grown. The belief that they do not grow well with vines, oregano and cyclamen stems from Classical times. In the 16th century, it was well known that "Vineyards where Coleworts grow, doe yeeld the worser Wines."

 medicinal

Eating cabbage is said to reduce the risk of colonic cancer, stimulate the immune system and kill bacteria. Drinking the juice is alleged to prevent and heal ulcers. Some active principles are partly destroyed on cooking, so cabbage is much more nutritious eaten raw.

According to folklore, placing heated cabbage leaves on the soles of the feet reduces fever; placed on a septic wound, they draw out pus or a splinter.

 culinary

Traditionally cabbage is cooked by boiling — preferably as briefly as possible — in a small amount of water, to preserve the nutrients. Add the cabbage to boiling water, which should not stop boiling while you place the younger leaves from the heart on top of the older leaves below. Cover, cook briefly for 3 minutes, then drain. Or steam for about 6–8 minutes.

Stir-frying, the Asian way, is almost as fast; alternatively, bake, braise or stuff. Use as a substitute for vine leaves in dolmades.

Eat shredded white or red cabbage raw in salads. Coleslaw is a mixture of shredded cabbage, carrot, apple and celery with French dressing or a mayonnaise/sour cream blend; its name derives from "cole," the old name for cabbage, and the Dutch *slaw*, meaning salad.

Pickle red cabbage in vinegar and white cabbage in brine (as *sauerkraut*).

Czerwona Kapusta
Serves 6

The Polish and Czechs are extremely keen on red cabbage. This dish combines subtle flavours to make a refreshing change from our usual ways of cooking the vegetable.

2 pounds red cabbage, finely sliced
Salt and freshly ground black pepper
1 tablespoon butter
1 tablespoon plain flour
½ cup red wine
2 teaspoons sugar
Pinch ground cloves
Pinch ground cinnamon

Put the cabbage in a colander and sprinkle with 1 teaspoon salt; leave for 15 minutes then rinse well under cold water. Transfer to a pan of boiling water and simmer gently until the cabbage is just cooked. Drain and keep warm. Reserve a little of the liquid.

Heat the butter in a saucepan over a medium heat and mix in the flour to make a roux. Cook for 2 minutes without burning. Dilute with the cooking liquid to make a thick sauce and stir in the cabbage. Season and add the red wine, sugar, cloves and cinnamon. Mix well and simmer for a further 5 minutes. Serve.

Czerwona Kapusta

Colcannon
Serves 4

Probably the most famous Irish dish, some believe this was traditionally made with kale but today it is commonly made with cabbage. Use a Savoy.

1 pound cabbage, sliced and cooked
1 pound potatoes, peeled and cooked
1 leek, cleaned, sliced and cooked in a little cream
  or milk
4 tablespoons butter
Salt and freshly ground black pepper

Mash the potatoes and season them before stirring in the slices of leek and juices in which they were cooked. Then add the cabbage and mix thoroughly over a low heat. Arrange on a warmed serving dish and make a hole in the center. Keep warm. Partly melt the butter, season, and pour it into the cavity. Serve immediately, piping hot.

BRUSSELS SPROUT

Biennial grown as annual for leafy buds and "tops." Hardy. Value: excellent source of vitamin C, rich in beta carotene, folic acid, vitamin E and potassium.

First recorded as a spontaneous sport from a cabbage plant found in the Brussels region of Belgium around 1750, this vegetable had reached England and France by 1800. The Brussels version may not have been the first occurrence: a plant described as *brassica capitata polycephalos* (a many-headed brassica with knoblike heads) was illustrated in D'Alechaps's *Historia Generalis Plantarum* in 1587. A stalwart among winter vegetables in cool temperate climates, sprouts are extremely hardy and crop heavily, but are rather fiddly to prepare. As with all vegetables, home-grown ones taste far better than those bought from a shop. If you have never eaten sprouts harvested fresh from the garden, try them: they are absolutely delicious.

 ## varieties

Sprouts are divided into early, mid-season and late varieties, harvested from early to mid-autumn, mid-autumn to midwinter and midwinter to early spring respectively. "Earlies" are shorter and faster-growing than the hardier "lates," which are taller with higher yields. To extend the season, grow one variety from each group if you have space; alternatively, grow midseason and late types for midwinter to early spring crops, when other vegetables are scarce.

Although older open-pollinated varieties are very tasty, it is generally accepted that the modern, compact F1 hybrids are a better buy. They produce a heavy crop of uniform "buttons" all the way up the stem, which remain in good condition for a long period without "blowing"; plants are also less likely to fall over.

'Braveheart'* is vigorous, high yielding and easy to pick, with a nutty flavor. **'Falstaff'** is a vigorous, high-yielding red cultivar with tasty "buttons." The red coloration disappears when boiled so steaming is a good method of cooking. **'Noisette'** is a "gourmet" sprout with a nutty flavor. **'Oliver'*** (very early) is a high-yielding variety with large, tasty sprouts and good resistance to powdery mildew. **'Rampart'** (late) has tasty sprouts that last for a long time before "blowing" but tend to become bitter late in the season. It has good resistance to powdery mildew and some resistance to ringspot. **'Romulus'*** grows tall and vigorous, crops well and is very reliable and tasty. **'Rubine'**, a red form, is worth a place in an ornamental border and produces small crops of good-tasting sprouts.

BRUSSELS SPROUT

cultivation

Sprouts need a sheltered, sunny spot; wind rock can be a problem in exposed sites. Soil should be moisture-retentive yet free-draining, with a pH of 6.5.

Propagation

Sow early varieties from late winter to early spring, midseason varieties from mid- to late spring and late varieties from mid-spring. Sow seeds thinly, 1 inch deep in a half tray of moist seed or multi-purpose compost and put them in an unheated greenhouse, cold frame or sheltered spot outdoors to germinate. Transplant seedlings when they are large enough to handle into a larger seed tray, in potting or multipurpose compost, about 1½–2 inches apart.

Sowing in modules reduces root disturbance when transplanting. Put 2 seeds in each module and retain the strongest after germination. Sow early varieties from late winter in a propagator at 50–55°F (10–13°C) and transplant them into their permanent position after

Brussels sprouts can be harvested in autumn and winter

The tops can be eaten too

hardening off. Some taller varieties are prone to falling over when grown in modules, but when planted deeply, a long tap root develops.

The previous two methods are preferable to sowing in a seedbed, which takes up space that could be used for other crops, and leaves seedlings vulnerable to pests and diseases; I do not recommend it. If necessary, warm the soil with cloches or black plastic. Protect earlier sowings from cold weather; later sowings can be made without shelter. Water before sowing if the soil is dry. Level, firm and rake the seedbed to a fine tilth before sowing seed thinly, 1 inch deep in rows 8 inches apart, thinning seedlings to 3–4 inches apart when they are large enough to handle. Transplant into their final position when they are about 4–6 inches tall. Gradually harden off those grown under cover before planting them in their final positions.

Growing

Dig in plenty of well-rotted manure or compost several months before planting, particularly on light, poor or heavy soils. The ground should not be freshly manured, as excessive nitrogen causes sprouts to "blow."

Plant earlier, smaller varieties about 24 inches apart each way, those of moderate size 30 inches apart and taller varieties 36 inches apart. Wider spacing encourages larger sprouts, improves air circulation and reduces fungal problems, while closer spacing means smaller, compact "buttons" that will mature at the same time.

Plant with the lowest leaves just above the soil surface. Tug a leaf — if the whole plant moves it has not been planted firmly enough. On light soils, make a drill 3–4 inches deep, plant sprouts in the bottom and refill it with soil. The extra support makes the plants more stable. Water immediately after transplanting for 3–4 weeks until plants have become established and, if available, mulch with straw to a depth of 2–3 inches.

Keep the beds weed-free. Watering is not normally needed once plants are established except during drought, when each plant can be given up to ½ cup per day to maintain the growth necessary for good cropping. Remove any diseased or yellowing leaves as they appear. Earthing up around the stem base to a depth of 3–5 inches provides support against winter winds, although tall varieties will usually need staking. In exposed gardens, even dwarf varieties need staking.

"Stopping" by removing the growing point is only beneficial for autumn-maturing F1 cultivars being grown for freezing. Plants can be stopped when lowest sprouts reach ½ inch diameter, to encourage even development of sprouts on the stem. When left unstopped, sprouts can be picked over a longer period.

Grow sprouts on a 3- or 4-year rotation, preferably following peas and beans (where they benefit from the nitrogen left in the soil). In late summer, feeding with a liquid high-potassium fertilizer gives plants a useful boost. Plant small lettuces like 'Little Gem' between

BRUSSELS SPROUT

sprouts for summer and autumn cropping, and winter purslane or land cress for early winter crops.

Lift plants immediately after harvesting, put leaves on the compost heap and shred the stems.

Maintenance
Spring Sow outdoors in seedbeds, thin and keep weed-free.
Summer Transplant outdoors and water during drought.
Autumn Harvest early varieties; stake tall varieties if needed.
Winter Sow early varieties indoors. Harvest later crops.

Protected Cropping
Earlier sowings made outdoors in a seedbed should be protected with cloches or fleece. Continued protection with horticultural fleece provides a physical barrier against pests such as cabbage root fly, flea beetle, aphids and birds.

Harvest sprouts that are tightly closed

Harvesting and Storing
Pick sprouts when those at the base are walnut-sized and tightly closed. Snap them off with a sharp downward tug or cut with a knife, removing "blown" sprouts and any yellow, diseased leaves. When harvest is over, the tops can be cooked as cabbage. During severe winter weather, lift a few plants to hang in a shed where they can be easily harvested. They will last for several weeks.

Pests and Diseases
Sprouts are very robust yet subject to the usual brassica problems. Downy mildew shows as yellow patches on the leaves, with patches of fluffy mold on the underside in humid conditions. Remove all affected leaves or dust with sulfur. If downy mildew appears on seedlings, improve ventilation and increase spacing.

Powdery mildew is a white powdery deposit over shoots, stems and leaves. In severe cases, plants become yellow and die. It is more of a problem when plants are dry at the roots. Water and mulch, remove diseased leaves and spray with fungicide.

Clubroot, affecting members of the *Brassicaceae* family, is a disease to be avoided at all costs. Roots swell and distort, young plants wilt on hot days but recover overnight, growth is stunted and crops ruined. It is more of a problem on poorly drained, acid soils. Spores remain in the soil for up to 20 years. Never buy brassicas from unknown sources: grow them yourself. Potting plants into 4–6 inch pots allows the roots to become established before they are planted out, which lessens the effects of clubroot. Improve drainage; lime acidic soils to create a neutral pH. Earthing up often encourages new roots to form and reduces the effects. Remove all diseased plants, with the whole root system if possible, and destroy them.

Ringspot is worse in cool wet seasons and on well-manured land. It is most evident on older leaves as round brown spots with dark centers. Remove and burn any affected plants and rotate crops.

 companion planting

When planted among maturing onions, sprouts benefit from their root residues and the firm soil.

 culinary

Steam or boil sprouts briskly for the minimum time required to cook through — they should not turn mushy. Small sprouts can be shredded in salads — 'Rubine' and 'Falstaff' are particularly attractive.

They can be stored for up to 3 days in a plastic bag in the refrigerator. Freeze sprouts only if they are small. Blanch for 3 minutes, cool and drain before drying and packing them into freezer bags.

Stir-fried Sprouts
Serves 4

This can look quite spectacular made with a red variety such as 'Falstaff' or 'Rubine'.

1 pound Brussels sprouts, trimmed and finely sliced
2 tablespoons vegetable oil
2 tablespoons soy sauce
2 tablespoons hazelnuts, roughly ground
Salt and freshly ground black pepper

Heat the oil in a wok, stir in the soy sauce and, over a high heat, cook the sprouts for 2–3 minutes. Sprinkle over the hazelnuts. Season and serve.

Brassica oleracea (Gongylodes Group). *Brassicaceae*
KOHLRABI

Biennial grown as annual for rounded, swollen roots. Hardy. Value: rich in vitamin C, traces of minerals.

This odd-looking vegetable with a distinctive name has a rounded, swollen stem which, with the leaves removed, looks like a sputnik! Its common name, derived from the German *Kohl*, meaning cabbage and *rabi*, turnip, accurately describes its taste when boiled. Raw, it has a fresh, nutty flavor. Found in northern Europe in the 15th century, it may already have existed for centuries, as a similar-sounding vegetable was described by Pliny around 70 CE. This highly nutritious, tasty vegetable is more drought-resistant than most brassicas, succeeding where rutabagas and turnips fail. It deserves to be more widely grown and eaten.

 ## varieties

'Blusta' is fast-maturing, has a sweet, nutty flavor and is resistant to bolting. **'Domino'***, an early variety, is good for growing under cover. **'Kongo'*** is top-quality; fast-growing, very sweet and juicy and high yields. **'Korist'*** produces a good-sized crop of mildly flavored, tender, juicy bulbs. **'Lanro'*** is a white-fleshed, green-skinned variety. Juicy and mild-flavored, it is a good mini vegetable. **'Olivia'*** produces good-sized bulbs and is crisp and mild-flavored. **'Trero'** is sweet, uniform, vigorous and slow to become "woody." **'White Vienna'** has a pale green skin and is delicately flavored.

 ## cultivation

Propagation

As a general rule, green varieties are sown from mid-spring to midsummer for summer crops and the hardier purple-skinned types from midsummer to mid-autumn for winter use. Sow successionally for a regular harvest. Early sowings in seed or multi-purpose compost in a propagator at 55–65°F (10–15°C) can be made during midwinter to early spring. Transplant after hardening off in mid-spring when they are no more than 2 inches high; if you let them grow taller or sow seed when soil temperatures are below 50°F (10°C), they are liable to run to seed. Protect with cloches or horticultural fleece until the plants are established.

Pick when small for the finest flavor

Purple Vienna

Water the drills before sowing and sow later crops thinly in drills ½ inch deep in rows 12 inches apart. Thin seedlings when they are about 1 inch high and the first true leaves appear, to a final spacing 6–8 inches apart. Prompt thinning is vital, as growth is easily checked. Alternatively, plant 3 seeds together in "stations" 6 inches apart and thin to leave the strongest seedling. Kohlrabi can also be grown successfully in modules and then transplanted at their final spacing.

Kohlrabi grown as a mini vegetable is ideal for the small garden. Sow cultivars like **'Rolano'**, **'Logo'**, 'Korist' and **'Kolibri'** and thin to about 1 inch apart between the plants and rows. Harvest after 9–10 weeks when about the size of golf balls.

Growing

The ideal situation is a sunny position on light, fertile, humus-rich, well-drained soil. Incorporate organic matter the winter before planting if necessary and lime acidic soils to create a pH of 6–7. The ground must be firm before planting, as (in common with other brassicas), kohlrabi does not grow well on loose soil. Lightly fork the area, removing any debris, then gently tread down the surface or firm it with the head of a rake. Finally, rake in a general fertilizer at 6 ounces/sq yd and level. Kohlrabi must receive a constant supply of water throughout the season. This is because if growth is checked they can become "woody." During drought periods, they need up to 2 gallons/sq yd of water per week. If growth slows down, liquid feed with a high-nitrogen fertilizer. Keep crops weed-free and mulch with compost to suppress weeds and retain moisture.

Rotate kohlrabi with brassicas.

Maintenance

Spring Prepare the seedbed and sow seed *in situ* under cloches.
Summer Sow regularly for successional cropping. Sow hardier purple varieties later in the season. Weed and water as necessary.
Autumn Sow in mid-autumn and protect with cloches for early winter harvest.
Winter From late winter, sow early crops in modules or trays. Prepare the ground for outdoor sowings.

Protected Cropping

Early and late outdoor crops should be protected with cloches or crop covers.

Harvesting and Storing

Kohlrabi matures rapidly and is ready for harvest 2 months after sowing. Lift when plants are somewhere in size between a golf and a tennis ball. Larger "bulbs" tend to become woody and unpalatable, but this is less of a problem with newer cultivars.

Harvest as required. In severe weather they can be stored in boxes of sand or sawdust. Remove the outer leaves, keeping the central tuft of leaves to keep them fresh. Some flavor tends to be lost during storage.

Pests and Diseases

As it matures quickly, kohlrabi is untroubled by many of the usual brassica problems, including clubroot.

Birds can cause severe damage, particularly to young plants. You should protect crops with netting, cages, humming wire or with bird deterrents.

Flea beetles — tiny and black with yellow stripes — nibble holes in leaves of seedlings, checking growth. Dust plants and the surrounding soil thoroughly with derris or insecticide when symptoms appear. They can also be controlled by brushing a yellow sticky trap or piece of wood covered in glue along the tops of the plants: the insects jump out, stick to the glue and can be disposed of.

Cabbage root fly larvae cause stunted growth, wilting and death. Protect the seedlings when transplanting with 5-inch squares of plastic, cardboard or rubberized carpet underlay, slit from edge to center and fitted around the stems. This stops adults from laying eggs.

 companion planting

Kohlrabi grows well with beet and onions.

 container growing

Kohlrabi are ideal for containers, particularly when grown as "mini vegetables." Plant in a loam-based compost with a moderate fertilizer content and maintain a regular supply of water. Feed every 2–3 weeks with a general liquid fertilizer.

 culinary

There is no need to peel tiny kohlrabi, but peel off the tough outer skin of older globes before cooking. Young ones can be trimmed, scrubbed and boiled whole or sliced for 20–30 minutes, then drained, peeled and served with melted butter, white sauce, or mashed.

Boiled kohlrabi can be made into fritters by frying with egg and breadcrumbs. Add kohlrabi to soups and stews, serve stuffed, cook like celeriac, or eat in a cheese sauce. It complements basil and is excellent steamed.

Kohlrabi globes can also be eaten raw, grated or sliced into salads, and the leaves are good boiled.

BROCCOLI

Brassica oleracea (Italica Group). *Brassicaceae*

Also known as Sprouting Broccoli, Calabrese. Perennial or annual grown for immature flowerheads. Hardy or half hardy. High in beta carotene, vitamin C, folic acid and iron. Moderate levels of calcium.

Said to have originated in the eastern Mediterranean, early forms of broccoli were highly esteemed by the Romans and described by Pliny in the first century CE. It spread from Italy to northern Europe, arriving in England in the 18th century. Philip Miller in his *Gardener's Dictionary* of 1724 called it "sprout cauliflower" or "Italian asparagus." Broccoli is an Italian word, derived from the Latin *brachium*, meaning "arm" or "branch." Calabrese, a similar plant with the same botanical origin, grown for its larger immature flowerheads, also takes its name from the Italian — meaning "from Calabria." This delicious vegetable was introduced to France by Catherine de Medici in 1560, spreading from there to the rest of Europe. "Green broccoli" was first mentioned in North American literature in 1806, but was certainly in cultivation long before that. It is said to have been introduced by Italian settlers and is extensively grown around New York and Boston.

Purple Sprouting Early

 varieties

Old varieties of perennial broccoli are still available; outstanding among them all is **'Nine Star Perennial'**, a multiheaded variety with small white heads. Cropping improves if unused heads are removed before they go to seed.

Sprouting broccoli

This excellent winter vegetable produces a succession of small flowerheads for cropping over a long season from early winter to late spring and is suitable for poor soils and cold areas. "Purple" varieties are hardier than the "white," which have a better taste and crop later, but tend to be less productive. Sow **'Summer Purple'** in early spring, **'Rudolph'** from early to late spring and **'Cardinal'** in late spring for a harvest lasting almost twelve months.

'Bordeaux'*, if sown early, can produce an early flowering harvest from July. **'Purple Sprouting Early'** is easy, prolific and extremely hardy and can be eady for harvesting from late winter. **'Purple Sprouting Late'** is similar, but ready for picking from mid-spring. **'White Sprouting'** is delicious, with shoots like tiny cauliflowers and **'White Sprouting Early'** is the white equivalent of **'Purple Sprouting'**. **'White Sprouting Late'** is ready to harvest from mid-spring.

Calabrese

Also known as American, Italian or green sprouting broccoli, this produces a large central flowerhead surrounded by smaller sideshoots, which develop after the main head has been harvested. Maturing about

3 months after sowing, it crops from summer until the onset of the first frosts.

'**Broccoletto**' is quick-maturing and sweet, with a single head. '**Fiesta**'* is excellent for summer and autumn cropping with large, domed heads of small buds. '**Flash**'* produces small to medium buds over a long season. '**Green Sprouting**', an old Italian variety, matures early. '**Paragon Enhanced**' has hybrid, umbrella like spears and tender, slim, sweet-tasting stems. '**Ramoso**' ('**DeCicco**'), an old Italian variety for spring or autumn cropping, produces heads over a long period. Tasty, tender and freezes well. '**Trixie**'* is high yielding with domed heads of small buds.

 ## cultivation

Propagation

Prepare the seedbed for sprouting broccoli by raking the soil to a fine texture. Sow over several weeks from mid- to late spring, planting the earlier varieties first. Sow thinly in drills in a seedbed, 12 inches apart and ½ inch deep, thinning to 6 inches apart before transplanting at their final spacing. Alternatively, sow 2–3 seeds in "stations" 6 inches apart, thinning to leave the strongest seedling.

For early spring crops, sow early maturing cultivars indoors in trays from late summer to early autumn. Transplant seedlings when they are about 5 inches tall into an unheated greenhouse or cold frame. Harden off and transplant outdoors from late winter to mid-spring. Alternatively, sow 2 seeds per module and thin to

Ready for harvesting

leave the stronger seedling. The final spacing for plants should be about 26–30 inches apart in and between the rows. It is worth noting that they take up a lot of space and have a long growing season!

Calabrese can be sown successively from mid-spring to midsummer for cropping from early summer to autumn. It does not transplant well and is better sown *in situ*. Sow 2–3 seeds at "stations," thinning to leave the strongest seedling. Close spacing suppresses side shoots and encourages small terminal spears to form, which are useful for freezing. Wider spacing means higher yields. While they can be as close as 3 inches apart with 24 inches between rows, the optimum spacing is 6 inches apart with 12 inches between the rows.

Growing

Sprouting broccoli thrives in a warm, sunny position. Soil should be deep, moisture-retentive and free-draining. Nitrogen levels should be moderate; excessive amounts encourage soft, leafy growth. You should avoid shallow or sandy soils and windy sites.

Sprouting broccoli tends to be top-heavy, so earth up round the stem to a depth of 3–5 inches to prevent wind rock, or stake larger varieties. Firm stems loosened by wind or frost.

Keep crops weed-free with regular hoeing or mulch with a 2-inch layer of organic matter. Water crops regularly before the onset of dry weather: do not let them dry out. Calabrese needs at least 6 gallons/sq yd every 2 weeks, though a single thorough watering 2–3 weeks before harvesting is a useful option for those under watering restrictions!

Feed with a general liquid fertiliser, or scatter and water in 1 ounce/sq yd of granular fertilizer after the main head has been removed to encourage side shoots to grow.

Maintenance

Spring Sow early broccoli indoors and later crops in seedbeds. Sow calabrese.
Summer Water crops and keep weed-free. Feed calabrese after harvesting the terminal bud.
Autumn Harvest calabrese, remove and dispose of crop debris.
Winter Harvest broccoli.

Steam florets to keep the color and goodness

Harvesting and Storing

Cut sprouting broccoli when the heads have formed, well before the flowers open, when the stems are 6–8 inches long. Regular harvesting is essential, as this encourages side-shoot formation and should ensure a 6–8 week harvest. Never strip the plant completely, or let it flower, as this stops the side shoots forming and makes existing "spears" woody and tasteless.

Sprouting broccoli can be stored in a plastic bag in the refrigerator. It will keep for about 3 days. To freeze, soak in salted water for 15 minutes, rinse and dry. Blanch for 3–4 minutes, cool and drain. Pack it in containers and then freeze.

Cut the mature central heads of calabrese with a sharp knife, while still firm and the buds tight. This encourages growth of side shoots within about 2–3 weeks. Pick regularly as for sprouting broccoli.

Calabrese can be stored in the refrigerator for up to 5 days, and freezes well.

 ## companion planting

Plant with rosemary, thyme, sage, onions, garlic, beet and chards.

culinary

Remove any tough leaves attached to the stalks and wash florets carefully in cold water before cooking. For the best flavor cook immediately after picking in boiling salted water for 10 minutes, or steam by standing spears upright in 2 inches of gently boiling water for 15 minutes with the pan covered. Drain carefully and serve hot with white, hollandaise or béarnaise sauce, melted butter, or vinaigrette. An Italian recipe book recommends braising calabrese in white wine or sautéing it in oil and sprinkling with grated Parmesan cheese. In Sicily, it is braised with anchovies, olives and red wine. Broccoli fritters are dipped in batter, then deep-fried.

Stir-fried florets can be blanched for 1 minute and fried with squid and shellfish. On a more mundane (but practical) level, broccoli and calabrese can be used as a fine substitute in cauliflower cheese.

Penne with Broccoli, Mascarpone and Dolcelatte
Serves 4

1 pound broccoli florets
½ cup mascarpone cheese
⅔ cup dolcelatte or Gorgonzola cheese
2 tablespoons crème fraîche
1 tablespoon balsamic vinegar
1 tablespoon dry white wine
1 pound penne
2 tablespoons capers
4 tablespoons black olives
1 tablespoon hazelnuts, crushed
Salt and freshly ground black pepper

Steam the broccoli florets over a pan of boiling water for 2–3 minutes. Run under cold water and set aside. In a heavy pan, gently heat the mascarpone, dolcelatte, crème fraîche, vinegar and wine.

Add the broccoli florets. Cook the pasta until it is just tender and drain well. Pour over the hot sauce, sprinkle with the capers, olives and hazelnuts and toss well. Adjust the seasoning and serve.

Brassica rapa (Rapifera Group). *Brassicaceae*

TURNIP

Biennial grown as an annual for globular, swollen root and young leaves. Hardy. Value: low in calories and carbohydrate; small amounts of vitamins and minerals.

This ancient root crop was known to Theophrastus in 400 BC and many early varieties were given Greek place names. Pliny listed 12 distinct types under *rapa* and *napus* — which became *naep* in Anglo-Saxon, and together with the word 'turn' (meaning 'made round'), gave us the common name. Introduced to Canada in 1541, the turnip was brought to Virginia by the colonists in 1609 and was rapidly adopted by the native Americans. In Britain they have found a role in folklore. In Northern Ireland, turnips were made into lamps for Hallowe'en (31 October), and in the Shetland Islands of Scotland slices were shaped into letters and put into a tub of water for young revellers to retrieve with their mouths; they usually tried to pick the initial of someone they loved.

varieties

Earlies
'Oasis'* has virus-resistant white roots and is delicious when raw. **'Purple Top Milan'*** produces flattish roots with purple markings and white flesh. Tender when young, early maturing and good for overwintering, it has an excellent flavor. **'Primera'*** is succulent and full of flavor. **'Snowball'** is a delicately flavored, fast-maturing white variety with cut leaves. **'Tokyo Cross'*** is an excellent F1 hybrid that matures rapidly, in about 35–40 days, and produces small, tasty white globes. A "mini vegetable" that is also tasty when larger, it is suitable as a late summer to early autumn crop.

Maincrops
'Golden Ball' (**'Golden Perfection'** or **'Orange Jelly'**) is a small, round yellow variety that should be grown quickly to keep the flesh succulent. Tasty, hardy, excellent for storing. **'Green Globe'** is white-fleshed with round roots; excellent for turnip tops. **'Shogoin'** (Japanese for "greens" or "root") is crispy and great for cooking and pickling.

cultivation

Turnips flourish at about 68°F (20°C) and prefer a sheltered, open site in light, fertile, well-drained but moisture-retentive soil. Summer sowings can be made in moderate shade provided they receive sufficient moisture. Turnips prefer a pH of 5.5–7.0; very acidic soil will need liming.

Propagation
Sow early turnips in mid-spring, as soon as the ground is workable, or in late winter or early spring under cloches or fleece.

Prepare the seedbed carefully and sow early turnips thinly in drills about 1 inch deep, in rows 9 inches apart. Then thin to a final spacing of 4–5 inches. They can also be grown in a grid pattern: mark 5-inch squares in the ground with a cane and sow 3 seeds where the "stations" cross, thinning after germination to leave the strongest seedling.

Sow maincrop varieties from mid- to late summer in drills 1 inch deep and 12 inches apart, thinning to 4–5 inches apart. It is important to thin seedlings when no more than 1 inch high, when the first true leaves appear, to ensure the roots develop properly. Firm the soil after thinning; do not thin turnips grown for tops.

When growing for their tops, prepare the seedbed and broadcast seed over a small area or sow thinly in rows 4–6 inches apart as soon as soil conditions allow. Sow early cultivars in spring for summer cropping and hardy varieties in late summer or early autumn. Small seedlings of "maincrops" overwinter and grow rapidly in spring, making them a useful early crop, particularly

Purple Top Milan

when covered with cloches or fleece. To ensure a prolonged harvest, make successional sowings of "earlies" from early spring until early summer.

Growing
If the ground has not been manured for the previous crop, double dig in autumn, working plenty of well-rotted organic matter into the soil and allowing it to weather over winter. About a week to 10 days before sowing, remove any weeds or debris and rake general fertiliser into the soil at 4 ounces/sq yd. In common

with other brassicas, turnips grow poorly on loose soil, so rake the soil to a fine tilth and firm it with the head of a rake or by carefully treading. If the soil is dry, water thoroughly before sowing and stand on a planting board to avoid compacting the soil. Mark each row with canes or twigs, and label and date the crop.

Keep crops weed-free by hand weeding or careful hoeing. Turnips must have a constant supply of water throughout the growing season, otherwise they tend to run to seed or produce small woody roots, while sudden watering or rain after a period of drought causes them to split. They will need up to 2 gallons/sq yd per week during dry periods. This improves the size and quality of the crop, but usually reduces the flavor. Turnips should be rotated with other brassicas.

Maintenance
Spring Prepare seedbed, sow early varieties under cloches.
Summer Sow earlies every 2–3 weeks for successional cropping. Keep crops weed-free and water as necessary. From mid- to late summer, sow maincrop varieties.
Autumn Sow "earlies" under cloches mid- to late autumn. Thin maincrop varieties.
Winter Harvest and store maincrop turnips.

Protected Cropping
Cover ground with cloches, fleece or black plastic for 2–3 weeks in late winter to early spring to warm the ground before sowing early crops. In late summer, protect sowings of early cultivars. Maincrop turnips grown for their tops can be grown under cloches after sowing in autumn and picked during winter.

Shogoin

Harvesting and Storing
Harvest early varieties when young and tender. Gather those to be eaten raw when they are the size of a golf ball; any time up to tennis ball-size if they are to be cooked. Hand pull them in the same way as radishes. Maincrop turnips that are lifted in mid-autumn for winter use are much larger, hardier and slower to mature. To keep the flavor, harvest at maturity as they soon become woody and unpalatable. Turnips can be left in the soil and lifted as required using a garden fork. Keep them in a cool place and use within a few days. In cold wet climates, roots are better lifted to prevent deterioration. Twist off the leaves, remove any soil, put the roots between layers of dry peat substitute, sawdust or sand in a box, then store in a cool shed.

Turnips grown for their tops can be harvested when about 4–6 inches high, cutting about 1 inch above ground level. Keep soil moist and they will resprout several times before finally running to seed.

Pests and Diseases
Flea beetle, tiny and black with yellow stripes, nibble holes in leaves of seedlings, checking growth. Large infestations of mealy aphid may kill young plants or cause black "sooty mold" on leaves. Cabbage root fly larvae feed on roots; transplanted brassicas are particularly vulnerable. Powdery mildew, a white deposit over shoots, stems and leaves, causes stunted growth. In severe cases, leaves yellow and die.

 ## companion planting

Growing with peas and hairy tares deters aphids. Turnips are useful for intercropping between taller crops and for catch-cropping.

 ## container growing

Fast-maturing early varieties grow well in large containers of well-drained, soil-based compost with added organic matter. Water crops well.

 ## medicinal

The liquor from turnips sprinkled with demerara sugar was used in folk medicine to cure colds.

 ## culinary

Both turnips and their leaves (turnip tops) are tasty. Eat early turnips raw in salads or boiled, tossed in butter and chopped parsley. Peel maincrop turnips before cooking. They are good mashed, roasted and in casseroles and soups.

Glazed Turnips
Use small, young turnips. Scrub them and cut into ½ inch dice (or use whole). Drop into boiling water for 3 minutes. Drain. Melt a little butter and olive oil in a frying pan, add the turnips, sprinkled with a little sugar, and fry over a high heat, stirring constantly, until browned and caramelized. This is particularly delicious with the 'Snowball' variety.

Turnip Tops
Wash well, removing stringy stalks. Chop roughly into manageable pieces. Steam over boiling water until just tender. Serve warm, tossed in olive oil and lemon juice vinaigrette, sprinkled with a finely chopped garlic clove. Or cook like spinach: put the washed leaves in a pan, add salt, pepper and a small pat of butter and steam for 10 minutes in only the water remaining on the leaves. Drain thoroughly and serve immediately.

Brassica rapa var. *chinensis*. Brassicaceae

BOK CHOY

Also known as Pak choi. Hardy biennial, grown as an annual. Value: rich in carotenes, calcium, fiber, potassium and folic acid.

Bok choy, translated as "white vegetable" from Cantonese, has been grown in China since the fifth century CE, cultivated in Europe since the 18th century and is one of the most familiar oriental vegetables. Relatively few varieties are grown in the west; there are 20 varieties in Hong Kong alone and many more on mainland China and Taiwan. In 1751 a friend of the Swedish taxonomist Carl Linneaus brought seeds to Europe, at the same time as Jesuit missionaries handed similar races to German scientists working in Russia, where it also spread rapidly.

Bok choy

Harvesting and Storing
Pick when the leaves are fresh and crisp, either by removing a few leaves from plants as required or cutting them off at the base, so they can resprout.

Pests and Diseases
They are susceptible to all the standard *brassica* problems. Flea beetle is a major problem; grow crops under horticultural fleece or mesh to avoid, cabbage root fly, slugs, cutworm, and powdery and downy mildew.

 ## varieties

Joy Larcom, in her definitive work, *Oriental Vegetables*, a "must have" book for anyone interested in the ingredients and cultivation of vegetables for eastern cuisine, identifies four types based on their appearance.

Chinese White types
These have thick, light to deep green leaves, usually curving outward, with wide, white, short and straight leaf blades, often overlapping at the base. They vary in their cold tolerance and tendency to bolt. **'Joi Choi'** is slow to bolt and has good frost resistance.

Soup Spoon types
These are vigorous and versatile, tolerating warm or cool conditions and have narrow "waists" with thin leaves and leaf stalks; the leaves are shallowly concave, like soup spoons. Most are tall, reaching around 18 inches when mature, and have the best flavor. **'Japanese White Celery Mustard'** is particularly delicious.

Green Leaf Stalk types
These varieties produce broad, light green leaf stalks on compact, robust, fast-growing plants.

Canton types
The smallest bok choy come from this group, with dense, white leaf stalks and compact, deep green leaves; they can be harvested as young greens and have a fine flavor. They are more warm-weather tolerant than most and inclined to run to seed in cold weather. **'Canton Dwarf'** is compact with dark green leaves.

 ## cultivation

Propagation
Sow seeds about ½ inch deep and spaced according to the recommendations on the seed packet, which is dictated by the size of the plant required at harvest. Sow small varieties up to 2 inches apart with 7 inches between rows; large plants should be up to 18 inches apart.

Growing
Most are cool season crops for late summer and autumn, growing best between 59–68°F (15–20°C). Spring-sown seedlings are best grown as "cut and come again" or for harvesting as young plants. Alternatively, choose cold-tolerant varieties like **'Tai Sai'**. Protect early sowings with crop covers.

Most varieties only tolerate light frost though green-stalk varieties are much tougher. They thrive in rich, fertile, well-drained soil and bolt if the soil dries out though 'Canton' and green-stemmed varieties are the most resistant to drought; keep the soil constantly moist and grow in shade during summer.

Maintenance
Spring Sow seedling crops under cover; harvest early sowings.
Summer Sow seeds in shade and harvest earlier crops.
Autumn Sow seedling crops under cover.
Winter Sow under glass.

Protected Cropping
Grow early- and late-season crops under glass. In winter, seed can be sown in modules at 68°F (20°C) and temperatures lowered by 50% after germination.

 ## medicinal

Dried leaves have been used to alleviate the effects of dysentery.

 ## culinary

Bok choy has a mild flavor in the way that Swiss chard does. Wash well with several changes of water before use. Bok choy leaves, from "cut and come again" to mature leaves, stems and flower shoots are used in stir-fries, soups, salads and are an ingredient in many forms of oriental cooking including pickles. Young flower heads from "bolting" plants can be used as a "choy sum" substitute.

Tempting, tender and tasty

MIZUNA & MIBUNA GREENS

Brassica rapa var. *japonica*. Brassicaceae

Hardy annual. Value: rich in vitamin A and C, folic acid and antioxidants.

Mizuna greens are a Chinese vegetable but have long been cultivated in Japan. They are fast growing, productive over a long period of time and can tolerate several degrees of frost without damage; making them an excellent all-around crop for cool conditions. Both Mizuna and 'Mibuna' greens have the characteristics of the parent plant, thought to be a natural hybrid which occurred in times past. There is chromosome evidence from *brassica rapa*, the "turnip" which has several leafy forms, particularly in Italian cooking where they are known as *cima de rapa* and *Brassica juncea* or "Chinese mustard" that is grown as an oil seed in China and Japan.

Crab salad served on mizuna leaves

Mizuna greens add texture and taste to salads

 varieties

Mizuna greens form a vigorous clump of finely-cut, dark green leaves with white, juicy stems. **Mibuna** greens have long been cultivated in Japan; they have slender stems and long straplike leaves of varying length, which are dark or light green. They are normally referred to as "early" or "late" according to the timing of their sowing and harvest.

 cultivation

Propagation

Sow outdoors from late spring and late summer to early autumn or under cover, either direct sown or sown in seed trays or a seedbed; transplant 2–3 weeks later. For small plants sow 1½ inches apart, for medium-sized 7 inches and large up to 18 inches apart.

Growing

Both are tolerant of cool, wet conditions and dislike extreme heat; drought may stunt plants and make the leaves tough. Mibuna and mizuna greens are cool weather plants and ideal for early- and late-season sowings; both need an open, sunny site in moisture-retentive soil with shade if sown in summer. Improve the soil by adding well-rotted organic matter if necessary. Keep plants weed free and watered when necessary to ensure a constant supply of young leaves.

Maintenance

Spring Sow seedlings under cover when the soil warms; sow in trays for transplanting into cloche- or fleece-warmed soil.
Summer Sow in shade, harvest regularly and keep crops well watered.
Autumn Sow under cover for "cut and come again" seedling crops.
Winter Harvest. Ventilate the greenhouse on hot days.

Protected Cropping

Mizuna and mibuna greens flourish in unheated greenhouses, cloches or cold frames over winter and tolerate low, winter light levels.

 culinary

Use mizuna and mibuna greens in stir-fries and salads. Mizuna can be used in soups, steamed, with fish or poultry, seeds can be dry roasted for use in curries and pickles, sprouted seeds can be used in salads. Use fresh to retain the highest level of nutrients. Wash in several changes of water and dry thoroughly before use. Leaves can be stored for up to five days in the salad compartment of a fridge.

Harvesting and Storing

Mibuna and mizuna greens can be grown as "cut and come again" crops, juvenile or mature plants. Harvest regularly for a constant supply of tender leaves, up to five cuts can be made per plant, according to the level of maturity and time of year. Older leaves gradually become more fibrous.

Pests and Diseases

Flea beetles and slugs can be a problem, grow under horticultural fleece or mesh.

 container growing

They are ideal for growing in containers and growing bags, provided there is adequate space to form a good root system.

Brassica rapa var. *komatsuna*. *Brassicaceae*
KOMATSUNA

Also known as Japanese Mustard Spinach, Turnip Tops. Hardy annual or biennial. Value: rich in calcium, vitamin A, C, folic acid and antioxidants.

This oriental vegetable of Japanese origin is another leafy form of the wild turnip; with large, wide, dark green, often glossy leaves it is believed to have been developed from bok choy. Valued for its versatility, it is grown as a food crop in Taiwan and Korea, and as a fodder crop in several Asian countries. It is tough, vigorous, fast growing, impervious to the effects of all but the worst weather and is an ideal winter crop in cool climates.

varieties

'Green Boy' is often listed as a form of bok choy. It is heat tolerant with dark green leaves and thick leaf stems. **'Hybrid Kojisan'** is top quality with bright green leaves. **'Komatsuna'** is an all season variety, with fleshy, rounded, green stems, and dark green leaves; disease and heat resistant, best in early spring or late summer. Originally found growing near Tokyo. **'Nozawana'** is highly cold- and heat tolerant with long green leaves. It is popular in Japan for pickling. The variety **'Summer Fest'** is similar. **'Natsu Rakuten — Summer Fest'** hybrid, has thick, dark green leaves and an upright habit. Sow spring to autumn. **'Red Komatsuna'** is ideal as micro- or baby greens; the flat, round leaves are tinted red above and green with red veins below. It is heat-tolerant. Sow spring to autumn. **'Tokyo Early'** has glossy leaves and thin, light green stalks and is slow to bolt. Sow from spring to autumn. **'Toriksan'** is heat-tolerant.

cultivation

Propagation
Sow seeds in wide drills or broadcast, thinning seedlings to leave 1 inch between "cut and come again" plants. The spacing of crops growing to maturity depends on the variety; large plants should be up to 18 inches apart in and between the rows, those being harvested at other stages of growth can be spaced accordingly and "thinnings" can be eaten at any stage.

Growing
Komatsuna greens are easy to grow, very prolific and almost the perfect winter-hardy crop, recovering from temperatures down to 7°F (-14°C). This characteristic ensures that they are less likely to "bolt" in cold spring weather than other oriental vegetables. They need an open, sunny site and rich, fertile, moisture-retentive soil; incorporate well-rotted organic matter if necessary before planting. Sow ⅛–½ inch deep and keep plants well watered at all times.

"Cut and come again" seedlings can be sown in spring and autumn under cover and in late spring and summer outdoors. Crops being grown to maturity can be sown in late summer and transplanted under cover in autumn or midsummer, if being grown outdoors, so they are well established before the onset of winter.

Maintenance
Spring Make early sowings under unheated protection; harvest mature crops.
Summer Sow in modules or trays in late summer for transplanting under protection.
Autumn Make late sowings under unheated protection.
Winter Harvest crops.

Protected Cropping
Although very hardy, the quality of the leaves is improved when crops are grown under protection. Protect early and late sowings under cloches, in cold frames or in a cold greenhouse.

Harvesting and Storing
Harvest seedlings from 4 inches; cut juvenile plants back to 1 inch above ground level and they will regrow. Water plants well to boost regrowth and feed with dilute liquid fertilizer. Cut leaves from mature plants as needed.

Pests and Diseases
Plants are susceptible to the usual Brassica problems like slugs, flea beetle and pigeons. Grow under fleece and protect mature plants with netting.

container growing

Growing bags or containers of organic-based compost can be used for growing "cut and come again" or semi-mature crops.

culinary

Komatsuna greens have a mellow flavor between spinach and Asian mustard. They can be eaten from "cut and come again" to maturity; flowering shoots can be eaten too and are sweet and juicy. Steam or lightly boil younger leaves as spinach; older leaves taste stronger and are more like cabbage — they become stronger and hotter as they mature, so are better cooked. Eat young leaves raw in salad, stir-fry, boil, pickle, add to soups or braise.

Broth with Komatsuna and Tofu
Serves 2

¼ pound komatsuna, cleaned and trimmed
2 sheets deep-fried tofu
Pinch of salt

For the Broth:
2 cups dashi stock
1 tablespoon sake
1 tablespoon mirin
2 tablespoons light soy sauce
Pinch of salt

Put the tofu in a colander and pour boiling water over it to remove the excess oil. Cut lengthways in half and slice thinly.

Discard any roots of the komatsuna and wash it well. Bring a large pan of water to a boil and add a pinch of salt. Blanch the komatsuna and transfer immediately to a bowl of cold water. Squeeze the komatsuna dry and chop it into 1-inch lengths.

Put all the ingredients for the simmering broth into a large pan and bring to the boil. Add the tofu and simmer over a medium heat for 2 minutes before adding the chopped komatsuna. Simmer for another 2–3 minutes and serve.

Brassica rapa (Pekinensis Group). *Brassicaceae*

CHINESE CABBAGE

Also known as Chinese Leaves, Celery Cabbage, Pe Tsai, Peking Cabbage. Annual or biennial grown as annual for edible leaves, stems and flowering shoots. Half hardy. Value: moderate levels of folic acid and vitamin C.

Chinese cabbage was first recorded in China around the fifth century CE, and has never been found in the wild. It is thought to have been a spontaneous cross in cultivation between the bok choy and turnips. Taken to the East Indies and Malaya by Chinese traders and settlers who established communities and maintained their own culture, in the 1400s Chinese cabbage could be found in the Chinese colony in Malacca. By 1751 European missionaries had sent seeds back home, but the vegetable was regarded as little more than a curiosity. Another attempt at introduction was made by a French seedsman in 1845, but the supply became exhausted and the seed was lost. In 1970 the first large-scale commercial crop was produced by the Israelis and distributed in Europe; about the same time it was marketed in the United States as the Napa cabbage, after the valley in California where it was grown. It has become a moderately popular vegetable in the West.

 varieties

There are many groups, but three have become popular: the "tall cylindrical," the "hearted" or "barrel-shaped" and the "loose-headed."

The cylindrical type has long, upright leaves and forms a compact head, which can be loosely tied to blanch the inner leaves. It is slow-growing, takes about 70 days from sowing to harvest and is most susceptible to bolting. This type is sweet and stores well.

Hearted types have compact, barrel-shaped heads with tightly wrapped leaves and a dense heart. They mature after about 55 days and are generally slow to bolt.

Loose-headed types are lax and open-headed, often with textured leaves. The "self-blanching" ones have creamy centers and textured leaves. They are also less liable to bolt than headed types. **'Jade Pagoda'*** is cylindrical with a firm, crisp head. It takes about 65 days to mature and is cold-tolerant. **'Kasumi'***, a barrel type, has a compact head and is resistant to bolting. **'Monument'** is strong, vigorous, uniform and very tasty. **'Nerva'*** is similar, matures quickly, and has dark green leaves with dense heads. **'Ruffles'** is delicious and early-maturing, with lax, pale green heads and a creamy white heart. However, early sowings are liable to bolt. **'Shantung'** has a spreading habit, with tender, light green leaves and a dense heart. **'Tip Top'** is an early variety for spring planting and can be harvested around 70 days after sowing. It is vigorous and produces good-sized heads. **'Wa Wa Sai'** is sweet and very tender. Sow closely for baby leaves.

cultivation

Propagation

A cool-weather crop, Chinese cabbage is more likely to bolt in late spring and summer. Use resistant varieties or sow after midsummer. The chance of bolting increases if young plants are subjected to low temperatures or dry conditions, or suffer from transplanting check.

Sow the main crop *in situ* from mid- to late summer, 2–3 seeds per "station," spaced 12–14 inches apart in and between the rows. Thin to leave the strongest seedling. Alternatively, sow sparingly in drills and thin.

Otherwise it can be sown in modules or pots, transplanting carefully to avoid root disturbance when there are 4–6 leaves. If the soil is dry, water thoroughly. Broadcast or sow loose-headed types as "cut and come again" seedlings.

Make first sowings in a cold greenhouse or cold frame in early spring, sow outdoors under cloches or fleece as the weather improves and the soil becomes workable. Summer sowings tend to grow too rapidly and become "tough," unless it is a cool summer. Make the last sowing under cover in early autumn.

Cut seedlings when they have reached a few inches tall, leaving them to resprout. Seeds can also be sprouted, as for alfalfa.

Growing

Chinese cabbage needs a deep, moisture-retentive, free-draining soil with plenty of organic matter. Excessively light, heavy or poor soils should be avoided unless they are improved by incorporating organic matter or grit. Alternatively, grow in raised beds or on ridges. Dig the soil thoroughly before planting; acidic soils should be limed, as the ideal pH is 6.5–7.0. Slightly more alkaline soils are advisable where there is a risk of clubroot.

Chinese cabbage prefers an open site, but tolerates some shade in midsummer. Rotate Chinese cabbage with other brassicas.

Water crops thoroughly throughout the growing season; do not let them dry out. They are shallow-rooted and so need water little and often. Mulching is also

Chinese cabbage harvest in Thailand

advisable. Erratic watering can result in damage to the developing head, encouraging rot. Scatter general fertilizer around the base of transplants or feed with a general liquid fertilizer as necessary to boost growth — this is particularly important on poorer soils. Keep crops weed-free.

In late summer, tie up the leaves of hearting varieties with soft twine or raffia. (With self-hearting varieties, this is unnecessary.)

Maintenance

Spring Sow early "cut and come again" seedling crops under cover. Sow later crops outdoors.
Summer Sow in drills from mid- to late summer. Water a little and often, mulch and keep weed-free. Harvest.
Autumn Sow quick-maturing varieties or "cut and come again" crops outdoors; sow later crops under cover.
Winter Harvest "cut and come again" crops grown under cover.

Protected Cropping

Earlier crops can be achieved by sowing bolting-resistant cultivars from late spring to early summer. They need temperatures of 68–77°F (20–25°C) for the first 3 weeks after germination to prevent bolting. Harden off, transplant, then protect the plants with cloches or with crop covers.

Late summer-sown crops should be transplanted under cover. Space plants about 5 inches apart and grow them as a semi-mature "cut and come again" crop.

Harvesting and Storing

In autumn, cold-tolerant varieties can stay outside for several weeks provided it is dry. Protect from wet and cold using cloches. Lift developing crops and replant in cold frames, or uproot and lay plants on straw or similar, covering them with the same material if temperatures fall below freezing point. Ventilate on warm days.

CHINESE CABBAGE

Harvest as "cut and come again" seedlings, semi-mature or mature plants and for the flowering shoots. Cut seedlings when they are 1–2 inches tall. Semi-mature or mature plants can be cut with a sharp knife about 1 inch above the ground and will then resprout; after several harvests they will send up a flower head. Harvest the flowering shoots when they are young, before the flowers open. Harvest mature heads when they are firm.

Chinese cabbage keeps in the fridge for several weeks. Wash thoroughly before storing. Heads can be stored in a cool, frost-free shed or cellar for up to 3 months. When storing, check plants every 3–4 weeks and remove any diseased or damaged leaves immediately.

Pests and Diseases
Chinese cabbage can be affected by any of the usual brassica pests and diseases. You should take precautions in particular against flea beetle, slugs, snails, caterpillars, clubroot and powdery mildew. Crops grow well under horticultural fleece or fine netting.

 ## companion planting

Plant with garlic and dill to discourage caterpillars. Main crops are ideal after peas, early potatoes and broad beans; late crops are good companions for Brussels sprouts. It is good for cropping between slower-growing vegetables.

Chinese cabbages are sometimes grown as sacrificial crops so that slugs, flea beetles and aphids are attracted to them rather than other crops. In the United States they are used among maize, as they attract corn worms.

 ## container growing

The fast-growing varieties give the best results. Use a 10-inch pot or container and loam-based compost with added organic matter and a thick basal layer of drainage material. Sow seeds ½ inch deep and 1 inch apart in shallow pots or modules in mid-spring. Transplant seedlings singly into pots when they have 3–4 leaves.

 ## warning

To minimize the risk of listeria, you should never store Chinese cabbage in plastic bags.

 ## culinary

Cook Chinese cabbage only lightly to retain the flavor and nutrients. Steam, quickly boil, stir-fry — or eat raw. (Seedlings are better cooked.) Leaves blend well in raw salads of lettuce, green pepper, celery, mooli and tomato. They also make a delicious warm salad, stir-fried and mixed with orange. Otherwise use in soups, cook with fish, meat, poultry and use in stuffing.

Outer stalks can be shredded, cooked like celery and tossed in butter. In Korea, China and Japan heads are used to make fermented and salted pickles.

Sweet and Sour Chinese Cabbage
Serves 4

1 ½ pounds Chinese cabbage, finely shredded
2 tablespoons olive oil
1 onion or several shallots, sliced
2 tablespoons white wine vinegar
2 teaspoons sugar
6 tablespoons chopped tomatoes in their juices
Salt and freshly ground black pepper

Heat the oil in a heavy-bottomed pan and cook the onions until soft. Stir in the vinegar, sugar and tomatoes and blend well. Add the Chinese cabbage and seasoning. Cook for 10 minutes with the lid on, stirring occasionally, until the cabbage is tender.

Serve hot.

PEPPER & CHILI

Capsicum annuum. Solanaceae

Also known as Sweet Pepper, Bell Pepper, Capsicum, Pimento, Chilli peppers, Chile peppers. Annuals and short-lived perennials grown for edible fruits. Half hardy. Value: very rich in vitamin C and beta carotene.

Both hot and mild peppers come from one wild species, which is native to Central and South America. The name capsicum comes from the Latin *capsa*, meaning "a box." It is thought that the hot types were the first to be cultivated; seeds have been found in Mexican settlements dating from 7000 BCE, and the Aztecs are known to have grown them extensively. They are one of the discoveries made in the New World by Columbus. He thought he had discovered black pepper, which at the time was extremely expensive, and used the name "pepper" for this new fiery spice. Spanish and Portuguese explorers then distributed the new kinds of peppers around the world.

Sweet (or Bell) peppers were introduced to Spain in 1493 and were known in England by 1548 and Central Europe by 1585. The Spanish use red sweet peppers to make the spice pimentón and for stuffing green olives. Chili peppers are notorious for their fieriness. Their heat is caused by the alkaloid capsaicin, which is measured in Scoville Units. Mild chilies are around 600 units. Beware the 'Dorset Naga' and 'Bhut Jolokia' both measured at over one million units!

varieties

The larger, bell-shaped, mild-tasting sweet peppers eaten as vegetables are members of the *Capsicum annuum* Grossum Group. Green when immature, different cultivars ripen to yellow, orange, red or 'black'.

Hungarian Hot Wax

The smaller, hotter chilies used for flavoring are classed in the *C. a.* Longum Group.

Sweet (or Bell) peppers
'Big Bertha' is one of the largest sweet peppers, growing to 7 inches long by 4 inches wide. Excellent for growing in cooler climates and for stuffing. 'Californian Wonder' has a mild flavor, is good for stuffing and crops well over a long period. 'Calwonder Wonder Early' grows well in short seasons and is prolific. 'Gypsy' is an early cropper with slightly tapered fruits and is also resistant to tobacco mosaic virus. 'Redskin'* is compact and ideal for pots and growbags. 'Sweet Chocolate' is an unusual chocolate-brown color and good when frozen whole.

Chili peppers
'Anaheim' produces tapered, moderately hot fruits over a long period. The moderately hot yellow fruits of 'Hungarian Hot Wax'* ripen to become crimson and are good for salad and stuffing. 'Italian White Wax' has pointed fruits which pickle well and are mild-tasting when young. 'Large Red Cherry' is extremely hot, with flattened fruits ripening to cherry red. Good for drying and ideal in curries, pickles and sauces. 'Serrano' is extremely hot with orange-red fruits. It is prolific and can be dried. 'Tabasco Habanero' is extremely hot — beware! 'Tam Jalapeno' has a good, mild flavor and is high yielding. 'Thai Burapa' is small and pointed; ideal for Asian dishes. 'Thai Denchai', tapering to 5 inches, is great for all Thai dishes. 'Tunisian Baklouti' has large, tapering pods and is hot.

Chili peppers drying in India

 ## cultivation

Propagation

Sow seed indoors from late winter to mid-spring in trays, modules or pots of moist seed compost at 70°F (21°C). Lower temperature gradually after germination. Transplant into 3-inch pots when three true leaves appear, repotting again into 4–5-inch pots when sufficient roots have formed. Move plants into their final position when about 4 inches high and the first flowers appear.

Harden off outdoor crops in cool temperate zones and transplant in late spring to early summer when the soil is warm and there is no danger of frost.

Space standard varieties 15–18 inches apart; dwarf varieties should be spaced 12 inches apart.

Growing

Sweet peppers and chilies flourish outdoors in warmer climates. More successful under cover in cooler zones, they can be grown outside in mild areas or warm microclimates but benefit from protection with cloches or fleece. Chillies tend to be more tolerant of fluctuating temperatures and high or low rainfall and grow in marginally less fertile soil. Blossom drops when night temperatures fall below 59°F (15°C). Soil should be moisture-retentive and free-draining on ground

manured for the previous crop. Alternatively, dig in plenty of well-rotted organic matter in autumn or winter prior to planting. Rake in a granular general fertilizer at 8 ounces/sq ft before planting.

Keep the soil moist and weed-free; mulching is recommended. Feed with a general liquid fertilizer if plants need a boost. Excessive nitrogen can result in flower drop.

If branches are weak and thin, when the plant is about 12 inches tall remove the growth tips from the stems to encourage branching. Normally, they branch naturally. Support with a cane if necessary.

Maintenance

Spring Sow seeds under cover. Transplant when the danger of frost is passed or grow in an unheated greenhouse.
Summer Keep crops weed-free; wet down the greenhouse in warm weather. Harvest.
Autumn Cover outdoor crops where necessary. Harvest.
Winter Prepare the ground for outdoor crops.

Protected Cropping

Crops are better grown under glass, clear plastic, cold frames or cloches in cool temperate climates. In greenhouse borders, prepare the soil as for "Growing." Keep it moist but not waterlogged and mist with tepid water to maintain humidity and help fruit set.

Sow in mid-spring for growing in a greenhouse and in late spring for under cloches. Ventilate well during hot weather. If you are growing dwarf varieties on a sunny windowsill, turn pots daily to ensure even growth.

Plants grown under cloches may outgrow their space: rigid cloches can be turned vertically and supported with canes. Alternatively, use polycarbonate sheeting.

Harvesting and Storing

Harvest with scissors or secateurs when sweet peppers or chilies are green, or leave on the plant for 2–3 weeks to ripen and change color. Picking them when they are green increases the yield.

Peppers may be stored in a cool, humid place for up to 14 days at temperatures of 55–59°F (13–15°C). Toward the end of the season, uproot plants and hang them by the roots in a frost-free shed or greenhouse; fruits will continue to ripen for several months.

The heat of chilies increases with the maturity of the fruit. Fresh chilies keep for up to 3 weeks in the fridge in a paper bag. Or store them in an airtight jar in a dark cupboard. Chilies can either be dried and used whole or ground into powder. Both sweet peppers and chilies freeze successfully.

Pests and Diseases

Red spider mite can be a nuisance under cover. Slugs can damage seedlings, stems, leaves and fruits. Remove any decaying flowers or foliage immediately.

 ## companion planting

Capsicums grow well with basil, okra and tomatoes.

 ## container growing

Grow under cover or outdoors. Plant in 8–10-inch pots of loam-based compost with moderate fertilizer levels or in growbags. Dwarf varieties can be grown successfully in pots on windowsills. Keep the compost moist but not waterlogged and mist with tepid water, particularly during flowering to assist fruit set. Water frequently in warm weather, less at other times.

 ## medicinal

Capsaicin increases the blood flow and is used in muscle aches. It is said to help the body metabolize alcohol, acts as an expectorant, and prevents and alleviates bronchitis and emphysema. Drinking 10–20 drops of red-hot chili sauce in a glass of water daily (or hot spicy meals three times a week) can keep airways free of congestion, preventing or treating chronic bronchitis and colds. It stimulates endorphins, killing pain and inducing a sense of wellbeing.

 ## warning

Ventilate the kitchen when using chilies. If you have sensitive skin, wear rubber gloves to handle them and always avoid touching your eyes or other sensitive areas after handling.

culinary

Sweet peppers add both color and taste to the table. They can be eaten raw in salads, roasted or barbecued, fried or stir-fried, stuffed with rice, fish or meat mixtures, and used in countless casseroles and rice dishes.

Chilies are used in chili con carne, curries and hotpots. Removing the internal ribs and seeds reduces the heat intensity. Paprika is the dried and powdered fruits of sweet peppers. Cayenne pepper is dried and ground powder made from chilies.

If chili is too strong, it can cause intestinal burning — cucumber, rice, bread and beans are a good antidote. By coating the tongue, the fat content of yogurt and butter soothes a chili-burnt mouth. Water only makes things worse.

If you're uninitiated at eating chili peppers, start with small doses and build up heat tolerance. Excessively hot peppers can cause jaloproctitis or perianal discomfiture.

Mrs. Krause's Pepper Hash
Serves 6

William Woys Weaver, in *Pennsylvania Dutch Country Cooking*, quotes this recipe from Mrs. Eugene F. Krause of Bethlehem, who lived in the early part of the 20th century and was renowned for her peppery hashes.

6 green peppers, deseeded and finely chopped
6 red peppers, deseeded and finely chopped
4 onions, finely chopped
2 small pods hot chili peppers, deseeded and finely chopped
1½ tablespoons celery seeds
1½ cups cider vinegar
1¼ cups brown sugar
1½ teaspoons sea salt

Combine the peppers, onion, hot chili peppers and celery seeds in a nonreactive preserving pan. Heat the vinegar in a nonreactive pan and dissolve the sugar and salt in it. Bring to a vigorous boil, then pour over the pepper mixture. Then cook over a medium heat for 15 minutes, or until the peppers begin to discolor. Pack into hot sterilized preserving jars, seal, and place in a 15-minute water bath. Let the pepper hash mature in the jars for 2 weeks before using.

Jean-Christophe Novelli's Andalouse of Sole
Serves 6

For the piperade:
Carton of sun-dried tomato juice
½ pound sun-dried tomatoes
3 star anise
Fresh thyme

Mrs. Krause's Pepper Hash

1⅔ cup olive oil
1 large zucchini, sliced at an angle
2 medium eggplants, sliced at an angle, then halved
8 large shallots, peeled
8 baby fennel, trimmed
2 red peppers, deseeded and cut in half
2 yellow peppers, deseeded and cut in half
2 green peppers, deseeded and cut in half
10 red cherry tomatoes
1 head of garlic, cloves separated and peeled
Sugar
Freshly ground salt and pepper
Good handful of black olives
20 basil leaves

For the Sole Fillets:
6 large sole fillets
olive oil
1 vanilla pod, split and seeds scraped out

To Serve:
Handful of mixed fresh herbs
Freshly grated Parmesan
1 tablespoon truffle oil

To make the piperade, start by heating the tomato juice in a pan with the sun-dried tomatoes, star anise and thyme and cook steadily until it's reduced by one-third.

Heat the olive oil in a pan. Add the vegetables, garlic, a little sugar and the sun-dried tomato juice and season. Cover with a tight fitting lid and leave over a low heat until the vegetables are just soft to the touch. Remove the vegetables from the heat and add the olives and basil to warm through.

Preheat the grill. Brush the sole fillets with a little olive oil and the vanilla seeds. Season and grill for about 2–3 minutes on each side, skin-side up first. If the fillets are quite thick, they may require 4 minutes on each side.

Carefully arrange the vegetables on the plates. Place a sole fillet on each dish and garnish with fresh herbs, grated Parmesan and a splash of truffle oil.

Chrysanthemum coronarium. Compositae

CHRYSANTHEMUM GREENS

Also known as Shungiku, Chop suey greens. Hardy annual. Value: rich in vitamin B, moderate vitamin C and minerals.

There are few Chrysanthemums or their close relatives with culinary value. Tanacetum balsamita, a stalwart of the cottage garden was once classified in the same group and, in times past, its leaves were used to flavor ale, while Dioscorides notes that the stalks and leaves of marguerites were "eaten as other pot herbes are." It is a mystery how an attractive plant of Mediterranean hillsides, valued as an ornamental for its pretty flowers, spread east to China, Vietnam and Japan where its foliage became widely eaten as "greens." It is not only the leaves that are used; the Japanese dip the flowers in sake and eat them at the beginning of a meal to confer health and long life.

Wash thoroughly before eating

 culinary

Eat young aromatic shoots and stems raw, in salads, sushi or with pickles; leaves can be cooked or steamed, dipped into tempura batter and deep-fried. Try not to overcook the leaves as they can become bitter. Kikumi, a Japanese pickle, is made from the edible flower petals. Garnish stews with young leaves. Harvest just before use as the leaves wilt quickly.

Chrysanthemum in bloom

 varieties

There are no cultivars; just three forms are in cultivation. One has pale green, finely-cut, almost feathery leaves, with good low and high temperature tolerance and a strong flavor. Another, bushier, high-yielding plant with broader, thicker, shallowly-lobed leaves is tender and mildly flavored; the third, which is intermediate in appearance between the two, is fast growing, bushy and high yielding, thriving in both warm and cool climates.

 cultivation

Propagation
Sow, in drills or broadcast thinly, lightly covering the seed, every 2–3 weeks during spring and autumn for a constant harvest. Allow 6 inches in and between the rows for larger plants. Thinning is not usually required, for young plants, unless sowing is particularly dense, when they should thinned to 2 inches apart. Plants can also be grown from soft tip cuttings taken from overwintering plants in spring.

Growing
Chrysanthemum greens are primarily a cool-season crop, tolerating low light levels and withstanding light frosts. They are at their best in spring and autumn as temperatures over 77°F (25°C) impart bitterness to the leaves. They tolerate most soils but prefer a well-prepared seedbed on rich, fertile, moisture-retentive soil in full sun and a cool, shady position in summer. Plants can be grown as small "cut and come again" seedlings or leaves harvested from larger individual plants. Keep plants well watered and weed free by hoeing or hand weeding to prevent competition from annual weeds which suppresses growth.

Maintenance
Spring Sow outdoors once the danger of frost has passed. Harvest winter crops.
Summer Make the final sowings of the season outdoors around ten weeks before the last frost.
Autumn Sow winter crops under glass; harvest earlier crops.
Winter Harvest earlier sowings.

Protected Cropping
Sow seeds under glass in autumn for cropping over winter in an unheated greenhouse and in early spring for early crops.

Harvesting and Storing
As "cut and come again" crops, the first harvest can be made from 4 weeks after sowing during midsummer; plants recover rapidly and several cuts can be made from each sowing. Alternatively, cut back the top 8 inches of more mature plants leaving them to resprout from the base or pick side shoots from individual plants. Shoots can be harvested from flowering plants without any loss of quality and the flowers eaten in salads.

Pests and Diseases
It is pest and disease free.

 container growing

Plants can be grown in containers or growing bags throughout the season and respond well to cutting back.

 medicinal

Leaves are used to calm the stomach and as an expectorant.

Cicer arietinum. Papilionaceae

CHICKPEA

Also known as Dal, Egyptian Pea, Garbanzo, Gram. Annual grown for seed sprouts, seeds, young shoots and leaves. Tender. Value: high in protein, phosphorus, potassium, most B vitamins, iron and dietary fiber.

Chickpeas originated in the northern regions of the fertile crescent. Evidence of their ancient use as a domesticated crop was found at a site in Jericho and dated to around 6500 BCE. Seeds excavated in Greece indicate that the chickpea must have been introduced to Europe with the first food crops arriving from the Near East. Today it is cultivated worldwide in subtropical or Mediterranean climates as a cool-season crop, needing about 4 to 6 months of moderately warm, dry conditions to flourish. It is the world's third most important legume after peas and beans, and 80% of the crop is produced in India. It is eaten fresh or dried, made into flour, used as a coffee substitute and grown as a fodder crop. The plant grows about 12 inches tall, with compound leaves of up to eight toothed leaflets. Its tiny white- or blue-tinged flowers are followed by a small flat pod containing one or two round seeds, each with a small "beak" — hence the common name "chickpea."

 varieties

The following are Indian cultivars: **'Annegeri'** is a semi-spreading, high-yielding variety with yellowish brown seeds. It is deep-rooting and likes good soil but a coarse tilth is adequate. **'Avrodhi'** has medium-sized brown seeds and is wilt-resistant. **'Bheema'**, a semi-spreading variety, has large, light brown, smooth seeds and is suitable for drought-prone or low-rainfall areas. **'Brown Seeded'** is good for the home gardener, particularly in short, dry seasons. **'Kabuli Black'**, with 2 black seeds per pod, is very hardy, vigorous and fast maturing. It has some tolerance of cold soils and is drought-resistant.

 cultivation

Chickpeas need a fertile, well-drained soil in full sun.

Propagation
Seeds can be broadcast or sown in drills during winter in Mediterranean regions or after the rains in subtropical climates. Broadcasting is very simple. Prepare the soil using the "stale seedbed" method, raking and leveling, allowing the weeds to germinate and hoeing them off before sowing. Then scatter the seed evenly, raking the soil twice — first in one direction, then again at 90 degrees to ensure even coverage.

Chickpeas can also be sown in drills 2½–4 inches deep with the rows 20 inches apart, thinning to 10 inches between plants after germination. Alternatively, sow 3–4 seeds in "stations," 10 inches apart, and thin to leave the strongest seedling standing.

Growing
Dig over the area thoroughly before planting, adding organic matter to poor soil. Rake over the area to create a fine tilth and water well before sowing if the seedbed is dry. Alternatively, soak the seeds for an hour. Keep crops weed-free during the early stages; as plants mature, their spreading habit naturally stifles weed growth.

Chickpeas are drought-tolerant, but watering just before flowering and as the peas begin to swell improves productivity. Rotate with other legumes and leave the roots in the ground after harvest to provide nitrogen for the following crop.

The flowers are delicate and pretty

Maintenance

Spring Dig over the planting area, adding organic matter where needed.
Summer Keep crops weed-free. Water in prolonged drought, just before flowering and as the peas swell.
Autumn Harvest crops.
Winter Dig over the planting area, adding organic matter where needed.

Protected Cropping

In cooler climates, sow seeds in early spring into small pots of moist seed compost in a greenhouse or on a windowsill. Harden off in late spring and plant outdoors once there is no danger of frost. Growing crops in cloches or plastic tunnels increases the yield.

Harvesting and Storing

Crops are ready after about 4–6 months. Harvest when leaves and pods turn brown; don't leave it too late, or the seeds will be lost when the pods split. Cut the stems at the base and tie them together before drying upside down in a dry, warm place. Collect the dry seeds and store in airtight jars. Peas can also be harvested fresh for cooking, but fresh ones deteriorate rapidly and should be used as soon as possible.

Sprouting Seeds

Always buy untreated chickpeas for sprouting, as seed sold for sowing is often treated with chemical dressings. Soak seeds overnight or for several hours in boiling water, tip into a sieve and rinse. Put several layers of moist paper towel or blotting paper in the base of a jar and cover with a layer of seed. Cut a square from a pair of nylons or piece of muslin and cover the top, securing with a rubber band. Place in a bright position, away from direct sunshine, maintaining constant temperatures around 68°F (20°C). Rinse the seed three to four times a day by filling the jar with water

and pouring off again. Harvest after 3–4 days when the "sprouts" are about ½ inch long.

Pests and Diseases

Plants can suffer from root rot. They turn black and finally dry up, leaves fall and the stems desiccate. Ensure the soil is well drained and destroy affected crops immediately. The acidic secretions from the glandular hairs are a good defence against most pests. Gram pod borer caterpillars feed on the crop from seedlings to maturity, damaging seedpods and the immature seeds. Spray with pyrethrum.

 container growing

They can be grown in containers, but seed production levels do not make them a worthwhile proposition as a crop plant.

 culinary

With a protein content of 20%, chickpeas are an important meat substitute and good for children and expectant and nursing mothers. Chickpeas are used fresh or dried. They are ground into "gram flour" (used in vegan cooking), and the ground meal is mixed with wheat and used for chapatis. Whole chickpeas are fried, roasted (to eat as a snack) and boiled. To make hummus, grind boiled chickpeas into a paste, mix with olive or sesame oil, flavor with lemon and garlic and eat on pita bread or crackers. Chickpeas are also used to make dal and are found in spicy side dishes, vegetable curries and soups. The young shoots and leaves are used as a vegetable and cooked like spinach — boiled in soups, added to curries or fried with spices.

Puréed Chickpeas

Serves 4

⅔ pound dried chickpeas, soaked overnight
2 tablespoons olive oil
1 onion, sliced finely
3 garlic cloves, crushed
⅔ pound tomatoes, peeled, deseeded and chopped
Salt and freshly ground black pepper

 medicinal

The leaves are astringent and used to treat bronchitis. They are also boiled and applied to sprains and dislocated bones; the exudate is used for indigestion, diarrhea and dysentery. The seeds are a stimulant, tonic and aphrodisiac. In Egypt they are used to gain weight, and to treat headaches, sore throat and coughs. Powdered seed is used as a facepack and also in dandruff treatment.

 warning

The whole plant and seed pods are covered with hairs containing skin irritants. You must always wear gloves when harvesting.

Drain the chickpeas, put in a heavy-bottomed saucepan, cover with fresh water and cook until tender. This will take up to 1½ hours, depending on the age of the chickpeas. Drain. Purée through a *mouli légumes*.

Heat the oil in a frying pan, sauté the onion until softened, add the garlic and cook for 30 seconds longer. Add the tomatoes and simmer for 5 minutes before adding the chickpea purée. Season well and serve immediately.

Cichorium endivia. Asteraceae

ENDIVE

Also known as Escarole, Batavian Endive, Grumolo. Annual or biennial grown as annual for blanched hearts and leaves. Value: rich in iron, potassium and beta carotene; moderate vitamin A and B complex.

The origins of this plant are obscure, but it was certainly eaten by the Egyptians long before the birth of Christ and is one of the bitter herbs used at Passover. Mentioned by Ovid, Horace, Pliny and Dioscorides, it was valued by the Greeks and Romans as a cultivated plant. It was introduced to England, Germany, Holland and France around 1548 and was described by several writers.

 ## varieties

There are two types. The upright Batavian, scarole or escarole has large, broad leaves. Curly or fringed frisée is a pretty plant, with a low rosette of delicately serrated leaves. Curled varieties are generally used for summer cropping; the more robust broad-leaved types tolerate cold, are disease-resistant and grow well in winter.

'Broad Leaved Batavian' has tightly packed heads of broad, deep green leaves that become creamy-white when blanched. **'En Cornet de Bordeaux'**, an old variety, is very tasty, extremely hardy and blanches well. **'Green Curled Ruffec'**, a curly type, is tasty blanched and makes a good garnish. Very hardy and cold resistant. **'Green Curled'** (**'Moss Curled'**) produces compact heads of dark green, fringed leaves. **'Lassie'** yields a large amount of deeply cut, well flavored leaves. **'Pancalieri'*** has very curly, dark green leaves with creamy white hearts. **'Salad King'** is prolific and extremely hardy, with large, dark green, finely cut leaves. **'Sanda'** is vigorous and resistant to tip burn,

cold and bolting. **'Scarola Verde'** has a large head of broad, green and white leaves. However it may bolt in hot weather. The pale, green leaves of **'Toujours Blanche'** are deeply cut and finely curled. **'Très Fine Maraichère'** (**'Coquette'**) has finely cut, curled leaves that are mild and delicious, and it grows well in most soils. **'Wallone Frisée Weschelkopf'** (**'Wallone'**) has a large, tightly packed head with finely cut leaves. It is vigorous, hardy and good as a "cut and come again."

 ## cultivation

Propagation
Sow thinly, ½ inch deep *in situ* or in a seedbed, pots or modules to transplant. Allow 12–15 inches between plants and rows.

Endive germinates best at 68–72°F (20–22°C). Sow early crops under cover and shade summer crops. Sow from early to midsummer for autumn crops, in late summer for winter crops, using curled or hardy Batavian types. Sow all year round for "cut and come again"

seedlings or semi-mature leaves, making early and late sowings under glass.

Growing
Endive needs an open site, though slimmer crops tolerate a little shade. Soils should be light, moderately rich and free-draining; this is particularly important for winter crops. If necessary, dig in plenty of well-rotted organic matter before planting. Excess nitrogen encourages lush growth and makes plants prone to fungal diseases.

Endive is a cool-season crop, flourishing between 50–68°F (10–20°C), yet it withstands light frosts; hardier cultivars withstand temperatures down to 15°F (-9°C). Higher temperatures tend to encourage bitterness, though "curled" types are heat-tolerant. Young plants tend to bolt if temperatures fall below 41°F (5°C) for long.

Keep crops weed-free; mulch and water thoroughly during dry weather, as dryness at the roots can cause bolting. Use a general liquid fertilizer to boost growth if necessary.

Blanch to reduce bitterness and make leaves more tender. Many newer cultivars have tight heads and some blanching occurs naturally. Damp leaves are likely to rot, so choose a dry period or dry plants under cloches for 2–3 days. Draw the outer leaves together and tie with raffia 2–3 weeks before harvest, placing a tile, piece of cardboard or dinner plate over the center

Endive is invaluable in winter salads

of the plant, and covering with a cloche to keep off the rain. Alternatively cover the whole plant with a bucket or a flower pot with its drainage holes covered. Blanching takes about 10 days. Blanch a few at a time; they rapidly deteriorate afterward.

Maintenance

Spring Sow early crops under glass or cloches. Harvest late crops under cover.

Summer Sow curly varieties outdoors in seedbeds for transplanting, or in situ. Keep early-sown crops weed-free and moist. Harvest.

Autumn Sow outdoors and under cover. Harvest.

Winter Sow under cover and harvest.

Protected Cropping

Sow hardy cultivars under cover in trays or modules at 68°F (20°C) in mid-spring for early summer crops. After germination, maintain a minimum temperature of 39°F (4°C) for 3 weeks after transplanting — this is to prevent bolting.

For winter and early spring crops, transplant in early autumn from seed trays or modules under cover. Sow 'cut and come again' crops under cover in early spring, and in early autumn.

Endive grows better than lettuce in low light and is also a useful crop for the greenhouse in winter.

Harvesting and Storing

Harvest endive from 7 weeks after sowing, depending on cultivar and season.

"Cut and come again" seedlings may be ready from 5 weeks. With some cultivars, only one or two cuts may be possible before they run to seed. Pick individual leaves as needed or harvest them using a sharp knife about 1 inch above the ground, leaving the root to resprout. The whole plant can be lifted in autumn and put in a cool, dark place to blanch.

Leaves do not store well and are better eaten fresh. They last about 3 days in a clear plastic bag in the salad drawer of a refrigerator.

Pests and Diseases

Protect plants from slugs and control aphids.

Keep winter crops well watered and mulched to prevent tip burn.

Eat endive immediately after harvest

companion planting

Endive is good for intersowing and intercropping.

container growing

Sow directly or transplant into large containers of loam-based compost with added well-rotted organic matter. Keep compost moist and weed-free. Use a general liquid fertilizer to boost growth if necessary.

culinary

Endive is used mainly in salads with — or instead of — lettuce and other greens; the slightly bitter taste and crisp texture gives it more of a "bite" than the usual lettuce combinations. It suits strongly flavored dressings. Crisp bacon or croutons are often included. With mature endive, use the inner leaves for salads; the outer ones can be cooked as greens. Endive can also be braised. Try serving it shredded and dressed with hot crushed garlic, anchovy fillets and a little olive oil and butter.

Warm Red and Yellow Pepper Salad

Serves 6

The slightly bitter taste of curly endive (escarole or frisée) is ideal combined with other lettuces such as lamb's lettuce or watercress in winter months. The sweetness of the peppers in this dish happily complements the endive.

1 large endive, washed and roughly chopped
Big bunch lamb's lettuce, washed
2 large red peppers
3 tablespoons olive oil
3 cloves garlic, crushed
1 tablespoon chopped fresh herbs
Salt and freshly ground black pepper

For the dressing:
3 tablespoons extra virgin olive oil
1 tablespoon white wine vinegar
Salt and freshly ground black pepper

Arrange the lettuces in a large bowl. Core and deseed the peppers and cut them into thin strips. Heat the oil in a heavy pan and sauté the peppers, stirring constantly. Add the garlic after 5 minutes and cook for a further minute.

Add the peppers to the salad. Make the dressing and toss in the herbs and seasoning. Serve the salad alongside plain grilled fish or chicken.

Cichorium intybus. Asteraceae
CHICORY

Also known as Radicchio, Belgian Endive, Witloof, Succory, Sugar Loaf Chicory. Hardy perennial grown as annual for blanched leaves or root. Very hardy. Value: moderate levels of potassium.

A native of Europe through to central Russia and western Asia, chicory has been cultivated for centuries. Pliny tells us that cichorium is a Greek adaptation of the Egyptian name; he also noted its medicinal use as a purgative and the blanching of leaves for salads.

Large-rooted varieties have long been used dried, ground and roasted as a substitute for coffee — particularly popular in England during the Napoleonic wars when a blockade of the French coast cut supplies. It has a distinctive fragrance and is often drunk by those who like the taste of coffee without the caffeine. John Lindley, in the 19th century, recorded that roasted chicory was adulterated with a multitude of substances as diverse as marigolds, oak bark, mahogany sawdust and even baked horse liver!

Chicory is a traditional ingredient in Belgium

 varieties

Chicory has a distinctive, slightly bitter flavor. Most varieties are hardy and make a good winter crop with colorful, attractive leaves. There are three types. "Forcing" chicories like 'Witloof' (that is, whiteleaf) produce plump, leafy heads (known as "chicons") when blanched. "Red chicory" or "radicchio" includes older cultivars that responded to the reduced daylength and lower temperatures of autumn by turning from green to red; newer cultivars are naturally red and heart earlier. "Nonforcing" or "sugarloaf" types produce large-hearted lettuce-like heads for autumn harvest.

'**Brussels Witloof**' ('**Witloof de Brussels**') is one of the most famous forcing types which is also grown for its root. '**Catalogna Frastagliata**' is upright with thin, white ribs. '**Large Rooted Magdeburg**' ('**Magdeburg**'), like '**Brussels Witloof**', is grown for its root, which is used to make coffee, but young leaves can also be harvested. '**Orchidea Rossa**' is crunchy with good flavor and texture; delicious eaten steamed, roasted or raw. '**Palla rossa Zorzi Precoce**'* is a radicchio with a tangy, delicate flavor. It colors better in cool weather. '**Radicchio di Treviso Black Svelta**' has dark red, upright leaves with white midribs. '**Rossa di Treviso**', another radicchio, has crisp, green leaves that become deep red and veined with white in cooler conditions. It dates back to the 16th century and tolerates light frost. '**Rossa di Verona**' is a radicchio with a spreading habit and withstands considerable frost.

 cultivation

Propagation
Sow seed of forcing varieties thinly in late spring to early summer in drills ½ inch deep and 9–12 inches apart. Thin when the first true leaves appear to 8 inches apart.

Sow early radicchio under cover in seed trays and modules before hardening off and transplanting from mid-spring for summer harvest, using early maturing types first. Sow for autumn harvest from early to midsummer, and in mid- to late summer for transplanting under cover in autumn and cropping over winter. Thin to 9–15 inches in and between the rows.

Nonforcing or sugarloaf types can be broadcast or sown in broad drills under cover in late winter. When the soil warms and the weather improves, sow successively outdoors until late summer. Sow the final crop during early autumn under cover.

Thin to a final spacing of 9–12 inches in and between the rows. For a semi-mature "cut and come again" winter crop, sow seed from mid- to late summer and transplant indoors in autumn.

Growing

Chicories prefer an open, sunny site, but tolerate a little shade. Soil should be fertile and free-draining, with organic matter added for the previous crop: avoid recently manured ground, this causes the roots to fork.

Radicchio tolerates most soils except gravel or very heavy clay. The ideal pH is 5.5–7. Rake soil to a fine texture before sowing. Apply a general balanced fertilizer at 2 ounces/sq yd.

Keep weed-free with regular hoeing or mulching. Water thoroughly during dry weather to prevent bolting. Force appropriate varieties in situ if soil is light and winters are mild.

In late autumn to early winter, cut back the leaves to 1 inch above ground level. Form a ridge of friable soil 6–8 inches high over the stumps and cover with straw or leaf mold. After about 8–12 weeks, when the tips are appearing, remove the soil and cut the heads off at about 1 inch above the neck. Keep the compost moist while the "chicons" are growing.

Maintenance

Spring Sow early radicchio under cover, transplant from mid-spring. Sow sugarloaf types as "cut and come again" crops.

Summer Harvest early radicchio and sow maincrop. Sow sugarloaf outdoors for "cut and come again" and autumn maincrop.

Autumn Harvest radicchio crops sown early to midsummer; sow late crops for winter. Lift forcing types or force outdoors. Sow sugarloaf indoors.

Winter Force roots indoors successively until spring. Sow sugarloaf indoors.

Protected Cropping

Nonforcing varieties can be grown under glass, for early or late crops.

In autumn, cover outdoor crops of radicchio with cloches, fleece or similar to extend the growing season.

Forcing

Force "chicons" indoors if soil is heavy, if winters are severe, or for earlier crops. In mid- to late autumn when the foliage dies down, lift roots carefully, discard any forked or damaged ones and keep those that are at least 1–2 inches in diameter at the top. Cut off the remaining leaves to within ½ inch of the crown, trim back the side and main roots to about 8–9 inches. Pack horizontally in boxes of dry sand, peat substitute or sawdust and store in a cool, frost-free place. For forcing, remove a few roots from storage at a time. Plant about 5 to 6 roots in a 9-inch pot of sand or light soil, ensuring that ½ inch of the crown is above the surface. Surround the roots with moist peat or compost, leaving the crown exposed above ground.

Radicchio

Water sparingly and cover with a black polyethylene bag, an empty flower pot with the holes blocked up, or an empty box. Maintain temperatures of 50–59°F (10–15°C). They can also be blanched in a dark cellar or shed or under greenhouse staging (see "Growing"). The blanched "chicons" should be ready for cutting within 4 weeks, depending on the temperature. Roots may resprout, producing several smaller shoots which can then be blanched.

Harvesting and Storing

Harvest chicories grown for roots after the first frost. Cut heads of mature sugarloaf varieties with a sharp knife 1 inch above the soil in late autumn; use immediately or store in a frost-free place.

Allow the plants to resprout as a "cut and come again" crop under cloches.

Pick radicchio leaves as required, taking care not to overharvest, as this weakens plants. Alternatively, cut the whole head and leave the roots to resprout.

"Chicons" can be stored in the refrigerator, wrapped in foil or paper to prevent them from becoming bitter. Nonforcing chicory will stay fresh for up to 1 month.

Pests and Diseases

Though seldom troubled by pests and diseases, crops can rot outdoors in cold weather.

 ## companion planting

The blue flowers of chicory are attractive in the ornamental border.

 ## container growing

Chicories can be grown in large containers or growing bags as "cut and come again."

 ## medicinal

Chicory is said to be a digestive, diuretic and laxative, reducing inflammation. A liver and gall bladder tonic, it is used for rheumatism, gout and hemorrhoids. Culpeper suggests its use "for swooning and passions of the heart."

CHICORY

 culinary

All types of chicory make a wonderful winter salad, particularly if you mix the colors of red, green and white. Add tomatoes or a sweet dressing to take away some of the bitter taste. Home-grown chicons stored in the dark tend to be less bitter.

For a delicious light supper dish, pour a robust dressing (made with lemon juice rather than vinegar) over the leaves, add some anchovy fillets, crumbled hard-boiled eggs and top with a handful of kalamata olives.

As an accompaniment to cold meat and game, eat with sliced oranges, onion and chopped walnuts.

With roast meats, braise chicory with butter, lemon juice and cream. Radicchio can also be braised, but loses its color.

To make a chicory coffee substitute, dry roots immediately after harvest and grind thoroughly.

Chicory with Ham and Cheese Sauce

Serves 4

4 heads chicory
8 slices smoked Bayonne ham
2 tablespoons butter
2 tablespoons plain flour
2 teaspoons Dijon mustard
½ cup milk
Light cream
4 tablespoons grated Gruyère cheese
Salt and freshly ground black pepper

Blanch the chicory heads in a pan of salted water for 5 minutes, drain and gently squeeze out as much water as you can. Cut each chicory in half and wrap in a slice of the ham. Then arrange in one layer in an ovenproof dish.

Preheat the oven to 400°F (200°C). Make the cheese sauce: melt the butter in a heavy pan and stir in the flour. Cook for 2 minutes, then stir in the mustard. Pour in the milk gradually, stirring vigorously as the sauce thickens, then add the cheese and enough cream to accomplish a smooth consistency. Stir over a gentle heat for 5 minutes to let the cheese melt. Season to taste.

Pour the cheese sauce over the chicory wrapped in ham and cook in the oven for 20 minutes until nicely browned. Serve immediately.

Braised Chicory

Braised Chicory

Serves 4

The French, especially in the South-West and in Provence, braise chicory or Belgian endives and serve them with roasted meats such as lamb and beef.

4 heads chicory, trimmed
2 tablespoons butter
1 red onion, finely chopped
2 slices bacon, diced
½ cup chicken stock and white wine combined
Juice of ½ a lemon
Salt and freshly ground black pepper

Liberally coat the sides and bottom of a heavy, lidded casserole with half the butter and heat the remaining butter in a small pan over a medium flame. Gently fry the onion and bacon, and set aside.

Arrange the endives in the casserole. Add some of the stock and white wine, season with salt and pepper and cover. Allow to sweat over a low heat until just turning color. Roll them over and cook on the other side.

Add a little more liquid as required. The liquid should evaporate from the endives by the end, so that they are browned and tender (you may have to remove the lid for a short while). Add the onion and bacon and quickly heat up. Drizzle over the lemon juice, season and serve immediately.

Chicory with Ham and Cheese Sauce

Colocasia esculenta var. *antiquorum*. *Araceae*

EDDOE

Perennial grown as annual for edible tubers. Tender. Value: rich in starch, magnesium, potassium and vitamin C.

This variety of taro, native of India and South-East Asia, was first recorded by the Chinese 2,000 years ago. It is now grown throughout the humid tropics. Eddoes flourish in moist soil alongside rivers and streams. The central tuber is surrounded by clusters of smaller tubers which are harvested, making it different from the single-tubered dasheen. The brown, hairy tubers can weigh up to 5 pounds, and when they are sliced reveal flesh which is usually white but can also be yellow, pink or orange. Their taste is similar to a garden potato but with an attractive nutty flavor. Tubers should never be eaten raw as all varieties contain calcium oxalate crystals, a skin irritant.

 culinary

Tubers can be boiled, baked, roasted, puréed and made into soup. They can also be fried.

Protected Cropping

If you have space in a greenhouse or plastic tunnel, it is worth trying to grow eddoes. Plant presprouted or chitted tubers in spring into growbags or 8–12-inch pots containing peat substitute compost. Maintain heat and high humidity: wet down the greenhouse floor or mist plants with soft tepid water.

Harvesting and Storing

Eddoes take 5–6 months to mature. Harvest when the stems begin to turn yellow and die back. Lift tubers carefully with a garden fork; select some for eating and save others for replanting. If they are undamaged and dried carefully, tubers can be stored for several months.

Pests and Diseases

Eddoes grown outdoors are generally problem-free but when grown under glass they are susceptible to aphids and fungal leaf spots; red spider mite can also be a problem, particularly when humidity is low.

Downy mildew can attack tubers after they have been lifted so it is important to ensure that they are dried well before being stored. Dispose of infected tubers and do not use them for propagation.

 varieties

'Euchlora' has dark green leaves with violet margins and leaf stems. **'Fontanesii'** produces leaf stems that are dark red-purple or violet. Its leaf blades are dark green with violet veins and margin.

 cultivation

Propagation

In the humid tropics, eddoes can be planted any time. In temperate climates, grow under glass or clear plastic at a minimum temperature of 70°F (21°C), and plant in spring. Plant small tubers or a tuber section containing some dormant buds in individual holes 24–30 inches apart. Cuttings consisting of the top of a tuber with several leaves and a growth point can be planted directly into the soil and will establish rapidly. Add general fertilizer to the planting hole.

Growing

Eddoes need humus-rich, slightly acid, moisture-retentive soil, in sunshine or partial shade. Cultivate the soil before planting and remove any weeds.

Maintenance

Spring Plant tubers if protected cropping.
Summer Feed every 3–4 weeks with a high potassium fertilizer; additional nitrogen may be needed. During drier periods, irrigate as needed to ensure swelling of the tubers and earth up. Keep weed-free.
Autumn Harvest as required.
Winter Prepare beds for the following year's crop if growing in a greenhouse.

 warning

When handling and peeling eddoes, be sure to wear gloves or cover the hands with a layer of cooking oil to prevent a nasty rash.

Colocasia esculenta var. esculenta. Araceae
DASHEEN

Also known as Elephant's Ear, Arvi Leaves, West Indian Kale, Taro, Coco Yam. Herbaceous perennial grown for its edible leaves, shoots and tubers. Tender. Value: tuber rich in starch; leaves high in vitamin A, good source of B_2.

In cultivation for around 7,000 years, dasheen is said to have been first grown in India on terraces where rice now flourishes. The common name derives from *de Chine* (from China): the root was imported from South-East Asia following a competition organized by the Royal Geographical Society to find a cheap food source for the slaves on West Indian sugar plantations.

Dasheen thrives in flooded conditions

 ## varieties

Dasheen have a cylindrical main tuber with fibrous roots and a few side tubers. The upright stems up to 6 feet tall are topped with large, heart-shaped leaves with prominent ribs on the underside. Cultivated types rarely flower and are grouped by the color of their flesh, ranging from pink to yellow, and leaf stems of green, pinkish purple to almost black.

 ## cultivation

Propagation
Dasheen are propagated from "tops" with a small section of tuber, small side tubers or "suckers." Plant 24 inches apart with 40 inches between rows, or 24–36 inches apart; add general fertilizer to the hole before planting.

Growing
Dasheen tolerate quite heavy, fertile, moisture-retentive soil rich in organic matter with a pH of 5.5–6.5. Dig in compost or well-rotted manure if necessary. As dasheen need plenty of water and tolerate waterlogging, they are ideal for areas by streams and rivers. Where the water table is high, mound or ridge planting is advised. Irrigate heavily during dry weather.

In well-manured soil, a second crop can be planted between the rows 12 weeks before the main crop is harvested.

DASHEEN

Maintenance

Spring Plant presprouted tubers with protection.
Summer Keep crops well fed and watered and weed-free.
Autumn Harvest crops.
Winter Prepare for the following year.

Protected Cropping

Plant pre-sprouted tubers in spring into greenhouse borders. Keep temperatures around 70°F (21°C), and maintain high humidity by misting plants with soft tepid water or wetting down the greenhouse floor. Do not worry about overwatering.

Feed every 3–4 weeks with a high-potassium fertilizer; extra nitrogen may be needed if growth slows.

 ## container growing

Dasheen can be grown as a "novelty" crop in 8–12 inches pots of peat-substitute compost. Soak thoroughly after planting and stand the pot in a shallow tray of tepid water throughout the growing season. Treat as for "Protected Cropping."

Dasheen roots

 ## culinary

Tubers can be roasted, baked or boiled, served with spicy sauces and in stews. Larger tubers, which tend to be dry and coarse, should be braised and cooked slowly.

Leaves (with midrib removed) can be stuffed, boiled or steamed and eaten with a pat of butter. Avoid particularly large leaves; they are often tough. In the West Indies, Callaloo Soup is made from dasheen leaves, okra, crab meat and coconut milk. Young blanched shoots can be eaten like asparagus.

Pests and Diseases

Taro leaf blight causes circular water-soaked spots on leaves followed by collapse of the plant. Those grown under glass are susceptible to aphids. Red spider mite and downy mildew can also be a problem. Take the necessary precautions.

Harvesting and Storing

Dasheen take 7 to 11 months to mature. Harvest by lifting the main tuber, saving some of the small side tubers for eating and others for replanting. Undamaged tubers can be dried and stored for up to 4 weeks, while washed leaves keep for several days in a refrigerator.

Palusima

This is a Western Samoan or Polynesian dish. Allow about ½ pound dasheen per person. Peel and chop roughly, then parboil in plain salted water for 5–10 minutes. Drain, then boil until reduced in coconut milk (enough to come to half the height of the dasheen in the pan) until thickish. Mash. Stuff the mashed dasheen into parboiled leaves and secure with a toothpick. (Alternatively, wrap it in banana leaves, and even spinach or cabbage.) Bake for 15 minutes in a lightly greased dish in a preheated oven at 350°F (180°C). Serve with any good white fish such as cod.

 ## warning

Although selection has, over the years, reduced calcium oxalate levels in the skin of dasheen, it is extremely important to wear gloves or to cover the hands with a layer of cooking oil. This prevents skin irritation when peeling the vegetables.

Always make sure dasheen are cooked thoroughly before eating.

Crambe maritima. Brassicaceae
SEA KALE

Perennial grown for its blanched young shoots. Hardy. Value: an excellent source of vitamin C.

Found on the seashores of northern Europe, the Baltic and the Black Seas, sea kale was harvested from the wild and sold in markets long before it came into cultivation. In Victorian times it was seen as an aristocrat of the vegetable garden and widely cultivated by armies of gardeners in the enormous kitchen gardens attached to great houses. Today it is rarely grown, perhaps because the scale on which it was forced for Victorian tables gave it a reputation for being labor-intensive. However, it is easy to grow at home, and quite delicious; so it is high time it experienced a revival!

Two essentials: healthy plants and a blancher

 varieties

'Lily White' crops heavily with pale stems and has a good flavor. Unnamed selections of the wild species are also available from nurseries.

 cultivation

Propagation

Sea kale can be grown from seed, but it is usually propagated from crowns or root cuttings from the side roots, taken in autumn after the leaves have died back. These are called "thongs." Buy them from a nursery or select roots that are pencil-thick and 3–6 inches long.

Make a straight cut across the top of the root and an angled cut at the base (so top and bottom are distinguishable). Store in sand until planting.

Growing

Sea kale needs a sunny position on deep, rich, well-drained light soil with a pH of around neutral.

The winter before planting, dig in some well-rotted compost; on heavier soils, add horticultural sand or grit, or plant on a raised bed.

culinary

Eat while the stalk end is still firm. Some people remain adamant that peeled cucumbers are best: others think the flavor and appearance of the skin enhance the vegetable.

They are frequently sliced and eaten in salads, and are good in sandwiches with salmon. Mix with yogurt and mint as a side dish to Middle Eastern dishes or curries. Make into a delicious cold soup.

To eat them as a vegetable, peel, seed, dice and stew them in a little water and butter for 20 minutes, until soft. Thicken with cream and serve with mild- or rich-flavored fish.

Cucumber and Cream Cheese Mousse
Serves 4

½ a cucumber, in chunks
8 ounces cream cheese
1–2 tablespoons mint leaves
2 teaspoons white wine vinegar
2½ teaspoons gelatin
⅔ cup vegetable stock
Salt and freshly ground black pepper
Radicchio leaves and sprigs of fresh mint, to serve

Put the cucumber into a blender with the cream cheese, mint and vinegar and purée until smooth. Dissolve the gelatin in a little stock over a low heat. Leave to cool, then stir in the balance of the stock. Add this to the cream cheese, season and blend. Chill for at least 2 hours before serving, arranged individually with radicchio leaves, garnished with a few fine slices of cucumber and sprigs of mint.

Plenty to enjoy and give away

Harvesting and Storing

Fruits should never be harvested until they are fully ripe, and the 16th-century practice of leaving fruit on until they were mottled brown and yellow with a rich flavor may be to your taste!

Outdoor cucumbers crop midsummer to early autumn: cut with a sharp knife when they are large enough to use. For maximum yields, you should pick fruit regularly. Cucumbers last for several days in the salad drawer of a refrigerator. Cover the cut end with plastic wrap and use as rapidly as possible. Or stand it stalk end down in a tall jug with a little water in the bottom. Like squash, they can be stored in nets in a cool place.

Pests and Diseases

Red spider mite, aphids, slugs and powdery mildew can be troublesome.

Cucumber mosaic virus shows as mottled, distorted leaves. Burn young infected plants and leaves from older plants. Older plants may recover, though yields will be lower.

 companion planting

Ridge cucumbers thrive in the shade of maize or sunflowers, and grow well with peas and beans, beets or carrots.

Climbing cucumbers flourish, scrambling over sweetcorn and beans.

 container growing

Sow indoor types in pots or growbags (see "Protected Cropping"). Smooth-skinned varieties can be grown in a growbag or container 12 inches wide by 8 inches deep in a sunny position outdoors. Sow 3 seeds 1 inch deep in late spring or early summer.

Thin out to leave the strongest seedling; pinch out growing tips when the plant develops 6–7 leaves. Train the side shoots on netting or canes. Keep soil moist. Feed with high-potassium fertilizer when fruits form. 'Bush Champion' is ideal.

 medicinal

Cucumbers were used by the Romans against scorpion bites, bad eyesight and to scare away mice.

Wives wishing for children wore cucumbers tied around their waists, and they were carried by midwives and thrown away once the child was born.

PUMPKIN & SQUASH
COURGETTE, ZUCCHINI, POTIRON

"On the coast of Coromandel
Where the early pumpkins blow
In the middle of the woods
Lived the Yonghy-Bonghy-Bo..."
Edward Lear (1812–88)

Annuals grown for edible fruits, often colorful, which can be extremely large. Tender. Value: high in beta carotene, moderate amounts of vitamin C and folic acid.

The name "pumpkin" appeared in the 17th century, shortly before Perrault wrote Cinderella, the tale about a poor girl whose fairy godmother turned a pumpkin into a golden coach that took her to the ball. "Pumpkin" comes from the Greek word for melon — *pepon* or "cooked by the sun" — while one French name, *potiron*, means "large mushroom," from the Arabic for morel mushrooms. "Squash" is an abbreviation of the native North American Indian word *askutasquash*, meaning "eaten raw or uncooked."

The squashes originated in the Americas and are believed to have been cultivated for between five thousand and ten thousand years. Wild forms were originally gathered for their seeds and were only later found to have sweet flesh. Many varieties arrived in Europe soon after the discovery of the New World in the 16th century. Not only were they eaten, but the seeds were pounded in oatmeal and applied to the face, to bleach freckles and other blemishes.

Estienne and Liébault wrote in 1570: "To make pompions keep long and not spoiled or rotted, you must sprinkle them with the juice of a houseleek." In the 17th century they were mashed to bulk up bread, or boiled and buttered.

This group contains a wealth of edible and outstandingly ornamental fruits. One of the most beautiful sights in the kitchen garden is that of pumpkins ripening in golden sunshine during the autumn.

PUMPKIN & SQUASH

Provide enough space to spread

 ## varieties

Members of the genus *Cucurbita* are bushy or trailing annuals — sometimes extremely vigorous plants — bearing a wide range of edible and/or ornamental fruit. The fruits from all of these species are often grouped together according to their shape or time of harvest — crookneck, summer squash, winter squash and so on; in practice, categories overlap and some are multipurpose, being served differently when young and when mature. Additional confusion arises because of local variation in what is grown and what it is called. Here they are classed according to species.

The *Cucurbita maxima* group has large, variable fruits and includes most traditional pumpkins and winter squashes, containing several ornamentals like the banana, buttercup, hubbard and turban types. They tend to have hard skins when mature, and keep well; the yellow flesh needs cooking. They flourish in low humidity from 68–80°F (20–27°C), though some tolerate cooler conditions.

'Atlantic Giant' is not for the faint-hearted as it can grow to 700 pounds. **'Banana Pink'** is long, broad and curved, with pale pink skin. **'Big Max'** is a massive pumpkin with rough, red-orange skin and bright flesh. It is excellent for pies, exhibitions and as a "giant" vegetable. **'Buttercup'** is delicious with firm, dense, sweet flesh. The skin is dark green with pale narrow stripes and the flavor is perfect for soups, roasting and pumpkin pie. **'Crown Prince'** is small with tender orange flesh. It's tasty and keeps well. **'Queensland Blue'** is an attractive small variety with blue-gray skin — very tasty. **'Turk's Turban'** ('Turk's Cap') is a

wonderful ornamental squash; orange with cream and green markings. The name aptly describes the shape. **'Warted Hubbard'** is a small, round fruit with extraordinary dark green, warty skin and orange-yellow flesh. It keeps well. **'Whangaparoa Crown Pumpkin'** is a hard, gray-skinned variety with a pronounced crown and orange flesh. It also stores well.

Cucurbita pepo embraces summer squashes (including zucchini), nonkeeping winter pumpkins and ornamental gourds such as custard squash, plus straight and crook-necked types. The fruits are usually soft-skinned, especially when young, and may be served raw when small. One variety, **'Little Gem'**, is slow to mature, taking about 4 months. It doesn't perform well in cooler conditions but is good for storage.

Summer Squash
'Early Golden Summer Crookneck' is an early cropper with bright yellow fruits and excellent flavor. Harvest when 4 inches long. **'Early Prolific Straight Neck'** is yellow with finely textured flesh. Pick at 6 inches. **'Vegetable Spaghetti'** ('Spaghetti Squash') is pale yellow when mature. Boil or bake fruits whole and then scoop out the flesh inside; it looks like spaghetti. **'White Pattypan'** ('White Bush Scallop') has an unusual flattened shape with a

Zucchini or *Cucurbita pepo*

Even the 'Atlantic Giant' starts small

scalloped edge. It is better harvested and cooked whole when about 3 inches in diameter. It is bushy and ideal for small gardens. **'Yellow Bush Scallop'** is an old variety with bright yellow skin and coarse, pale yellow flesh that has a distinctive flavor.

Zucchini
'Long Green Trailing' is a prolific, long-fruited, dark green variety — fine quality and flavor. **'Tiger Cross'*** is an early, green bush-type that crops well and yields good-quality fruits. Resistant to cucumber mosaic virus. **'Badger Cross'*** is compact, high yielding and crops early. Ideal for containers or small gardens.

There are varieties of zucchini bred for picking when small; the following are all bush types and ideal for the smaller garden. **'Ambassador'** is high-yielding with dark green fruit and reliable cropping. **'Defender'*** produces high yields of mid-green fruits. Harvest regularly. Resistant to cucumber mosaic virus. **'De Nice à Fruit Rond'**, a round variety, should be picked when the size of a golf ball — delicious flavor. **'Partenon'** fruits without pollination and is good for early crops or in cool weather. **'Spacemiser'** is a compact and prolific gourmet variety. **'Supremo'** produces very tasty, dark green fruit.

PUMPKIN & SQUASH

Winter squash

These usually have white or pale yellow flesh, whereas pumpkins have coarse, orange flesh. **'Ebony Acorn'** ('Table Queen') is early-cropping with thin, dark green skin and sweet, pale yellow flesh; delicious baked with honey. It is a semi-bush but can be temperamental. **'Jack be Little'** is a miniature pumpkin with deep ribbed, orange-skinned fruits about 2 x 3 inches in diameter. You can eat them but they are often more attractive as an autumn decoration. **'Small Sugar'** has rounded orange fruits growing to 7 inches in diameter. The flesh is tender, yellow and excellent in sweet or savoury dishes. It matures from late autumn.

Cucurbita moschata includes the early butternut, butternut, Kentucky Field and crookneck squashes, harvested in autumn and winter. They are large, rounded and usually have smooth, tough skin. Possibly one of the earliest species in cultivation, they are widely grown and found throughout the tropics. Particularly heat-tolerant.

'Butternut' has pale tan, club-shaped fruits with bright orange flesh. It succeeds in cooler areas and the flavor improves with keeping. **'Early Butternut'** is a curved, narrow fruit with a swollen tip. This bush variety matures rapidly and keeps well. **'Neck'** squash, with straight or curled necks, is tasty, high-yielding and the best for pies. **'Triple Treat'** is a bright orange, round fruit. Its seeds are particularly good eaten raw, fried or roasted. It is easy to carve and is therefore a variety that is often grown for Halloween. **'Waltham Butternut'** has a smooth, pale tan skin, yellow-orange flesh and a nutty taste. It is very good for storing and yields extremely well.

 cultivation

Propagation

Sow *in situ* or in pots in cooler climates as seeds do not germinate if the soil is below 56°F (13°C).

From mid- to late spring, soak the seed overnight, then sow one seed edgeways, about 1-inch deep in a 3-inch pot or module of moist multipurpose or seed compost and place in a propagator or on a warm windowsill, preferably at 68–77°F (20–25°C). After germination transplant the seedlings when they are large enough to handle into 5-inch pots, taking care not to damage the roots. Keep compost moist but not waterlogged. Harden off gradually and transplant from late spring to early summer when the danger of frost has passed. Protect with cloches until the plants are established.

Alternatively, sow *in situ* when the soil is warm and workable and there is no danger of frost, from late spring to early summer. Dig out a hole at least 12–18 inches square and half fill with well-rotted manure 7–10 days before planting. Sow 2–3 seeds 1 inch deep in the center of the mound and cover with a jam jar or cut the base from a plastic bottle and use as a crop cover. After germination, thin to leave the strongest seedling, remove the cover and mark the position with a cane so you know where to water the plant among the mass of stems. Alternatively, prepare the ground as described and transplant seedlings.

Space cultivars according to their vigor. Sow bush varieties on mounds or ridges, 24–36 inches apart with 3–4 feet between rows. Trailing varieties should be 4–6 feet apart with 6–12 feet between rows.

Growing

Pumpkins and squashes need a sunny position in rich, moisture-retentive soil with plenty of well-rotted organic matter and a pH of 5.5–6.8.

Even the flowers are edible

Only female flowers produce fruit

It is a good idea to plant through a black polyethylene mulch laid over the soil with the edges buried to hold it in place. This warms the soil, suppresses weeds, conserves moisture and protects ripening fruit. A thick layer of straw or horticultural fleece are useful alternatives, or you can lay the ripening fruit on a roof tile, a piece of board or similar object to protect it from the soil and prevent rotting.

Hand-pollination is recommended, particularly in cold weather when insect activity is reduced. Female flowers have a small swelling, the embryonic squash, immediately behind the petals, while male flowers have only a thin stalk.

When the weather is dry, remove a mature male flower, fold back or remove the petals and dust pollen on to the stigma of the female flowers. Alternatively, transfer the pollen with a fine paintbrush. Periods of hot weather can reduce the ratio of female to male flowers.

Plants need copious amounts of food and water, particularly when flowers and fruits are forming, up to 3 gallons of water per week, but they should never be allowed to become waterlogged.

Feed with a liquid general fertilizer every 2 weeks. Plants grown with a black plastic mulch also need an occasional foliar feed to boost growth.

Pinch out tips of main shoots of trailing varieties when they reach 24 inches to encourage branching and trim back those that outgrow their position.

Trailing types can also be trained over trellis or supports. Where space is limited, you can push a circle of pegs into the soil and trail the stems around the pegs.

To guarantee large fruits, allow only 2–3 to develop on each plant.

Keep crops weed-free.

Maintenance
Spring Sow seeds under glass or outdoors.
Summer Feed and water copiously; keep crops weed-free. Harvest zucchinis.
Autumn Harvest pumpkins and winter squashes, allow to ripen and protect from frost.
Winter Store winter squashes until midwinter or later.

Protected Cropping
In cooler climates or to advance growth, sow seed indoors and transplant. Protect with cloches or crop covers until they are well established. Use bush varieties for earlier crops.

Harvesting and Storing
Pick zucchini and summer squashes when they are about 4 inches long and still young and tender. Bigger zucchini breeds are harvested when they have reached full size. Push your thumbnail gently into the skin near the stalk; if it goes in easily then the bigger zucchini breed is ready for harvest.

Cut them from the stem, leaving a short stalk on the fruit, and handle with care to avoid bruising. Harvest regularly for continual cropping.

They can be stored in a cool place for about 8 weeks. Zucchini can be kept in a plastic bag in the refrigerator and will stay fresh for about a week.

Zucchini are suitable for freezing. Cut into ½-inch slices, blanch for 2 minutes, cool, drain and dry. Freeze in plastic bags. Flesh of winter squashes and pumpkins can be cooked, then frozen, without any loss of flavor.

Plenty of sunshine ensures early ripening

Toward the end of the growing season, remove any foliage that shades the fruits. Harvest pumpkins and winter squashes from late summer to autumn, though they must be brought into storage before the first heavy frosts. On maturity, the foliage rapidly dies, the skin hardens and stem starts to crack.

After harvest, leave them outdoors for about 14 days, as cold weather improves the taste and sugar content, hardening the skin and sealing the stem. Protect from heavy frost with a covering of hessian, straw or similar.

In cooler areas, they can be ripened in a greenhouse or on a sunny windowsill. Pumpkins will last until midwinter when stored in a frost-free shed.

Store winter squashes at a minimum temperature of 50°F (10°C); they can last for up to 6 months. Some Japanese varieties will last even longer.

Good air circulation means healthy plants

Pests and Diseases
If fruits show signs of withering, water and feed more often. Aphids, powdery and downy mildew and slugs can be a problem.

Cucumber mosaic virus causes yellow mottling and puckering of the leaves and rotting of the fruit. Destroy infected plants immediately and control aphids, which transmit this virus.

 ## companion planting

Grow zucchini alongside sweetcorn for support and shade, and with legumes, which provide essential nitrogen.

 ## container growing

Zucchini, bush varieties of other squashes and those that are moderately vigorous can be grown in growbags or containers that are at least 14 inches by 12 inches deep. Use a loam-based compost with additional well-rotted organic matter. Sow indoors to transplant later or sow directly outdoors. Keep plants well watered and do not allow the compost to dry out. Plants can be grown up strong canes 7 feet tall. Pinch out growing points when stems reach the top; tie the main stem and side shoots firmly to the supporting canes.

Hand-pollinate for successful cropping.

 ## other uses

Pumpkins are hollowed out and made into Halloween "Jack o' Lanterns." Mature large zucchinis can be used for wine making.

 ## medicinal

In Ethiopia, seeds from squashes are used as laxatives and purgatives; they are used worldwide to expel intestinal worms. Eating winter squash and pumpkin is said to reduce the risk of prostate cancer.

 ## warning

Be careful when lifting large squashes: bend from the knees, not the back!

 ## culinary

Flowers of all varieties can be used in salads or stuffed with rice or minced meat and fried in batter. Prepare the meat, rice and batter before picking the flowers, as they wilt quickly. They can also be puréed and made into soup. Young shoots are steamed or boiled. Pumpkin flesh is used for pies; their seeds are deep-fried in oil, salted and are known as "pepitos." The fruits can be stuffed, steamed, stir-fried, added to curries, made into jam or pickles, and the seeds are edible too.

Pumpkin Kibbeh
Serves 4

A centerpiece of many Middle Eastern meals, these "balls" should be served warm, rather than hot. This recipe was given to me by Arto der Haroutunian.

1 cup freshly boiled pumpkin flesh
2 cups bulgar wheat
1 ½ cups all-purpose flour
1 onion, finely chopped
Salt and freshly ground black pepper

For the filling:
2 shallots, finely chopped
½ pound spinach, washed
¾ cup cooked chickpeas, drained
⅓ cup walnuts, chopped
⅓ cup dried apricots
¼ teaspoon sumac
1 tablespoon lemon juice
Salt and freshly ground black pepper
Oil for frying

In a large bowl, purée the pumpkin, using a fork. Sieve the bulgar and flour into the bowl and mix in the onion and seasoning. Leave in a cool place for 10–15 minutes. If the dough is too hard to handle, you may need to add a tablespoon of water and knead well. To make the filling, sauté the shallots in the oil until they just turn brown. Mix in the spinach and allow to wilt, stirring constantly, for a couple of minutes. Then add the rest of the ingredients, mixing well.

Make the kibbehs with wet hands to prevent the mixture from sticking. Form the bulgar and pumpkin mixture into oval patties — they should be about 3 inches long and

PUMPKIN & SQUASH

just big enough to stuff. Create an opening at one end and fill each kibbeh with the spinach and apricot stuffing. Using your fingers, seal up the ends.

Fry the kibbehs in hot oil for a couple of minutes on each side and drain on kitchen paper. There should be enough to make between 20 and 24 kibbehs.

Zucchini Omelette
Serves 2

⅔ pound zucchini
5 eggs
4 tablespoons olive oil

1 tablespoon fresh (purple) basil leaves
1 tablespoon fresh thyme leaves
Salt and freshly ground black pepper

Whisk the eggs with salt and pepper and set aside. Slice the zucchini into coarse dice. Heat half the oil and sauté the zucchini for a couple of minutes. Then remove from the heat.

In an omelette pan, heat the balance of the oil and pour in the eggs, zucchini and herbs. Stir gently over a low heat while the omelette sets. Turn it on to a plate and slide back into the pan to cook the second side for a minute or so until nicely browned. Serve as a refreshing Sunday supper dish.

Acorn Squash with Balsamic Vinegar

Zucchini omelette

Acorn Squash with Balsamic Vinegar

Allow ¼ pound of acorn squash per person. Cut in half and remove the seeds and fibres. Place in a buttered ovenproof dish and pour over 1 tablespoon balsamic vinegar, 2 tablespoons liquid honey and 1 tablespoon lemon juice for each serving. Cook in a preheated oven, 350°F (180°C) for 40 minutes, turning over halfway.

Pattypan squash with Bacon and Cheese
Serves 2–4

1 pound pattypan squash, roughly diced
2 tablespoons butter
1 small onion, finely sliced
⅓ cup smoked back bacon, diced
⅔ cup crème fraîche
4 tablespoons grated mature Cheddar cheese
Salt and freshly ground black pepper

Steam the pattypan squash until just tender. Keep warm. Make a sauce by heating the butter and cooking the onion until softened. Add the bacon and continue cooking for 5 minutes, stirring from time to time. Mix in the crème fraîche, the squash and seasoning and pour into a greased ovenproof dish. Top with the cheese and cook in a preheated oven, 425°F (225°C), for 15 minutes.

Cynara cardunculus. Asteraceae
CARDOON

Also known as Cardon. Perennial grown as annual for "heart" and blanched leaf midribs. Half hardy. Value: rich in potassium.

This close relative of the globe artichoke is found in the wild through much of the Mediterranean and North Africa. Cultivated versions are valued as a vegetable and in the ornamental garden. When grown as a food crop, the stems are blanched during autumn in a similar manner to celery. Its delights have been enjoyed for centuries; it was grown before the birth of Christ and was esteemed by the Romans, who paid high prices for it in their markets as an ingredient for stews and salads. Cardoons reached England by 1658 and North America by the following century, but never established themselves as a major crop, despite their popularity in Europe. Today they are more likely to be found in a herbaceous border, where the bold angular foliage and tall candelabras of thistle-like purple flowers are outstanding.

The leaves are ready for blanching

 ## varieties

'**Gigante di Romagna**' is a reliable variety with long stalks. '**Gobbo di Nizza Monferrato**' is a large plant with a strong celery flavor. Use in soups or eat fried, sautéed or raw, dipped in olive oil. '**Plein Blanc Inerma Ameliora**' grows to 4 feet tall, with white ribs that are well textured and tasty.

 ## cultivation

Cardoons need a sunny, sheltered site on light, fertile, well-drained soil.

Propagation
Sow *in situ* in mid-spring, planting 3–4 seeds 1 inch deep in "stations" 20 inches apart with 5 feet between rows. Thin after germination to retain the strongest seedling. In cooler areas or if spring is late and the soil is yet to warm up, sow indoors. Place 3 seeds in 3-inch pots or modules of moist seed compost in a propagator or greenhouse at 55°F (13°C). Thin, leaving the strongest seedling, then harden off before planting outdoors in mid- to late spring, when there is no danger of frost. Water well after planting and protect from scorching sunshine until they have established.

Growing
The autumn or early spring before seed sowing or planting out seedlings, double dig the site, adding well-rotted organic matter. Alternatively, plant in trenches 15–20 inches wide and 12 inches deep; dig these in late autumn or early spring, incorporating plenty of rotted manure or compost into the base and refilling to 3–4 inches below the surface. Leave the remaining soil alongside for earthing up. Before planting, rake in general fertilizer at 4 ounces/sq yd.

Cardoons make attractive ornamentals

In late summer to early autumn, on a day when the leaves and hearts are dry, begin blanching: pull stems into a large bunch (wear long sleeves and gloves for protection), and tie with raffia or soft string just below the leaves. Wrap cardoons with "collars" of newspaper, corrugated cardboard, brown wrapping paper or black polyethylene tied firmly around the stems. Weeping tile and plastic guttering are just as effective at excluding the light. Support collars with a stake, particularly on exposed sites. Alternatively, cardoons can be earthed up. Cover stems with dry hay, bracken or straw held firmly at several points with twine and cover with soil, banked at an angle of 45°. The first method is easier, cleaner and quicker.

Cardoons need a regular water supply from early summer through to early autumn, and feeding with liquid general fertilizer every 2 weeks. Keep them weed-free by hand weeding, hoeing or, preferably, mulching with a 2-inch layer of organic matter once plants are established.

Maintenance

Spring Sow seeds *in situ* or under glass.
Summer Feed and water regularly. Keep weed-free.
Autumn Harvest crops using a sharp knife. Prepare the planting bed.
Winter Store in a cool, dry place until required.

Protected Cropping

Protect transplants or seedlings under cloches or horticultural fleece if late spring frosts are forecast.

Harvesting and Storing

Blanching takes about 3–4 weeks. When ready to harvest, lift plants with a garden fork, trim off roots and remove outer leaves. Cardoons can remain in the ground until needed, but protect with bracken, straw or other insulating material in moderate frosts. If hard frosts are forecast, lift and store in a cool shed or cellar.

Pests and Diseases

Cardoons are robust and have few problems. They can be affected by powdery mildew, which is worse when plants are dry at the roots and if nights are cold and days warm and dry. Mice will eat the seeds. An old remedy is to dip the seeds in paraffin; otherwise buy humane traps or a cat!

 container growing

Grow in large containers of loam-based compost with added organic matter or in free-draining, moisture-retentive soil. Allow plenty of room for leaves to grow. Water and feed regularly: do not let the compost dry out. Blanch using "collars."

 culinary

The leaf midribs and thinly sliced hearts are eaten raw in salads, in soups and stews or as an alternative to fennel or celery. They can be boiled in salted water with a squeeze of lemon juice for about 30 minutes until tender. Once cardoons are cut, drop them into water with a squeeze of lemon juice, as the cut surfaces do tend to blacken.

The dried flowers are used as a substitute for rennet in Spain and some parts of South America.

Lamb Tagine with Cardoons
Serves 4

Tagines (or stews) are popular in northern Africa. Cardoons give this traditional Moroccan dish a rich flavor.

1 ½–2 pounds cardoons
1 ½ pounds chunks lamb
3 cloves garlic, crushed
1 teaspoon ground ginger
Pinch saffron
¼ teaspoon turmeric
2–3 tablespoons vegetable oil
2 tablespoons chopped fresh coriander
1 onion, peeled and sliced
2 preserved lemons, quartered
4 tablespoons black olives
Juice of 2 lemons
Salt and freshly ground black pepper

Put the lamb, garlic, ginger, saffron, turmeric, oil, chopped coriander and onion in a heavy pan and mix well. Pour over a cup or two of water and bring to the boil.

Skim, if need be, then simmer, covered, for 1 hour, adding more water if necessary, to just cook the lamb.

Then add the cleaned cardoons and enough water to cover them (this is important), and continue cooking for a further 30–40 minutes.

Stir in the preserved lemon quarters and the olives and enough lemon juice, to taste, and ensure the tagine is well mixed. Taste and adjust the seasoning before serving piping hot.

Cynara scolymus. Asteraceae

GLOBE ARTICHOKE

Also known as French artichoke, green artichoke. Tall, upright perennial grown for edible flower buds. Half hardy. Value: 85% water; half carbohydrate indigestible inulin, turning to fructose in storage; moderate iodine and iron content.

Originating in the Mediterranean, globe artichokes were grown by the Greeks and Romans, who regarded them as a delicacy. The common name comes from the Italian *articoclos*, deriving from *cocali*, or pine cone — an apt description of the appearance of the flower bud. Artichokes waned in popularity in the Dark Ages, but were restored to favor when Catherine de Medici introduced them to France in the 16th century. From there they spread around the world. Globe artichokes reached the United States in 1806, traveling with French and Spanish settlers.

In Italy, its bitter principal flavors the aperitif Cynar, which is popular as a vermouth and definitely an acquired taste!

Growing to about 4–5 feet tall, with a 3-foot spread, attractive leaves and large thistle-like flowers, globe artichokes always look wonderful in the flower border and make excellent dual-purpose plants.

 varieties

'Green Globe' has large green heads with thick, fleshy scales and needs winter protection in cooler climates. **'Gros Camus de Bretagne'** is only suitable for warmer climates, but is worth growing for its large, well-flavored heads. **'Purple Globe'** is hardier than the green form but not as tasty. **'Purple Sicilian'** has small, deep purple-colored artichokes that are excellent for eating raw when they are very young. However it is not frost-hardy. **'Vert de Laon'** is hardy with an excellent flavor and **'Violetta di Chioggia'**, a purple-headed variety, is excellent in a flower border.

 cultivation

Artichokes need an open, sheltered site on light, fertile, well-drained soil.

Propagation
Artichokes can be grown from seed or divided, but are usually propagated from rooted "suckers" — shoots arising from the plant's root system. Suckers are bought or removed from established plants in mid-spring. They should be healthy, about 8–9 inches long and well

Purple Globe

rooted, with at least 2 shoots. Clear soil from around the roots of the parent plant and remove them with a sharp knife, cutting close to the main stem between the sticker and parent plant. Alternatively, divide established plants in spring by lifting the roots and easing them apart with 2 garden forks, a spade or an old knife and replanting the sections; these, too, should have at least 2 shoots and a good root system. To keep your stocks vigorous and productive, renew the oldest one-third of your plants every year. This extends the cropping season, too, as mature plants are ready for harvest in late spring to early summer and young plants in late summer.

You can grow from seed and select the best plants, but this is time-consuming, uses valuable space and is not recommended; it is far better to grow proven, named cultivars. If you have the time and inclination, then sow seed in trays of moist seed compost in an unheated greenhouse during late winter or outdoors in early spring. Thin to leave the strongest seedlings and harden off before planting out at their final spacing in late spring. Once flower buds have been produced, retain the best plants for harvest and for future propagation, discarding the rest.

Growing

If necessary, improve the soil by digging in plenty of well-rotted organic matter in spring or autumn before planting. This prevents summer drought and winter waterlogging, conditions that globe artichokes dislike. Before planting, rake in general fertilizer at 4 ounces/sq yd.

Plant suckers or divisions 24 inches apart with 24–30 inches between each row, trimming the leaves back to 5 inches, which helps to reduce water loss, and shading them from full sun until they are established. Water thoroughly after planting and during periods of dry weather, applying a high-potassium liquid fertilizer every 2 weeks when the plants are actively growing.

Keep the beds weed-free and mulch with organic matter in spring. During autumn and winter, if heavy frosts are forecast, protect plants by earthing up with soil, then covering them with a thick layer of straw, bracken or other organic insulation. Remove the covering in spring.

Maintenance

Spring Divide or remove suckers from existing plants and replant.

Buds ready to be enjoyed

Summer Keep weed-free and water thoroughly during periods of drought.
Autumn In areas with moderate temperatures, retain leaves and stems as frost protection.
Winter If severe frost is forecast, remove the decayed leaves, earth up, and protect plants with a layer of insulating material. Remove the materials in spring before growth begins.

Harvesting and Storing

Each flowering stem normally produces one large artichoke at the tip and several smaller ones below. A few flower heads will be produced in the first year; these are best removed so that the energy goes into establishing the plant, but if you cannot resist the temptation, harvest in late summer. In the second and third years more stems will be produced and are ready for cutting in midsummer. Harvest when the scales are tightly closed, removing the terminal bud first with 2 or 3 inches of stem, then the remaining side buds as they grow large enough. Alternatively, remove the lower artichokes for eating when they are about 1½ inches long.

Once the scales begin to open, globe artichokes become inedible.

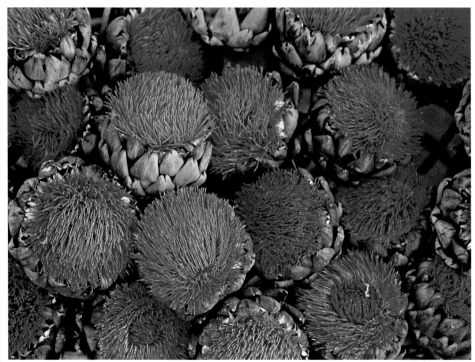

The flowers are pretty, too

Pests and Diseases

Slugs attack young shoots and leaves — the problem is worse in damp conditions. Keep the area free of plant debris, use biological controls, scatter ferric phosphate-based slug pellets around plants or make traps from plastic cartons half-buried in the ground and filled with milk or beer. Lay newspaper, old lettuce leaves or other tempting vegetation on the ground and hand pick regularly from beneath. Or put a barrier of grit around plants, or attract predators such as birds to the garden. Lettuce root aphid can be a problem. Creamy yellow aphids appear on the roots during summer, sucking sap and weakening plants. Water well in dry weather; spray with insecticidal soap.

 # medicinal

Artichokes are highly nutritious and are especially good for the liver, aiding detoxification and regeneration. They reduce blood sugar and cholesterol levels, stimulating the gall bladder and helping the metabolism of fat. Artichoke is also a diuretic and used to treat hepatitis and jaundice. It was formerly used as a contraceptive and aphrodisiac, but its potency is not recorded!

Bees are attracted to the flowers

 # culinary

Artichokes can be stored for up to a week in a plastic bag in a refrigerator.

The edible parts are the fleshy base of the outer scales, the central "heart" and the bottom of the artichoke itself. Wash the artichoke thoroughly before use and sprinkle any cut parts with lemon juice to prevent them from turning black. Boil artichokes in a nonmetallic pan of salted water with lemon juice for 30–45 minutes, until soft. Check if they are ready by pushing a knife through the heart, or try a basal leaf to check it for tenderness.

Eat artichokes by hand, pulling off the leaves one by one and dipping the base in mayonnaise, hollandaise, lemon sauce, melted butter or plain yogurt before scraping off the fleshy leaf base between your teeth. Pull off the hairy central "choke," or remove it with a spoon, and then eat the fleshy heart.

Bottoms can be a garnish for roasts, filled with vegetables or sauces. Cook "Cypriot-style" with oil, red wine and coriander seeds, or toss in oil and lemon dressing as an hors-d'oeuvre. Make a salad of cubed artichoke bottoms and new potatoes (leftovers are suitable) and season well. Toss in mayonnaise and crumble over finely chopped hard-boiled egg and good-quality black olives. Sprinkle with chives and flat-leaved parsley. Whole baby artichokes can be battered and deep-fried or cooked in oil. Eat them cold with vinaigrette.

A 17th-century herbalist and apothecary wrote that even the youngest housewife knew how to cook artichokes and serve them with melted butter, seasoned with vinegar and pepper. Florence White, a founder of the English Folk Cookery Association and member of the American Home Economics Association, gives a recipe for artichokes in *Good Things in England* (1929) from the time of Queen Anne:

A Tart of Artichoke Bottoms

"Line a dish with fine pastry. Put in the artichoke bottoms, with a little finely minced onion and some finely minced sweet herbs. Season with salt, pepper and nutmeg. Add some butter in tiny pieces. Cover with pastry and bake in a quick oven. When cooked, put into the tart a little white sauce thickened with yolk of egg and sharpened with tarragon vinegar."

varieties

There is a huge choice of carrot varieties; many new varieties have been bred for increased sweetness and higher beta carotene content. Carrots are grouped into categories according to their root shape and harvesting time. This is indicated on the package or in the catalog.

'Adelaide'* is one of the earliest to mature, with cylindrical, stump-shaped roots that are deep orange in color. **'Amsterdam Forcing 3'*** is fast-maturing and produces small, good quality roots with little core. Ideal for early sowings under unheated cover and good for "finger" carrots. **'Autumn King 2'*** is an excellent "maincrop" with top quality roots up to 12 inches long. Ideal for eating fresh or winter storage. **'Bangor'*** produces large, top-quality cylindrical roots with excellent color and flavor. It resists greening and cracking and stores well and is one of the best maincrops for the gardener. **'Belgian White'** is a tasty white variety for summer harvesting. **'Carson'*** has a rich, crunchy orange core and is one of the best 'Chantenay' hybrids for flavor — a good "maincrop" for autumn use and winter storage. **'Eskimo'*** has excellent cold tolerance, so is good for late cropping or storing in the ground. Rich in vitamin A, it also has good resistance to cavity and leaf spot and is suitable for deep freezing. **'Giant Flakee'** is a reliable old "maincrop" with huge, juicy roots and exceptional flavor. **'Healthmaster'** grows up to 10 inches long and is said to contain up to 35% more beta carotene than any other carrot. The roots

Parmex — ideal for children

Eat carrots immediately for the finest flavour

are deep orange-red and are resistant to cracking and greening. **'Honeysnack'** is juicy, sweet and delicious. The creamy-yellow roots reach 6 inches and are perfect for slicing or cutting into cubes for snacks or salads. The early-maturing Nantes variety **'Jeanette'** has a high level of pest and disease resistance and so is ideal for organic growers. It is well flavored, vigorous and ideal for salads. **'Kazan'*** **'Autumn King'** hybrid is one of the best late varieties for color and flavor and stores well. **'Kingston'*** is one of the best for taste, color and uniformity. Another Nantes type, **'Maestro'***, is vigorous, resists pests (including carrot fly) and is good for organic production. **'Mokum'*** is high-yielding, very juicy, crisp and sweet, so ideal for juicing or eating fresh. Grow early under glass or in containers. **'Nantes Frubund'** is the first autumn sowing carrot. It is very cold-resistant and ideal for early spring crops. **'Parmex'***, a round-rooted type, is ideal for shallow or stony soils. **'Paris Market Baron'** is a similar shape. **'Parano'*** is a very early bunching type with a smooth skin and delicious cylindrical roots that are ideal for salads. Good carrot fly resistance. **'Samuari'** ('**Red Samurai'**) has sweet, slender, red-skinned roots with pink-tinted flesh that retains its color after steaming and lends color to a salad. **'Purple Dragon'** is similar but with an orange core. **'Sugarsnax 54'*** and earlier-maturing **'Tendersnax'** both have long, juicy, tender roots that are tantalizingly sweet. Ideal juiced, in salads or lightly cooked. **'Flyaway'***, **'Sytan'*** and **'Resistafly'** are reliably carrot fly-resistant and **'Edible leaf carrot'** is grown for the leaves which are good in salads.

cultivation

Propagation

Germination is poor at soil temperatures below 45°F (7.5°C): warm the soil before sowing early crops. Another option is available for the small Paris Market varieties — sow 3–4 seeds per module and plant out after hardening off in mid-spring.

Carrot seed is very small and is easier to sow when mixed with sand or "fluid sown." Sow sparingly to reduce thinning and associated problems with carrot fly.

Seeds should be in drills 1 inch deep in rows 6 inches apart; allow 4 inches between plants in the rows for early crops and 1½–2½ inches apart for maincrops, depending on the size of roots you require.

Sow all but the '**Berlicum**' and 'Autumn King' types from mid- to late spring for cropping from late summer to early autumn.

Sow '**Chantenay**', 'Autumn King' and 'Berlicum' types from mid- to late spring for mid- to late autumn crops. Sow 'Autumn King' and 'Berlicum' types in late spring for mid- to late winter harvesting.

Growing

Early carrots need an open, sheltered position; maincrops are less fussy. Soils should be deep, light and free-draining, warming early in spring, and with a pH of 6.5–7.5. Carrots are the ideal crop for light sandy soils — you should be able to push your index finger right down into the seedbed.

Let's hope they all germinate

Thin when the soil is damp

Avoid walking on prepared ground to ensure maximum root growth.

Dig in plenty of well-rotted organic matter in the autumn before planting. On heavy or stony soils, grow round or short-rooted varieties, or plant in raised beds or containers.

Rake the seedbed to a fine texture about 3 weeks before sowing and use the "stale seedbed" method, allowing the weeds to germinate and hoeing off before sowing.

Keep crops weed-free at first by mulching, hand weeding or careful hoeing, to avoid damaging the roots. In later stages of growth, the foliage canopy will suppress weed growth.

Keep the soil moist to avoid root splitting and bolting. Water at a rate of 40–60 gallons/sq ft every 2–3 weeks, taking particular care with beds surrounded by barriers as a protection against carrot fly, as these create an artificial rain-shadow.

Maintenance

Spring Sow crops successionally from mid-spring when the soil is workable.
Summer Harvest early crops, sow maincrops. Keep well watered.

Autumn Sow under cover for a mid-spring crop. Harvest.
Winter Harvest and store.

Protected Cropping
Sow 'Nantes' types in an unheated greenhouse, under cloches or fleece in mid-autumn for a mid-spring crop. Sow 'Paris Market', 'Nantes' and 'Amsterdam Forcing' in mid-spring for early to midsummer crops.

Harvesting and Storing
Early cultivars are ready to harvest after around 8 weeks, maincrops from 10 weeks. In light soils, roots can be pulled straight from the ground, but on heavier soils they should be eased out with a garden fork. Water the soil beforehand if it is dry.

On good soils, maincrop carrots can be left in the ground until required. Cover with a thick layer of straw, bracken or similar material before the onset of inclement weather to make lifting easier.

Alternatively, lift roots, cut or twist off foliage and store healthy roots in boxes of sand in a cool, dry, frost-free place for up to 5 months. Check regularly and remove any that are damaged.

Freeze finger-sized carrots in polythene bags. Top and tail, wash and blanch for 5 minutes. Cool and rub off the skins.

Carrots will stay fresh for about 2 weeks in a cool room or in a plastic bag in the refrigerator.

Pests and Diseases
Carrot fly is the most serious problem. Attracted by the smell of the juice from the root, their larvae tunnel into the roots, making them inedible. Leaves turn bronze. Sow resistant cultivars, sow sparingly to avoid thinning, thin on a damp overcast day (or water before and after), pinch off the tops of thinnings just above the soil level and dispose of them in the compost pile. Lift and dispose of affected roots immediately. Lift "earlies" by early autumn and maincrops by mid-autumn. Since these pests do not fly very high, grow carrots under fleece or mesh, or surround with a barrier of fine netting or fleece 24 inches high, or grow in raised beds or boxes.

Root and leaf aphids can also be a problem.

Carrot juice is tasty and packed with goodness

companion planting

Intercropping carrots with onions reduces carrot fly attacks; leeks and salsify have also been used with some success.

Mixing with seeds of annual flowers also seems to discourage carrot fly.

Carrots grow well with lettuce, radishes and tomatoes and encourage peas to grow. They dislike anise and dill. If left to flower, carrots attract hoverflies and other beneficial predatory insects to the garden.

container growing

Choose short-rooted or round varieties for containers, window boxes or growbags. Sow in loam-based compost; keep moist throughout the growing season.

medicinal

Reputed to be therapeutic against asthma, general nervousness, dropsy and skin disorders.

Recent research suggests that high intake of beta carotene may slow cancerous growths. Beet and carrot juice is reported to prevent diarrhea.

culinary

Young carrots are sweet and can be eaten raw. Older carrots need to be peeled and the hard core discarded. Grated, they can be made into salads They're especially good mixed with raisins and chopped onion and tossed in a French dressing or mayonnaise, thinned with some extra virgin olive oil.

Try freshly picked baby carrots, rinsed under the tap, topped and tailed, very lightly boiled in as little water as possible, then sprinkled with chopped parsley, a little sugar and freshly ground black pepper, or just a pat of butter. Add a sprinkling of sugar, a tablespoon of butter and a pinch of salt, cover and gently steam until tender. Cook in a cream sauce seasoned with tarragon, nutmeg and dill, or steam with mint leaves.

Cut into sticks as raw snacks, slice for stews and casseroles, pickle, stir-fry, use for jams, wine and carrot cake. Carrots are an essential ingredient in stocks, soups and many sauces.

Balkali Havuçi

Balkali Havuçi
Serves 4

Serve this Armenian-Turkish dish with pilaf and salad; it can be topped with a dollop of yogurt.

2 carrots, cut into 1 inch disks
1 pound broad beans, shelled
1 onion, chopped
2 cloves garlic, finely chopped
2 tablespoons chopped fresh dill or mint
1 teaspoon salt
Freshly ground black pepper
Pinch sugar
3 tablespoons extra virgin olive oil

Rinse the beans. Put 1¼ cups water into a large saucepan and bring to a boil; add the onion and beans, bring to a boil, cover and simmer until tender.

Stir in the remaining ingredients and cook until the vegetables are just tender, about 20 minutes more. Serve hot with chunks of good bread as a starter.

Carrot and Raisin Cake

This spicy dough mixture can also be used to make cookies; drop heaped tablespoonfuls of dough on to a lightly greased baking sheet 2 inches apart and bake for 12–15 minutes until golden. Cool on a rack.

½ cup carrots, grated
1½ cups all-purpose flour
2 teaspoons baking powder
1 teaspoon ground cinnamon
Pinch mace
Pinch salt
2 heaped tablespoons seedless raisins
Zest of ½ an orange
2 tablespoons orange juice
½ cup butter
⅔ cup brown sugar
2 large eggs

Sift the flour, baking powder, spices and salt into a large bowl and set aside. Mix the raisins, carrots, orange zest and juice and set aside. Cream the butter and sugar thoroughly in a mixer and beat until light. Add the eggs, one at a time, with the blender on slow. Combine the batter with the flour and carrot mixtures and blend well.

Pour into a greased and lined 8-inch pan and bake in a preheated oven 350°F (180°C) for 40–60 minutes. Test with a toothpick to ensure the cake is cooked and allow to cool in the pan for 15 minutes before turning out onto a wire rack.

Dioscorea alata. Dioscoreaceae
YAM

Also known as Greater Yam, Asiatic Yam, White Yam, Winged Yam, Water Yam. Twining climber grown for large edible tubers. Tender. Value: rich in carbohydrate and potassium; small amounts of B vitamins.

The "greater yam" is believed to have originated in east Asia and is widely cultivated as a staple crop throughout the humid tropics. It was said to have reached Madagascar by 1000 CE and by the 16th century Portuguese and Spanish traders had taken it to West Africa and the New World, often as a food on slave-trading ships. Christopher Columbus knew of the plant as *nyame* and the tubers were regularly used for ships' supplies, because they stored for several months without deteriorating and were easy to handle. There are hundreds of different forms producing tubers with an average weight of 10–20 pounds, although specimens with massive tubers up to 135 pounds have been recorded.

varieties

Dioscorea alata has square, four-winged or angled twining stems with pointed, heart-shaped, leaves. Small bulbils are often produced on the stems. The tubers are brown on the outside with white flesh, vary in size and are usually produced singly. There is a great number of cultivars which vary in the color and shape of the stems, leaves and tubers.

'White Lisbon', one of the most widely grown, is high-yielding, shallow-rooted and tasty and it will store for up to 6 months. 'Belep', 'Lupias', 'Kinbayo', and 'Pyramid' are also high-yielding.

cultivation

Propagation

Yams are usually planted on banks, mounds or ridges at the end of the dry season while they are still dormant, as they need the long rainy season to develop. Small tubers, bulbils or sections with 2–3 buds or "eyes" taken from the tops of larger tubers are used for propagation. The latter are preferable, as they sprout quickly and produce higher-yielding plants.

They can be "sprouted" in a shady position before planting 6 inches deep and 12–36 inches apart on mounds 48 inches across or ridges 48 inches apart. Spacing depends on the site, soil and the variety.

Growing

Yams need a humid, tropical climate, 60–70 inches of rain in a 6–12 month growing season and a site in sun or partial shade. Soils must be rich, moisture-retentive and free-draining, as yams can survive drought but not waterlogging. Dig in plenty of well-rotted organic matter before planting and grow plants up trellising, arbours, poles or netting at least 6 feet high, or allow them to grow into surrounding trees.

Keep crops weed-free.

Tropical crops do not grow well below 68°F (20°C). Growth increases with temperature and the crucial time for rain is 14–20 weeks after planting, when food reserves are nearly depleted and the shoots are growing rapidly.

A flowering yam plant

reduce watering during the resting season as the stems die back, gradually increasing the amount in spring when plants resume active growth.

Harvesting and Storing

Depending on the variety and weather conditions, tubers are ready to harvest from 7–12 months after planting as the leaves and stems die back. Lift them carefully, as damaged tubers cannot be stored.

Tubers are normally dried on a shaded vertical frame or in an open-sided shed before being stored in a dark, cool, airy place where they can last for several months. Do not store yams at temperatures below 50°F (10°C).

Pests and Diseases

Leaf spot appears as brown or black spots on stems and leaves. Storage rot can be a serious problem and yam beetles feed on tubers and damage the shoots of newly planted sets. Scale insect also causes problems.

 ## companion planting

Grows well with taro, ginger, maize, okra and cucurbits.

 ## medicinal

Yams have been used as a diuretic and expectorant.

 ## warning

All yams except *Dioscorea esculenta* contain a toxin, dioscorine, which is destroyed by thorough cooking.

Maintenance

Spring Increase watering as new shoots appear when growing under cover.
Summer Maintain high temperatures and humidity.
Autumn Reduce watering as stems turn yellow.
Winter Keep compost slightly moist.

Protected Cropping

If you are able to provide an environment and cultural conditions similar to those described under "Growing," yams can be grown indoors. The minimum temperature for active growth is 68°F (20°C); wet down greenhouse paths and mist with tepid water during summer, and

 ## culinary

Yam can be peeled and then boiled, mashed, roasted and fried in oil. In West Africa, they are pounded into *fufu* in a similar way to cassava, and are added to a thick soup made of spices, meat, oil, fish and vegetables. Yams are tasty cooked with palm oil, candied, casseroled with orange juice or curried. They can be peeled and boiled in water with a pinch of salt, then brushed with melted butter and grilled or barbecued until brown; serve with more butter.

In China, they are mashed with lotus root, wrapped in lotus leaves and steamed.

They can also be peeled, rubbed with oil and baked at 350°F (180°C) for 1^1/$_2$ hours, then slit like a baked potato and eaten with seasoned butter or a similar filling.

Yellow Yam Salad

Serves 6

3 pounds yellow yams
1 large onion, sliced
3 tablespoons chopped chives
1 green pepper, deseeded and diced
½ cup mayonnaise
½ teaspoon cayenne pepper

Salt and freshly ground black pepper
4 hard-boiled eggs, chopped
1 tablespoon black olives, stoned and sliced

Clean the yams and cook in boiling salted water until tender but firm. Drain and allow to cool slightly, then cut into cubes. Add the onions, chives and pepper and mix well.

Season the mayonnaise with the cayenne, salt and pepper and stir into the yam mixture, folding in the eggs and olives carefully.

Check the seasoning. Chill for an hour before serving.

Eleocharis dulcis. Cyperaceae

WATER CHESTNUT

Half-hardy aquatic perennial. Value: good source of potassium, B6 and fiber; high in carbohydrates.

Eleocharis dulcis **has been cultivated for centuries. It has become naturalized on the edge of paddy fields in China and Southeast Asia, is popular in oriental cuisine and is used for making salt in Zimbabwe. Like the tiger nut and lotus root, the water chestnut is notable for remaining crisp even after cooking or canning — this is because its cell walls are cross-linked and strengthened by the presence of aromatic phenolic compounds that also give plants such as cloves their fragrance.**

 ## varieties

Eleocharis dulcis is a tropical or subtropical marginal plant, with dense tufts of thin, hollow, sedgelike leaves that grow to 3¼ feet tall.

 ## cultivation

Propagation
Use water chestnuts bought from specialized suppliers or the market; choose ones free of wrinkles and soft spots. Plant in 6 inches pots of loam-based compost with the base submerged in warm water in a heated propagator or on a sunny windowsill, at a minimum of 79°F (26°C), from mid-spring. Transfer them into their final position as temperatures rise. Alternatively, plant them by hand directly into their final position, 12–16 inches apart, once the danger of frost has passed.

Growing
Water chestnut needs an open, sunny site and to be grown in water. Use a wading pool, an old bathtub or similar, or create a temporary pond by digging a hole or trench in the ground and lining it with polyethylene. The "pond" should be deep enough to allow a 8 inch layer of loam or garden soil (with a low organic matter content) to be spread over the base with 4 inch of water above. If a paddling pool is being used, sweep the standing area before inflating and put a layer of old carpet, corrugated cardboard or similar under the base to prevent it from being punctured by stones.

Plant water chestnut when the soil and water has warmed; a small pond or swimming pool heater boosts water temperatures and is useful in cooler summers. It needs plenty of warmth to grow, at least six months in temperatures from 86–95°F (30–35°C) is ideal, though it can crop in cooler conditions.

Maintenance
Spring Plant corms in pot and put in a warm place.
Summer Keep water levels topped up in the container.
Autumn Harvest corms.
Winter Store propagation material in damp conditions.

Protected Cropping
In cooler climates, growing under glass or in polythene tunnels encourages heavier cropping. Starting crops off under protection, even if they are then grown outdoors, extends the growing season.

Harvesting and Storing
Tubers form from late summer and are ready to harvest when the stems turn yellow and die down in autumn. Allow the water to evaporate, then drain any remaining water; it is easier to harvest tubers when soil is moist, rather than waterlogged. Store tubers for propagation the following year in a damp, frost-free place.

Pests and Diseases
There are no problems with pests and diseases.

 ## medicinal

Chinese herbalists use water chestnuts for sweetening breath. The juice of the tuber is said to be bactericidal.

 ## culinary

The onion-shaped tubers of the water chestnut are sweet, nutty and crisp. Remove the papery tunic before cooking them, or eating them raw or lightly cooked. A familiar ingredient in Chinese cooking, they can be seasoned or combined with other vegetables and are eaten in chop suey. Soaked lightly in salted water and threaded on to thin bamboo stalks, they are sold by street vendors in China. Dried tubers are ground into flour that is used for thickening, coating vegetables or giving a crispy coating to deep-fried food. They store for up to two weeks in a plastic bag in the fridge, but are better eaten fresh.

Stir-fried Shrimp with Vegetables
Serves 4

3 ounces water chestnuts from a can, drained and sliced
½ pound raw tiger shrimp, peeled
1 teaspoon salt
1 tablespoon egg white
2 tablespoons cornstarch paste
2½ cups vegetable oil
⅓ cup snow peas
1 carrot, peeled and finely sliced
3 ounces straw mushrooms from a can, drained and halved lengthways
2 spring onions, cut into ½-inch pieces
2 tablespoons peeled and finely sliced fresh ginger
½ teaspoon sugar
1 tablespoon light soy sauce
2 teaspoons rice wine
A few drops sesame oil

Cut the shrimp in half lengthways and remove the black vein. Mix the shrimp with the salt, egg white and cornstarch.

Heat the oil in a wok, then deep-fry the shrimp for 1 minute until they turn pink. Remove them with a slotted spoon on to some paper towel to drain.

Pour off the oil, leaving roughly 1 tablespoon in the wok. Add the snow peas and carrot and stir-fry for about 1 minute. Then add the rest of the vegetables, the ginger, sugar, soy sauce and rice wine and stir well. Stir-fry for 1 more minute.

Drizzle over the sesame oil and serve piping hot with noodles or boiled rice.

Eruca vesicaria subsp. *sativa*. Brassicaceae

ARUGULA

Also known as Rocket Salad, Roquette, Italian Cress, Rucola, Rocket. Annual grown for tender edible leaves. Hardy. Value: high in potassium and vitamin C.

Arugula has been cultivated since Roman times and is native to the Mediterranean and Eastern Asia, though it grows in many areas. *Eruca* means 'downy-stemmed'; *vesicaria*, 'bladder-like', describes the slender seed pods. Introduced to North America by Italian settlers, the spicy leaves were particularly popular in Elizabethan England.

 ## varieties

Eruca vesicaria subsp. *sativa*, an erect plant growing to 3¼ feet, has hairy stems, broadly toothed leaves and cross-shaped, creamy flowers. **'Apollo'** and **'Runway'** are fast growing forms and **'Sky Rocket'** combines the flavor of wild arugula with the fast growth of salad arugula.

 ## cultivation

Propagation
Sow seed successively every 2–3 weeks, from mid-spring to early summer, in drills ½ inch deep and 12 inches apart. Thin when large enough to handle, until 6 inches apart. Arugula germinates at fairly low temperatures. In warmer climates sow in winter or early spring.

Growing
Arugula needs rich, moisture-retentive soil in partial shade. It may need extra shading in hot weather, otherwise it produces less palatable leaves. Keep weed-free and water regularly.

Maintenance
Spring Sow seeds from mid-spring; thin when large enough to handle.
Summer Continue sowing until midsummer. Water and feed as necessary. Harvest regularly to encourage tender growth and keep from bolting.
Autumn Harvest, prepare the ground for the following year's sowing and sow seeds for protected crops.
Winter Harvest winter crops.

Protected Cropping
Although arugula is a hardy plant, protect against severe frosts with cloches. Sow autumn/winter crops from late summer in a cool greenhouse, cold frame, or under cloches.

Harvesting
Plants are ready to harvest after 6–8 weeks. Pick frequently to encourage a regular supply of good-quality leaves and to prevent plants from running to seed in hot weather. Discard any damaged leaves. Either pull leaves as required or treat as a "cut and come again" crop, cutting the plant 1 inch above the ground.

Pests and Diseases
Arugula is usually trouble-free, but flea beetle can damage seedlings. Protect with horticultural fleece or mesh.

 ## culinary

The increasingly popular leaves are delicious in salads — younger leaves are milder. They can be lightly boiled or steamed, added to sauces, stir-fried, sautéed in olive oil and tossed with pasta. The flowers are edible and can decorate salads.

Penne with Merguez and Arugula
Serves 4

3 ounces arugula leaves, washed and shredded
1 pound penne
2 tablespoons olive oil
⅔ pound merguez sausages, cut into bite-size pieces
1 red onion, thinly sliced
2 tablespoons dry white wine
12 cherry tomatoes, halved
Salt and freshly ground black pepper
¼ cup freshly grated Parmesan

Bring a pan of salted water to a boil and cook the penne. Meanwhile, heat the oil in a large frying pan, add the merguez and onion and fry for 2–3 minutes. Add the wine and simmer for 10 minutes. Then add the tomatoes. When the pasta is cooked, drain well and toss in the sauce with the arugula. Mix well, season and serve at once with Parmesan.

 ## container growing

Arugula is not the perfect plant for pots, but it can be grown in a soil-based compost with low fertilizer levels with added peat-substitute compost. Sow seed *in situ*. Water thoroughly.

 ## medicinal

Young leaves are said to be a good tonic and are used in cough medicine. Dioscorides described arugula as "a digestive and good for ye belly."

Foeniculum vulgare var. *azoricum. Apiaceae*

FENNEL

Also known as Florence Fennel, Sweet Fennel, Finocchio. Biennial or perennial grown as annual for pungent swollen leaf bases, leaves and seeds. Half hardy. Value: good source of potassium; small amounts of beta carotene.

This outstanding vegetable with a strong aniseed flavor, swollen leafbases (known as "bulbs") the texture of tender celery, and delicate feathery leaves has been cultivated for centuries as an ornamental vegetable. Its close relative, wild fennel, which lacks the swollen base, is used as a herb. When Portuguese explorers first landed on Madeira in 1418, they found the air fragrant with the aroma of wild fennel, so the city of Funchal was named after *funcho*, the Portuguese name for the plant. Florence fennel was popular with the Greeks and Romans, whose soldiers ate it to maintain good health — while the ladies used it to ward off obesity. In medieval times, seeds were eaten during Lent to alleviate hunger, and dieters still chew raw stalks to suppress their appetite. The first records of its cultivation in England date from the early 18th century, when the third Earl of Peterborough cultivated and ate it as a dessert.

In 1824 Thomas Jefferson received seeds from the American consul in Livorno and sowed them in his garden in Virginia. He enthused: "Fennel is beyond every other vegetable, delicious... perfectly white. No vegetable equals it in flavor." However, it has become a weed in those countries where conditions are particularly favorable.

varieties

'**Amigo**' is early cropping and vigorous with medium, white bulbs. '**Heracles**'* is fast-maturing and produces top quality bulbs. '**Perfection**', a French variety, has medium-sized bulbs and a delicate aniseed flavor. Resistant to bolting, it is ideal for early sowing. '**Pronto**' is an early variety with round, white bulbs. '**Sirio**', from Italy, is compact with large, sweet white bulbs and matures rapidly. '**Sweet Florence**' is moderately sized and should be sown from mid-spring to late summer. '**Victoria**' produces dense, top-quality, greenish white bulbs. '**Zefa Fino**' is particularly vigorous and ornamental with uniform bulbs of excellent quality.

cultivation

Propagation
Fennel thrives in a warm climate and is inclined to bolt prematurely if growth is checked by cold, drought or transplanting. For early sowings, choose cultivars that are bolt-resistant.

Grow successively from late spring to late summer for summer and autumn crops. Sow thinly in drills ½ inch deep and 18–20 inches apart, thinning when seedlings are large enough to handle to a final spacing of 9–12 inches apart.

Where possible, fennel is better sown *in situ* to reduce problems with bolting. Modules are preferred for plants started under cover. Growing in trays is fine if transplants are treated carefully enough.

Growing
Fennel flourishes in temperate to subtropical climates, though mature plants can withstand light frosts. The largest bulbs are formed during warm, sunny summers. Plants should be grown as rapidly as possible, so incorporate a slow-release general fertilizer into the soil before planting at 2–4 ounces/sq yd.

Plants need a sunny, warm, sheltered position and well-drained, moisture-retentive, slightly alkaline soil. A light, sandy soil with well-rotted organic matter dug in the winter before planting is ideal. Stony soils and heavy clays should be avoided. Never allow the soil to

FENNEL

A fine filigree of fennel foliage

dry out; mulch in spring and hand weed around bulbs to avoid damage.

When the stem bases start to swell, earth up to half their height to blanch and sweeten the bulbs. Or tie cardboard "collars" around the base.

Maintenance

Spring Sow early crops under cover. Warm the soil with cloches before sowing early crops outdoors.
Summer Keep the soil constantly moist and weed-free. Harvest mature bulbs.
Autumn Cover later crops in order to prolong the growing season.
Winter Transplant later sowings for an early winter crop.

Protected Cropping

Cover early outdoor crops with cloches. Sow from mid-spring, in modules or trays of seed compost at 60°F (16°C). Pot seedlings grown in trays when very small, with a maximum of 4 leaves, into 3-inch peat pots. Transplant in the pots a month after hardening off.

Harden off and plant out those grown in modules at a similar size. Late sowings can be made for transplanting under cover in early winter. Plants do not always produce "bulbs," but the leaves and stems can still be used in cooking.

Harvesting and Storing

Harvest about 15 weeks after sowing or 2–4 weeks after earthing up, when the bulbs are about 2–3 inches across and slightly larger than a tennis ball. Cut the bulb with a sharp knife, just above the ground, and the stump should resprout, producing sprigs of ferny foliage. Bulbs do not store and should be eaten when fresh.

Leaves can be harvested throughout summer and used fresh in salads, or deep-frozen.

Pests and Diseases

Slugs can damage young plants. Lack of water, fluctuating temperatures and transplanting check can cause bolting.

 ## companion planting

Allow a few plants to flower; they are extremely attractive to a large number of beneficial insects that prey on garden pests.

Fennel has a detrimental effect on beans, kohlrabi and on tomatoes.

 ## container growing

Grow single plants in a container at least 10 inches wide by 12 inches deep containing loam-based compost with added sharp sand. Apply a general liquid fertilizer monthly from late spring to late summer.

 ## medicinal

An infusion aids wind, colic, urinary disorders and constipation. Recent research indicates that fennel may reduce the effects of alcohol.

Use in an eye bath or as a compress to reduce inflammation. Chew to sweeten breath or infuse as a mouthwash or gargle for gum disease and sore throats, to alleviate hunger and ease indigestion.

 ## warning

Do not take excessive doses of the oil; nor should it be given to pregnant women.

 ## culinary

Use bulbs in the same way as celery, removing green stalks and outer leaves. For salads, slice inner leaf stalks and chill before serving. (To ensure that bulbs are crisp, slice and place in a bowl of water and ice cubes in the fridge for an hour.)

Fennel can be parboiled with leeks and is suitable for egg and fish dishes. Steam, grill or boil and serve with cheese sauce or butter. Infuse fresh leaves in oil or vinegar, add to a bouquet garni or snip as a garnish over soups or salads. Gives characteristic flavour to *finocchiona*, an Italian salami, and the French liqueur, *fenouillette*.

Fennel Sautéed with Peas and Red Peppers
Serves 4

1 pound fennel, trimmed and finely sliced
2 tablespoons olive oil
2 sweet red peppers, deseeded and cut in thin strips
2 cloves garlic, crushed
½ pound peas, shelled
Salt and freshly ground black pepper

In a wok or heavy-based frying pan heat the oil, add the peppers and fennel and cook for 10–15 minutes over a moderate heat until crunchy, stirring occasionally. Add the garlic and peas and continue cooking for 2 minutes. Season and serve.

Glycine max (syn. *Glycine soja*). *Leguminosae*

SOY BEAN

Also known as Soya Bean. Annual grown for seed sprouts and seeds. Half hardy. Value: rich in potassium, protein, fiber, vitamins E, B and iron. Seed sprouts are rich in vitamin C.

One of the most nutritious of all vegetables, this Asian native is thought to have been the plant that Chinese emperor Shen Nung used to introduce people to the art of cultivation. It is mentioned in his *Materia Medica* from around 2900 BCE. Soy beans were first known in Europe through Engelbert Kaempfer, physician to the governor of the Dutch East India company on an island off Japan in 1690–92. The Japanese guarded their culture, but, by bribing the guards and picking plants along the route, Kaempfer was able to get his botanical specimens. Benjamin Franklin sent seeds back from France to North America in the late 18th century. One of the first Americans to be interested in soy beans was Henry Ford, who saw their potential for manufactured goods and is said to have eaten soy beans at every meal, had a suit made from "soy fabric" and sponsored a 16-course soy bean dinner at the 1934 "Century of Progress" show in Chicago.

 ## varieties

Glycine max is a herb, usually with trilobed leaves and white to pale violet flowers. The pods, containing 2–4 seeds, are mainly on the lower parts of the stem. **'Black Jet'** is early-maturing and one of the best. The seeds have a good flavor and it is ideal for a short growing season. **'Beer Friend'** is a cool climate variety with 70 days to maturity. It has good flavor and productivity and is a perfect accompaniment to a pint of beer. **'Friskeby'**, a Swedish variety, is ideal for cool climates and **'Prize'** is widely used for sprouting. **'Sayamusume'** produces robust plants, large, moderately sweet seed and consistent crops. **'Ustie'**, is self-pollinating and 100% GM-free.

 ## cultivation

Propagation

Sow when danger of frost has passed and the soil has warmed. Sow 2–3 seeds 1 inch deep in heavy soil and 1¼ inches deep in lighter soils in "stations" 3–4 inches apart with 18–24 inches between rows. After germination, thin, leaving the strongest seedling. Alternatively, sow thinly and thin to the final spacing when large enough.

Sprouting Seed

Seeds can also be sprouted. Use untreated seed and remove any that are damaged or moldy. Soak overnight in cold water. The following morning rinse them thoroughly. Put a layer of moist paper towel over the base of a flat-bottomed bowl, tray or "seed sprouter." Spread over a layer of soy beans ½ inch deep and cover with plastic wrap. Exclude light by putting the bowl in a dark cupboard or wrapping it in newspaper or aluminum foil. Temperatures should be 20–25°C (68–75°F). Check that the absorbent layer stays damp, rinsing morning and night. They should be ready to harvest in 4–10 days, when shoots are 1–2 inches long. Remove sprouts from the shell, and rinse well before eating.

Growing

Soy beans flourish in an open site with rich, free-draining soil and a pH of 5.7–6.2, although there are now cultivars to suit most soils. Where necessary, lime soils and dig in well-rotted organic matter before

Just a little taste

planting. They are not frost hardy; they prefer 68–75°F (20–25°C); exceeding 100°F (38°C) may retard growth.

Keep plants well watered during drought and early stages of growth. Remove weeds regularly, or suppress by mulching in spring.

Maintenance
Spring Sow seeds under cover or outdoors when there is no danger of frost.
Summer Keep crops weed-free. Water during drought.
Autumn Harvest before the pods are completely ripe.
Winter Hang in bunches in a cool shed and collect seed when the pods open.

Protected Cropping
In cooler climates, sow seeds in pots, modules or trays of seed compost, planting out when the soil is warm. Harden off before transplanting and protect under cloches until established. In cooler climates, sow crops in a heated greenhouse.

Harvesting and Storing
Soy needs a hot summer and nice autumn for the seeds to ripen. Harvesting should be carefully timed so that the seeds are ripe but the pods have not yet split. If conditions are unfavorable, pull up plants when the pods turn yellow and hang up to ripen in a dry place. Do not harvest when plants are wet, as the seeds are easily bruised. Harvest for green beans as soon as pods are plump and the seeds are almost full size.

Pests and Diseases
Fungal diseases can be a problem if plants are harvested when wet and pods are bruised or broken.

container growing

This is only worth growing in containers as a "novelty" crop. Use 8–10-inch pots and loam-based compost with moderate fertilizer levels, adding well-rotted organic matter. Keep well watered and weed-free.

other uses

Soy oil is used in a range of products, including ice cream, margarine, soaps and paint; milk substitute is made from the crushed beans, and fermented they make soy sauce and tofu, and also Worcestershire sauce. Also firefighting foam and meat substitute. A valuable plant indeed!

medicinal

Said to control blood sugar levels, lower cholesterol, regulate the bowels and relieve constipation.

warning

Soy beans should be cooked before drying; they can cause stomach upset.

culinary

Used mainly when green or sprouted for salads or stir-fries. Remove shell by plunging into boiling salted water for 5 minutes, then allow to cool and squeeze out the seeds. Cook for 15 minutes, then sauté with butter. Juvenile pods can be cooked and eaten whole.

Soak dried beans before eating. A shortcut is to cover with water in a kettle, boil for 2 minutes, allow to stand for one hour, then cook until tender.

Soy Bean and Walnut Croquettes
Serves 4

4 ounces soy beans, soaked and well rinsed
1 onion, finely chopped
1 clove garlic, crushed
5 teaspoons butter
1¼ cups walnuts, ground in a blender
½ teaspoon dried thyme
½ cup wholewheat breadcrumbs
1 tablespoon tomato purée
2 tablespoons chopped fresh parsley
½ teaspoon mace
1 egg
Salt and freshly ground black pepper

Wholewheat flour
1 egg, beaten
Dried breadcrumbs
Vegetable oil, for frying

Cook the beans until very tender, drain, then mash with a fork, enough to break them up. Fry the onion and garlic in the butter for 10 minutes, then remove from the heat and stir in the beans. Add the walnuts and thyme, together with the breadcrumbs, tomato purée, parsley, mace and egg. (You may need to add more liquid; otherwise use fewer breadcrumbs.) Mix well and season to taste.

Using your hands, shape into small croquettes, then roll in the flour, dip into the egg and roll in the crumbs. Fry in hot oil until crisp and drain on paper towel. Serve hot. Particularly good with a spicy tomato sauce.

JERUSALEM ARTICHOKE

Helianthus tuberosus. Asteraceae

Also known as Girasole, Sunchoke. Tall perennial grown as annual for edible tubers. Hardy. Value: high in carbohydrate but mostly inulin, turning to fructose in storage; moderate vitamin B_1, B_5, low in calories.

This vegetable is not from Jerusalem, nor is it any relative of the globe artichoke. "Jerusalem" is said to be a corruption of the Italian *girasole* or "sunflower" — a close relative; the nutty-flavored tubers were thought to taste similar to globe artichokes, hence the adoption of that name. Frost-hardy, these tall, upright perennials are native to North America, where they grow in damp places. The tubers contain a carbohydrate that causes flatulence; in 1621 John Goodyear wrote that "they stirre and cause a filthie loathsome wind within the bodie." In the 1920s they were a commercial source of fructose and were expected to replace beet and cane as a source of sugar.

 varieties

'**Boston Red**' has large, "knobbly" tubers with rose-red skin. '**Dwarf Sunray**' is a short-stemmed, crisp, tender variety that does not need peeling. It flowers freely and is good for the ornamental border. '**French Mammoth White**' is round, white-skinned and frost-hardy. '**Fuseau**', a traditional French variety, has long, smooth, white tubers. The plants are compact, reaching 5–6 feet. '**Gerrard**', purple-skinned and round, is smooth and easy to peel. '**Golden Nugget**' has tubers that are good for slicing. '**Originals**' produces traditional rounded tubers and also makes an excellent windbreak or temporary screen in the garden. '**Stampede**' is a quick-maturing variety with large tubers and is also very cold hardy. The tubers of '**Sun Choke**' have a fresh nutty flavor and are excellent raw in salads, cooked or creamed.

 cultivation

Jerusalem artichokes prefer a sunny position, but will grow in shade. They tolerate most soils, though tubers are small on poor ground; the best are grown on sandy, moisture-retentive soil.

They will grow in heavy clay provided it is not extremely acidic or subject to winter waterlogging. The fibrous root system makes them useful for breaking up uncultivated ground. The tall stems make excellent temporary screens or windbreaks in sheltered areas, but need staking in more exposed sites.

Propagation
Tubers bought from the grocery store can be used for planting. Choose tubers the size of chicken eggs, and plant from early to late spring, when the soil becomes workable, 4–6 inches deep, 12 inches apart and 36 inches between rows; cover the tubers carefully. During harvest, save a few tubers to replant or leave some in the soil for the following year.

Growing
Incorporate organic matter in autumn or early winter before planting. Earth up the base of stems to improve stability when plants are 12 inches high. Water during dry weather. Remove flower buds as they appear. Shorten stems to 5–6 feet in late summer to stop them from being blown over; on windy sites they

JERUSALEM ARTICHOKE

Jerusalem artichoke makes a wonderful windbreak

may also need staking. On poor soil, feed with liquid general fertilizer every 2–3 weeks.

Maintenance
Spring Plant tubers.
Summer Keep weed-free, water and stake if necessary. Remove flower buds.
Autumn Cut back stems and begin harvesting.
Winter Save tubers for next year's crop.

Harvesting and Storing
In autumn, as the foliage turns yellow, cut back stems to within 3–6 inches of the ground. Use the cut stems as a mulch to protect the soil from frost, making lifting easier; alternatively, cover with straw.

Lift tubers from late autumn to midwinter. They keep better in the ground, but in cold climates or on heavy ground, lift in early winter and store for up to 5 months in a cool cellar in moist peat substitute or sand.

Pests and Diseases
Slugs tend to hollow out tubers. Set traps, aluminum sulfate pellets, or pick off manually.

Sclerotinia rot causes stem bases to become covered with fluffy white mold. Lift and burn diseased plants; water healthy plants with fungicide. Cutworms eat stems at ground level; damaged plants wilt. Keep crops weed-free, cultivate well or scatter an appropriate insecticide in the soil before planting.

 ## medicinal

The carbohydrate inulin is difficult to digest; tubers are low calorie and suitable for diabetics.

 ## warning

Jerusalem artichokes can become invasive. After harvesting, lift even the smallest tuber from the ground.

 ## culinary

Jerusalem artichokes are versatile vegetables when the weather is cold: they can be kept in the ground until you want to cook them and then dug up root by root. Fresh tubers have a better flavor, but they become more digestible if stored; they will keep in a plastic bag in the salad drawer of the fridge for anywhere up to 2 weeks.

There is no need to peel them painstakingly unless you want a very smooth, creamy-white purée — the vitamins are, after all, just below the skin. (If you do want them peeled, steaming or boiling "knobbly" varieties makes the job easier.) To serve as a vegetable, scrub tubers immediately after picking, boil for 20–25 minutes in their skins in water with a teaspoon of vinegar; peel before serving if desired. The addition of a little grated nutmeg always does wonders in bringing out the unusual flavor.

To make rissoles, form boiled, mashed artichokes into flat cakes and deep-fry. Jerusalem artichokes can also be fried, baked, roasted or stewed — or eaten raw. Artichokes gratinéed in a sauce made with good, strong Cheddar make an excellent accompaniment to plain meat dishes such as baked ham or roast lamb. Parboil the artichokes and drain when they are just tender. Roughly slice and layer into a dish. Pour over a béchamel sauce flavored with French mustard and well-matured cheese and bake in a hot oven (400°F/200°C) until browned.

Artichoke Soup
Serves 4

1 pound Jerusalem artichokes
2 tablespoons olive oil
2 large onions, sliced
1 large clove garlic, crushed
2½ cups chicken stock
Strip of orange peel
Salt and freshly ground black pepper
4 tablespoons thick cream

Scrub the artichokes, discard any hard knobs and roughly chop. Heat the oil in a heavy-based pan and add the onions. Cook until translucent, add the garlic, continue cooking for a couple of minutes and add the artichokes. Toss well to coat with oil and pour in the chicken stock. Bring to the boil, add the orange peel and season. Cover and simmer for 15–20 minutes, until cooked. Remove from the heat, discard the peel and blend in a food processor. Return to the pan, adjust the seasoning, stir in the cream and serve.

Hibiscus esculentus (syn. *Abelmoschus esculentus*). *Malvaceae*

OKRA

Also known as Gumbo, Lady's Fingers, Bhindi. Annual grown for its edible pods. Tender. Value: rich in calcium, iron, potassium, vitamin C and fiber.

The okra, a close relative of the ornamental hibiscus, with slender edible pods, has been cultivated for centuries. It is thought to have originated in northern Africa around the upper Nile and Ethiopia, spreading eastward to Saudi Arabia and to India. One of the earliest records of it — growing in Egypt — describes the plant, its cultivation and uses. It was introduced to the Caribbean and southern North America by slaves who brought the crop from Africa; the name "gumbo" comes from a Portuguese corruption of the plant's Angolan common name.

distance between plants. Alternatively, sow in "stations" 8–12 inches apart, thinning to leave the strongest seedling. Plant seedlings grown in trays or modules into 3-inch pots when they are large enough to handle and later harden them off ready for transplanting when they are about 4–6 inches tall.

Growing

Okra needs a rich, fertile, well-drained soil, so incorporate organic matter several weeks before sowing. Put a stake in place before transplanting and tie in the plant as it grows, pinching out the growing tip on the main stems when plants are around 9–12 inches tall to encourage bushy growth. Apply a general liquid fertilizer until plants become established, then change to a liquid high-potassium feed every 2 weeks or scatter potassium sulfate around the plant base. In cool temperate conditions, warm the soil for several days before planting outdoors, spacing plants 24 inches apart once the danger of frost has passed.

Maintenance

Spring Sow seeds under cover or outdoors in warmer

 ## varieties

'Cow Horn' has a good flavor and texture and is slow to go fibrous. **'Clemson Spineless'** is a popular, reliable variety with high yields over a long period of dark, fleshy pods. It grows well under cover. **'Dwarf Green Long Pod'** is only about 3 feet tall but crops well, producing dark green, spineless pods. **'Emerald'** grows prolifically, with deep green pods on tall plants. It pods early and is slow to go "seedy." **'Little Lucy'**, a dwarf variety growing to 2 feet, is ideal for containers. Its attractive flowers and 4 inches pods are held erect above the plant. **'Mammoth Spineless Long Pod'** is vigorous and high-yielding, with pods that stay tender for a long time. It is excellent fresh or bottled. **'Red Velvet'**, another spectacular red variety, is vigorous, reaching 4–5 feet. **'Star of David'**, an Israeli heirloom variety growing to 6–8 feet tall, is very tasty and high-yielding. The pods grow to 9 inches long, but are better eaten when small; great in soups and stews.

 ## cultivation

A garden plant for the tropics and warm temperate climates, okra can be tried outdoors in cooler climates during hot summers, though success is better guaranteed if it is sown under cover.

Propagation

Soak the seeds in warm water for 24 hours before planting. My friend Robert Fleming, who gardens in Memphis, Tennessee, has been successful with several other methods that reduce germination time from 15 down to 5 days: soak the seed in bleach for 45–60 minutes, rinse, then plant; pour boiling water over seed, soak overnight, then plant; or place 3 seeds in each section of an ice-cube tray, allow to freeze for a few hours, then plant.

When soil temperatures are about 61°F (16°C), sow seeds in rows about 24 inches apart, leaving the same

Okra growing in Southern India

OKRA

climates when the soil is warm enough. Pinch out the growth tips as they appear.
Summer Water, feed and tie in plants to their supporting stakes. Keep crops weed-free. Harvest young pods.
Autumn Protect outdoor crops in cooler climates to extend the cropping season.
Winter Prepare the ground for the following season.

Protected Cropping
In cooler climates, plant okra in heated greenhouses or polyethylene tunnels from early spring, waiting until mid-spring if heat is not provided. Plant them about 24 inches apart in beds or borders. Insert a supporting cane before planting.

Temperatures should be a minimum of 70°F (21°C) with moderate humidity. Feed plants every 2 weeks with a liquid general fertilizer, changing to a high-potash fertilizer once they are established.

Harvesting and Storing
Harvest with a sharp knife or scissors while seed pods are young, picking regularly for a constant supply of new pods. Handle gently: the soft skin marks easily. Pods keep for up to 10 days wrapped in a plastic bag in the salad drawer of the fridge.

Pests and Diseases
Precautions should be taken against heavy infestations of aphids, which weaken and distort growth, and powdery mildew, which stunts growth and, in severe cases, causes death. This is more of a problem when plants are underwatered. Whitefly can cause yellowing, stickiness and mold formation on the leaves. They form clusters on the leaf undersides and fly into the air when the foliage is disturbed.

companion planting

Okra flourishes when it is grown with melons and cucumbers, as it enjoys the same conditions.

container growing

Okra can be grown in 10-inch pots or growbags, in peat-substitute compost, under cover or outdoors. Water regularly and feed every 2 weeks with a high-potassium liquid fertilizer during the growing season.

medicinal

The mucilage from okra is effectively used as a demulcent, soothing inflammation. In India, infusions of the pods are used to treat urogenital problems as well as chest infections.

Okra is also added as an ingredient of artificial blood plasma products.

culinary

Okra is used in soups, stews and curries, can be sautéed or fried and eaten to accompany meat or poultry. To deep-fry, remove the stalks, trim around the "cone" near the base, simmer for about 10 minutes, drain and dry each pod, then deep-fry until crisp. In the Middle East, pods are soaked in lemon juice and salt, then fried and eaten as a vegetable. In Indian cooking, bhindi is used as a vegetable or as a bhaji to accompany curries.

Okra should not be cooked in iron, brass or copper pans, otherwise it will discolor.

Overcooked, the pods become very slimy. Any "gluey" texture can be overcome by adding a little lemon juice to the pan and the fine, velvety covering over the pod can easily be removed by scrubbing the pod gently under running water.

Okra can also be eaten raw in salads or used as a "dip." Wash pods, carefully trimming off the ends. To reduce stickiness, soak them for about 30 minutes in water with a dash of lemon juice, then drain, rinse and dry.

Okra seed oil is also used in cookery.

Gumbo
Serves 4

This spicy Creole dish is known for its good use of okra.

1 pound okra
1 tablespoon olive oil
½ pound cooked ham, cubed
1⅓ cups onion, finely sliced
1 cup celery, chopped
1 red pepper, deseeded and chopped
2 teaspoons tomato purée
1 pound tomatoes, skinned and chopped
1 dried chili, finely chopped
Salt and freshly ground black pepper

Trim the stalk ends of the okra to expose the seeds, then soak for 30 minutes in acidulated water. In the meantime, heat the oil and gently cook the ham, onion, celery and pepper until the onion begins to color. Add the tomato purée and the tomatoes, mix in well, and cook over a high heat for a minute or so.

Stir in the drained okra and season well. Cover and cook gently until stewed. Add a little water if the mixture gets dry.

Serve with plain grilled chicken.

Ipomoea aquatica. Convolvulaceae
WATER SPINACH

Also known as Swamp Cabbage, Aquatic Morning Glory, Bindweed, Water Convolvulus, Kangkong, Ung Choi, Rau Muong, Entsai Water Spinach. Tropical aquatic/semi-aquatic perennial. Value: high in vitamin A, calcium, phosphorus and potassium.

This close relative of the sweet potato has a long history of cultivation in southeastern China, probably originated in southern India, grows throughout the tropics and has become a pestilent weed, now banned, in America. Once a staple crop of the poor in Vietnam, it gradually became an important ingredient of Vietnamese cuisine and has potential as a food crop for rabbits grown for meat production in Cambodia. It was first mentioned in *Nanfang Zaomu Zhuang*, a Vietnamese botanical work of the fifth century CE, and is a worthwhile "novelty" crop for those who like to grow horticultural and culinary oddities.

Pak Quat flowers

 varieties

There are two types: **'Ching Quat'** is narrow leaved with green stems and white flowers, **'Pak Quat'** has broad, arrow-shaped leaves, white stems and pink flowers. The former is more cold-tolerant and robust; the latter is of better culinary quality.

 cultivation

Propagation
In temperate climates they are best grown from seed sown just below the surface of loam-based compost at 72°F (22°C); plant several seeds in a 9-inch pot, standing in a tray of tepid water from mid-spring. Alternatively, sow directly into their final position from mid-spring or start off in modules, transplanting to the final position when they are at least 4 inches high. They can also be propagated from 12-inch-long stem cuttings with five or more joints on the stem and the basal cut just below a node, in water or damp sand.

Growing
Water spinach can be grown as an aquatic or in waterlogged compost or rich soil, in a sheltered, sunny site. It stops growing and starts flowering as day length shortens, so is grown as an annual. Transplant seedlings into loam-based compost in an old sink or wading pool, topped up with water, depending on the volume required. Temperatures should be around 77°F (25°C) from mid-spring. Growth stops below 50°F (10°C) and lower temperatures can be damaging to water spinach. Plants grown in soil should be spaced in blocks, with

 A farmer in Vietnam collecting water spinach plants

Harvesting and Storing

Harvest regularly, removing the tips to encourage tender regrowth or cut back plants to within a few inches of the base to encourage regrowth of young, tender shoots. Towards the end of the season, the whole plant can be lifted for harvesting.

Pests and Diseases

None in cooler climates; they suffer from the same diseases as sweet potato in warmer climates.

 ## container growing

Grow plants in old sinks or wading pools of water to ensure plenty of soft, tender growth.

medicinal

In Burma, the plant is used as an emetic for opium poisoning; also used as a diuretic and to treat constipation.

around 6 inches between rows. Keep the soil moist, or growth becomes coarse. Add well-rotted compost to aid water retention.

Maintenance

Spring Sow seeds and take cuttings.
Summer Keep compost moist and water levels topped up. Harvest regularly.

Autumn Harvest regularly.
Winter Buy seed for next year.

Protected Cropping

Water spinach is best grown in a polyethylene tunnel or greenhouse in cooler climates.

 ## culinary

Use immediately after harvesting, as the water-filled stems wilt rapidly. Water spinach is used extensively in Chinese and Malayan cuisine. It is mucilaginous, slightly sweet and takes up the surrounding flavours during cooking. The crispy stems are made into a pickle in the Philippines. The edible young shoots and leaves are eaten raw or cooked and eaten like spinach. Eat water spinach as the Chinese do, with fermented bean curd or shrimp sauce; it can also be fried with garlic, chilies and dried prawns or with cuttlefish and sweet, spicy sauce.

Chicken and Water Spinach with Spicy Peanut Sauce

Serves 4

2 cooked chicken breasts, shredded
1⅓ pounds water spinach, stems discarded, washed and dried
1 tablespoon oil
3 cloves garlic, finely chopped
1 tablespoon Thai red curry paste
½ cup thick coconut milk
1 tablespoon fish sauce (nam pla)
1 teaspoon palm sugar, finely shaved, or brown sugar
4 tablespoons dry-roasted peanuts, coarsely ground
Salt

In a large saucepan of boiling water quickly blanch the water spinach for about 2 minutes. Drain and cool it under running water to stop the cooking process, then drain again. Arrange on a large platter and scatter the shredded chicken over it.

Heat the oil in a small pan and stir-fry the garlic for a minute or so until fragrant, then add the red curry paste and continue cooking for another 30 seconds. Pour in the coconut milk and bring up to simmering point. Stir in the fish sauce and the sugar, then add the peanuts, seasoning with salt to taste.

Pour over the water spinach and chicken and serve.

SWEET POTATO

Ipomoea batatas. Convolvulaceae

Also known as Kumara, Louisiana Yam, Yellow Yam, Yam. Trailing perennials grown as annuals for starchy roots and leaves. Tender. Value: excellent source of beta carotene, rich in carbohydrates, moderate potassium and vitamins B and C. Orange type is a superior source of vitamin A.

The "sweet potato" is unrelated to the "Irish" potato and the "yam" but is a relative of the bindweed, in the Morning Glory family. The names became interchangeable when the USDA ruled that canned sweet potatoes must also be labeled as yams. Sweet potato was cultivated in prehistoric Peru and is now found throughout the tropics; it is also a staple crop in Polynesia. Its arrival there is something of a mystery; some suggest it was taken there by Polynesians who visited South America, others think it arrived on vines clinging to logs swept out to sea. It was cultivated in Polynesia before 1250 and reached New Zealand by the 14th century. Columbus observed sweet potato growing in the West Indies and introduced it to Spain, where it was widely cultivated, predating the "Irish" potato by nearly half a century, and De Soto later found sweet potato in what is now Louisiana. Native Americans were reportedly growing sweet potato in present-day Georgia when English settlers arrrived. It was grown in Virginia in 1648.

Closely related to Morning Glory

 varieties

There are hundreds of sweet potato varieties worldwide. They are classified under three groups: dry and mealy-fleshed, soft and moist-fleshed, and coarse-fleshed types used as animal feed. White or pale types are floury with a chestnut-caramel flavor, while yellow and orange varieties are sweet and watery.

'Centennial' grows vigorously (to 16 feet) and prolifically in short seasons. Its high-quality tubers have bright copper-orange skin and deep orange flesh. The deep orange flesh of **'Georgia Jet'** has a superb flavor. It matures early and is very reliable. **'T65'** has creamy-white flesh and is the most reliable in cool climates. **'Beauregard Improved'** is a virus-free clone, smaller than T65, but with orange flesh and a more pronounced flavor. **'Tokatoka Gold'** is large, rounded and smooth-textured, and popular in New Zealand.

 cultivation

Propagation
Take cuttings from healthy shoots 8–10 inches long. Cut just below a leaf joint, remove basal leaves. Alternatively, pack several healthy tubers in a tray of moist and sharp sand, vermiculite or perlite in a warm greenhouse, or plant into hotbeds. When shoots reach 9–12 inches, cut them off 2 inches above the soil and take the cuttings as described above. Three potatoes should produce about 24 cuttings, enough for a 30-foot row.

culinary

A sweet potato contains roughly one and a half times the calories and vitamin C of the "Irish" potato. Before cooking, wash carefully and peel or cook whole. Parboil and cut into fries, grate raw and make into fritters or roast with meat.

Glazed with butter, brown sugar and orange juice, sweet potatoes accompany Thanksgiving dinner. In Latin America and the Caribbean they are used in spiced puddings, casseroles, soufflés and sweetmeats. The leaves can be steamed.

Tzimmes
Serves 4

This one-pot meal is based on Olga Phklebin's recipe from *Russian Cooking* but adapted to our ingredients.

1–2 sweet potatoes, depending on size
2 large potatoes
Olive oil

2 pounds stewing steak, cubed
1 large onion, chopped
2 carrots, chopped
3 cups vegetable stock
3 tablespoons honey
½ teaspoon ground cinnamon
1 tablespoon all-purpose flour
Chopped fresh parsley, to garnish
Salt and freshly ground black pepper

Peel both types of potatoes and coarsely chop. Heat the oil in a heavy pan and sauté the meat well to brown it on all sides. Remove from the pan and keep warm. Brown the onion, adding the carrots and the meat and sufficient stock to cover. Season with salt and pepper and bring to a boil, then simmer for 45 minutes.

Stir in the potatoes, the honey, cinnamon and more seasoning if required. Bring back to a boil and simmer for a further 45 minutes, covered. If the stew is too liquid, allow it to boil fast at this stage. Remove ⅓ cup of the stock and mix with the flour. Pour this back into the pot, bring to the boil and cook for a further

30 minutes or until the meat is tender and the potatoes are cooked. Sprinkle with parsley and serve with a green salad.

In the humid tropics and subtropics, cuttings are rooted *in situ* at the start of the rainy season. Plant on ridges 6–12 inches high and 3–5 feet apart. Just below the ridge top, insert cuttings 9–12 inches apart, leaving half of the stem exposed. Or plant small tubers 3–4 inches deep along the top of the ridge. On sandy, free-draining soil plant cuttings and tubers on level ground.

Growing
Sweet potatoes thrive in a tropical or sub-tropical climate with an annual temperature of 70–78°F (21–26°C). Light frost kills leaves and damages tubers. Ideal annual rainfall is 30–48 inches, with wet weather in the growing period and dry conditions for the tubers to ripen. Tuber production is fastest and sugar production highest when day lengths exceed 14 hours.

Soils should be moisture-retentive and free-draining with a pH of 5.5–6.5. If necessary, dig in well-rotted organic matter before planting. In cool climates, plant cuttings outdoors when there is no danger of frost. Plant through black polyethylene after hardening off. Once established, scatter a high-potassium granular fertilizer around plants. Occasionally lift vines from the ground to prevent rooting at the leaf joints. Rotate crops.

Maintenance
Spring Take cuttings under cover, keep warm and moist.
Summer Keep cuttings weed-free, water well and feed. Prune as necessary.
Autumn Harvest. Save some tubers for the next crop.
Winter Keep compost slightly moist.

Protected Cropping
Grow under cover in cool temperate climates at a minimum temperature of 79°F (26°C).

Take cuttings as normal from healthy shoots of mature plants, and insert about 4 cuttings round the outside of a 6-inch pot filled with cuttings compost. Keep moist with tepid water. Transplant into a greenhouse border once a good root system has formed. Mist regularly. Prune stems longer than 24 inches to encourage sideshoots and also from late winter to thin out congested growth.

Harvesting and Storing
In good conditions, tubers ripen in 4–5 months. Lift when slightly immature; otherwise wait until vines begin to yellow. Lift carefully to avoid bruising. Use fresh or store, once dried, in a cool dark place for up to a week.

Pests and Diseases
Leaves can suffer from leaf spot and sooty mold. Black rot appears at the base of the stem and brown rot on the tuber. Check stored tubers regularly. Also susceptible to whitefly or red spider mite under cover.

 container growing

Grow in pots or containers 12 inches deep and 15 inches wide using loam-based compost with moderate fertilizer levels. Provide supports.

 medicinal

Sweet potatoes and their leaves contain antibacterial and fungicidal substances and are used in folk medicine. In Shakespeare's day they were sold in crystallized slices with sea holly ("eringo") as an aphrodisiac. In *The Merry Wives of Windsor*, Falstaff cries: "Let the sky rain potatoes… hail kissing-comforts and snow eringoes." The Empress Josephine introduced sweet potatoes to her companions, who were soon serving them to stimulate the passion of their lovers. The results are not recorded!

Lactuca sativa. Asteraceae

LETTUCE

Annual grown for edible leaves. Half hardy to hardy. Value: rich in beta carotene, particularly outer leaves.

The garden lettuce is believed to be a selected form of the bitter-leaved wild species *Lactuca serriola*, which is found throughout Europe, Asia and North Africa. The ancient Egyptians were said to have been the first to cultivate lettuces and there are examples of tomb wall paintings depicting a form of Romaine lettuce, which is said to have originated on the Greek island of the same name. They believed it was an aphrodisiac and also used its white sap and leaves in a concoction alongside fresh beef, frankincense and juniper berries as a remedy for stomach ache. The Romans, too, attributed medicinal properties to the lettuce and the Emperor Augustus erected an altar and statue in its honor; they believed that it upheld morals, temperance and chastity. The Romans were said to have introduced it to Great Britain with their conquering armies and even after many centuries the lettuce is still regarded as the foundation of a good salad.

 varieties

The many cultivars are divided into three main categories — cabbage, leaf and Romaine types. They can be grown all year round, and many modern cultivars are disease-resistant (see p249–250).

Cabbage Lettuce
More tolerant of drought and drier soils than the other kinds, this group includes "Butterhead" types, with soft buttery-textured leaves that are usually grown in summer, and "Crisphead" types, which have crisp leaves forming compact hearts.

Butterhead
'Action' has thick, pale green leaves and is resistant to mosaic virus and downy mildew. **'All Year Round'** is tasty and compact, with pale green leaves. It is slow to bolt and hardy. **'Arctic King'** is highly resistant to cold and ideal for autumn or early spring sowing. **'Avon defiance'*** is an excellent, high-yielding, dark green lettuce which withstands drought and high temperatures. It is ideal for summer crops, particularly those sown from mid- to late summer, and is resistant to root aphid and downy mildew. **'Buttercrunch'** has compact, crisp, dark green heads and a beautiful "buttery" heart. It is slow to bolt and heat-resistant. **'Cassandra'*** is top quality with pale green leaves and large "hearts." Resistant to downy mildew and lettuce mosaic virus, it is good for growing all year round. **'Dolly'** is a large lettuce for midsummer to mid-autumn cropping. It has good resistance to downy mildew and

Pandero

Sangria

lettuce mosaic virus. **'Kwiek'**, a large-headed variety for winter cropping, is resistant to downy mildew. Sow in late summer for harvesting in midwinter or force as an early spring crop. **'Musette'** has dark green, succulent leaves and is resistant to root aphid, lettuce mosaic virus and downy mildew. **'Sabine'** is resistant to root aphid and downy mildew. The outer leaves of **'Sangria'*** are tinged red, the inner a pale green and it has some resistance to mildew and mosaic virus. **'Soraya'** also has some resistance to downy mildew and lettuce mosaic virus. **'Valdor'**, which has firm, dark green hearts, is a very hardy lettuce for overwintering outdoors. **'Yugoslavian Red'** has red tips to the leaves and a bright greeny-yellow heart. It is mild-flavored and ideal for the ornamental vegetable garden.

Crisphead

'Avoncrisp' has some resistance to mildew and root aphid, but can suffer from "tip burn." **'Iceberg'** is ideal for spring or summer sowing and has very crisp tender leaves with large ice-white hearts (the heart has the best-quality leaves). **'Malika'*** grows very rapidly and should be harvested soon after it matures. It has some resistance to mildew and bolting. **'Premier Great Lakes'** is large, crisp and matures rapidly. It is heat- and "tip-burn"-resistant. **'Saladin'** is excellent for summer cropping and is resistant to mildew and bolting. **'Vienna'** has crisp, medium-sized heads of fresh, green leaves and is resistant to leaf aphids and mildew. **'Webb's Wonderful'** is extremely popular, and rightly so. It is a good-quality lettuce that lasts well at maturity.

Leaf lettuce

These are loose leaf varieties that sometimes form an insignificant head. Cut to resprout, or remove single leaves as needed. They stand longer before bolting than other types and can be grown at any time of year; however, growth is slower in winter.

'Cocarde'* is a large, bronze, "oak leaf" type with an excellent flavor. **'Grand Rapids'** has crinkled, pale green leaves and is resistant to tip burn. **'Lollo Blonda'** is similar to **'Lollo Rossa'***, but with fresh pale green leaves and some resistance to lettuce root aphid. **'Lollo Rossa'*** adds color to salads. The leaves are tinged red with serrated, wavy margins and it is good mixed with cos or iceberg lettuces. It is also attractive as an edging plant in the flower border or vegetable plot. **'Oak Leaf'** has several different color forms, from pale green to brown. It is tasty and ornamental. **'Red Salad Bowl'*** has bronze-green to crimson leaves. **'Ruby'** is crinkled and pale green with deep red tints and has good heat resistance. **'Salad Bowl'*** was one of the first leaf lettuces with masses of green, deeply lobed leaves that are crisp but tender. Good resistance to bolting.

Romaine or Cos

These flourish in humus-rich, moist soil, take longer to mature than other varieties and are better in cooler weather. Some can overwinter outdoors or be grown as leaf lettuce if closely spaced. They are generally very tasty.

'Bubbles'* has heavily textured leaves and is mildew-resistant. **'Chartwell'** is one of the tastiest and sweetest with firm hearts. It is downy mildew resistant and slow to bolt. Grows well in hot weather. **'Counter'** is very sweet and crisp and is resistant to tip burn, bremia and bolting. **'Freckles'** is very tasty, with attractive, red mottling over the leaves. It is warm weather-tolerant and slow to bolt. **'Lobjoits Green'***, is a large, good-quality, old variety which is deep green, crisp and tasty. It can be grown as closely as leaf lettuce but is subject to tip burn. **'Little Gem'*** is a compact, quick-maturing, semi-Romaine with a firm, sweet heart. It is ideal as a catch crop, for early crops under cover and for small gardens and has remained a popular variety since the late 19th century. **'Nymans'*** has burgundy leaves that blend towards a bright green heart. It is slow to bolt and has good mildew resistance. **'Pandero'*** is a well flavored, red-leaved baby Romaine. It is mildew-resistant and ideal as a colorful

"cut and come again." **'Parris Island'** has upright conical heads with light green outer leaves and a white heart. They have a wonderful flavor. **'Valmaine'** is good for growing as a "cut and come again" or for close planting and use as leaf lettuce. **'Winter Density'** has dark green heads and crisp, refreshing leaves, and also outstanding cold hardiness.

 ## cultivation

Propagation

Germination is poor, particularly with Butterhead types, if soil temperatures exceed 77°F (25°C), with the critical period being a few hours after planting. During hot weather sow in late afternoon or evening, when soil temperatures are lower, water after sowing to reduce soil temperature, shade before and after sowing, germinate in trays or modules in a cool place and transplant, or fluid sow. Lettuces do not transplant well in dry soil and hot weather; where possible, summer sowings are better made *in situ* or in modules. Sow thinly in drills about ½ inch deep; seeds sown too deeply are slow or fail to germinate. Thin to the final spacing when plants are large enough to handle

Sow lettuce early, then transplant

Beauty in a bell jar

(overcrowding checks growth and can cause bolting). In cool weather, thinnings can be transplanted if lifted with care to avoid root damage.

Sow those grown in trays or modules in loam-based potting compost to maintain strong growth and harden off before transplanting when they have 4 to 5 true leaves. Do not transplant when the weather is hot and dry, unless shading can be provided, and do not plant them too deeply.

Sow summer crops from mid-spring to midsummer. Sow winter-hardy varieties from late summer to early autumn, thinning to the final spacing in spring. As they do not last long after maturity, maintain a continuous supply of lettuce by sowing successionally, about every 2 weeks, just as the seedlings from the previous sowing appear. Thin when the seedlings are large enough to handle, where possible staggering them in a triangular pattern to make optimum use of the area.

Space small lettuces 8 inches apart in and between the rows, butterheads with about 11 inches in and between the rows, or 10 inches apart in rows 12 inches apart. Crispheads should be planted 15 inches apart or 12 inches apart with the rows 15 inches apart. Plant 'Salad Bowl' or Romaine about 14 inches apart in and between the rows.

Leaf lettuce can also be grown as "cut and come again" seedlings, providing 2 or 3 harvests before bolting, while summer crops tend to run to seed more rapidly. Make sure you sow thinly.

Romaine varieties like 'Lobjoits Green' can be grown as leaf lettuce. Sow in rows 5 inches apart, thinning to 1 inch. Sow weekly from late spring to early summer and again in 3 consecutive weeks from late summer. This technique was developed at the Horticulture Research International in the United Kingdom.

Growing

Lettuce prefer cool growing conditions, from 50–68°F (10–20°C), and need an open, sunny site on light, rich, moisture-retentive soil, with a pH of around neutral. They struggle on dry or impoverished soil, so dig in plenty of well-rotted organic matter the autumn before sowing or grow on ground manured for the previous crop. Lightly fork in a base dressing of general fertilizer at 4 ounces/sq yd about 10 days before sowing and create a seedbed by raking to a fine tilth.

Hoe and hand weed regularly to remove any weeds. A constant supply of moisture is vital for success. Lettuce need 6 gallons/sq yd per week in dry weather. Water in the mornings on sunny days so that the water evaporates quickly, reducing the risk of disease. If water is scarce, apply only on the last 7–10 days before harvest.

Boost growth of winter-hardy outdoor crops with a liquid general fertilizer in mid-spring and use the same treatment for slow-growing crops at any time of year. Rotate crops every 2 years to avoid the build-up of pests and diseases.

Maintenance

Spring Sow crops under glass or outdoors under cloches in early spring. Sow later crops outdoors. Harvest early crops.
Summer Sow successionally and harvest overwintered crops. Keep crops weed-free; water as needed. Harvest.
Autumn Sow and protect crops under cloches. Harvest.
Winter Sow crops under cover. Harvest.

Protected Cropping

Sow from late winter to early spring in modules or trays for transplanting under cloches or cold frames from mid- to late spring. Alternatively, they can be sown *in situ* in cold frames or under cloches for growing on or transplanting outdoors in a protected part of the garden and covered with floating cloches.

Protect late spring and summer transplants under cloches until they become established and protect late summer sowings under cloches to maintain the quality of autumn crops. Grow hardier varieties under floating cloches or in a greenhouse or a cold frame over winter, ideally with a gentle heat around 45°F (7°C).

Germination is better in cool conditions

LETTUCE

Lettuce seedlings in a vegetable garden

Sow from late summer to mid-autumn for transplanting. Earlier sowings can be made outdoors in a seedbed for transplanting; others can be sown in modules or seed trays. Ventilate well to avoid disease problems.

Harvest from late autumn to mid-spring. Cover outdoor winter-hardy crops with glass or floating cloches to ensure a good-quality crop and provide protection during severe weather.

Sow early crops of "cut and come again" seedlings under cover in late winter or spring, and also from mid-autumn.

Harvesting and Storing

Summer maincrop lettuce are ready to harvest from early summer to mid-autumn, around 12 weeks after sowing. Romaine stand for quite a time in cool weather but Butterheads deteriorate within a few days of maturity. Crispheads last for about 10 days before deteriorating. Leaf lettuces can be picked over a long period. Harvest hardy overwintered outdoor crops from late spring to early summer.

Harvest "cut and come again" seedlings about 4 weeks after sowing and Romaine types grown as leaf lettuce about 1 inch above the ground when they are 3–5 inches high. A second crop can be harvested from 3 to 8 weeks later, depending on the growing conditions.

Cut mature lettuces at the base, just below the lower leaves. Do not squeeze hearting lettuces to check if they are ready for harvesting, as this can damage the leaves: press them gently but firmly with the back of your hand. Pull single leaves from leaf lettuce as required or cut 1 inch above the base and allow the plant to resprout.

Store lettuce in the refrigerator in the salad drawer or in a plastic bag for up to 6 days. Romaine lettuce stores the longest.

Pests and Diseases

Root aphids appear in clusters on the roots and are usually covered in a white powdery wax. The symptoms are stunted growth and yellowing leaves; plants may collapse in hot weather. They are less of a problem in cool, damp conditions. Pick and destroy affected plants or grow resistant varieties.

Aphids can also be a problem.

Leaf tips become brown and dry when affected by tip burn, caused by sudden water loss in warm weather. Water well and shade, if necessary; do not allow lettuces to grow excessively large; grow resistant varieties where possible.

Botrytis or grey mold can be a problem in cool, damp conditions. Do not plant seedlings too deeply, handle transplants carefully to avoid damage, thin early, remove diseased material, improve ventilation and spray with a systemic or copper-based fungicide. Grow resistant varieties.

Bolting or running to seed is caused by check during transplanting, drought, temperatures over 70°F (21°C), or long days; otherwise lettuces will only bolt after hearting. Grow resistant varieties or leaf lettuce. Pigeons and sparrows can damage seedlings. Grow under horticultural fleece, tie thread between bamboo canes, use humming line or other deterrents.

Lettuce mosaic virus is a disease that causes the leaves to become puckered and mottled; veins become transparent and growth is stunted — more of a problem on overwintering crops. Destroy those that are affected, control aphids and grow resistant varieties.

 ## companion planting

Lettuce grow well with cucumbers, onions, radishes and carrots. Dill and chervil protect them from aphids.

 ## container growing

Compact varieties are suitable for growing in pots, containers and window boxes. Use a soil-based compost, mix in a slow-release granular fertilizer and water regularly. Sow either *in situ* or in modules for transplanting.

 ## medicinal

Lettuce is used as a mild sedative and narcotic, and lettuce soup is reported to be effective in treating nervous tension and insomnia. Lettuce sap dissolved in wine is said to make a good painkiller.

Lettuce soothes inflammation — lotions for the treatment of sunburn and rough skin are made from its extracts.

Lettuce can also be used as a poultice on bruises or taken internally for stomach ulcers and for irritable bowel syndrome.

It is also antispasmodic and can be used to soothe coughs and bronchial problems; it is reputed to cool the ardor.

culinary

Wash leaves thoroughly before use. Use fresh or wilted in salads, braise with butter and flavor with nutmeg or braise with peas and shallots and serve with butter. Stir-fry with onions and mushrooms, steam and add to chicken soup or make cream of lettuce soup and garnish with hardboiled eggs and a sprinkling of curry powder. Stalks can be sliced and steamed.

Cypriot Salad
Serves 2

3–4 large lettuce leaves, torn into pieces
1¾ ounces haloumi cheese, cut into thin slices
4 medium tomatoes
¼ cucumber, sliced
¼ yellow pepper, cored, deseeded and diced
Handful of fresh flat-leaf parsley, roughly chopped
10 black olives, stoned
½ red onion, thinly sliced

For the Dressing:
2 tablespoons extra virgin olive oil
1 tablespoon white wine vinegar
1–2 teaspoons lemon juice
Sea salt and freshly ground black pepper

Toast the cheese under a medium grill on a non-stick baking sheet until golden brown. Turn once and brown the other side. Mix with the other ingredients in a large salad bowl. Shake all the dressing ingredients together in a glass jar until well combined. Pour over the salad, gently toss to mix and serve immediately.

Lettuce-wrapped Minced Shrimp
Serves 6–8 as a side dish

1 head crisp lettuce (Webb's or iceberg)
30 raw shrimp, shelled and deveined
¼ teaspoon salt
2 teaspoons cornstarch
2 tablespoons egg white
4 tablespoons peanut or vegetable oil
50g Szechuan zhacai, trimmed and finely chopped
1 teaspoon crushed garlic

Cypriot Salad

Mince the shrimp coarsely and put in a large mixing bowl. Season with salt. Add the cornstarch and egg white and stir in the same direction until the egg white is absorbed and the mixture is elastic. Refrigerate, covered, for 1 hour.

Arrange the separated lettuce leaves, preferably cup-shaped, on a plate on the dining room table.

Heat a wok until hot. Add 1 tablespoon of oil and the *zhacai* (pickled mustard stem, from specialized stores) and cook for a few seconds, stirring. Scoop on to a dish and keep nearby. Wipe the wok clean.

Reheat the wok until the smoke rises. Add the rest of the oil and coat the wok with it. Add the garlic and the shrimp, stirring vigorously. Add the *zhacai* and continue cooking until the shrimp turn pink and are cooked. Then place on a plate next to the lettuce.

To serve, each person takes a lettuce leaf, spoons some shrimp mixture into the center and wraps the lettuce around it: perfect finger-food.

Papaya salad
Serves 4

A selection of firm seasonal green vegetables, e.g. iceberg lettuce, cucumber and cabbage, to serve
2 garlic cloves, peeled
3–4 small fresh red or green chilies
2 yard-long beans or 20 French beans, chopped into 2-inch lengths
1 cup fresh papaya, peeled, deseeded
1 tomato, cut into wedges
2 tablespoons nam pla (Thai fish sauce)
1 tablespoon granulated sugar
2 tablespoons lime juice

Pound the garlic in a large mortar, then add the chilies and pound again. Add the long beans, breaking them up slightly. Cut the papaya into fine slivers. Now take a spoon and stir in the papaya. Lightly pound together, then stir in the tomato and lightly pound again.

Add the fish sauce, sugar and lime juice, stirring well, then turn into a serving dish. Serve with fresh raw vegetables — any leaves, such as white cabbage, can be used as a scoop for the spicy mixture.

Braised Lettuce
Serves 4

4–5 heads of small lettuce, trimmed
A little oil or butter
¼ cup bacon, roughly diced
1 carrot, roughly diced
1 red onion, sliced
1¼ cups vegetable stock
2 tablespoons chopped fresh thyme and parsley
Salt and freshly ground black pepper

In a saucepan of salted water, cook the lettuce for 5 minutes. Drain and refresh in cold water. Drain again and remove as much liquid as possible: you can blot the leaves lightly with paper towel.

Grease an ovenproof dish and sprinkle the base with the bacon, carrot, onion and seasoning. Arrange the lettuce neatly in the dish and pour in the stock. Cover the dish with wax paper and braise in a preheated oven, 350°F/180°C, for 30–40 minutes.

Remove the lettuces and other ingredients and keep hot. Then reduce the cooking liquid and pour it over the vegetables. Sprinkle with the fresh herbs and serve very hot.

Papaya salad

Lactuca sativa var. augustana. Asteraceae.

CELTUCE

Also known as Stem Lettuce, Asparagus Lettuce, Chinese Lettuce. Annual grown for edible leaves. Value: little nutritive value; low in carbohydrate and calories; a source of potassium.

Introduced from China, where it has been grown for centuries, this "oriental vegetable" consists of a short-stemmed mutation lettuce. It has been listed in European catalogs since 1885, but the name "celtuce" was adopted by an American seed company that first offered seeds in 1942. It aptly describes its characteristics: the stems are used like celery; the leaves make a lettuce substitute.

 ## varieties

'Zulu' is a variety for cooler climates, with narrow, dull-textured leaves. Others are sold in seed mixes of broad, dull, glossy or red-leaved varieties.

 ## cultivation

Celtuce needs well-drained, rich, fertile soil, with a pH of 6.5–7.5, around neutral. Celtuce tolerates a range of temperatures from light frosts to over 80°F (27°C).

It tends to bolt prematurely in extremely hot conditions, but is still more heat-resistant than lettuce. Grow celtuce as a winter crop in mild areas.

Propagation
For successional cropping, sow every 2 weeks from mid-spring until midsummer in drills ½ inch deep and 12 inches apart. When large enough to handle, thin to 3½ inches.

Germination is poor in temperatures above 80°F (27°C). In hot summers, sow in seed trays or modules in a cool, partially shaded position. Modules tend to produce better plants than seed trays; weak seedlings rarely produce good stems. Transplant when 3–4 leaves have been produced, generally after 3–4 weeks.

Mulch after planting to conserve moisture and suppress weeds; the shallow roots are easily damaged by hoeing.

Growing
In poor soils, add copious amounts of organic matter the winter before planting. Celtuce grows well on light soil, but develops a stronger root system and more robust plants on heavier soils.

Water well as leaves develop, to keep them tender. As the stems develop, reduce watering, but take care to keep the supply steady: if the soil becomes too wet or too dry, the stems may crack. Feed with a liquid general fertilizer every 3 weeks.

Maintenance
Spring Sow seed.
Summer Water and remove weeds.
Autumn Transplant seedlings for winter crops.
Winter Grow under cover; harvest mature crops.

Why not give it a try?

CELTUCE

Protected Cropping

Grow in cloches, unheated greenhouses, tunnels or under horticultural fleece to extend the season. Raise early crops by sowing and planting under cover in early spring and late crops by transplanting summer-sown seedlings under cover in autumn.

Harvesting and Storing

Harvest 3–4 months after sowing, when 12 inches high and 1 inch diameter. Cut the stalks, pull up the plant or cut it off at ground level. Trim the leaves from the stem but do not touch the top rosette of leaves, in order to keep the stem fresh.

Celtuce stems can be kept for a few weeks if stored in cool conditions.

Pests and Diseases

Celtuce is susceptible to the same problems as lettuce. Pick off slugs, set traps or use ferric phosphate pellets. Downy mildew is worse in cool, damp conditions: treat with fungicide, and remove infected plants and debris at the end of the season.

companion planting

Plant with chervil and dill to protect from aphids. Interplant between slower-growing crops such as cauliflower, self-blanching celery or Chinese chives.

container growing

Sow in containers or pots in a loam-based compost with moderate levels of added fertilizer.

culinary

Celtuce is excellent raw and cooked. Prepare the stems by peeling off the outer layer. Cut into thin slices for salads, or into larger pieces for cooking. In salads, it can either be eaten raw or cooked and cooled, served with a spicy dressing.

Cook lightly, for 4 minutes at most. Stir-fry with white meat, poultry, fish, other vegetables, or on its own seasoned with garlic, chili, pepper, soy or oyster sauce. It is also delicious served with a creamed sauce or baked *au gratin*. In China it is used in soups and pickles. Young leaves can be cooked like "greens."

Crispy Spring Rolls
Serves 4–6

½ pound celtuce stems
20 frozen spring roll skins, defrosted
½ pound fresh beansprouts, washed and husked
½ cup bamboo shoots
½ cup white mushrooms
½ cup carrots
Vegetable oil, for frying
1 teaspoon sugar
1 tablespoon light soy sauce
1 tablespoon rice wine
1 tablespoon all-purpose flour mixed with
    1 tablespoon water
Salt and freshly ground black pepper

Prepare the beansprouts and roughly chop all the other vegetables to the same size. Heat a little oil in a wok until smoking and stir-fry the vegetables for a minute, then add the sugar, soy sauce, rice wine and seasoning, and cook for a further minute or two. Set aside to cool.

Cut the spring roll skins in half diagonally. Place a teaspoon of the vegetable mixture in the center of each and roll up neatly, folding in all the corners. Place on a lightly floured plate and brush the upper edge with a little flour paste to seal.

Heat enough oil to deep-fry until steaming and drop in the spring rolls for 3–4 minutes, until crispy, cooking in batches. Drain and serve with chili sauce.

CALABASH

Lagenaria siceraria. Cucurbitaceae

Also known as Bottle Gourd, Calabash Gourd, Doodhi, White-flowered Gourd, Trumpet Gourd. Vigorous annual climber grown for edible young fruits, shoots and seeds. Tender. Value: little nutritive value; a moderate source of vitamin C; small quantities of B vitamins and protein.

Early evidence for the cultivation of this versatile tropical gourd comes from South America around 7000 BCE, though it is thought to have originated in Africa, south of the Sahara, or India. Some sources suggest that it may have dispersed naturally by floating on oceanic currents from one continent to another: experiments have found that seed will germinate after surviving over seven months in seawater. One of the earliest crops cultivated in the tropics, these gourds with their narrow necks have developed in many shapes and sizes, some reaching up to 7 feet long. The young fruits are edible, but mature shells become extremely hard when dried and have been used to make bottles, kitchen utensils, musical instruments, floats for fishing nets and even gunpowder flasks. In the past *Lagenaria* leaves were used as a protective charm when elephant hunting.

varieties

Lagenaria siceraria is a vigorous annual, climbing or scrambling by means of tendrils to more than 30 feet. The leaves are broad and oval with wavy margins. Its solitary, fragrant, white flowers open in the evenings. Its fruits are pale green to cream or yellow, with a narrow "neck," and contain white, spongy flesh and flat, creamy-colored seeds. The names of selected forms (like "bottle," "trumpet," "club" or "powderhorn" gourd) relate to their use and appearance.

cultivation

They flourish in warm conditions, around 68–86°F (20–30°C) and plenty of sunshine, but will grow outdoors in warm temperate climates where humidity levels are moderate to high. Plants need to be trained over supporting structures.

Propagation
Soak seeds overnight in lukewarm water before sowing on mounds of soil about 12 inches apart, containing copious amounts of well-rotted manure. Plant 3 seeds, edgeways, and thin to leave the strongest seedling.

Seeds can be sown in a nursery bed and transplanted when they have 2 to 3 leaves. Seeds are usually sown at the start of the rainy season.

Growing
Calabash needs fertile, well-drained soil, preferably with a pH of 7. Add a granular general fertilizer to the planting hole or scatter it around the germinated seedling.

Train the stems into trees, or over fences, arbors or frames covered with 6 inches mesh netting. Erect stakes or trellis on the beds or among the groups of mounds. Alternatively, grow plants in beds 4–6 feet square, planting a seedling at each corner and training towards the center. Pinch out the terminal shoots when they are 1–1½ inches long, to encourage branching. The best yields are obtained in warm-climate areas with rainfall around 32–48 inches per annum, but they grow well in drier regions if they are kept well watered. Feed with a high-nitrogen fertilizer every 3 weeks during the growing season, keep crops weed-free and mulch with a layer of organic matter.

Plants can grow extremely rapidly in hot weather: 2 feet in 24 hours has been recorded. Where conditions are suitable they can be grown all year round. To grow outdoors in cooler climates, harden off under cloches or cold frames and plant in a sheltered, sunny position when the danger of frost has passed.

The chance of success is greater in hot summers; they should reach edible size, though they rarely have a long enough season to mature fully.

Maintenance
Spring Sow seeds under glass in warm conditions.
Summer Train vines over trellis or netting. Water regularly; feed as necessary. Wet down the greenhouse to maintain humid conditions and harvest young fruits.
Autumn In cooler climates, harvest mature gourds for preserving before the onset of the first frosts.

Protected Cropping
In cool, temperate climates, sow seeds 6–8 weeks before the anticipated planting out time. Sow 2–3 seeds in a 6-inch pot of peat-substitute compost in late winter or early spring at 70–77°F (21–25°C).

Germination takes 3–5 days. If the ideal temperatures cannot be achieved and maintained, delay sowing until mid- to late spring. Transplant when seedlings are 4–6 inches high. They will grow at temperatures down to 50°F (10°C), but flourish at high temperatures and in humid conditions in bright, filtered light.

Wet down the greenhouse floor at least twice a day, depending on outside weather conditions. Dig in plenty of well-rotted manure and horticultural grit or sharp sand into the greenhouse border, or grow in containers.

Keep the compost constantly moist, using lukewarm water, and feed with a liquid general fertilizer every 2 weeks. Train up a trellis, wires or netting. Flowers will appear from early summer and only 1 or 2 should be allowed to grow to maturity.

Harvesting and Storing
Vines begin to fruit 3–4 months after planting. Harvest immature fruits when an inch or two long, 70–90 days after sowing. Mature fruits can be harvested and dried slowly as ornaments.

Pests and Diseases
This very robust plant is rarely troubled by disease. Whitefly can occasionally be a problem when plants are grown under cover. In warm, humid climates, anthracnose appears as pinhead-sized, water-soaked lesions on the fruits, combining to form a small black mass. Fruit rot can also be a problem. Spray with a

copper-based compound and remove badly affected leaves. Harvest fruits carefully to avoid damage.

 ## container growing

Pot as plants grow, until they are in 12-inch pots, or grow in large containers of loam-based compost with added organic matter and horticultural grit or sharp sand to improve drainage. Keep the compost moist, with lukewarm water. Growth is better restricted when they are grown in pots and is preferable in the greenhouse border, increasing the chance of successful fruiting.

Stop the shoot tips when the stems are 5 feet long and train the side stems along a wire. (It is worth noting that even with this method, plants still need a considerable amount of space.) Hand-pollination ensures a good crop. (Male and female flowers are on the same plant: females are recognizable by the ovary at the back of the flower, covered in glandular hairs.) Once a flower has formed, allow 2 more leaves to appear, then pinch out the growing tip. If it is a male flower or a fruit is not going to form, cut the stem back to the first leaf. A replacement will be formed.

The ornamental gourd tunnel in Rosemoor Gardens, UK

 ## culinary

Young fruits, which are rich in pectin, are popular in tropical Africa and Asia. They have a mild, somewhat bland taste, are peeled before eating and any large seeds removed. They can be cubed or sliced, sautéed with spices to accompany curries and other Indian dishes and added to stews or curries. Young shoots and leaves can be steamed or lightly boiled. Seeds are used in soups in Africa and are boiled in salt water and eaten as an appetizer in India. The seed oil is used for cooking.

 ## medicinal

The fruit pulp around seeds is emetic and purgative and is sometimes given to horses! Juice from the fruit is used to treat baldness; mixed with lime juice, it is used for pimples; boiled with oil, it is used for rheumatism. Seeds and roots are used to treat dropsy and the seed oil used externally for headaches.

Languas galanga (syn. *Alpinia galanga*). *Zingiberaceae*

GREATER GALANGAL

Also known as Greater Galingale, Siamese Ginger. Herbaceous perennial; rhizomatous rootstock used as flavoring. Tender. Value: negligible nutritive value.

Two species, greater and lesser galangal, have been grown for centuries for their pungent, aromatic roots, which are used as spices and medicinally. The earliest records date from around 550 CE, while Marco Polo noted its cultivation in southern China and Java in the 13th century. In the Middle Ages it was known as "galangale," a name also used for the roots of sweet sedge, whose violet-scented rhizomes are used in perfumery.

The word galangal came from the Chinese, meaning "a mild ginger from Ko," a region of the Canton province. It is an essential ingredient of many Malaysian and Thai dishes. The spicy rhizomes have a somewhat different use in the Middle East, where they have been used to "spike" horses!

 cultivation

The plant is a herbaceous perennial with pale orange-flushed cream bulbous rhizomes. Stems grow to 7 feet tall, with dark green lance-shaped leaves up to 20 inches long. Flowers are pale green and white with pink markings; the fruit is a round red capsule. There are many different races in cultivation, including types with red and white rhizomes. Lesser galangal is regarded as superior, as it is more pungent and aromatic, but is uncommon in cultivation.

Propagation

Sow fresh seed in pots of peat-substitute compost at 68°F (20°C). Keep the compost moist, using lukewarm water, and transplant seedlings when they are large enough to handle. In tropical and subtropical regions they can be sown outdoors in a seedbed (for ground preparation, see "Growing").

Divide rhizomes in spring, when the young shoots are about 1 inch long. Remove young, vigorous sections from the perimeter of the clump, using a sharp knife, dust the cuts with fungicide and transplant just below the soil or compost surface. Soak thoroughly with lukewarm water and maintain high humidity and temperatures.

Growing

Galangal grows outdoors in tropical or subtropical climates, thriving in sunshine or partial shade. It needs a rich, free-draining soil, so dig in plenty of well-rotted compost and allow the ground to settle for a few weeks before planting. Allow 3 feet between plants. Keep crops weed-free and water during dry periods. Mulch with well-rotted compost when plants have become well established.

Protected Cropping

In temperate zones, plants can be grown in a heated polyethylene tunnel or greenhouse in bright filtered light, with a minimum temperature of 59°F (15°C). Maintain high humidity by misting plants with lukewarm water and "wetting down" paths. Prepare borders as for "Growing" and allow 3 feet between plants.

Keep the compost constantly moist with lukewarm water and reduce watering in lower temperatures. Remove flower stems before they flower and reduce

culinary

Before use, scrape or peel off the skin. The raw chopped or minced root is used in Malaysian and Indonesian dishes with bean curd, meat, poultry, fish, curries and sauces. It is also used as a marinade to flavor barbecued chicken. The fruits are a substitute for cardamom, the buds can be pickled and the flowers are eaten raw with vegetables or pickles in parts of Java. In Thai cooking, it is preferred to ginger. In medieval England, a sauce was made from bread crusts, galangal, cinnamon and ginger pulverized and moistened with stock. It was heated with a dash of vinegar and strained over fish or meat.

Galangal Soup
Serves 4

This Vietnamese recipe has many variations. First, make a stock from the following, by simmering for about three hours, topping up as necessary:

4 cups water
1 chicken carcass

4 bulbs lemon grass, bruised
5-inch piece galangal, peeled and sliced
1 onion, roughly sliced
2 red dried chilies
6 kaffir lime leaves
Salt and freshly ground black pepper

Then strain the stock through some fine cheesecloth. Reheat in a heavy saucepan, adding the meat from the chicken carcass, chopped finely, together with 1 tablespoon of fish sauce and 4 tablespoons of lime juice.

Simmer for 5 minutes, then add ¼ pound shiitake mushrooms, left whole. Simmer for a further 3 minutes, then stir in ½ cup thick coconut milk. Do not allow to reboil, and check the seasoning. Serve hot.

---

watering. The foliage gradually becomes yellow and dies back in winter. The compost should remain slightly moist throughout the dormant period. Increase watering when new shoots emerge the following spring. Feed regularly with a liquid general fertilizer every 2 weeks while the plant is actively growing. Mulch plants grown in borders annually in spring with well-rotted manure.

Harvesting and Storing
Rhizomes are ready to harvest after 3–4 years. Lift plants towards the end of the growing season and remove mature rhizomes, retaining younger ones for transplanting. It is a good idea to divide and replant a few each year to ensure a constant supply.

Galangal are better used immediately after harvest but will keep for at least a week in a cool place. Alternatively, they can be frozen whole in a plastic bag and segments removed as required. Keep dried roots in airtight containers in a cool dark place.

Pests and Diseases
Red spider mite can be a problem under glass. Check plants regularly, as small infestations are easily controlled. Speckling, mottling and bronzing of the leaf surface are the usual symptoms; in later stages, fine webbing appears on leaves and stems. They prefer hot, dry conditions. Control by maintaining high humidity or spray with derris or a similar insecticide.

container growing

Plants can be grown in containers under cover in a compost mix of 2 parts each of loam and leaf mold, 1 part horticultural grit or sharp sand and 3 parts medium-grade bark. Repot and divide in spring when the rhizomes outgrow their allotted space.

medicinal

Plants contain cineol, an aromatic, antiseptic substance. The essential oil acts as a decongestant and respiratory germicide and digestive aid. In India it is used as a breath purifier and deodorant, and a paste is made from the rhizomes to treat skin infections. It is also said to be an aphrodisiac. Infusions are taken after childbirth.

other uses

Roots of lesser galangal are used in Russia for flavoring tea and a liqueur called Nastoika. The rhizomes produce a yellow or yellow-green dye.

KAEMPFERIA GALANGA
(Chinese keys)

The rhizomes, common in the markets of South-East Asia, produce a distinctive cluster of fingerlike roots that are pale brown with bright yellow flesh and a pungent aroma. They have a very strong taste and should be used sparingly in green curry paste, sauces, soups and curries.

The rhizomes may be eaten raw when young, or steamed and eaten as a vegetable. Young shoots are cooked as a vegetable, pickled or eaten raw. Chinese keys are used as a carminative, stomachic, expectorant, analgesic, and to treat dandruff and sore throats.

Lens culinaris. Leguminosae

LENTIL

Also known as Split Pea, Dhal, Masur, Dal. Annual herb grown for edible, flattened seeds. Tender. Value: rich in protein, fiber, iron, carbohydrate, zinc and B vitamins.

Presumed to be native to southwest Europe and temperate Asia, lentils are one of the oldest cultivated crop plants. Carbonized seeds found in Neolithic villages in the Middle East have been dated at 7000–6000 BCE, and it is believed that they were domesticated long before that. By 2200 BCE plants appeared in Egyptian tombs; they are referred to in the Bible as the "mess of pottage" for which Esau traded his birthright (Genesis 25: 30, 34). The English "lens," describing the glass in optical instruments, comes from their Latin name — its cross-section resembles a lentil seed. Christian Lent has the same origin, as it was traditionally eaten during the fast.

Grown throughout the world, lentils have become naturalized in drier areas of the tropics. Because of their relatively high drought tolerance, they are suitable for semi-arid regions. The quick-maturing plant is rarely more than 18 inches tall and has branched stems, forming a small bush. The white to rose and violet flowers lead to two to three seeded pods.

varieties

Lentils have been selected over many centuries for their size and color. Today many different races and cultivars exist. Two main races predominate: the larger, round-seeded types usually grown in Europe and North America, and the smaller, flatter-seeded types common in the East.

The choice is yours

Frequently encountered is the split red or Persian lentil, which is extremely tender and quick to cook.

Among round-seeded types grown in Europe, the **'Lentille du Puy'**, a tiny green form, is the tastiest and tenderest. Similar but coarser is the **'Lentille Blonde'** or **'Yellow Lentil'** commonly grown in northern France, while **'German or Brown Lentils'** are coarser still and need lengthy cooking to make them tender. Of varieties grown in North America, **'O'Odham'** has flat gray-brown to tan-colored seeds and **'Tarahumara Pinks'** from Mexico has mottled seeds and thrives well in semi-arid conditions.

cultivation

Propagation
Prepare the seedbed by removing any debris from the soil surface and raking to a moderate texture. Sow in spring, when the soil is warm, in drills 1 inch deep, thinning seedlings to 8–12 inches apart with 18 inches between rows. They can also be broadcast and then thinned after germination to 8–12 inches apart.

Growing
Lentils are not frost-hardy but flourish in a range of climatic conditions. They prefer a warm, sunny, sheltered position on light, free-draining, moisture-retentive soil. Sandy soils with added well-rotted organic matter are ideal, though equally good crops are grown on silty soil.

Keep crops weed-free and irrigate if necessary during periods of prolonged drought. Excessive watering can lead to overproduction of leaves and poor cropping.

Lentils can be grown as a "novelty" crop in cool temperate climates, but yields are not high enough to make it worthwhile on a large scale.

Maintenance
Spring Prepare the seedbed and sow when soil is warm.
Summer Keep crops weed-free and irrigate if needed.
Autumn Harvest before the seeds split.
Winter Store seeds or pods in a cool dry place, for use as required.

culinary

As their protein content is about 25%, lentils are an important meat substitute. They also have the lowest fat content of any protein-rich food.

Soak lentils overnight, drain and replace the water. Boil rapidly for 10 minutes, then simmer for 25 minutes until tender. Use in soups, thick broth or grind into flour.

Lentils are commonly used for "dal." Seeds are moistened with water and oil and dried before milling 2–3 times, each time separating the "chaff" from the meal.

Puy Lentils with Roasted Red Peppers and Goat's Cheese
Serves 4

¾ cup Puy lentils
3 red peppers
1 red onion
1 carrot
Sprig each of fresh parsley, marjoram and thyme

2 tablespoons sun-dried tomatoes, chopped
6 ounces crumbled goat's cheese
1 tablespoon freshly chopped herbs

For the Dressing:
4 tablespoons extra virgin olive oil
1 ½ tablespoons lemon juice
Salt and freshly ground black pepper

Roast the peppers on a baking sheet in a preheated oven 475°F (250°C) for 30 minutes. Put them into a plastic bag in the fridge. When cooled, deseed and peel the peppers, then cut into strips. Set aside.

Wash the Puy lentils thoroughly and cook them, covered in 1 ½ cups water, with the whole onion, carrot and herbs. These lentils cook faster than other types, in about 15 minutes. Drain. Roughly chop the onion and add back into the lentils. Discard the carrot and herbs. While still warm, add the tomatoes and goat's cheese and stir gently. Season.

Make the dressing and toss the lentil mixture in it. Arrange the lentils with the slices of red pepper on individual plates.

Sprinkle with the herbs and serve.

Protected Cropping
In cool temperate climates, sow seeds in spring in trays, pots or modules of seed compost. Keep compost moist and pot on when seedlings are large enough to handle. Harden off before planting outdoors when the soil is warm and workable and there is no danger of frosts. Protect plants under cloches until they are properly established. Seeds can be sprouted.

Harvesting and Storing
Lentils take about 90 days to reach maturity. Harvest as foliage begins to yellow, before the pods split and the seeds are shed. Lift the whole plant and lay on trays or mats in the sunshine to air-dry or put them in an airy shed. When the pods dry and split, remove the seed and store in a cool, dry place.

Pests and Diseases
Lentils suffer from few pests and diseases. Leaf rust can occur; burn plants after harvest and use treated seed.

Companion Planting
Lentils can be grown as a "green manure."

container growing

Grow in containers of soil-based compost with moderate fertilizer levels. Water well and keep the plants weed-free. To avoid the need for transplanting, seeds can be sown in a container that can then be moved outdoors into a suitable sunny spot after germination.

other uses

Dried leaves and stems are used as forage crops. Lentils have also been used as a source of commercial starch in the textile and printing industries, the by-products being used as cattle feed. Plants are used fresh, or dried as hay and fodder.

warning

Never eat lentils raw.

A protein-packed field

Lycopersicon esculentum. Solanaceae

TOMATO

Also known as Love Apple. Short-lived perennial grown as annual for fleshy, succulent berry. Half hardy. Value: rich in beta carotene and vitamin C; some vitamin B.

The wild species is believed to have originated in the Andean regions of north and central South America, spreading to Central and North America along with maize during human migrations over 2,000 years ago. The fruits had been cultivated in Mexico for centuries when European explorers found them growing under local names including *tomati*, *tomatl*, *tumatle* and *tomatas*. When they were first brought to Europe around 1523, tomatoes were considered to be poisonous, due to their strong odor and bright white, red and yellow berries, and were grown only as ornamentals. Dodoens in his *Historie of Plants* of 1578 records, "This is a strange plant and not found in this country, except in the gardens of some herborists… and is dangerous to be used."

In Europe, it was first used for food in Italy. Like many vegetable introductions from the New World, it was considered to be an aphrodisiac. The Italian name *pommi dei mori* was corrupted during translation to the French *pomme d'amour* or "apple of love," as it was thought to excite the passions. Not all believed it to have this effect. Estienne and Liébault wrote that tomatoes were boiled or fried, but gave rise to wind, choler and "infinite obstructions" — hardly an inducement to romance!

The use of tomatoes by North American settlers was not recorded until after Independence, but they were regularly used as food by Italian immigrants to New England and French settlers living in New Orleans, who were making ketchup by 1779. Thomas Jefferson was certainly growing them in his garden in 1781 and they were introduced to Philadelphia eight years later.

varieties

Most greenhouse varieties are "indeterminate," with a main stem that can become several yards long — these are usually grown as "cordons." Most of those grown outdoors are bush types that do not need supporting and can be grown under crop covers or cloches. Low-yielding, dwarf varieties are good for pots or window boxes.

As you will see from any seed catalog, there are many hundreds of tomato varieties. Those for cultivation under cover in a cold greenhouse and outdoor varieties are generally interchangeable. They range in size from the large ribbed, "beefsteak" types to small "cherry," "pear-shaped" and "currant" tomatoes in a fantastic range of colors including mottled, dark skinned, pink and yellow.

'Ailsa Craig' grows well indoors/outdoors. It is a reliable, tasty, heavy-cropping variety. **'Alicante'***, another indoor/outdoor variety, crops heavily and matures early. It produces smooth, tasty fruit and does well in growbags. The large, black-tinted fruit of **'Black Krim'** have a delicious, smoky flavor. It sets well in

Yellow Pear

Roma

heat but is also prone to cracking. However, don't let that deter you. **'Brandywine'** is a delicious old variety and the fruit can become quite sizeable. The skin is rosy pink or tinged slightly purplish red. It performs best in cooler climates. **'Dombito'** is an excellent variety that produces large, round, sweet "beefsteak" fruits; perfect for salads or slicing. **'Gardener's Delight'*** is extremely popular, producing long trusses of delicious, sweet, "cherry" tomatoes over a long period. It grows indoors but has better flavor outdoors, is ideal for containers and generally trouble-free. **'Ildi'** is very prolific indeed, producing masses of tiny fruits. **'Jaune Flammée'** is deep orange and shaped like an apricot; prolific, tasty and good for drying. **'Marmande'*** is a delicious outdoor variety with deep, red ribbed fruits. It crops early and is resistant to fusarium and verticillium wilt. **'Oaxacan Pink'** has small, flattened, pink fruits. **'Orange Banana'** has orange fruit up to 4 inches long, which are excellent for drying. **'Red Alert'** is an early bush variety for the greenhouse or outdoors with small, sweet, oval fruits. **'Roma VF'** is an outdoor bush "plum" tomato, ideal for paste, ketchup, bottling, soups or juice. It crops heavily and sometimes needs supporting, and has high resistance to fusarium and verticillium wilt. **'San Marzano'**, another Italian tomato, also crops heavily and is good for soups, sauces or garnishing salads. **'Shirley'*** is grown commercially and has good quality, tender, tasty, disease-resistant fruit. Withstanding

lower temperatures than most types, it does not suffer from "greenback," is highly resistant to tobacco mosaic virus, leaf mold and fusarium and is therefore an ideal tomato for organic growers. **'Siberia Tomato'** is a bush variety that crops extremely early, around seven weeks after transplanting and sets fruit at temperatures as low as 38°F (5°C). **'Stupice'** crops heavily and extremely early, producing fruit with an excellent balance between sweetness and tartness; delicious! **'Sungold'** is one of the sweetest tomatoes ever produced.

'Tasty Evergreen' has light yellow to green skin and the flesh remains green when ripe; succulent, tender and sweet. **'Tigerella'*** produces tasty, small orange-red fruits with pale stripes and crops well over a long period. **'Tiny Tim'** is compact, bushy and ideal for pots, window boxes and hanging baskets. The fruits are cherry-sized and tasty. **'Tumbler'** was originally bred for hanging baskets. It has flexible, hanging stems, and the bright red fruits ripen quickly and are sweet to the taste. **'Wapsipinicon Peach'** has fuzzy skin like a peach and was a U.S. taste test winner; delicious and sweet — recommended. **'Yellow Pearshaped'** are well described by their name. The dense clusters of fruit are sweet-tasting and have few seeds and the plants are vigorous and high-yielding. **'Yellow Perfection'*** crops early and is prolific, producing tasty, bright yellow fruits — an excellent tomato.

Modern greenhouse varieties such as **'Aromata'**, **'Moravi'** and **'Merlot'** are significantly disease-resistant compared with older types.

The Black Krim has a fabulous flavor

There's plenty of light by the window

 ## cultivation

Propagation
A minimum temperature of 60°F (16°C) is needed for germination, but seedlings can tolerate lower night temperatures if those during the day are above this level.

In cool climates, for growing in heated greenhouses, sow from midwinter. For growing outdoors or in an unheated greenhouse, sow seed indoors 1 inch deep in trays of seed compost, 6–8 weeks before the last frost is due or sow 2–3 seeds in 3-inch pots or modules, thinning to leave the strongest seedling.

Transplant tray- or module-grown seedlings into 3-inch pots when 2–3 leaves have formed, keeping the plants in a light, well ventilated position. Harden off carefully and plant out when there is no danger of frost and air temperatures are at least 45°F (7°C) with soil temperatures at a minimum of 50°F (10°C).

Transplant, with the first true leaves just above the soil level, when the flowers on the first truss appear. Do not worry if your plants have become spindly; planting them deeply stimulates the formation of roots on the buried stems, making the plants more stable.

Tomatoes can also be fluid-sown from mid-spring *in situ* or in a cold frame for transplanting after warming the soil. Germinate on moist paper towel at 70°F (21°C), sowing when the rootlets are a maximum of ⅕ inch long (see advice on fluid sowing). Sow outdoors in drills and thin to leave the strongest seedling or in "stations" at their final spacing. Cover the drills with compost and protect them with cloches until the first flowers appear.

When sowing in cold frames, sow seed in rows 5–6 inches apart, thinning to 4–5 inches apart in the rows. Transplant carefully when the plants are 6–8 inches tall.

Alternatively, buy plants grown individually in pots rather than packed in boxes or trays, using a reliable supplier. Plant "cordon" types 15–18 inches apart, or in double rows with 36 inches between each pair of rows. Bush types should be planted 18–24 inches apart and dwarf cultivars 8–12 inches apart, depending on the variety.

Closer spacing produces earlier crops; wider spacing generally produces slightly higher yields.

Growing
Outdoor tomatoes need a warm, sheltered position, ideally against a sunny wall, in a moisture-retentive, well-drained soil. Add well-rotted organic matter where necessary and lime acidic soils to create a pH of 5.5–7. If tomatoes are grown in very rich soil or are fed with too much nitrogen they produce excessive leaf growth at the expense of flowers and fruit. Fruit will not set at night temperatures below 55°F (12°C) and day temperatures above 90°F (33°C). Night temperatures around 76°F (25°C) may well cause blossom to drop. Tomatoes should be fed with a liquid general fertilizer until established, then with a high-potassium fertilizer to encourage flowering and fruiting. Use lukewarm water to avoid shocking plants.

Keep crops weed-free by hoeing and hand weeding, taking care not to damage the stems, or mulch with a layer of organic matter.

Keep them constantly moist but not waterlogged; erratic watering causes the fruits to split and also encourages blossom end rot, particularly when plants are grown in containers or growbags. Use lukewarm water. In dry conditions or when the first flowers appear they need about 3 gallons water each week. Careful watering and feeding is essential (be restrained!), particularly near harvest time to ensure that the fruits are not excessively

Be prepared to recycle and improvise

watery and have a good flavor. Feed with tomato fertilizer according to the manufacturer's instructions.

Cordons need supporting with canes, strings or a frame. Using a sharp knife or by pinching between the finger and thumb, remove sideshoots when they appear and "stop" plants by removing the growing tip 2–3 leaves above the top truss when 3–5 trusses have been formed or when the plant has reached the top of the support. The number of trusses on each plant depends on the growing season: in shorter growing seasons, leave fewer trusses. Remove leaves below the lowest truss to encourage air circulation, but not too many.

In seasons when ripening is slow, remove some of the leaves near to the trusses with a sharp knife, exposing fruits to the sunshine.

To keep the fruit clean and stop fruit from rotting, grow bush tomatoes on a mulch of straw, felt or crop covers laid over the soil. Black polyethylene or even a split bin liner (with the edges anchored by burying them in the soil) absorbs heat, warms the soil, conserves moisture and helps fruit to ripen. Rotate crops annually.

Maintenance

Spring Sow crops under cover and, later, outdoors.
Summer Keep crops watered, fed and weed-free. Shade and ventilate as necessary. Remove any sideshoots. Harvest.
Autumn Ripen later outdoor crops under cloches or indoors.
Winter Harvest crops in midwinter from cuttings taken in late summer.

Protected Cropping

In cooler climates, more reliable harvests can be achieved by growing tomatoes in an unheated greenhouse or polyethylene tunnels. Rotate crops to avoid the build-up of pests and diseases and sterilize or replace the soil every 2–3 years, or use containers. To assist pollination and fruit set, particularly of plants grown indoors, mist occasionally and tap the trusses once the flowers have formed; do this around midday if possible. (It is not so important for outdoor crops, as wind movement assists pollination.) Shade greenhouses before the heat of summer and ventilate well in warm conditions.

A fascinating innovation is the "Wall-o-Water," a series of connected plastic tubes filled with water that absorbs

A tomato plant supported by a trellis

heat during the day and warms by radiated heat at night. This is reusable and offers protection down to 16°F (-8°C), extending the growing season and warming the soil. Adding roughly 1 part bleach to 500 parts water will prevent the formation of algae on the inside of the tubes.

For tomatoes at Christmas, take cuttings in midsummer from sideshoots 5 inches long and root them in a container of sharp sand or perlite and water. When roots appear they can be potted into 4 inch pots and grown on under cover.

Protect newly planted outdoor tomatoes with cloches or floating crop covers until they become established. Once the first flowers are pushing against the cover, make slits along the center; about 7–10 days later slit the remainder of the cover and leave as a shelter alongside the plants. "Indeterminate" varieties can then be tied to canes.

Harvesting and Storing

Harvest fruits as they ripen, about 7–8 weeks after planting for bush types and 10–12 weeks for "cordon" varieties. Lift and break the stem at the "joint" just above the fruit. Outdoor crops should be harvested before the first frosts. Towards the end of the season, "cordon" varieties with unripe fruit can be lifted by the roots and hung upside down in a frost-free shed to ripen.

Alternatively, they can be detached from their support, laid on straw and covered with cloches or put in a drawer or a paper bag with a ripe banana or apple (the

ethylene these produce ripens the fruit). Bush and dwarf types can be ripened under cloches.

Tomatoes can be cooked and jarred in airtight jars. To freeze, skin and core when ripe, simmer for 5 minutes, then sieve, cool and pack in a rigid container.

Tomatoes stay fresh for about a week in a plastic bag or the salad drawer of a refrigerator. To retain flavor they are better stored at 59°F (15°C).

Dry large "meaty" tomatoes in the sun or the oven. Cut into halves or thirds and put skin side down on a tray and cover with a gauze frame as a protection from insects. Ideal drying conditions are in warm, dry windy weather, but they should be brought indoors at night if dew is likely to form. Humid conditions are not suitable for outdoor drying. Oven-dry just below 145°F (65°C) until tomatoes are dried but flexible. Stored in airtight containers in a cool place, they can last for up to 9 months. Before use, put the tomatoes in boiling water or a 50:50 mix of boiling water and vinegar and allow them to stand until soft. Drain and marinate for

Growing bags can be productive

several hours in olive oil with added garlic to suit your taste. They last in the marinade for about a month and are excellent with pasta and tomato sauce.

Pests and Diseases

Blossom end rot appears as a hard, dark, flattened patch at the end of the fruit away from the stalk. This indicates a deficiency in calcium, usually caused by erratic watering. It is often a problem with plants grown in growbags. Water and feed regularly, particularly during hot weather. Erratic watering causes fruit to split, which may also happen with sudden growth after overcast weather. Pick and use split fruits immediately.

Greenback — hard, green patches appearing near the stalk, caused by sun scorch and overheating — is more of a problem with plants growing under glass. Sometimes this becomes an internal condition known as whitewall. Shade and ventilate well, water regularly and feed with a high-potassium liquid fertilizer.

Curled leaves are caused by extreme temperature fluctuations between day and night. It is often a

Alicante

problem in greenhouses: shade, ventilate and wet down. Close ventilation before temperatures drop. Whitefly, aphids and red spider mite can be a problem, as can potato blight in wet summers: dark blotches with lighter margins appear on the leaves. Spray with a copper fungicide or grow resistant varieties.

Plants with verticillium wilt droop during the day and usually recover overnight. Lower leaves turn yellow and cut stems have brown markings on the inside. Do not plant when the soil is cold, rotate crops regularly, replace the soil, mist regularly and shade. Mounding moist compost round the stem encourages the formation of a secondary root system. The symptoms and control of fusarium wilt are similar.

Tobacco mosaic and other viruses show as mottling on the leaves, some of which may be misshapen; inside the fruit is browned and pitted and growth is stunted. Dispose of affected plants, wash your hands and sterilize tools by passing them through a flame. Grow the following year's plants in sterilized compost or in growbags.

Tomato moth caterpillars eat the fruit. They are about 1½ inches long and green or brown with a pale lemon line along the body. They appear from late spring to early summer. Check the underside of leaves and squash the eggs. Check over fruits thoroughly and remove by hand.

The symptoms of magnesium deficiency are yellowing between the leaf veins, older leaves being affected first. Spray, drench or scatter magnesium sulfate around the base. Wherever possible, grow disease-resistant varieties.

 container growing

Tomatoes are excellent for containers, pots or growbags, indoors or outside where they can be included in "edible" displays in window boxes, pots and hanging baskets.

Grow in 9-inch pots of loam-based compost with high fertilizer levels. For requirements see "Growing" and "Protected Cropping." Bushy varieties are ideal. Plants in containers dry out rapidly, so careful feeding and watering is essential. Water regularly and remember to label your plants.

Marigolds keep whitefly away

 companion planting

Grow with French marigolds to deter whitefly. Tomatoes grow well with basil, parsley, alliums, nasturtiums and asparagus.

 medicinal

Tomatoes contain lycopene and are believed to reduce the risk of cancer and appendicitis.

In American herbal medicine, tomatoes have been used to treat dyspepsia, liver and kidney complaints and are also said to cure constipation.

 warning

Some doctors believe that tomatoes aggravate arthritis and may be responsible for food allergies. The leaves and stems are poisonous.

culinary

In salads, tomatoes are particularly good with mozzarella, basil and olive oil. They are also good with chives. Some people prefer to peel them first, by immersing in boiled water for 1 minute to loosen the skins. Use in soups, stews, sauces and omelettes.

Tomatoes are wonderful grilled: cut them in half and cover the cut surface with olive oil, pepper and sugar. Grill for 5 minutes. Alternatively, glaze them with wine and brown sugar and grill.

Try a BLT — a cold bacon, lettuce and tomato sandwich. Eat "currant" and "cherry" varieties as a snack. Use "beefsteak" varieties as a garnish with steak or hollow out and stuff with shrimp, potato salad, cold salmon, cottage cheese or egg salad filling. Serve hot or cold.

Green tomatoes can be sliced, dipped in batter and then breadcrumbs, and fried in hot oil, made into chutney or jam or be added to orange marmalade.

Jean-Christophe Novelli's Gazpacho Soup
Serves 6

1 pound very ripe cherry tomatoes
2 large over-ripe tomatoes
2 tablespoons truffle oil
⅓ cup olive oil
4 teaspoons white wine vinegar
Unrefined superfine sugar
Salt and freshly ground black pepper
1 pound bright red peppers, chopped
6 sprigs fresh coriander

Place the tomatoes, truffle oil and olive oil in a blender and add half the vinegar, 2 teaspoons sugar and a little seasoning. Blend together, thin with water if necessary, and season to taste. Put through a fine sieve and chill for at least 2 hours.

Rinse out the blender, then blend the peppers with 3 tablespoons water to a purée. Pass through a fine sieve and stir in 1½ tablespoons sugar and the remaining vinegar. Put the sieved purée in a pan and simmer until reduced to a syrup. Allow to cool to room temperature.

Stuffed Tomatoes

To finish, carefully pour the chilled gazpacho soup into a bowl, drizzle some red pepper syrup over the surface and serve garnished with coriander.

Stuffed Tomatoes
Serves 4

In times gone by Catholics all over Europe ate these on fast days, when meat was not allowed.

4 large ripe tomatoes
3 cups white breadcrumbs (day-old bread)
⅔ cup milk
2 eggs, lightly beaten
2 cloves garlic, finely crushed
2 tablespoons chopped fresh basil
2 tablespoons finely chopped fresh parsley
1 onion, finely chopped

2 tablespoons toasted breadcrumbs
5–6 tablespoons grated Gruyère cheese
Olive oil
Salt and freshly ground black pepper

Remove a slice from the top of each tomato and scoop out the pulp. Season the insides of the tomatoes with salt and pepper, and arrange in a greased baking dish.

Preheat the oven to 350°F (180°C). To make the stuffing, combine the white breadcrumbs with the milk and eggs in a bowl and add the garlic, herbs and onions. Season with salt and pepper and fill the tomatoes. Sprinkle over the toasted breadcrumbs and Gruyère and drizzle over a little olive oil to prevent burning. Bake until the tomatoes are tender, about 30 minutes.

Manihot esculenta (syn. *M. utilissima*). Euphorbiaceae
CASSAVA

Also known as Tapioca, Yucca, Manioc. Tall herbaceous perennial grown for edible tubers and leaves. Tender. Value: mainly starch; small amounts of vitamin B, C and protein.

One of the most important food crops in the humid tropics, cassava is believed to have been cultivated since at least 2500 BCE. Unknown as a wild plant, it may have originated in equatorial South America in the Andean foothills, the Amazon basin or regions of savannah vegetation. The earliest archaeological records, from coastal Peru, date from 1000 BCE. Tubers contain highly toxic cyanide, which is removed by cooking; accounts tell of starving European explorers eating raw manioc and dying at the moment they thought sustenance had been found. The indigenous Indians tipped their arrows and blowpipe darts with its toxic sap; Arawak Indians committed suicide by biting into uncooked tubers rather than be tortured by the Conquistadors.

The Portuguese brought the crop to West Africa, whence it quickly spread, reaching Sri Lanka in 1786, India in 1794 and Java by 1835. An estimated 62 million tons of cassava is produced annually, much of it in West Africa, where it is eaten as "fufu."

 varieties

Manihot esculenta is tall and branched and its stems becoming woody with age. The leaves are long-stalked, with 5–9 lobes; toxic latex is present in all parts of the plant. The swollen tubers are cylindrical or tapering, forming a cluster just below the soil surface, and weigh 10–20 pounds.

There are two types. **"White Cassava"** is sweet, soft and used as a source of starch; **"yellow"** varieties are bitter and usually grown as a vegetable. The more primitive bitter varieties contain larger quantities of cyanide, which is washed out by boiling in several changes of water before cooking. In recent selections of "sweet" varieties, most of the toxin is in the skin, and tubers are edible after simple cooking.

There are well over 100 different forms with local names. **'Nandeeba'**, quick to mature, and **'Macapera'**, used for boiling, are both from Brazil.

 cultivation

Propagation
Take cuttings from mature stems 6–12 inches long; plant 48 inches apart in rows 39 inches apart or 'pits' 36–41 inches square in a grid pattern. Planting cuttings upright, leaving the top 2 inches exposed, gives best results. Plant cuttings at the start of the rainy season.

Growing
Cassava flourishes where the warm rainy season is followed by a dry period. It has good resistance to drought; in a constantly wet climate, there is excessive stem growth and tuber formation is poor. Soils should be deep, rich and free-draining. It is often grown on ridges or mounds as it dislikes waterlogging. Dig deeply before planting, adding well-rotted organic matter. Earth up as necessary. Cassava is a heavy feeder and cannot usually be grown for more than 3 years on the same ground.

Maintenance
Spring Dig in organic matter before planting.
Summer Plant cuttings at the start of the rainy season.
Autumn Keep weed-free.
Winter Harvest at maturity.

CASSAVA

Typically tropical

Protected Cropping

In cool temperate zones, plants can be grown as a "novelty crop" in a hothouse. Prepare the borders and cultivate as for "Growing." Water well during the growing season and reduce watering during winter.

Harvesting and Storing

Varieties are harvested from 8 months to 2 years after planting, depending on the locality and variety. Harvest when plants have flowered and the leaves are yellow. Lift the whole plant and carefully remove the tubers. They store for up to 2 years in the ground, but should be used within 4–5 days of lifting.

Pests and Diseases

Whitefly and fungal diseases can be a problem.

Bacterial diseases, scale and cassava mosaic are a real problem in Africa. Plants are highly resistant to locusts.

 other uses

Cassava is also a source of starch for the manufacture of plywood, textiles, adhesives and paper.

 warning

All parts of the plant contain toxic latex. Prepare tubers thoroughly before eating. Inhabitants of Guyana take chilies steeped in rum as an antidote to yucca poisoning, but do not rely on it!

 culinary

The fresh root is equivalent in starch to 33% of its weight in rice and 50% in bread, but its nutritional value is unbalanced and high consumption often leads to protein deficiency.

Wash thoroughly and remove the skin and rind with a sharp knife or potato peeler. Boil in several changes of water and allow to dry before cooking.

It can be eaten mashed or boiled as a vegetable or made into dumplings and cakes. Mix with coconut and sugar to make biscuits. The juice from grated cassava is boiled down and flavored with cinnamon, cloves and brown sugar to make "cassareep," a powerful antiseptic and essential to the West Indian dish, Pepperpot. Tapioca flour is made from ground chips.

In Africa, the fresh root is washed, peeled, boiled and pounded with a wooden pestle to make "fufu." Cook cassava chunks in boiling water for 45–50 minutes, drain, cool, pound into dough and shape into egg-sized balls to add to soups and stews as a traditional African accompaniment.

Roots of "sweet" forms can be roasted like sweet potato, baked or fried in slices.

Young leaves can be boiled or steamed and eaten with a pat of butter.

Cassava Chips (Singkong)

These thin, crispy wafers are perfect served as a snack or as a garnish. Allow ½ pound per person to accompany a plain meat course.

Slice the cassava very thinly and leave to dry. Heat some peanut or vegetable oil (do not allow it to smoke) in a wok or a deep pan. Deep-fry 1–3 slices at a time by immediately submerging each below the surface of the oil. Remove quickly from the heat and drain well on layers of paper towels.

Cooked Singkong can be stored in an airtight container for several weeks, but is best served immediately.

Medicago sativa. Papilionacae

ALFALFA

Also known as Lucerne, Purple Medick. Grown as annual or short-lived perennial for seed sprouts and young leaf shoots. Hardy. Value: good source of iron, and protein.

"Medick" comes from the Latin *Herba medica*, the Median or Persian herb, imported to Greece after Darius found it in the kingdom of the Medes. It was a vital fodder crop of ancient civilizations in the Near East and Mediterranean, and known in Britain by 1757. Today, alfalfa is valued by gardeners as a green manure as well as a nutritious vegetable. Its blooms in the wildflower meadow are rich in nectar, while the leaves are a commercial source of chlorophyll.

 varieties

The species *Medicago sativa* is a fast-growing evergreen legume with cloverlike leaves; growing ultimately to 3 feet, it has spikes of violet and blue flowers. It produces quality crops on poor soils, as it is highly effective at fixing nitrogen in the root nodules.

Penetrating up to 20 feet into the ground, the roots draw up nutrients and aerate the soil. Agricultural varieties are available. If you want to sprout alfalfa seeds, buy untreated seed; that sold for sowing as a crop is usually chemically treated.

 cultivation

Alfalfa can be grown as a short-lived perennial, a "cut and come again" crop or as seedsprouts. It tolerates low rainfall and can be grown in any soil, in temperate to subtropical conditions or at altitude in the tropics.

Propagation
Sow in spring or from late summer to autumn. Thin those grown as perennials to 10 inches apart when

Alfalfa flowering in California

ALFALFA

culinary

Young shoot tips and sprouted seeds can be used raw in salads or cooked lightly.

For a tasty salad, try it with hard-boiled eggs (1 per person), anchovies and capers served on a bed of endive and radicchio leaves. To stir-fry, pour a little oil in a pan, add the alfalfa, stir briskly for 2 minutes; serve immediately.

companion planting

Alfalfa accumulates phosphorus, potassium, iron and magnesium; it keeps grass green longer in drought.

container growing

Sow "cut and come again" crops in a bright open position in a loam-based compost with low fertilizer levels; water pots regularly.

medicinal

An infusion of young leaves in water is used to increase vitality, appetite and weight. The young shoots, rich in minerals and vitamin B, are highly nutritious and the seeds appear to reduce cholesterol levels.

large enough to handle. Sow "cut and come again" crops, spaced evenly, by broadcasting or in shallow drills 4–5 inches wide.

Growing

Prepare seedbeds in winter, fork the area, remove debris and stones, rake level. Keep weed-free until established. Cut perennials to within a few inches of the base after flowering and renew every 3–4 years, as old plants become straggly.

Maintenance

Spring Sow seed outdoors.
Summer Harvest young shoots from perennials.
Autumn Sow protected crops.
Winter Prepare seedbed.

Protected Cropping

Sow alfalfa seeds under cloches, horticultural fleece or glass in late summer to autumn to harvest a winter crop.

Harvesting

Harvest "cut and come again" crops when about 2 inches long a few weeks after sowing. Cut back plants regularly to encourage new growth; they provide young growths for many harvests.

Sprouting Seeds

To sprout alfalfa, soak seeds overnight or for several hours, pour seeds into a sieve and rinse. Put several layers of moist paper towel in the base of a jar and cover with a ⅕ inch layer of seed. Cut a square from a pair of nylons or piece of muslin to cover the top, securing with a band. Place in a bright position, away from direct sun, maintaining constant temperatures around 68°F (20°C). Rinse seed daily by filling the jar with water and pouring off again. Harvest shoots after 3–7 days, when they have nearly filled the jar. Wash and dry sprouts and use as required; do not store more than 2 days, as salmonella develops quickly.

Pests and Diseases

Rabbits can be a problem.

Healthy eating for all

Momordica charantia. Cucurbitaceae
KARELA

Also known as Bitter Melon, Bitter Gourd, Balsam Pear, Fu Gua, Momordica, Peria. Annual climber grown for edible fruits and leaves. Tender. Value: fruit a good source of iron, ascorbic acid and vitamin C; leaves and young shoots contain traces of minerals.

This strange-looking fruit with skin the texture of a crocodile has been grown throughout the humid tropics for centuries. Rudyard Kipling's description in Mowgli's "Song Against People" conveys the plant's vigor as it climbs to 13 feet with the aid of tendrils:

I will let loose against you the fleet-footed vines,
I will call in the Jungle to stamp out your lines.
The roofs shall fade before it, the house-beams shall fall;
And the Karela shall cover it all.

The strongly vanilla-scented flowers are followed by the elongated fruit. When ripe, it splits at the tip into three sections, exposing brown or white seeds surrounded by blood-red pulp. Fruits are best eaten young.

Go on, try it!

 varieties

Male and female flowers are borne on the same plant. Male flowers are 2–4 inches long; females are similar, but with a slender basal bract. The fruit can grow up to 10 inches — which ripens to become orange-yellow, though a white variety is grown in India and eastern Asia.

'Baby Doll' has top-quality, small fruit and is easy to grow. 'Bankok Large' produces dark green fruit of excellent quality and 'Japan Green Spindle' produces spindle-shaped fruit. 'Taiwan Large' is high-yielding. 'Taiwan White' is highly ornamental with white fruit and 'Winter Beauty' is creamy white in color.

 cultivation

Propagation
In humid tropical climates, sow at the start of the rainy season, placing 2–3 seeds outdoors in "stations" 3 feet apart, in and between the rows. Thin after germination, leaving the strongest seedling. Water plants as needed.

The first flowers appear 30–35 days after sowing. In temperate zones, sow seed in early spring under glass at 68°F (20°C) in peat-substitute compost. Keep the compost moist with tepid water and repot as necessary when roots become visible through the drainage holes.

Growing

Karela flourish in moderate to high temperatures with sunshine and high humidity. Plant in beds or mounds of rich, moisture-retentive, free-draining soil. Dig in plenty of well-rotted manure or similar organic matter before sowing.

Pinch out the terminal shoots when they are 1–1½ inches long to encourage branching, then train the stems into trees or over fences, trellis or frames covered with 6-inch mesh netting. Keep plants moist and weed-free.

Maintenance

Spring Sow seed under glass in peat-substitute compost.
Summer Keep plants well fed and watered.
Autumn When cropping finishes, add leaves and stems to your compost heap
Winter Prepare the greenhouse border for the following year's crop.

Protected Cropping

Grow under cover in temperate zones. Plants need hot, humid conditions in bright light. When growing plants in the greenhouse border, prepare the soil as for "Growing."

Growth is better restricted in borders and containers. Stop the shoot tips when the main stems are 5 feet long, training the lateral stems along wires or trellis.

Appearances are deceiving

Once a flower has formed, allow 2 more leaves to appear, then pinch out the growing tip. If it is a male flower or a flower does not form, cut the stem back to the first leaf to allow a replacement to form. Flowers should be hand-pollinated.

You should damp down the greenhouse floor regularly during hot weather.

Harvesting and Storing

The first fruits appear about 2 months after sowing, are yellow-green in color and should be harvested when they are about 1½ inches long. They can be eaten when longer.

Fruits can be kept in a cool dark place for several days or stored in the salad drawer of a refrigerator for 4 weeks. Karela can also be sliced and dried for use out of season.

Pests and Diseases

Fruit fly is common; spray with contact insecticide or protect the fruits with a piece of paper wrapped around the fruit and tied with string round the stalk. Red spider mite is a common pest under cover. Leaves become mottled and bronzed. Check plants regularly; small infestations are easily controlled — isolate young plants. The mite prefer hot, dry conditions, so keep humidity high or use biological control.

 ## container growing

Plants can be grown indoors in containers containing a rich, well-drained potting mixture of equal parts loam-based compost and well-rotted organic matter with added peat and grit.

Keep the compost moist with tepid water and feed every 2 weeks with a liquid general fertilizer.

 ## medicinal

The fruits are said to be tonic, stomachic and carminative and are a herbal remedy for rheumatism, gout, and diseases of the liver and spleen. In Brazil, the seeds are used as an anthelmintic. Its fruits, leaves and roots are used in India and Puerto Rico for diabetes. In India, leaves are applied to burns and used as a poultice for headaches and the roots used to treat hemorrhoids. In Malaya they are used as a poultice for elephants with sore eyes.

culinary

Remove the seeds from mature fruit, and remove any bitterness by salting. Young fruits do not need to be salted.

Karela are ideal diced in curries, chop suey or pickles, stuffed with meat, shrimps, spices and onions and fried or added to meat and fish dishes. Mature fruits can be parboiled before being added to a dish or cooked like zucchini and eaten as a vegetable.

Young shoots and leaves are cooked like spinach.

Pelecing Peria
Serves 4

Sri Owen gives this recipe in her marvellous book, *Indonesian Food and Cookery*. Some of the ingredients need determination to track down, but it is worth the trouble.

3–4 karela (peria)
Salt
6 cabé rawit (or hot red chilies)
3 candlenuts
2 cloves garlic
1 piece terasi (shrimp paste, available at Thai shops)
1 tablespoon vegetable oil
Juice of 1 lime

Cut the karela lengthwise in half, take out the seeds, then slice like cucumbers. Put the slices into a colander, sprinkle liberally with salt and leave for at least 30 minutes. Wash under cold running water before boiling for 3 minutes with a little salt.

Pound the cabé rawit, candlenuts, garlic and terasi in a mortar until smooth. Heat the oil in a wok or frying pan and fry for about 1 minute. Add the karela and stir-fry for 2 minutes; season with salt and lime juice. Serve hot or cold.

Oxalis tuberosa. Oxalidaceae
OCA

Also known as Iribia, cuiba, New Zealand yam. Perennial grown for tubers. Half hardy. Value: about 85% water; some carbohydrates; small amounts of protein.

This is common in the high-altitude Andes from Venezuela to northern Argentina, where it is second only to the potato in popularity. At the northern end of Lake Titicaca, more than 150 steep terraces dating from the Incas are still cultivated. Oca is grown in New Zealand, where it was introduced from Chile in 1869. Today it is rarely found in European or American gardens, though it was once grown as a potato substitute. Tubers form in autumn when day lengths are less than 9 hours.

 varieties

Oxalis tuberosa is bushy to 10 inches tall, with tri-lobed leaves and orange-yellow flowers. It produces small tubers 2–4 inches long which are yellow, white, pink, black or piebald.

 cultivation

Propagation
Plant single tubers or slice into several sections, each with an "eye" or dormant bud, and dust the cut surfaces with fungicide. Plant 5 inches deep and 12 inches apart with 12 inches between rows.

In frost-free climates plant in mid-spring; in cooler areas propagate under cover in 5–8-inch pots of compost before planting out once frosts have passed.

Growing
Oca flourish in deep fertile soils, so incorporate organic matter before planting. Earthing up before planting increases the yield.

Maintenance
Spring Plant tubers.
Summer Water as necessary.
Autumn Tubers can be lifted when needed.
Winter Store tubers in sand.

Protected Cropping
Where early or late frosts are likely, grow under cover to extend the harvest season. Plant in mid-spring in greenhouse borders. Harvest from mid-autumn to early winter.

Extend outdoor cropping by protecting with horticultural fleece or cloches.

Harvesting and Storing
Tubers are formed in autumn and can be stored in sand in a dry frost-free place. Lift just before the first frosts or protect with fleece and harvest later.

Pests and Diseases
Slugs are often a problem.

 culinary

Tubers have been selected over the centuries for flavor and reduced levels of calcium oxalate crystals, which otherwise render them inedible. Leave them for a few days to become soft before eating. In South America they are dried in the sun until floury and less acidic. If dried for several weeks, they become sweet, tasting similar to dried figs.

The acidity can be removed by boiling in several changes of water. The flavor of tubers even improves once frozen. Oca can be eaten raw, roasted, boiled, candied like sweet potato and added to soups and stews. Use leaves and young shoots in salads or cook them like sorrel.

Oca and Bacon
Clean 1 pound oca and cut into cubes. Boil in salted water until just tender; drain and combine with ½ pound bacon that has been diced and fried. Coat with mayonnaise, sprinkle over fresh chives and season. Serve warm.

 container growing

Oca grow well in containers, although yields are lower. Tubers should be planted in spring in 12-inch pots in loam-based compost with moderate fertilizer levels, with added organic matter. Regular watering is vital, particularly as tubers begin to form. Allow the compost surface to dry out before rewatering. An occasional feed with liquid fertilizer helps to boost growth.

 companion planting

Oca grow well with potatoes and can be grown under runner beans, maize or crops of a similar height.

 warning

Prepare tubers correctly before eating to remove calcium oxalate crystals.

Pachyrrhizus erosus. Leguminosae
JICAMA

Also known as Yam Bean, Potato Bean, Mexican Water Chestnut, Dou Shou, Sha Kot. Tender, vining perennial. Value: low in starch and calories, high in fiber, a good source of vitamin C and potassium.

Originating in tropical American and naturalized in Florida, the Jicama is very popular in the local cuisine of southern China and the Philippines. In Mexico, it is one of four foods included in rituals for the "Festival of the Dead" celebrated on November 1, alongside sugar, tangerines and peanuts.

Grown as a novelty crop in cooler climates, its attractive flowers also give it considerable value as an ornamental plant.

 ## varieties

Pachyrrhizus erosus is a scrambling perennial with attractive violet and purple flowers. Two major types are grown in Mexico, where it is a popular edible crop; **'Jicama de leche'** with dark skin and spindle-shaped roots, which is rather dry and **'Jicama de agua'** with light skin and a succulent, sweet, watery flavor to the tubers.

 ## cultivation

Propagation
From mid-spring, sow two seeds in a 4-inch pot filled with seed compost and place in a propagator or on a warm windowsill at 68°F (20°C). Thin after germination, leaving the strongest seedling and transplant regularly as the plants grow, supporting the stems with a stick. Plants grow rapidly: allow as much growing time as possible before they are planted outdoors (if that is what you intend to do); ideally the seeds should be sown around 6 to 8 weeks before the final frosts in spring. Although tubers can be stored at temperatures from 54–59°F (12.5–15°C) for replanting, they are very sensitive to chilling. It is much easier to save or buy fresh seeds the following year.

Growing jicama is day-length sensitive and the edible tubers are not formed until autumn when there are fewer than 9 hours of daylight; unfortunately, this often coincides with the first frosts. Vines are best grown indoors in temperate climates, so they have enough

energy to produce sizable tubers at the end of the growing season, before light and cold restrict growth.

If growing plants outdoors, warm the soil with cloches before planting the large ones, covering them with cloches for 2 to 3 weeks until they become acclimatized. Grow them like runner beans, along rows of canes or up "wigwams," in a sunny position in well-prepared, deep, light, rich, moisture-retentive soil, incorporating plenty of well-rotted organic matter, if necessary. Pinch out growth tips if plants become too large, and remove the flower buds, too; this has the added advantage of encouraging tuber growth.

Maintenance
Spring Sow seeds early in the season.
Summer Keep plants well watered.
Autumn Harvest after the first frosts.
Winter Order seed.

Protected Cropping
Grow in large tubs in the greenhouse or polyethylene tunnel border, then feed and water well during the

 ## culinary

Like water chestnut, jicama is very refreshing when peeled and eaten raw. Tubers can be fried, braised, boiled, eaten in casseroles, used as a bamboo shoot, water chestnut or mooli substitute, added to custards, puddings and fruit salads or eaten as a snack. In California it is commonly sliced and added to salads, in Mexico it is marinated with lime then served topped with chili powder; sometimes sour orange is used as a lime substitute. Crunchiness is retained after cooking. The best quality roots are about 4½ pounds in weight; older tubers become "woody" growing up to 7 feet long and weighing 45 pounds, at this stage they become fibrous and inedible. Only the young pods are edible, boil them thoroughly before eating and use as French beans.

growing season. A hot, humid environment encourages heavy cropping, so they are best grown under protection in temperate climates.

Harvesting and Storing
Cropping is most productive in temperate zones during hot summers. Harvest the tubers as late in the season as possible, once the top growth has been frosted. Harvest seed pods while immature.

Pests and Diseases
Bean seed weevil can be a problem; the seeds show evidence of tiny holes but usually germinate if sown. Alternatively, dry the seed, in silica gel, then freeze them for 48 hours.

 ## container growing

Plants can be grown in raised beds or very large containers, if preferred.

 ## warning

Mature seed pods contain rotenone: do not eat.

Pastinaca sativa. Apiaceae

PARSNIP

Biennial grown as annual for edible root. Hardy. Value: some carbohydrate, moderate vitamin E, smaller amounts of vitamins B and C.

This ancient vegetable is thought to have originated around the eastern Mediterranean. Exactly when it was introduced into cultivation is uncertain, as references to parsnips and carrots seem interchangeable in Greek and Roman literature: Pliny used the word *pastinaca* in the first century CE when referring to both. Tiberius Caesar was said to have imported parsnips from Germany, where they flourished along the Rhine — though it is possible that the Celts brought them back from their forays to the east long before that. In the Middle Ages, the roots were valued medicinally for treating problems as diverse as toothache, swollen testicles and stomach ache. In 16th-century Europe parsnips were used as animal fodder, and the country name of "madneps" or "madde neaps" reflects the fear that delirium and madness would be brought about by eating the roots.

Introduced to North America by early settlers, they were grown in Virginia by 1609 and were soon accepted by the Native North Americans, who readily took up parsnip growing. They were used as a sweetener until the development of beets in the 19th century; the juices were evaporated and the brown residue used as honey. Parsnip wine was considered by some to be equal in quality to Malmsey and parsnip beer was often drunk in Ireland. In Italy pigs bred for the best-quality Parma ham are fed on parsnips.

Avonresister

 varieties

Roots are "bulbous" (stocky, with rounded shoulders), "wedge" types (broad and long-rooted) or "bayonet" (similar, but long and narrow in shape).

'Alba' has small, thin, wedge- and bayonet-shaped roots and good canker resistance; top quality. 'All American' has wedge-shaped roots and is sweet-tasting. 'Arrow' should be sown in succession from mid-spring to midsummer for young roots and harvested from mid- to late summer for small roots. 'Avonresister' is small with bulbous roots, is sweet-tasting, performs well on poorer soil and grows rapidly. It also has excellent resistance to canker and bruising. 'Bugi Bijeli' is a Yugoslavian variety with a large, sweet root. 'Cobham Improved Marrow'* is wedge-shaped, medium in size and well-flavored, and resistant to canker. 'Exhibition Long' is extra-long with an excellent flavor. 'Gladiator'* produces large, vigorous, well-shaped and fine-flavored roots with good canker resistance. 'Javelin' is wedge- or bayonet-shaped, high-yielding and canker-resistant; "fanging" rarely occurs. 'Student' has long slender roots and is very tasty. It originated around 1810 from a wild parsnip found in the grounds of the Royal Agricultural College, England. 'Tender and True'* is an old variety that is very tasty, tender and sweet. It has very little core. 'White Gem' has wedge-shaped to bulbous smooth roots, with delicious flesh and good canker resistance. It is ideal for heavier soils.

PARSNIP

cultivation

Propagation

Parsnip seed must always be sown fresh, as it rapidly loses the ability to germinate. Seeds are also renowned for erratic, slow germination in the cold, wet conditions that often prevail early in the year when they are traditionally sown.

To avoid poor germination, sow later, from mid- to late spring, depending on the weather and soil conditions, when the ground is workable and temperatures are over 45°F (7°C).

Warm the soil with cloches or horticultural fleece a few weeks before sowing. Rake in a granular general fertilizer at 1½ pounds/sq ft 1–2 weeks before sowing. Rake the seedbed to a fine texture before sowing. Sow *in situ* on a still day so the light, papery seeds are not blown away.

In dry conditions, water drills before sowing 2–3 seeds at the recommended final spacing in "stations," thinning to leave the strongest seedling after germination. Sow radishes between the stations to act as a marker crop indicating where slower-germinating parsnip seeds are sown.

Alternatively, parsnip seeds can be sown thinly in drills ⅕–⅓ inch deep, sowing shorter-rooted varieties in rows 6–8 inches apart, thinning them to 2–4 inches, and larger types in rows 12 inches apart, thinning them to 5–8 inches.

In stony soil, make a hole up to 6 x 36 inches with a crowbar, fill with finely sieved soil or compost, sow 2–3 seeds in the center of the hole and thin to leave the strongest seedling. Grow short-rooted varieties in shallow soils.

Growing

Parsnips thrive in an open or lightly shaded site on light, free-draining, stone-free soil which was manured the previous year.

Traditionally, parsnips are not grown on freshly manured soil as this causes "fanging," or forking of the roots; however, recent research has not supported this. Dig the plot and add plenty of well-rotted organic matter in autumn or early winter the previous year. Deep digging is particularly important when growing long-rooted varieties.

The ideal pH is 6.5–7.0; lime where necessary, as roots grown in acidic soil are prone to canker. Rotate with other roots.

Parsnip flowers attract beneficial insects

Keep crops weed-free, by hoeing or hand weeding carefully to avoid damaging the roots, or by mulching with well-rotted organic matter. Do not let the soil dry out, as erratic watering causes roots to split. Water at 4–6 gallons/sq yd every 2 weeks during dry weather when the roots are swelling.

Maintenance

Spring Rake the seedbed to a fine tilth, apply general fertilizer, sow seed in modules, "fluid sow," or sow *in situ* when the soil is warm.
Summer Keep crops weed-free by mulching, hand weeding or careful hoeing.
Autumn Harvest crops.
Winter Cover crops with straw or bracken before the onset of inclement weather. Dig the soil for the following year's crop.

Protected Cropping

Possible germination problems can be avoided by pregerminating and fluid-sowing seed, or by sowing in modules under cover and transplanting before the tap root starts to develop.

Parsnip — an essential ingredient in winter

Harvesting and Storing

Most parsnips are a long-term crop and occupy the ground for around 8 months — a factor worth bearing in mind if your garden is small. Roots are extremely hardy and can remain in the ground until required.

Harvest from mid-autumn onwards, covering plants with straw, bracken or hessian for ease of lifting in frosty weather. Make sure you lift them carefully with a fork to avoid root damage.

Lift all your roots by winter and store them in boxes of moist sand, peat substitute or wood shavings in a cool shed.

Parsnips have a better flavor when they have been exposed for a few weeks to temperatures around freezing point. (This changes stored starch to sugar, increasing sweetness and improving the flavor.) Stored in a plastic bag in the refrigerator, they remain fresh for up to 2 weeks.

Wash, trim and peel roots, then cube and blanch in boiling water for 5 minutes before freezing them in plastic bags.

Peeled parsnips, ready for cooking

Seeds only have a short life

Pests and Diseases

Parsnip canker is a black, purple or orange-brown rot, often starting in the crown, which can be a problem during drought, when the crown is damaged or the soil is too rich. There is no chemical control. Sow crops later, improve drainage, keep the pH around neutral, rotate crops and sow canker-resistant varieties. Carrot fly can also be a problem.

 ## companion planting

Sow rapidly germinating plants such as lettuces between rows. Parsnips grow well alongside peas and lettuce, provided they are not in the shade.

Plant next to carrots and leave a few to flower the following year, as they attract beneficial insects.

 ## container growing

Shorter-rooted varieties can be grown in large containers of loam-based compost. Longer types are grown in large barrels, making a deep hole in the compost, as described above for stony soil. Make sure that containers are well drained.

 ## medicinal

In Roman times, parsnip seeds and roots were regarded as an aphrodisiac.

culinary

In 17th-century England, there are records of parsnip bread and "sweet and delicate parsnip cakes." They were often eaten with salt fish and were a staple during Lent.

Scrub or peel parsnips, and use boiled, baked, mashed or roasted with beef, pork or chicken. They combine particularly well with carrots.

Parsnips can be lightly cooked and eaten cold. Parboil and prepare like fries or slice into rings, dip in batter and eat as fritters. Grate into salads, add chopped and peeled to casseroles or soups. Or parboil, drain, then stew in butter and garnish with parsley. They are also good parboiled, then grilled with a sprinkling of Parmesan. Try steaming them whole, slicing them lengthwise and pan-glazing with butter, brown sugar and nutmeg, or garnishing them with chopped walnuts and a dash of sweet sherry.

Purée of Parsnips

Boil some parsnips and mix them with an equal quantity of mashed potatoes, plenty of salt and freshly ground black pepper, a little grated orange zest, a splash of thick cream and enough butter to make a smooth dish. Sprinkle with chopped flat-leaf parsley and serve piping hot. (Puréed parsnips are also wonderful combined with carrots and seasoned with nutmeg.)

Curried Parsnip Soup

Serves 4–6

2 pounds parsnips
1 large onion, sliced
1 tablespoon butter
2 cloves garlic, crushed
1 teaspoon curry powder
1 x 14-ounce can chopped tomatoes
4 cups vegetable stock
1 bay leaf
Sprig each of fresh thyme and parsley
4–6 teaspoons yogurt
Salt and freshly ground black pepper
Chopped fresh parsley, to garnish

Clean the parsnips and peel, if old. Chop them coarsely. Add the onion to a large soup pot with the butter and garlic and sauté over a medium heat until lightly browned (this helps to give the flavor of Indian cuisine). Stir in the curry powder and continue to cook for 1 minute, stirring constantly.

Add the parsnips and stir, coating them well in the curry and onion mixture, and add the tomatoes, stock and herbs. Stir thoroughly. Season, bring to the boil and simmer, covered, for about 15–20 minutes, until the parsnips are tender.

Remove the herbs. Then liquidize the soup, adjust the seasoning and garnish with yoghurt and parsley. This is delicious served with crusty bread.

Persea americana. Lauraceae

AVOCADO

Also known as Alligator Pear, Avocado Pear. Evergreen tree or shrub. Tender. Value: very rich in vitamin E, average fat content, high in monounsaturated fatty acids. A good source of protein.

This subtropical tree from Central America was originally introduced to Europe by the Conquistadors and has since been planted in many parts of the world. Its anglicized name is a corruption of the Aztec word *ahuacatl*, which was used to describe both its fruit and the testicle! There are three main races: Guatemalan fruits are large with a warty skin; Mexican ones are small; and large, smooth-skinned types come from the West Indies. All have been hybridized, producing hundreds of cultivars suitable for Mediterranean to tropical climates.

 ## varieties

'Anaheim' was found in California in 1910 and has glossy green skin of medium thickness and peels easily. **'Bacon'** is a Mexican type, commonly grown in Spain, with smooth green skin and pale yellow flesh. **'Edranol'** has butter-yellow flesh and an excellent flavor. **'Ettinger'** has pale green flesh and shiny, bright green skin. **'Hass'** is self-fertile, the skin dark purple when it matures, and the flesh is rich and creamy. More than 95 percent of avocados grown in California — the top avocado-producing State — are of the Haas variety.

cultivation

Avocados flourish in shelter and sunshine. The ideal soil is a slightly acid, moisture-retentive, free-draining loam. Improve sandy or clay soils by adding organic matter. Temperatures should be between 68–82°F (20–28°C) with humidity greater than 60 percent all year round.

Some can withstand temperatures down to 48–58°F (10–15°C). Allow 20 feet between the trees and the rows. In exposed areas, plant windbreaks to prevent damage.

During the growing season, apply 3–4½ pounds of general fertilizer in 2 or 3 doses. Mulch around the base to suppress weeds. Water during times of drought until trees are established.

Shape young trees to ensure a balanced crown. Remove diseased, damaged or crossing branches after fruiting. They withstand hard pruning. Plant several cultivars with overlapping or simultaneous flowering periods to produce fruit.

Growing under Glass

Grow in a large greenhouse, maintaining moderate temperatures and humidity according to the origin of the cultivar. Flowers and fruit are rarely produced in cool temperate zones, owing to low light intensity and reduced daylight hours.

 ## container growing

Repot young plants as the compost becomes congested with roots. Every 2–3 years repot established plants into a pot one size larger, using a loam-based compost with moderate fertilizer levels. Top-dress in the intervening years by removing and replacing the top 2–3 inches of compost in spring. Apply a general fertilizer every 2–3 weeks when plants are actively growing. Water as the compost surface dries out. Reduce watering in winter and do not feed.

In spring, prune side branches to encourage bushy growth. Containerised plants can be placed outdoors in summer in a warm, sheltered position when there is no danger of frost. During winter, they need a light, cool position with temperatures no lower than 61°F (16°C).

Maintenance
Spring Repot containerized plants.
Summer Feed, harvest and water as necessary.
Autumn Bring containerized plants indoors in cool temperate zones.
Winter Reduce watering and stop feeding avocados grown under glass.

Try growing your own

culinary

Bean sprouts can be eaten raw, in salads, with a suitable dressing or lightly cooked for about 2 minutes only in slightly salted water. (Be warned: overcooked shoots lose their taste.)

To stir-fry, use only a little oil, stirring briskly for about 2 minutes. In Oriental cooking, bean sprouts combine well with other vegetables, eggs, red meat, chicken and fish and can be used to stuff savoury pancakes, egg rolls and tortillas.

Stir-fried Mung Beans
Serves 2

1 bag mung beans
Groundnut oil, for frying
2 cloves garlic, crushed
½ cup chicken stock
1 tablespoon light soy sauce
1½ teaspoons cornstarch
2–3 spring onions, coarsely chopped

Rinse the mung beans well. Heat the oil and the garlic in a wok, then add the mung beans. Fry for 1 minute, stirring constantly.

Cover with chicken stock and cook until tender and the liquid has evaporated. Then stir in the soy sauce and the cornstarch. Cook for 2 minutes more.

Garnish with the spring onions and serve with rice.

Maintenance
Outdoors Broadcast or sow seed in drills; water when needed, as the soil dries out. Harvest before the pods split.

Sprouting Keep seeds moist. Harvest regularly.

Harvesting and Storing
Harvest shoots from 3 days onwards, when they are about 1–2 inches long. If the seed coats remain attached to the sprouts, soak them in water, then "top and tail," removing the seed and shoot tip. Store in the fridge. When growing for seed, gather before they split, to prevent the seeds being lost.

Pests and Diseases
Powdery mildew is a problem when plants are dry at the roots. Mulch and water regularly, remove diseased leaves immediately, spray with bicarbonate of soda, improve air circulation by thinning crops and destroy plant debris at the end of the season.

medicinal

The seeds are said to have a cooling and astringent effect on fever and an infusion is used as a diuretic when treating beriberi. In Malaya it is prescribed for vertigo.

warning

Do not let sprouted seeds become waterlogged, as they rapidly become moldy.

In 2002, the U.S. Food and Drug Administration issued a warning against eating the sprouts raw after an outbreak of salmonella poisoning. Buy only refrigerated sprouts and cook them at a high heat.

Mung beans for sale

RUNNER BEAN

Also known as Scarlet Runner. Perennial climber grown as annual in temperate climates for edible pods and seeds. Half hardy. Value: moderate levels of iron, vitamin C and beta carotene.

A native of Mexico, the runner bean has been known as a food crop for more than 2,200 years. In the late 16th century, Gerard's *Herball* mentions it as an ornamental introduced by the plant collector John Tradescant the Elder: "Ladies did not…disdain to put the flowers in their nosegays and garlands," and in the garden it was grown around gazebos and arbors. Vilmorin Andrieux commented in 1885: "In small gardens they are often trained over wire or woodwork, so as to form summer houses or coverings for walks." Philip Miller, keeper of Chelsea Physic Garden, is credited with being the first gardener to cook them.

It was the fashion in 17th-century England to experiment with soaking seeds. Mr. Gifford, minister of Montacute in Somerset, noted in his diary: "May 10th 1679, I steep'd runner beans in sack five days, then I put them in sallet-oyle five days, then in brandy four days and about noon set them in an hot bed against a south wall casting all liquor wherein they had been infused negligently about the holes, within three hours space, eight of the nine came up, and were a foot high with all their leaves, and on the morrow a foot more in height… and in a week were podded and full ripe." You could try this for yourself — or perhaps you would prefer to stick to today's more conventional methods!

varieties

Older cultivars were rather stringy unless eaten young; newer varieties are "stringless." Besides the traditional tall-growing climbers, there is also a choice of dwarf varieties that do not need supporting and are ideal for smaller gardens, early crops under cloches and in exposed sites.

Non-stringless types
'Enorma'* is ornamental, with red flowers. It has long pods and is very tasty. **'Liberty'*** has good-quality pods to 18–20 inches long. **'Painted Lady'**, a variety grown since the 19th century, has delicate red and white flowers and long pods.

Stringless types
'Aintree' has red flowers that are followed by good quality green pods. Tolerant of high temperatures. **'Celebration'*** has pink flowers that are followed by plenty of straight, well-flavored, good-quality pods. **'Desiree'** has white flowers and seeds and is high-yielding and tasty. **'Kelvedon Marvel'** is tasty, matures early and crops heavily. **'Lady Di'*** grows long, slim stringless pods with outstanding taste and tenderness. **'Red Rum'*** is very early, high-yielding, tasty and resistant

White Lady

Scarlet Emperor

to halo blight. **'Scarlet Emperor'** is a traditional "all rounder," tolerating a wide range of conditions. **'Snowy'** is white flowered and "sets" even in hot conditions where night temperatures are above 59°F (15°C); pods to 12 inches. **'White Lady'*** is less likely to be attacked by birds. Its white flowers are followed by huge crops of straight fleshy pods (late). **'Wisley Magic'*** is one of the heaviest yielding red-flowered varieties, producing masses of pods with a traditional flavor.

Dwarf varieties
'Hammonds Dwarf Scarlet' is ideal for the small garden. The pods are easy to harvest but the tops may need to be pinched out. **'Hestia'** produces bicolored flowers and long, slim pods. Ideal for pots or containers.

 ## cultivation

Propagation
Runner beans are not frost-tolerant and need a minimum soil temperature of 50°F (10°C) to germinate. Sow from late spring to early summer 2–3 inches deep, 6 inches apart in double rows 24 inches apart. To shelter pollinating insects they are better grown in blocks or several short rows, rather

than a single long one. Allow 3–6 feet between rows for ease of harvesting, depending on the cultivar.

Climbing types can be encouraged to bush by pinching out the main stems when they are around 10 inches; the sideshoots can be pinched out at the second leaf joint for a bushy plant needing little or no staking.

Seed sown outdoors crops in about 14–16 weeks, depending on climatic and cultural conditions.

Growing
Runner beans are not frost-hardy and are less successful in cooler areas unless you have a suitable microclimate. They flourish from 57–85°F (14–29°C), needing a warm, sheltered position to minimize wind damage and encourage pollinating insects.

Soil should be deep, fertile and moisture-retentive. Dig a trench at least 12 inches deep and 24 inches wide in late autumn to early winter before planting, adding plenty of well-rotted organic matter to the backfill. Before sowing, rake in 1½–2 pounds/sq ft of granular general fertilizer.

Water well when flowering

Painted Lady

Keep crops weed-free during early stages of growth. Mulch after germination or after transplanting. Watering is essential for good bud set: the traditional method of spraying flowers has little effect. As the first buds are forming and again as the first flowers are fully open plants need 14–31 gallons/sq ft. Crops should be rotated.

Climbers can be up to 10 feet or more tall and a good sturdy support should be in place before sowing or transplanting. Traditionally, a "wigwam" of canes, or a longer row of crossed canes, were used; these may need supporting strings at the end of each row, like tent guy ropes. Do improvise: I once saw a wonderful structure like a V-shaped frame, designed so the beans would hang down and make picking easier. Use canes, strong wooden stakes, steel tubes, or make frameworks of netting. There should be one cane or length of strong twine for each plant.

Maintenance
Spring Sow crops under cover or outdoors in late spring. Erect supports.
Summer Keep crops weed-free and well watered. Harvest regularly.
Autumn Continue harvesting until the first frosts.
Winter Prepare the soil for the following year's crop.

Protected Cropping
For earlier crops and in cooler climates, sow in boxes or tall pots of seed or multipurpose compost under cover from mid-spring, harden off and plant out from late spring. Protect indoor and outdoor crops with cloches or horticultural fleece until they are established.

Harvesting and Storing
Harvest from midsummer to mid-autumn. Picking is essential to ensure regular cropping, high yields and to avoid any "stringiness." Runner beans freeze well.

Pests and Diseases
Slugs, black bean aphid and red spider mite may prove troublesome.

Grey mold (*botrytis*) and halo blight may cause problems in wet or humid weather.

Mice may eat seeds.

Root rots may kill plants in wet or poorly drained soils. Rotate crops to avoid this.

 companion planting

Runner beans are compatible with all plants except the *Allium* family.

Grow with maize to protect the latter from corn army worms. Nitrogen-fixing bacteria in the roots improve

Harvest regularly for continued cropping

soil fertility. After harvesting, cut off tops, leave roots in the soil or add to compost heaps. They thrive with brassicas; Brussels sprout transplants are sheltered and grow on once beans die back.

Late in the season, their shade can benefit celery and salad crops if enough water is available.

 container growing

Runner beans can be grown in containers at least 8 inches wide by 10 inches deep, depending on the vigour of the cultivar.

Sow seeds 2 inches deep and 4–5 inches apart indoors in late spring, moving the container outdoors into a sunny site. Water frequently in warm weather, less often at other times. Feed with liquid general fertilizer if plants need a boost.

Stake tall varieties, pinching out the growing points when plants reach the top of their supports. Otherwise use dwarf varieties.

Protect seedlings from rabbits

culinary

Wash, top and tail, pull off stringy edges, slice diagonally and boil for 5–7 minutes. Drain and serve with a pat of butter. Alternatively, cook whole and slice after cooking.

Runner Bean Chutney
Makes 3 pounds

Clare Walker and Gill Coleman give this recipe in *The Home Gardener's Cookbook*:

2 pounds runner beans
1 pound onions
1 tablespoon salt
1 tablespoon mustard seeds
½ cup sultanas
1½ teaspoons ground ginger
1 level teaspoon turmeric
6 dried red chilies, left whole
2½ cups spiced vinegar
1 pound demerara sugar

Wipe, top, tail and string the beans and cut them into small slices. Place in a jam pan with the peeled and finely chopped onions. Add 1⅓ cups water, the salt and mustard seeds and simmer gently for 20–25 minutes until the beans are just tender.

Then add the sultanas, ginger, turmeric, chilies and spiced vinegar, bring back to a boil and simmer for a further 30 minutes, or until the mixture is fairly thick.

Stir in the sugar, allow to dissolve, then boil steadily for about 20 minutes until the chutney is thick. Pour into warm, dry jars, cover with thick plastic and seal with a lid, if available. Label and store in a cool, dry place for at least 3 months before using. The chilies can be removed before potting.

Phaseolus vulgaris. Papilionaceae

FRENCH BEAN

Also known as Common, Kidney, Bush, Pole, Snap, String, Green, Wax Bean; Haricot; Baked Bean; Flageolet; Haricot Vert. Annual grown for edible pods and beans. Half hardy. Value: moderate potassium, folic acid and beta carotene. Very rich in protein.

Evidence of the wild form, found in Mexico, Guatemala and parts of the Andes, has been discovered in Peruvian settlements from 8000 BCE. Both bush and climbing varieties were introduced to Europe during the Spanish conquest in the early 16th century, though the dwarf varieties did not become popular for two more centuries. They were first referred to as "kidney beans" by the English in 1551, alluding to the shape of their seeds.

Gerard in his *Herball* calls them "sperage" beans and "long peason," while Parkinson wrote: "Kidney beans boiled in water and stewed with butter were esteemed more savory… than the common broad bean and were a dish more oftentimes at rich men's tables than at the poor." Another writer commented in 1681: "It is a plant lately brought into use among us and not yet sufficiently known."

In Europe, "haricot vert" was used in ships' stores in voyages of exploration during the early 1500s. When European colonists first explored the Americas, they found climbing beans planted with maize, providing starch and protein for indigenous tribes.

The Prince

 varieties

This group contains considerable variety. Plants are dwarf (ideal for smaller gardens or containers) or climbing, pods are flat, oval or round in cross-section and are green, yellow (waxpods) or purple, or marbled.

The seeds are colorful and often mottled. As well as being grown for the pods, seeds are eaten fresh as "flageolets," or dried as "haricots."

Drying beans
'**Cannellino**' is a dwarf variety with white seeds. '**Canadian Wonder**', a Victorian variety, should be picked while young and tender, or dry for the red seeds. '**Czar**' produces long, rough pods; tasty when green or can be dried. '**Saissons**' has flat pods and tasty pale green seeds.

Climbing types
'**Kingston Gold**'* is high-yielding with golden-yellow pods and a first-class flavor. '**Hunter**'* is flat-podded, and crops heavily over a long period. '**Kwintus**'* produces tender, tasty pods. '**Limka**' is ideal for early or late growing under glass. '**Musica**'* can be sown early and is full of flavor. '**Romano**', an old variety, is tender, tasty and prolific, and excellent for freezing.

Dwarf or bush types
'**Annabel**'* is high-yielding, round and tasty — perfect for the patio. '**Chevrier Vert**', a classic French flageolet from 1880, is tasty and tender. '**Delinel**'* is a prolific and tasty "filet"-type with stringless pods to 6 inches long. '**Golddeleaf**' (very early) is prolific with pale yellow pods. '**Purple Queen**' is delicious, producing heavy yields of glossy purple pods. '**Purple Teepee**' is high-yielding, ornamental and easy to spot when harvesting, as pods are held high above the foliage. '**Royalty**' crops heavily with dark purple pods that turn green when cooked and are delicately flavored.

'Safari'* produces slim, tasty beans but low yields. The dark green pods of **'Sprite'*** freeze well. **'The Prince'***, an old favorite, has magnificent taste and is also good for freezing.

 ## cultivation

Propagation
French beans dislike cold wet soils and are inclined to rot; for successful germination, do not sow until the soil is a minimum of 50°F (10°C).

For early sowings or in cold weather, warm the soil 3–4 weeks beforehand with cloches or black polyethylene.

Sow successively from mid-spring to early summer in staggered drills 1½–2 inches deep with 9 inches between the rows and plants for optimum yields. Climbing varieties should be in double rows 6 inches apart with 24 inches between rows.

Growing
French beans flourish in a sheltered, sunny site on a light, free-draining, fertile soil where organic matter was added for the previous crop. Alternatively, dig in plenty of well-rotted organic matter in late autumn or winter before planting.

Purple Queen

The plants need a pH of 6.5–7.0; lime acidic soils if necessary. Rake the soil to a medium tilth about 10–14 days before sowing, incorporating a balanced granular fertilizer at ¾–1½ pounds/sq ft.

Keep crops weed-free or mulch when the soil is moist. Earth up round the base of the stems for added support and push twigs under mature bush varieties to keep pods off the soil, or support plants with pea sticks. Support climbing varieties in the same way as runner beans.

Keep well watered during drought; plants are particularly sensitive to water stress when the flowers start to open and as pods swell. Apply 10–20 gallons/sq in per week.

Maintenance
Spring Sow early crops under cover or outdoors in late spring. Support climbers. Transplant when 2–3 inches tall.
Summer Keep crops weed-free, mulch, water in drought. Harvest regularly.
Autumn Continue harvesting until the first frosts. Protect later crops with cloches or fleece.
Winter Prepare the soil for the following year's crop.

Protected Cropping
For earlier crops and in cooler climates, sow in boxes, modules or pots of seed compost under cover from mid-spring. Warm the soil before transplanting. Harden off and plant out from late spring, depending on the weather and soil conditions. Protect crops sown indoors or *in situ* with cloches, polytunnels or with horticultural fleece until established.

For very early harvest, sow in pots in a heated greenhouse at 59°F (15°C) from late winter. Sow 4 seeds near the edge of a 9–10 inch pot containing loam-based compost with moderate fertilizer levels.

Seeds can also be pregerminated on moist kitchen towel in an airing cupboard or similar. Keep moist with tepid water, ventilate in warm weather and harvest in late spring.

Harvesting and Storing
Plants are self-pollinating, so expect a good harvest. Pick when pods are about 4 inches long, when they snap easily, before the seeds are visible. Pick regularly for maximum yields. Cut them with a pair of scissors or hold the stems as you pull the pods to avoid uprooting the plant.

French beans are great when lightly boiled or steamed

For dried or haricot beans, leave pods until they mature, sever the plant at the base and dry indoors. When pods begin to split, shell the beans and dry on paper for several days. Store in an airtight container.

French beans freeze well. Wash and trim young pods, blanch for 3 minutes, freeze in plastic bags or rigid containers. You should use within 12 months. They keep in a plastic bag in the refrigerator for up to a week and last about 4 days in a cool kitchen.

Pests and Diseases
Slugs, black bean aphid and red spider mite can be troublesome. Grey mold (*Botrytis*) and halo blight may be problems in wet or humid weather. Mice may eat seeds. Root rots can kill plants in wet or poorly drained soils. Rotate crops.

 ## companion planting

French beans do well with celery, maize, cucurbits, sweetcorn and melons. Intercrop with brassicas.

 ## container growing

French beans can be grown in containers that are at least 8 inches wide by 10 inches deep. Sow seeds 1½–2 inches deep indoors in mid-spring, moving the container outdoors into a sheltered, sunny site. Feed with liquid general fertilizer if necessary. Stake climbing varieties; pinch out growing points when plants reach the top of supports.

 ## medicinal

One cup of beans per day is said to lower cholesterol by about 12%.

FRENCH BEAN

culinary

Fresh French beans have such a delicate flavor that they hardly need more than boiling in water and serving as an accompaniment to meat and other dishes. Wash, top and tail pods and cook whole in boiling salted water for 5–7 minutes, preferably within an hour of harvesting. Cut large flat-podded types into 1-inch slices. Alternatively, steam them, serve cold in salads or try them stir-fried with other vegetables.

For haricot beans, place fresh beans in cold water, bring to the boil, remove from the heat and allow to stand for an hour. Drain and serve as a hot vegetable, or in vinaigrette as a salad.

Mussel Soup with French Beans

Serves 4

½ pound French beans, finely chopped
3 pounds mussels, cleaned and debearded
1⅓ cups dry white wine
3 tablespoons olive oil
1 onion, finely chopped
Salt and freshly ground black pepper
3 plum tomatoes, peeled, seeded and diced
Bunch fresh coriander, leaves picked and chopped

Start by discarding any mussels that won't close when they are lightly tapped. Heat a large pan over a high heat. Tip in the mussels and cover for 10–15 seconds, then pour over the wine and 1⅓ cups of water. Cover and cook, shaking the pan every now and then, for 5 minutes or until the mussels have opened. Discard any that stay closed.

Tip the mussels into a colander set over a large bowl. Sieve the cooking liquid once more and reserve. When cool enough to handle, remove the mussels from their shells and reserve, discarding the shells.

Heat 1 tablespoon of the oil in a pan and add the onion. Cook for a few minutes until softened, then pour in the reserved liquid and bring to the boil. Season to taste. Add the beans, mussels and tomatoes and just warm through. Ladle into bowls, scatter over the coriander and drizzle over the remaining olive oil. Serve immediately.

French Bean, Roquefort and Walnut Salad

Serves 4

⅔ pound French beans, topped and tailed
8 ounces Roquefort cheese
1 cup walnuts
1 small radicchio plus 2 little gem lettuces
3 tablespoons extra virgin olive oil
1 tablespoon balsamic vinegar
1 clove garlic, crushed
Salt and freshly ground black pepper

Wash the beans and steam them over a pan of boiling water until just crunchy. Keep warm. Crumble the Roquefort and lightly crush the walnuts. Wash the lettuces thoroughly and shake dry. Make a dressing with the remaining ingredients.

Arrange the lettuces in a large bowl, top with the beans, walnuts and cheese, and pour over the dressing. Toss and serve while the beans are still warm.

Phyllostachys spp. and others. *Graminae/Poaceae*

BAMBOO

Woody-stemmed, evergreen perennial. Hardy to tropical. Value: high in fiber, vitamin C, E and B$_6$ and several other elements, including phosphorus, potassium and zinc.

From creeping, grasslike species to giant fast-growing varieties climbing towards the heavens, bamboos are not only edible and ornamental but one of the most useful plants on earth. These fascinating, long-lived members of the grass family have influenced history and have many practical uses: from construction and scaffolding to the manufacture of fishing rods, paper and medicine. Bamboo has also inspired works of art, and writings about bamboo in Chinese literature date back many centuries. Silkworm eggs were first smuggled out of the country in a bamboo cane and the Chinese have drilled to over 3,000 feet for oil using bamboo canes since at least 200 BCE. Bamboos rarely flower, but when they do, every specimen of that particular clone does so simultaneously, wherever it is in the world. Bamboo shoots play a prominent role in the diets of many countries — generations of pandas can't be wrong!

Harvest bamboo before this stage

 varieties

There are clump-forming and spreading species of bamboo, so choose garden specimens carefully — those with spreading roots are often vigorous and invasive.

Phyllostachys dulcis has masses of green stems that grow rapidly to around 13 x 26 feet. It is highly productive in hot summers — produces sweet shoots, is one of the best for eating and thrives in sun or part shade. **P. edulis** can grow to a maximum of 16 x 65 feet but is usually smaller. Clump forming and slow to establish, with green canes. **Phyllostachys edulis 'Heterocycla'** grows to 16 x 65 feet; not for the faint hearted or those with small gardens. Happy in sun or part shade, **P. aurea** grows to 10 x 16 feet, the young shoots are bright green, becoming pale creamy-yellow and matt yellow in sun. Very graceful, yet tough and vigorous in warm climates. **P. aureosulcata** grows to 10 x 30 feet. The green canes with golden grooves often zigzag prominently at the base — very hardy and thrives in sun or part shade. **P. nigra**, the legendary black-caned bamboo, grows to 16 x 39 feet, though usually much smaller. Young canes are green and their transition to black is faster in sunshine; ideal in smaller gardens or containers. **P. nigra f. henonis** — the elegant canes of this clump-forming specimen reach 13 x 13 feet or more. It has dark green, glossy leaves and brown-yellow canes when mature and is excellent as a specimen plant. **P. nuda** grows to 8 x 16 feet and is tough and vigorous with dark green stems. **P. rubromarginata** is compact and upright with slender, pale olive-yellow canes. Grows to 5 x 20 feet and is ideal for the smaller garden. **P. viridiglaucescens** grows to 13 feet or more, in clumps up to 10 feet wide. It is leafy and graceful with tall, glossy, green canes.

BAMBOO

Pleioblastus hindsii forms clumps to 7 feet and sometimes dense thickets of olive-green canes up to 13 feet tall. Good in sun and dense shade, for maritime conditions and as a windbreak in sun or shade.

Pseudosasa japonica is adaptable, hardy and forms clumps to 10 feet and occasionally dense thickets of olive-green canes to 16 feet tall, which arch towards the tip. Good in shade, as a hedge or windbreak and easy to grow.

 ## cultivation

Propagation
Lift and divide clumps or rhizomes in spring, using a spade, and transplant in well-prepared ground.

Growing
Bamboos prefer rich, moist soils but are extremely tolerant, provided conditions are not waterlogged. Clear the ground of perennial weeds, add plenty of well-rotted organic matter to the soil and soak the rootball in a bucket of water before planting slightly lower than the level of the plant in the pot, then water in well. Mulch well after planting, using well-rotted organic matter, then do so annually, each spring, after feeding with general fertilizer. Keep the soil moist, particularly during the first 2–3 years, until the plants are established. Bamboos in containers need regular watering during the growing season; do not let the roots dry out in winter, particularly during mild periods.

Bamboo can be grown in a container

Although regular harvesting thins the clump, remove about a third or more of the old and weak stems at the base in spring to encourage regrowth.

Maintenance
Spring Cut out stems that were damaged over winter. Harvest young shoots.
Summer Water if necessary during drought.
Autumn Clear the ground ready for planting next spring.
Winter Order new varieties from plant catalogues.

Protected Cropping
Plants grown in containers can be protected under cover during winter and early spring, advancing shoot production for an earlier harvest.

 ## container growing

Grow in a 50:50 loam-based compost and peat substitute, or multi-purpose compost; mix with added grit for stability and a good layer of drainage material in the base. In cold winters, wrap the pot with hessian or bubble wrap and put the pot in a sheltered position. In spring, feed with slow-release fertilizer and repot into a container one size larger, if necessary. Bamboos dislike being transplanted into pots which are considerably larger than the existing rootball.

Harvesting and Storing
Harvest shoots that are ½ inch or more in diameter — plants may take more than 5 years to produce canes of this size — removing a few from each clump so plant growth is not affected; up to one-third of the new shoots can be removed without damaging the plants. New shoots grow rapidly, so check clumps daily and harvest from early to mid-spring, cutting shoots off at ground level with a sharp knife or clearing the soil and cutting at the point where they join the roots of spreading varieties. Shoots should be no more than 12 inches high; after this stage they become fibrous and inedible. Developing shoots that are blanched by covering with a box, bucket or layer of mulch are tenderer when eaten.

Pests and Diseases
In temperate climates, bamboos are almost disease-free and are resistant to honey fungus. Rabbits, squirrels and deer eat new shoots. Oriental bamboo spider mite can be a problem; spray to increase humidity or with an environmentally friendly insecticide.

 ## culinary

Most bamboos are edible but some are tastier than others. The sweetest are *Phyllostachys dulcis* and *Phyllostachys edulis*. Use the shoots immediately after harvest, in stir-fries and salads, or store them in a bowl of water; once they dry out, the taste deteriorates rapidly. Slice them lengthwise, removing the leafy outer sheath before cooking. Some varieties have a bitter flavor (called *egumi* in Japan) that can be removed by boiling in water for half an hour, either before or after the sheath has been removed. If there is still a hint of bitterness, cook the shoots again in fresh water. If you cannot find fresh bamboo shoots, you can buy them in jars or cans instead.

Fried Bamboo Shoot
Serves 3–4

1 tender bamboo shoot, about 12 inches long
2 teaspoons baking soda
1 teaspoon fenugreek seeds
4 dried red chilies
Salt
⅔ cup vegetable oil

Rinse the bamboo shoot and chop it into small cubes. Add the baking soda and mix well.

Fry the fenugreek seeds and chilies in a dry pan until they release their flavor and add a little salt. Pour in the oil, add the cubed bamboo shoot and continue cooking on a low heat. When the bamboo shoot dries up, add a couple of tablespoons of water and stir well. Serve piping hot.

PEA

Pisum sativum. Papilionaceae

Also known as Garden Pea, English Pea, Sweet Pea. Climbing or scrambling annual grown for seeds, pods and shoot tips. Half hardy. Value: good source of protein, carbohydrates, fiber, iron and vitamin C.

Like many legumes, peas are an ancient food crop. The earliest records are of smooth-skinned types, found in Mediterranean and European excavations dating from 7000 BCE. The Greeks and Romans cultivated and ate peas in abundance and it was the Romans who were said to have introduced them to Great Britain. In classical Greece they were known as *pison*, which was translated in English to "peason"; by the reign of Charles I they became "pease" and this was shortened to "pea" in the 18th century. During the reign of Elizabeth I types seen as "fit dainties for ladies, they come so far, and cost so dear" were imported from Holland.

In England "pease pudding," made from dried peas, butter and eggs, was traditionally eaten with pork and boiled bacon. It was obviously quite versatile, hence the nursery rhyme beginning, "Pease pudding hot, pease pudding cold, pease pudding in the pot nine days old." Peas were eaten dried or ground until the 16th century, when Italian gardeners developed tender varieties for cooking and eating when fresh. It took until the following century before this was accepted elsewhere.

 varieties

Peas are usually listed according to the timing of the crop — early, second early (or early maincrop) and maincrop types — but some descriptions refer to the pea itself, or to the pod.

Earlier varieties are lower-growing than later types, which are taller and consequently higher-yielding. Smooth-seeded types are hardy and are used for early and late crops. Wrinkle-seeded varieties are less hardy and generally sweeter.

"Petit pois" are small and well flavored. "Semi-leafless" peas have more tendrils than leaves, becoming intertwined and self-supporting as they grow.

"Sugar peas" or "snow peas" — varieties of *Pisum sativum* var. *macrocarpon* — are grown for their edible immature pods; of these, the 'Sugar Snap' type are particularly succulent and sweet. Some varieties can be allowed to mature and the peas eaten.

Early Peas
'Early Onward'* is a heavy cropper with large blunt pods and wrinkled seeds. **'Feltham First'** is an excellent early round-seeded variety with large, well-filled pods. **'Kelvedon Wonder'*** (early or main crop) produces pods packed with delicious peas. Dwarf.

Maincrop peas
'Alderman', an old variety, produces heavy crops to 5 feet with exquisite flavor. **'Cavalier'*** produces huge crops and is highly resistant to mildew. Easy to harvest, with wrinkled seeds and fusarium resistance. **'Darfon'** is a high-yielding "petit pois" type, its pods packed with small peas. It resists downy mildew and fusarium. **'Dorian'*** produces up to ten tasty peas per pod and harvests over a long period. **'Hurst Green Shaft'*** is sweet-tasting and heavy-cropping, maturing over a long period. Wrinkle-seeded and downy mildew and fusarium-resistant.

Sugar peas
'Oregon Sugar Pod'* is sweet and tasty; harvest as

Early Onward

Leaves can be harvested for their shoot tips

the peas form. Fusarium-resistant. **'Reuzensuiker'*** is a compact plant, needing little support. Its pods are wide and fleshy, and very sweet. **'Sugar Snap'** produces succulent, sweet edible pods or can be grown on for peas. Very sweet. Fusarium-resistant.

 cultivation

Propagation
Germination is erratic and poor on cold soils; do not sow outdoors when soil temperatures are below 50°F (10°C).

Sow earlies or second earlies successively every 14–28 days from mid-spring to midsummer. Avoid excessively hot times; these can affect germination.

According to the growing conditions, earlies mature after about 12 weeks, second earlies (or early maincrop) take 1–2 weeks longer, and maincrops take another 1–2 weeks longer again. As an alternative option, sow groups of earlies, second earlies and maincrops in mid- to late spring; the length of time taken for each type to reach maturity will give you a harvest over several weeks.

In midsummer, with at least 12 weeks before the first frosts are expected, sow an early cultivar for harvesting in autumn, and where winters are mild, sow earlies in mid- to late autumn for overwintering. Cloche protection may be necessary later in the season.

Peas can be sown in single V-shaped rows 1–2 inches deep and 2 inches apart, double rows 9 inches apart or broad or flat drills 10 inches wide. The distance between the rows or pairs of rows should equal the ultimate plant height.

Peas can also be sown in strips 3 rows wide with the seeds 4 inches apart in and between the rows and with 18 inches between the strips, or in blocks 3–4 feet wide with seeds 2–3 inches apart, or in compost in guttering that is then slid into place.

Yields are higher when plants are supported. Use pea sticks made from brushwood or netting. Place supports down one side of a single row, on either side or down the center of wide drills and around the outside of blocks of plants.

Growing
Peas are a cool-season crop, flourishing at 55–65°F (13–18°C), so crops will be higher in cooler summer temperatures. They do not tolerate drought, excessive temperatures or waterlogged soil. Peas should be grown in an open, sheltered position on moisture-retentive, deep, free-draining soil with a pH of 5.5–7.0.

Incorporate plenty of organic matter in the autumn or winter prior to sowing or plant where the ground was manured for the previous year's crop.

Keep crops weed-free by hoeing, hand weeding or mulching (which also keeps the roots cool and moist). Earth up overwintering and early crops to provide extra support.

Unless there are drought conditions, established plants do not need watering until the flowers appear, then, for a good harvest, they will need 60 gallons/sq ft each week until the harvest is complete.

Maintenance
Spring Sow early maincrops.
Summer Sow maincrops early in the season. Harvest, keep weed-free and water. Sow earlies for an autumn harvest.
Autumn Sow early overwintering crops under cover. Prepare the ground for the following year.
Winter Sow early crops under cover.

Protected Cropping
Warm the soil before sowing treated seed in spring. Sow the seed of dwarf cultivars under cover in early spring. Remove the covers when the plants need supporting.

Early spring and late autumn sowings can be made under cover, as flowers and pods cannot withstand frosty nights.

Harvesting and Storing
Harvest early types from late spring to early summer and maincrops from midsummer to early autumn. Pick regularly to ensure a high yield when the pods are swollen. Harvest those grown for their pods when the peas are just forming. If peas are to be dried, leave them on the plant as long as possible, lifting just before the seeds are shed; hang in a cool airy place or spread the pods out on trays to dry until they split and the peas can be harvested. Store in airtight containers.

Freeze young peas of any variety. Shell and blanch for 1 minute. Allow to drain, cool and freeze in plastic bags or containers. Use within 12 months.

A first-class pea support

Peas in a plastic bag in the refrigerator stay fresh for up to 3 days.

Pests and Diseases

Birds and mice can be a problem: net crops.

Pea moths are common, their larvae eating the peas. Protect with crop covers at flower bud stage. Autumn, early and midsummer sowings often avoid problems. Use bifenthrin or organic spray or cover with fleece.

Pea thrips attack developing pods, making pods distorted and silvery; peas do not develop. Spray with pyrethrum.

Mice may also be troublesome, eating seeds, particularly with overwintered crops; trap them.

Powdery mildew, downy mildew and fusarium wilt can be a problem: sow resistant varieties.

 ## companion planting

Peas grow well with other legumes, root crops, potatoes, cucurbits and sweetcorn.

 ## container growing

Sow early dwarf varieties successively through the season in large containers of loam-based compost with moderate fertilizer levels. Provide support, keep weed-free and well watered.

 ## medicinal

Peas are said to reduce fertility, prevent appendicitis, lower blood cholesterol and control blood sugar levels.

 ## culinary

Garden peas are eaten fresh or dried. When small and tender, they can be eaten raw in salads. Peas are traditionally boiled or steamed with a sprig of mint. Eat with butter, salt and pepper or herbs. Serve in a cream sauce with pearl onions, with celery, orange, carrots, wine or lemon sauce. Snow peas should be boiled for 3 minutes (or steamed), tossed in butter and served. Young pea shoot tips can be cooked and eaten.

Jean-Christophe Novelli's Cappuccino Soup
Serves 4

1 pound fresh or frozen peas
2 tablespoons butter
1 small onion, diced
¼ cup smoked pancetta, diced
3 cups light chicken stock
1 clove of garlic
1 sprig fresh mint
A pinch of superfine sugar
Salt and freshly ground black pepper
4 tablespoons whole milk
Cep powder

Heat the butter in large pan, add the onion and sweat gently until softened. Add the pancetta and quickly fry until crisp. Add the peas and stock, bring to the boil and cook until the peas are soft to the touch. Pour into a blender, add the garlic, mint, sugar and some seasoning and blend until smooth.

Warm up the milk and froth up using cappuccino frother or a hand blender. Pour the soup into individual soup terrines or coffee cups. Top with frothed milk and finish with crispy pancetta and a dusting of cep powder to resemble a large cappuccino.

Pasta and Snow Pea Salad
Serves 4

⅔ pound snow peas, topped and tailed
1 pound pasta — penne or fusilli
4 tablespoons olive oil
1 small onion, finely sliced
2 cloves garlic, crushed
8-ounce can tuna, drained and flaked
2 tablespoons heavy cream
2 tablespoons chopped fresh flat-leaf parsley
Salt and freshly ground black pepper

Cook the pasta in boiling salted water for 10 minutes, or until *al dente*, and drain. Drizzle over 1 tablespoon of the oil and toss well. Allow to cool.

Meanwhile, cook the snow peas in a steamer for 2–3 minutes; they should remain crunchy. In a separate pan, heat the oil and sauté the onion for a couple of minutes, then add the garlic and continue cooking for 1 minute. Remove from the heat and allow to cool.

Put the pasta into a large serving bowl and mix in all the ingredients. Taste for seasoning and serve.

Portulaca oleracea subsp. *sativa*. Portulacaceae
PURSLANE

Also known as Summer Purslane. Annual grown for succulent shoot tips, stems and leaves. Half hardy. Value: rich in beta carotene, folic acid, vitamin C; contains useful amounts of essential fatty acids.

Purslane has been grown for centuries in China, India and Egypt, and is now widespread in the warm temperate and tropical regions of the world. It was once believed to protect against evil spirits and "blastings by lightning or planets and burning of gunpowder." Its name in Malawi translates as "buttocks of the wife of a chief," referring to the plant's succulent, rounded leaves and juicy stems! The cultivated form has an erect habit and larger leaves than the wild species.

 varieties

Portulaca oleracea subsp. *sativa* is a vigorous, upright annual growing to 18 inches tall with thick, succulent stems, spoon-shaped leaves and bright yellow flowers. *P. o.* var. *aurea* is a yellow-leaved, less hardy form. It is more succulent, but has less flavor. Attractive in salads and as an ornamental.

 cultivation

Propagation
Sow in seed trays indoors in late spring and transplant seedlings into modules when large enough to handle. Harden off and plant when there is no danger of frost, 6 inches apart.

In frost-free climates or for later crops, sow directly, thinning to 6 inches apart. Sow in late spring for a summer crop and in late summer for autumn cropping.

Growing
Easily cultivated, purslane thrives in a sunny, warm, sheltered site on light, well-drained soil. Add organic matter and sand to improve drainage if needed. Remove flowers as they appear.

Maintenance
Spring Sow protected crops, or *in situ* once the danger of frost is passed.
Summer Keep plants weed-free and water as necessary. Harvest regularly.
Autumn Cut back mature plants to allow regrowth.
Winter In late winter sow early crops under glass.

Protected Cropping
To extend the season, sow in early to mid-spring and early to mid-autumn under cover. Make earlier and late summer sowings under cover as a "cut and come again" crop.

Harvesting
Pick young shoot tips, stems and leaves when about 1–2 inches long. "Cut and come again" crops are ready to harvest after about 5 weeks. Regular picking encourages young growth. As older plants deteriorate towards the end of the growing season, cut them back to within 2 inches of the ground, water them well and they should resprout.

Pests and Diseases
Purslane is prone to slug damage, particularly when young. Damping off can be a problem if sown at low temperatures or in cold soil.

The *aurea* variety

 culinary

Wash thoroughly; growing close to the ground, leaves can be gritty. It can be lightly cooked, although the taste is not memorable. Older leaves can be pickled.

Purslane Salad
Serves 4

Use young buds and stems as well as the leaves.

Handful purslane
4 ripe nectarines or peaches
Hazelnut oil
15 hazelnuts, toasted
½ teaspoon coriander seeds, crushed

Slice the nectarines or peaches and arrange on a plate brushed with hazelnut oil. Add the purslane leaves. Trickle over a little more oil, sprinkle with the chopped nuts and season with crushed coriander.

 container growing

Plant seedlings or sow seed in pots or containers when there is no danger of frost, using a soil-based compost with a low fertilizer content. Continue to water regularly.

 medicinal

A traditional remedy for dry coughs, swollen gums and, infused in water, for blood disorders. Research indicates that its high levels of fatty acids may help to prevent heart attacks and stimulate the body's immune system.

 warning

Expectant mothers and those with digestive disorders should not eat purslane in large quantities.

Early Champagne

affects cropping the following year. Keep weed-free and watered, removing dead leaves instantly. In early spring, scatter a balanced general fertilizer around the crowns.

Maintenance

Spring Force early crops under a bucket or similar.
Summer Harvest stems.
Autumn When stems die back, remove all plant debris.
Winter Mulch with well-rotted compost or manure.

Protected Cropping

For early crops lift a few crowns in late autumn, leave them above ground and let them be frosted, then bring indoors into a cool place for forcing. Put in a large container packed with soil, or plant under greenhouse staging. Exclude light with an upturned box or bucket 15–18 inches high to allow for stem growth. They can also be forced in garbage bags. Keep compost moist. Dispose of exhausted forced crowns after harvest.

Alternatively, from late winter, cover *in situ* with a 6-inch layer of straw or leaves or with an upturned can, bucket or blanching pot covered with straw or strawy manure. Harvest in early to mid-spring. Do not harvest from a crown for at least 2 years after forcing.

Harvesting and Storing

Do not harvest until 12–18 months after planting, taking only a few "sticks" in the second season and more in later years. Cropping can last from early spring to midsummer. To harvest, hold the stems near the base and twist off. Avoid breaking the stems, as it can cause fungal problems. Do not overpick; it can weaken the plant.

To freeze, chop the stems into sections and place on an open tray, then freeze for 1 hour before packing into plastic bags. This prevents the sections from sticking together. They can be stored for up to a year.

Pests and Diseases

Honey fungus may appear as white streaks in dead crown tissue; brown toadstools appear round the base. Dig out and burn diseased roots. Crown rot damages terminal buds and makes stems spindly. Dig out and burn badly infected plants. Do not replant in the area. Virus disease has no cure. Dig up and burn.

 ## companion planting

Rhubarb is reported to control red spider mite. A traditional remedy suggests putting rhubarb in planting holes to control clubroot. An infusion of leaves is effective as an aphicide and to check blackspot on roses.

 ## medicinal

Rhubarb is an astringent, stomachic and potent laxative. Dioscorides recommended it for chest, stomach and liver complaints, and ringworm. By the 16th century, in western Europe, it was taken as an infusion with parsley as a cure for venereal disease.

 ## warning

Do not eat the leaves, which are extremely poisonous!

Main course or dessert?

RHUBARB

 culinary

Forced rhubarb is tender and needs less sugar. Cook stems slowly with sugar. Very little or no water is required; do not overcook them. Do not use aluminum pans.

Rhubarb can be stewed for fruit pies, bottling or preserving, for fools, mousses and rhubarb crumble, and is delicious served with duck. The flavor can be improved by adding orange juice, marmalade or cinnamon. It can also be puréed with apple. Claudia Roden's *Middle Eastern Food* demonstrates that it is unexpectedly wonderful stewed with beef or lamb in Persian *khoresh*.

Preserved Rhubarb

8 pounds rhubarb
8 pounds preserving sugar
Zest and juice of 2 lemons
½ cup blanched almonds

Cut the rhubarb into 1-inch lengths and cook gently in a jam pan until the juices start to run. Add the sugar, lemon juice and zest and the almonds. Stir until the sugar dissolves, then boil until a good color and thickened. Pot up into sterilized jars and seal.

Rhubarb Sorbet
Serves 4

1 pound rhubarb
¾ cup superfine sugar
Juice of ½ a lemon

Cut the rhubarb into 1-inch lengths and put into a heavy-bottomed pan. Add ¼ cup water. Warm gently until the juices run, then stir in the sugar and lemon juice and simmer, covered, until tender. Freeze, whisking several times as it freezes, to break up the ice crystals. If you use a sorbetière, churn until smooth. Remove from the freezer 15 minutes before serving and leave in the fridge.

Rhubarb Sorbet

Rorippa nasturtium-aquaticum. Brassicaceae

WATERCRESS

Also known as Summer Watercress. Usually aquatic perennial grown for pungent, edible leaves and stems. Hardy. Value: excellent source of beta carotene, vitamins C and E, calcium, iron and iodine.

This highly nutritious aquatic herb, a native of Europe, North Africa and Asia, has been cultivated as a salad plant since Roman times and is grown throughout the world's temperate zones. It has become a weed in North America and New Zealand. Pliny records the Latin derivation of its original generic name as *Nasus tortus*, meaning "writhing nose" — referring to its spicy taste and pungent odor; *officinale* is often applied to plants with medicinal uses. Watercress was listed as an aphrodisiac in Dioscorides's *Materia Medica* of 77 CE.

It was mentioned in early Irish poetry around the 12th century — "Well of Traigh Dha Bhan, Lovely is your pure-topped cress," and, "Watercress, little green-topped one, on the brink of the blackbirds' well..." Early references to the shamrock are believed to be to watercress. Evidence to support this comes from Ireland's County Meath and Shamrock Well, the watercress of which was still remembered in the 1940s as "the finest in the district." Watercress was also known in Ireland as "St. Patrick's Cabbage." The first records of commercial cultivation are from Germany, around 1750, France, between 1800 and 1811, and in England, around 1808.

 ## cultivation

Found in and alongside fast-flowing rivers and streams, watercress has fleshy, glossy leaves on long stalks with 5–10 leaflets. Its long stems creep or float on the surface and root easily. Small whitish green flowers appear in flat-topped clusters from mid-spring to early autumn.

The best watercress is grown in pure, fast-flowing chalk or limestone streams with slightly alkaline water. This avoids the risk of contamination from pollution, which can cause stomach upsets.

Propagation
Propagate watercress is from shop-bought material but the cutway **'Aqua'** can be grown from seed. Cuttings 4 inches long take about a week to root in a glass of water.

If you live by a fast-flowing stream, plant rooted cuttings 6 inches apart in the banks. Firm well to prevent them from being dislodged.

To grow watercress in the garden, dig a trench 24 inches wide and 24 inches deep, and put a 6-inch layer of well-rotted farmyard manure or compost into the base. (Not use sheep manure, as it can carry dangerous liver fluke.) Mix in a little ground limestone if your soil is not alkaline, then cover with 3–4 inches of soil. Plant cuttings 6 inches apart in mid-spring. Alternatively, in spring, mark out an area and dig in well-rotted organic matter and ground limestone, firm and soak with water, then scatter seed thinly on the surface. Water daily.

Seeds can also be sown indoors from mid- to late spring, in a propagator or trays of peat-substitute seed compost on a window sill. Cover the seeds with 1/10 inch of compost, keep it constantly moist at around 50–59°F (10–15°C).

Transplant 3–4 seedlings into a 3-inch pot when large enough to handle, then plant out 4–6 inches apart from mid-spring onwards. When plants deteriorate, replace them with fresh cuttings.

Growing
Plants grown in the garden need a bright, sheltered position away from direct sunshine; never allow them to dry out, or plants run to seed. As a cool-season crop,

WATERCRESS

The leaves turn coarse after flowering

watercress grows most actively in spring and autumn, and during the winter in warmer climates. Occasional feeding with a diluted high-nitrogen liquid fertilizer or liquid seaweed may be needed. Do not grow in stagnant or still water.

Maintenance
Spring Take cuttings or sow seed mid- to late spring.
Summer Do not let compost-grown plants dry out. Keep weed-free. Harvest as needed. Remove flower heads as they appear.
Autumn Continue to harvest.
Winter Protect with cloches for continuous growth.

Protected Cropping
Cover plants with cloches, fleece or polyethylene tunnels before the first frosts. Make a watercress bed in an unheated greenhouse over winter, or grow in pots.

Harvesting and Storing
Younger leaves near the stem tips have the best flavor. Harvest lightly during the first season and annually towards autumn if plants are to be overwintered, cutting regularly for a constant supply of bushy shoots. Use leaves fresh or store in the salad compartment of a refrigerator for 2–3 days.

Pests and Diseases
Watercress is rarely troubled, but caterpillars of cabbage white butterfly may cause problems. Cover crops with netting.

 ## container growing

Grow in large pots or containers of moist peat-substitute compost, with a layer of gravel in the base, spacing 4–6 inches apart. Keep compost moist by standing the pot in a bowl of water that is replaced daily. Grow plants on a bright windowsill, but away from direct sunshine.

 ## medicinal

Watercress has been valued for its medicinal qualities since antiquity. It has been eaten to cure rheumatism, and used as a diuretic and as an expectorant for catarrh, colds and bronchitis; it is a stimulant, a digestive and a tonic to promote appetite, counteract anemia and to lower blood-sugar levels in diabetes. Externally it can be used as a hair tonic. Rubbed on the skin it is said to remove rashes. Culpeper recommended the bruised leaves or juice for clearing spots and freckles and a poultice was said to heal glandular tumors and lymphatic swellings.

Traditionally it was taken as a spring tonic. In the past, in isolated parts of the British Isles where the diet was predominantly shellfish and salt meat, it was often grown to prevent scurvy, and was so mentioned by Philip Miller in his *Gardener's Dictionary* of 1731.

 ## warning

Gathering from streams is not recommended if sheep are grazing nearby, as there is a risk of liver fluke. Fluke can be destroyed by thorough cooking.

 ## culinary

As with its relative, the radish, the hot, spicy taste of watercress comes from mustard oil. Remove discolored leaves and wash thoroughly, shaking off excess water. Eat in salads and stir-fries, or liquefy to make chilled soup. It makes a perfect garnish for sandwiches. Chop finely and add to butter, mashed potatoes, dumplings or a white sauce. Also sauté in butter for 10 minutes and serve as a vegetable.

Among her many tastebud-tingling recipes, Jane Grigson suggests cutting orange segments into quarters and mixing with watercress, olive oil vinaigrette and black pepper; add walnuts or black olives and eat as a salad with ham, duck or veal.

Salmon with Watercress Sauce
Serves 6

2 large bunches watercress, plus extra to garnish
6 salmon fillets, trimmed
4 tablespoons butter
4 tablespoons finely chopped shallots
⅔ cup heavy cream
Salt and freshly ground black pepper
Steam the salmon fillets, covered, on a steamer

rack over boiling water until cooked; this should take 10 minutes or so.

Meanwhile, prepare the sauce by melting the butter in a heavy frying pan and sautéing the shallots until softened. Add the watercress and, constantly stirring, allow the watercress to wilt for about 2 minutes; it should retain its bright green color. Stir in the cream and seasoning and bring to the boil. Remove from the heat and blend in a blender or food processor until smooth. Then reheat gently.

Arrange the salmon fillets in the center of individual plates and spoon sauce over each, garnishing with a little fresh watercress.

Rumex acetosa. Polygonaceae

SORREL

Also known as Spinach Dock, Bread and Cheese. Perennial often grown as annual for young leaves. Hardy. Value: rich in vitamin C.

Surele **in old French means "sour." It was popular in England until the 18th century. John Evelyn wrote that "Sorrel imparts a grateful quickness to the rest as supplying the want of oranges and lemons."**

 ## varieties

Rumex acetosa, upright, hardy, deep-rooted, grows to 4 feet. Its broad, lance-shaped leaves have backward-pointing basal lobes. Less acidic is *Rumex scutatus*, buckler-leaf or French sorrel, a low-growing ground-cover plant with oblong shield-shaped leaves.

 ## cultivation

Grow in a bright or lightly shaded position on fertile, moist soil. Its presence often indicates iron in the soil.

Propagation
In late spring, sow seeds in drills ⅕ inch deep and 18 inches apart, thinning to 9 inches when large enough to handle. Or sow in modules or seed trays and plant out in spring. Divide mature plants in spring or early autumn, while still dormant. Alternatively, leave a few to self-seed, then transplant into rows, or broadcast several seedheads.

Growing
Before planting enrich poor soils with organic matter. Mulch in spring with well-rotted manure or compost. Remove flowers as they appear. Renew plants after 3–5 years. Sorrel can also be grown as an annual. Sow in early spring, thin to 4 inches apart and lift plants with sufficient young leaves.

Maintenance
Spring Sow seed in beds, trays or modules.
Summer Mulch early and water well in dry weather.

Autumn Remove and compost dead leaves.
Winter Lift protected crops.

Protected Cropping
Overwinter under cloches or fleece by sowing seeds in trays or pots in late summer. Alternatively, transplant existing specimens into greenhouse borders, pots, or cold frames.

Harvesting
Harvest lightly until plants are established. Pick a few leaves from each; smaller leaves are tender, less bitter.

 ## container growing

This is advisable on chalk soils. Use large containers of loam-based compost with moderate levels of fertilizer and added organic matter. Keep the compost moist but not waterlogged and feed every 3 weeks with a diluted liquid general fertilizer.

 ## medicinal

Sorrel was added to ale as a treatment for fever and is said to increase the haemoglobin content of blood.

 ## warning

Sorrel contains high levels of oxalic acid, which in large doses causes kidney damage.

 ## culinary

Sorrel withers rapidly and should be used quickly. Add to salads; its tanginess is refreshing. Use in soup and stews, as a garnish, or cook like spinach.

Sorrel Tart
Serves 4

½ pound sorrel, washed
¼ cup butter
1 onion, finely sliced
1 tablespoon flour
1 teaspoon French mustard
1⅓ cups milk
8 ounces Cheddar, grated
salt and freshly ground pepper
8-inch pie plate, lined with shortcrust pastry

Gently cook the sorrel with half the butter, until dark green. Remove from the heat and chop finely. Add the rest of the butter and cook the onion until soft. Stir in the flour and cook for 2 minutes. Add the mustard, then the milk, and bring to the boil, stirring. Then add the cheese and cook gently until melted.

Mix in the sorrel and season. Pour into the pie plate and cook in a preheated oven, 400°F (200°C), for 20–30 minutes, until the top is golden. Turn off the heat and leave on the bottom shelf for 5 minutes. Serve with a green salad.

SCORZONERA

Also known as Black Salsify, False Salsify, Spanish Salsify. Grown as biennial for shoots, flower buds and flowers; annual for cylindrical tapering roots. Hardy. Value: contains indigestible carbohydrate inulin, which, when converted to fructose in storage, increases calorie content (27 calories per 100g); small amounts of vitamins and minerals.

Scorzonera is very similar to salsify, though scorzonera is perennial, not biennial, its skin is darker, the roots narrower and the flavor is not as strong. The name scorzonera may have come from the French *scorzon* or "serpent," as the root was used in Spain to cure snake bites. Another interpretation suggests it comes from the Italian *scorza*, "bark," and *nera*, "black," describing the roots. Native to central and southern Europe through to Russia and Siberia, scorzonera was known by the Greeks and Romans, who took little interest in its cultivation; it arrived in England by 1560 and in North America by 1806. It is widely grown in Europe as an excellent winter vegetable. The leaves have been used as food for silkworms.

varieties

'Duplex' produces long, tasty roots. **'Flandria Scorzonera'** has long roots, growing to 12 inches, with strongly flavored flesh. **'Habil'** is long-rooted with a delicious flavor. **'Lange Jan'** (**'Long John'**) has long, tapering, dark brown roots. **'Long Black'** is similar, but with black roots. **'Russian Giant'** lives up to its name, with long roots and a subtle, delicate flavor.

cultivation

Propagation

Sow fresh seed *in situ* from mid- to late spring, in drills ½–1 inch deep with rows 6 inches apart. Alternatively, sow 2 or 3 seeds in "stations" 6 inches apart, thinning to leave the strongest seedling when large enough to handle. Or sow in late summer for use early the following autumn.

Growing

It flourishes in a sunny position on a deep, light, well-drained soil that should have been manured for a previous crop. Do not grow on freshly manured or stony ground, as this causes "forking." A pH of 6.0–7.5 is ideal, so lime the soil if necessary.

The roots are very tasty when cooked

Flowering scorzonera

On heavy or stony soils, fill a narrow trench about 12 inches deep with finely sieved soil or free-draining compost, so that the roots grow straight. Dig soil deeply and rake in 1½–2 pounds/sq ft general balanced fertilizer 10 days before sowing.

Remove weeds around plants by hand, as roots bleed easily when damaged by a hoe. Mulching once the roots have established helps to smother weeds, conserves moisture and reduces the risk of bolting during dry weather. Water at a rate of 45–60 gallons/sq ft per week.

Roots can be left in the ground to produce "chards" (edible shoots) the following spring. In autumn cut off old leaves, leaving ½–1 inch above the soil. Earth up the roots to a depth of about 6 inches so the developing shoots are blanched during the winter. In late spring, scrape away the soil and harvest when the shoots are 5–6 inches long. They can also be blanched by covering to a similar depth with straw or leaves in early spring. Roots too small to harvest in the first year can be left to mature the following year.

Maintenance

Spring Sow thinly, from mid- to late spring. Thin when large enough to handle.
Summer Keep crops weed-free and water thoroughly as needed to keep soil moist.

Autumn Leave roots in the ground and lift carefully with a fork as needed.
Winter Continue harvesting. Prepare the ground for the next crop.

Protected Cropping

Scorzonera is hardy, but protection with straw or cloches before the onset of severe weather makes lifting much easier.

Harvesting and Storing

Plants need at least 4 months to reach maturity and are ready to harvest from mid-autumn to mid-spring. In a good year the roots may grow to 16 inches, but are more usually about 8 inches long.

Roots can either be left in the ground until needed or lifted — with care, as they are easily damaged. Clean and store in boxes of sand or sawdust in a cool place. They last up to 1 week in a fridge. Mature plants flower in spring or summer of the second year. The edible buds can be harvested with about 3 inches of stem.

If, while lifting, you see that your crop has many forked roots, the remaining plants can be kept for their young shoots and buds.

Pests and Diseases

Scorzonera suffers few problems but may develop "white blister," which looks like glistening paint splashes. Affected plants become distorted. Spray with Bordeaux mixture or destroy.

 ## companion planting

Scorzonera repels carrot root fly and the flowers attract beneficial insects.

 ## container growing

In shallow or stony soils, plants can be grown in deep containers of loam-based compost. Water regularly.

 ## medicinal

The name derived from the French reflects its reputation as an antidote to snake venom, "...and especially to cure the bitings of vipers (of which there may be very many in Spaine and other hot countries)," wrote Gerard in his *Herball* of 1636. This is not proven.

 ## culinary

Roots can be baked, puréed, dipped in batter, sautéed and made into croquettes and fritters, deep-fried or served *au gratin* with cheese and breadcrumbs.

Boiling allows you to fully appreciate the flavor. They discolor when cut, so drop into water with a dash of lemon juice, then boil for 25 minutes in salted water with a tablespoon of flour added. Peel after boiling as you would a hard-boiled egg. Toss with melted butter and chopped parsley. Young "chards" can be served raw in salads. The flower stalks and buds are cooked and eaten like asparagus.

Sautéed Scorzonera

Allow ⅓–⅖ pound per person of cleaned scorzonera; it should not be peeled. Chop roughly and cook in a heavy frying pan in a little extra virgin olive oil until *al dente*, turning to cook every side. Drain on paper towel and sprinkle with lemon juice mixed with 1 crushed garlic clove and 1 tablespoon finely chopped flat-leaf parsley.

Sechium edule. Cucurbitaceae
CHAYOTE

Also known as Vegetable Pear, Mirliton, Choko, Chow Chow, Christophine. Vigorous, scrambling, tuberous rooted perennial, grown for edible fruit and seed. Tender. Value: 90% water; low in calories; some vitamin C.

In good conditions, this climber spreads to 50 feet and produces huge tubers. It originated in Central America; "chayote" comes from the Aztec *chayotl*, while in the West Indies it is called "christophine" after Columbus, who reputedly introduced it to the islands. The pear-shaped fruits contain a single nutty-flavored seed, much prized by cooks.

 varieties

'**Ivory White**' is a small, pale-skinned variety.

 cultivation

Chayote needs rich, fertile, well-drained soil.

Propagation
Propagate cultivars from soft tip cuttings in spring at 65°F (18°C). Alternatively, plant the whole fruit laid on its side, at a slight angle, with the narrow end protruding from the soil.

Growing
Grow on mounds 12–16 inches high and 36 x 36 inches apart; cover a shovel full of well-rotted manure with 6 inches of soil. Lightly mulch.

Alternatively, grow on beds 10 feet square; dig in organic matter, plant seeds in the corners and grow vines towards the center. Or, plant in 36-inch wide ridges. Train the stems into trees, over trellising, fences, or 6-inch mesh netting. Water regularly in dry weather; optimum growth is during the wet season. A day length of just over 12 hours is required for flowering.

In the humid tropics, it grows better in moderate temperatures at altitude.

Germinating chayote fruit

Fruits are even better when suspended above ground

Maintenance

Spring Sow seed or take cuttings.
Summer Feed and water.
Autumn Harvest.
Winter Store fruit for next year's crop.

Protected Cropping

In cool temperate regions, grow under glass in bright light with moderate temperatures and humidity. In warmer areas, start off indoors and plant when the danger of frost has passed. Grow in the greenhouse border or in containers.

Harvesting and Storing

In tropical climates, plants last for several years, fruiting from 3 to 4 months after sowing, all year round. Harvest by cutting the stalk above the fruit with a knife. Fruit reaches its maximum size 25–30 days after fruit set. It will keep up to 3 months in a cool place.

Pests and Diseases

Root knot nematode causes wilting; powdery mildew can appear on leaves and stems; and red spider mite affects plants grown under glass.

 ## container growing

Propagate in spring from seed or cuttings. Pot on into loam-based compost with a high fertilizer content, adding well-rotted manure and grit to improve drainage. Water thoroughly, feed every two weeks with general liquid fertilizer and, once established, with a high-potassium fertilizer. Train the growth on to a trellis.

 ## medicinal

Chayote is said to be good for stomach ulcers. It contains some trace elements.

 ## culinary

This versatile vegetable can be made into soups, boiled, candied, puréed (spiced with chili powder) or added to stews, curries and chutneys. Its seeds can be cooked in butter, the young leaves cooked like spinach, and the tuber eaten when young. Its flesh stays firm after cooking. It makes a good substitute for avocado in a salad and is ideal for those on a diet.

For a stuffing, try a well-flavored bolognese sauce; add boiled chayote flesh and stuff back into halved chayote shells. Sprinkle with Cheddar and bake in an oven preheated to 350°F (180°C), for 30 minutes.

Chayote in Red Wine

Serves 6

Jane Grigson gives a recipe for this pudding.

6 pear-sized chayotes, peeled and left whole
¾ cup sugar
1⅓ cups water
½ cup red wine
2-inch cinnamon stick
4 cloves
Lemon juice
Whipped cream and icing sugar

Use a pan that will hold the chayote in a single layer. Put the sugar and water on to dissolve and simmer for 2 minutes. Carefully add the chayote, then the wine and spices.

Cover and simmer until tender. Remove the chayote to a bowl and arrange upright, like pears. Reduce the liquid until syrupy and add a little lemon juice to bring out the distinctive flavor. Strain the juice over the chayote and serve with whipped cream lightly sweetened with icing sugar.

EGGPLANT

Also known as Aubergine, Brinjal, Garden Egg, Guinea Squash, Pea Aubergine. Short-lived perennial grown as annual for fruits. Tender. Value: small amounts of most vitamins and minerals; very low in calories, with 3% carbohydrates and 1% protein.

This glossy-skinned fruit was known to 16th-century Spaniards as the "apple of love." In contrast, many botanists of the time called it *mala insana* or "mad apple," because of its alleged effects. The Chinese first cultivated eggplant in the fifth century BCE and they have been grown in India for centuries, yet they were unknown to the Greeks and Romans. Moorish invaders introduced them to Spain and the Spaniards later took them to the New World. "Aubergine" is a corruption of the Arabic name *al-badingan*.

 ## varieties

Fruits vary in shape from large, purple-skinned types to small, rounded white fruits 2 inches in diameter. Most modern F1 hybrids are bushy and grow about 3¼ feet tall. Unlike older varieties, they are almost spineless.

'Black Beauty' produces high yields of good quality, and dark purple fruits over a long period. **'Calliope'** is a dense, spineless plant. The white-skinned, purple striped fruits reach 4 inches at maturity. **'Mohican'*** and **'Baby Rosanna'** grow golf-ball-sized fruit and are ideal for containers in the greenhouse or on the patio. **'Diamond'**, from Ukraine, has dark purple fruit and flourishes in short summers and cool climates. The white and lavender-striped fruit of **'Listada de**

Listada de Gandida

Gandida' are very tasty. **'Long Purple'** produces good yields of dark purple fruits about 6 inches long. **'Moneymaker'** is a superb early variety with very tasty fruits. Tolerant of lower temperatures, it can be grown indoors as well as outside. **'Ova'** produces masses of small, white-skinned fruits. **'Pintung Long'** is one of the best — its ornamental, dark lavender fruits grow to 12 inches long and are tender and full of flavor. **'Rossa Bianca'**, a classic gourmet variety, produces white, violet-tinted fruit with a mild, creamy taste. **'Rosita'** bears gorgeous glossy, lavender pink fruit that taste sweet. **'Striped Toga'** is unusual for its orange, green-striped fruit that are only 3 inches long at maturity. **'Thai Green'**, with long, slender fruit, is renowned for its drought tolerance. **'Thai Green Pea'** is a tall plant covered with masses of tiny green fruit with a strong eggplant flavor. Ideal for stir-fries, curries and soups. The fruit of **'Thai Yellow Egg'** are a bright golden yellow and egg-sized; perfect for Thai dishes. **'Thai Long Green'** grows highly ornamental slim, light lime-green fruit to 12 inches long: a gourmet variety; tender and absolutely delicious. **'Violette di Firenze'** needs warmth to ripen fully. Its unusual yet very attractive dark mauve fruits make this an ideal plant for growing in a "potager."

 ## cultivation

Eggplants need long, hot summers, and are the ideal crop for warm climates. In cooler regions, they will grow outside, but better harvests come from those protected indoors. Constant temperatures between 77–86°F (25–30°C) with moderate to high humidity are needed for optimum flower and fruit production. Below 68°F (20°C) growth is often stalled.

Propagation

Temperatures of 59–70°F (15–21°C) are needed for good germination. Sow seed in early spring, in trays, pots or modules of moist seed compost in a propagator or warm greenhouse or on a windowsill. Soaking seed in warm water for 24 hours before sowing helps germination. When 3 leaves appear, pot on plants grown in seed trays into 2–3-inch pots, repotting as required until they are ready to plant outdoors or under cover. If you are growing eggplants outdoors, sow seeds 10–12 weeks before the last frosts are expected.

Growing

Eggplants flourish in a sunny, sheltered position on fertile, well-drained soil. Before planting, fork in a slow-release general fertilizer at ¾–1½ pounds/sq ft, improve the soil with the addition of organic matter and, in cooler climates, warm the soil before planting and leave the cloches in place until the plants are established for 2–3 weeks, allowing them to "harden off" before removing the cloches.

Space plants 20–24 inches apart. "Pinch out" the growth tip when plants are 16 inches tall, or 9–12 inches for smaller varieties. Stake the main stem or support branches with string, if necessary, as fruit begins to mature. Mulch outdoor plants to conserve moisture and suppress weeds.

Feed plants with a liquid general fertilizer until they are established, then water with a high-potassium liquid

EGGPLANT

Beautiful in bloom and fruit

feed every 10 days, once the first fruits are formed. When the flowers begin to open, a light spray with lukewarm water helps pollination; for large, high-quality fruits, allow only 4–5 to form on each plant, after which any new side shoots should be removed.

Maintenance
Spring Sow seeds under glass.
Summer Once frosts are over, transplant outdoors. Retain 4–6 fruits per plant, harvesting as they mature.
Autumn Protect outdoor crops from early frosts.
Winter Order seed for the following growing season.

Protected Cropping
When growing plants indoors, mist them regularly with tepid water or "wet down" the paths on hot days. Keep the compost moist throughout the growing season, but take care to avoid waterlogging.

Harvesting and Storing
Harvest when the skin is shiny: overripe fruits have dull skin and are horribly bitter. Using a knife, cut the fruit stalks close to the stem. They will keep for 2 weeks in a cool, humid place or in a refrigerator.

Pests and Diseases
Eggplants are susceptible to the typical problems of crops grown under glass.

Check plants for aphids, whitefly and red spider mite. Powdery mildew can stunt growth, and in severe cases leaves become yellow and die. Verticillium wilt turns lower leaves yellow; plants wilt, but recover overnight.

 ## companion planting

Eggplants flourish alongside the herbs thyme and tarragon, and peas.

 ## container growing

Eggplants can be grown in 8–12-inch pots or in growbags. Keep temperatures around 59–65°F (15–18°C); water regularly, keep the compost moist and feed with a half-strength high-potassium fertilizer every other watering.

 ## medicinal

In Indian herbal medicine, white varieties are used to treat diabetes and as a carminative. The Sanskrit *vatin-ganah* means "anti-wind vegetable." *Kama Sutra* prescribes it in a concoction for "enlarging the male organ for a period of 1 month." Neither claim is proven!

 ## warning

Always remove the fruit's bitter principle, as it irritates the mucous membranes.

 ## culinary

The large "berries" contain a bitter principle in the flesh: slice large varieties, sprinkle with salt and leave for 30 minutes before rinsing. Small and newer varieties do not need this treatment. Rub cut surfaces with lemon juice to prevent discoloration.

Eggplants can be made into soups, puréed, stewed, stuffed, fried and pickled. Slices can be dipped in batter to make fritters, or drizzled with olive oil and grilled or roasted. In the Middle East the skin is burned off over a naked flame, giving the flesh a smoky flavor.

In Provence, the vegetable stew *ratatouille* is made from eggplants, garlic, peppers, zucchini, onions and coriander seeds, all cooked in olive oil. The Greek *moussaka* contains minced meat and eggplants. In the Caribbean, small white varieties are stewed in coconut milk and sweet spices. Oriental eggplants have a sweetness that does not suit European cooking; use them in stir-fries.

Sautéed Eggplant with Mozzarella
Serves 4

This dish goes well with plain meats.

4 small, long, thin eggplants
1 clove garlic, crushed
1 tablespoon chopped parsley
Salt and freshly ground black pepper
¼ cup toasted breadcrumbs
3 tablespoons olive oil
4 ounces buffalo mozzarella, cut into ¼-inch slices

Cut the eggplants in half lengthwise. Score the flesh deeply, but do not cut the skin. Arrange in a shallow pan, skin side down. Mix the garlic, parsley, salt and pepper, the breadcrumbs and half the olive oil and press this into the scored eggplants. Drizzle over the rest of the oil and place in a preheated oven (350°F/180°C) until tender, about 20 minutes. Raise the heat to 400°F (200°C) and, as the oven warms, arrange the mozzarella on top of the eggplant. Return to the oven for 5 minutes. Serve this dish immediately after the mozzarella melts.

POTATO

Also known as Common Potato, Irish Potato. Perennial, grown as annual for edible starchy tubers. Half hardy. Value: rich in carbohydrates, magnesium, potassium; moderate amounts of vitamins B and C.

"Then a sentimental passion of a vegetable fashion must excite your languid spleen. An attachment à la Plato for a bashful young potato or a not too French French bean."
Sir William Gilbert (1836–1911)

The world's fourth most important food crop after wheat, corn and rice, the potato is a nutritious starchy staple grown throughout temperate zones. Hundreds of varieties have been developed since 5000 BCE, when potatoes were first cultivated in Chile and Peru. The name derives from *batatas*, the Carib Indian name for the sweet potato, or from *papa* or *patata*, as it was called by South American Indians.

The Spaniards introduced potatoes to Europe in the 16th century and Sir John Hawkins is reputed to have brought them to England in 1563. Extensive cultivation did not start until Sir Francis Drake brought more back in 1586, after battling with the Spaniards in the Caribbean. Sir Walter Raleigh introduced them to Ireland and later presented some to Elizabeth I. Her cook is said to have discarded the tubers and cooked the leaves, which did not help its popularity!

In England and Germany, potatoes were considered a curiosity; in France they were believed to cause leprosy and fever. However, in 1773 the French scientist Antoine Parmentier wrote a thesis extolling the potato's virtues as a famine food after eating them while a prisoner of war in Prussia. He established soup kitchens to feed the malnourished; potato soup is now known as *Potage Parmentier*, and there is also *Omelette Parmentier*. He created "French fries," which were served at a dinner honoring Benjamin Franklin, who was unimpressed; it was Thomas Jefferson who introduced French fries to the United States at a White House dinner.

Parmentier presented a bouquet of potato flowers to Louis XVI, who is said to have worn one in his buttonhole. Marie Antoinette wore them in her hair, which made it highly fashionable. By the early 19th century, the potato had become a staple in France.

Ireland's climate and plentiful rain produced large crops. Potatoes were propagated from small tubers that were passed from one household to another, so the whole crop came from a few original plants. These were susceptible to potato blight, and devastating crop failure in the 1840s caused the death of more than 1.5 million people. Almost a million others emigrated to North America.

During the American Civil War, potatoes were sent to the prisons and front lines. By eating the potatoes in their skins, soldiers received adequate supplies of vitamin C. The common name "spud" came from a tool that was once used to weed the potato patch.

varieties

Potatoes are classified as "first early," "second early" (or "midcrop") and "maincrop" varieties. Early and second early varieties grow rapidly, taking up less space for a shorter time than maincrops, so are better for small gardens. Yields are usually lower. They are also unaffected by some of the diseases afflicting maincrops.

Second earlies are planted about a month after earlies. Maincrop are for immediate consumption or winter storage.

Potatoes come in a huge range of shapes, sizes, colors and textures. The skin may be red, yellow, purple or white and the flesh pale cream or yellow,

Do not eat the leaves!

Maxine

mottled or blue. Their texture may be waxy or floury and shapes, variously, knobbly, round and oval. It is a wonderful time to grow potatoes. Hundreds of heritage varieties are available in catalogs; many from smaller, specialized producers and breeders are aiming to create more blight-resistant varieties. Grow some new varieties each year alongside your favorites for taste and performance. Use them or lose them!

'**Arran Pilot'** is an old favorite and a reliable cropper with tasty, firm, waxy flesh. '**Belle de Fontenay'** is a very old and rare French early variety that is excellent for salads. The yellow tubers are small and kidney-shaped with a waxy texture and fine flavor. '**Cara'** a late maincrop with pinkish red tubers, is good for baking and very disease-resistant. '**Charlotte'*** is a delicious second early salad variety with waxy flesh and a superb flavor hot and cold. '**Desirée'** is a popular maincrop with pink skin and pale yellow flesh that is good for fries and baking: crops well on most soils, but prefers medium to heavy; susceptible to mosaic and common scab. '**Golden Wonder'**, a late maincrop with floury, yellow flesh, is ideal for crisps and good for baking but usually disintegrates when boiled. It grows well in moist, humid climates, is resistant to scab but susceptible to slug damage and drought. '**Harlequin'**, a cross between 'Charlotte' and 'Pink Fir Apple', with pale yellow flesh, is an early maincrop salad potato with a delicious flavor — a taste test winner, both hot and cold. '**Highland Burgundy Red'** is an early maincrop with burgundy flesh and a mild taste. '**Maris Bard'** is a very early first early, with white skin and white waxy flesh. It is high-yielding and good under cover. Excellent quality and good virus resistance. '**Maris Piper'** is a prolific second early with waxy flesh when cooked. '**Mayan**

Maris Piper

Gold' is an early maincrop, "*phureja*"-type with different origins to traditional potatoes. Yellow-skinned with oval tubers, golden flesh and a nutty flavor and creamy but dry texture, it is good for fries, and pie toppings but not for roasting. **'King Edward'**, another famous high-yielding, good-quality maincrop, is good for baking but susceptible to blight, wart disease and drought. **'Lady Christl'*** is an excellent good textured first early with good disease resistance. **'Maxine'** is a maincrop that produces high yields of large, round, red-skinned tubers. The white waxy flesh remains firm when cooked; excellent for French fries. **'Mimi'***, a first early, produces tiny tubers that are superb in salads. Ideal for containers. First early **'Pentland Javelin'** produces high yields of oval, white-skinned tubers with white waxy flesh; resistant to common scab and golden eelworm. **'Pink Fir Apple'*** is a wonderful old late maincrop. The unusual elongated tubers are pink-skinned with pale yellow flesh. Remaining firm when cold, they are good in salads and make good fries. **'Ratte'***, a French classic early maincrop with a nutty flavor, is good for steaming. **'Red Duke of York'***, a first early with delicious yellow flesh, is a good all-rounder with a long harvesting season. **'Sarpo Axona'** is similar to 'Sarpo Mira' but with more regular-shaped tubers and creamier flesh. **'Sarpo Mira'** is heavy cropping with floury tubers that are good "all rounders" in the kitchen. It is also tolerant of a range of soils, not affected by slugs and 100% blight resistant. (Both late maincrops.) **'Sharpes Express'**, one of the best first early potatoes, has a wonderful flavor and is good for fries and new potatoes. **'Wilja'** is a high-yielding second early with long white tubers and pale yellow waxy flesh. Good for salads and excellent for cooking. Resistant to blight, it also has some resistance to scab and blackleg.

 cultivation

Propagation
Potatoes are normally grown from small tubers known as "seed potatoes." Buy "certified" virus-free stock from a reputable supplier to be certain of obtaining a good-quality crop.

First earlies
These are "sprouted" (or "chitted") about 6 weeks before planting to extend the growing season, which is particularly useful for early cultivars and in cooler climates. It is worth chitting second earlies and maincrops if they are to be planted late. Put a single layer of potatoes in a shallow tray or egg box with the "rose end" (where most of the "eyes" or dormant buds are) upwards, then put the tray in a light, cool, frost-free place to encourage growth. At 45°F (7°C) it takes about 6 weeks for shoots around 1 inch long to form. At this stage, they are ready for planting. They can be planted when the shoots are longer, but need handling with care, as they are easily broken off. For a smaller crop but larger potatoes, leave 3 shoots per tuber on earlies; otherwise leave all of the shoots for a higher yield.

Plant earlies from mid-spring and maincrops from late spring, when there is no longer any danger of hard frosts and soil temperatures are 45°F (7°C).

Make trenches or individual holes 3–6 inches deep, depending on the size of the tuber. Plant them upright with the shoots at the top and cover with at least 1 inch of soil. Take care not to damage the shoots. Earlies can be planted a little deeper to give more protection from cooler weather. Ideally the rows should face north-south, so that both sides receive sunshine.

Plant earlies 12–15 inches apart with 15–20 inches between the rows and maincrops 15 inches apart with 30 inches between the rows. Alternatively, plant earlies 14 inches apart and second earlies and maincrops 12–15 inches apart in and between the rows. Spacing can be varied according to the size of the tubers and also according to their subsequent cropping potential.

While the traditional method of propagation is very common, seed is also available, which is easy to handle and produces healthy crops. Seeds are sown indoors before potting on, hardening off and transplanting. "Plantlets" produced by tissue culture are also available;

these are healthy, virus-free and vigorous. These, too, will need growing on before hardening off and then transplanting.

Cutting large potatoes in half is not recommended; nor is the method I once saw being used — hollowing the tubers to leave a thin layer of flesh, then planting the skins only!

Growing
Potatoes flourish in an open, sunny, frost-free site on deep, rich, fertile, well-drained soil. They grow better in cool seasons, when temperatures are between 61–64°F (16–18°C), and are tolerant of most soils.

Lighter soils are better for growing earlies. Add organic matter to sandy soils. Alkaline soils or heavy liming encourages scab. Grow resistant varieties and lime acidic soils gradually to create a pH of 5–6, or cultivate in raised beds or containers. If necessary, dig in plenty of well-rotted organic matter in autumn, then rake to a rough tilth 10 days before planting, adding a general granular fertilizer at 2–3 pounds/sq ft.

Potatoes are an excellent crop for new or neglected gardens; while the crop may not be large, the root system breaks up the soil and improves its structure.

Mimi

Keep crops weed-free until they are established, when the dense canopy of foliage suppresses weeds.

Potatoes are "earthed up"; this prevents exposure to light, which makes them green and inedible, and also disturbs germinating weeds. When the plants are about 8–9 inches tall, use a rake or spade to draw loose soil carefully around the stems to a depth of 4–5 inches. Alternatively, begin earthing up in stages when the plants are about 4 inches tall, adding soil every 2–3 weeks.

To avoid having to earth up, plant small tubers about 5 inches deep and 9–10 inches apart on level ground. Wide spacing means tubers are not forced to the surface, yet still produce a moderate crop.

Potatoes need at least 20 inches of rainfall over the growing season for a good crop. During dry weather water earlies every 12–14 days at 45–60 gallons/sq ft. Except when there are drought conditions, do not water maincrops until the tubers are the size of marbles (check their development by scraping back the soil below a plant). At this point, a single, thorough soaking with at least 60 gallons/sq ft encourages the tubers to swell, increases the yield and makes them less prone to scab.

Fresh means full of flavor

Potatoes need a constant supply of water; erratic watering causes malformed, hollow or split potatoes. An organic liquid feed or nitrogenous top dressing helps plants to become established during the early stages of growth.

Early potatoes can be grown under black polyethylene, which also makes earthing up unnecessary. Prepare the soil, lay a sheet of black polyethylene over the area, anchor the edges by covering with soil and plant your potatoes through crosses cut in the polyethylene. Alternatively, plant the potatoes, cover them with plastic and when the foliage appears, make a cut in the polyethylene and pull through.

Where early frosts and windy conditions do not occur and the ground is excessively weedy or eelworm is a problem, potatoes can be grown in a bed of compost and straw. Clear the ground and cover the soil with a good layer of well-rotted manure or compost. Space the potatoes as required and cover them with a 2–3-inch layer of straw or hay, adding more as the potatoes grow, to a maximum of 6 inches. At this point, spread a 3–4-inch layer of lawn clippings over the area to exclude light from the developing tubers.

Rotate earlies every 3 and maincrops every 5 years.

Maintenance

Spring Chit potatoes before planting.
Summer Keep crops weed-free and water as necessary. Harvest and use, or store.
Autumn Plant winter crops under cover. Prepare the soil for the following year.
Winter Harvest winter crops.

Protected Cropping

To advance early crops and protect them from frost, cover early potatoes with cloches or floating crop covers, anchored by burying the edges under the soil. When the shoots appear, cut holes in the plastic and pull the foliage through. After 3–4 weeks cut the cover, leaving it in place to allow the potatoes to become acclimatized.

Protect the foliage and stems ("haulm") from heavy frosts by covering them at night with a layer of straw, bracken or newspaper, or a thin layer of soil. Light frosts do not generally cause problems.

For winter crops of new potatoes, in warm areas,

plant earlies in midsummer and cover with cloches in autumn. Alternatively, grow them in the borders of a frost-free greenhouse at 45–50°F (7–10°C). Provide warmth if necessary.

 ## companion planting

Growing horseradish in large sunken pots near to potatoes controls some diseases. Plant with corn, cabbage, beans and marigolds. Grow with eggplants, which are a greater attraction to Colorado beetle. Protect against scab by putting grass clippings and comfrey leaves in the planting hole or trench.

Harvesting and Storing

Earlies are ready to harvest from early to midsummer, second earlies from late summer to early autumn and maincrops mature from early to mid-autumn. Harvest earlies when they are about the size of a hen's egg: their readiness is often indicated by the flowers opening. Remove some soil from the side of a ridge and check them for size before lifting the root. Insert a flat-tined fork into the base of the ridge and lift the whole plant, bringing the new potatoes to the surface.

Harvest those grown under black polyethylene by folding back the sheeting: the crop of potatoes will be lying on the surface. Collect as required. Scrape away compost from those grown in containers to check their size before harvesting them.

Leave healthy maincrop potatoes in the soil for as long as possible, but beware of slugs! In early autumn cut back the haulm to about 2 inches above the soil, or wait until the foliage dies down naturally; leave the tubers in the ground for 2 weeks for the skins to harden before lifting.

Cut back the haulm and work along the side of each ridge, lifting the potatoes with a fork. Harvest on a dry sunny day when the soil is moderately moist, leave in the sun for a few hours to dry, then brush off the soil. If the weather is poor, dry them under cloches or on trays indoors. Store healthy tubers in paper or hessian sacks or boxes in a dark, cool, frost-free place. They should keep until spring. Check tubers weekly, removing those that are damaged or diseased.

When harvesting, ensure that all potatoes, however small, are removed from the soil, to prevent future

POTATO

problems occurring with pests and diseases. New potatoes do not store, but can be frozen: blanch whole in boiling water for 3 minutes; cool, drain, pack into rigid containers and freeze. Chips and French fries can also be frozen.

Pests and Diseases

Common potato scab shows as raised, corky scabs on the surface of the tuber. It does not usually affect the whole potato and can be removed by peeling. It is common in hot, dry summers, on light, free-draining and alkaline soils. Water well in dry conditions, add plenty of organic matter to the soil before planting, avoid excessive liming, or rotating after the soil has been limed for brassicas. Do not put infected potatoes or peelings on the compost heap. Grow resistant cultivars.

Potato blight appears on the leaves as brown patches, often with paler margins. The infection can spread to

Maxine leaves showing the first signs of blight

the stems and through the tuber, making it inedible. The disease spreads rapidly in warm, humid conditions and maincrops are more susceptible. Grow resistant cultivars and avoid overhead watering; before the problem appears, apply a systemic fungicide every 2 weeks from midsummer. Alternatively, use copper sulfate sprays such as Bordeaux mixture. Earthing up creates a protective barrier, slowing the infection of tubers. Lift early potatoes as soon as possible and in late summer, cut back the haulms of infected plants just above the ground and burn the infected material or put it in the garbage. Leave tubers in the ground for 2 weeks before lifting.

With potato cyst eelworm ("golden nematode" or "pale eelworm") growth is checked and yields can be severely reduced; badly affected plants turn yellow and die. Lift and burn infected plants, rotate crops, and do not grow potatoes or tomatoes in the soil for at least 6 years. Try to grow resistant varieties.

Wireworms are about 1 inch long and golden brown in color. They tunnel into the tubers, making them inedible. They are fairly easy to control. Cultivate the soil thoroughly over winter to expose to the weather and birds, keep crops weed-free, and lift maincrops as early as possible.

Blackleg shows when the upper leaves roll and wilt and the stem becomes black and rotten at the base. The tubers may be rotten. It is more severe in wet seasons; do not plant on waterlogged land. Remove affected plants immediately; burn or put in the garbage. Do not store damaged tubers.

Slugs tunnel into the tubers; damage is more severe the longer they remain in the ground. Use biological control.

 ## container growing

Potatoes can be grown in any container if it is at least 12 inches wide and deep and has drainage holes. It is possible to buy a potato barrel for this purpose — some models have sliding panels for ease of harvesting — but an old garbage can, flower pot or similar is just as good. Potatoes can also be grown in black garbage bags. Wider containers can, of course, hold more potatoes. Place a 4–5-inch layer of compost or good garden soil in a container, stand 2–3 chitted potatoes on the

surface and cover with a layer of compost about 4–5 inches deep. When the shoots are about 6 inches tall, cover with another 4–6-inch layer of compost, leaving the tips showing. Continue earthing up until the shoots are 2–3 inches below the rim of the container.

Winter crops of first earlies can also be grown in containers. Plant in midsummer for harvesting at Christmas. Cover the haulms in frosty weather or grow under glass.

Be sure to keep crops well fed and watered.

 ## other uses

Potatoes are made into flour and turned into bread. They can be boiled and the starch turned to glucose, which can be fermented to produce strong alcohol, like the poteen made in Ireland. In the past, they have also been a source of starch powder for whitening wigs. The juice of mature potatoes is particularly excellent for cleaning silks, cotton, wool and even furniture.

 ## medicinal

Potatoes are said to be good for rheumatism. One traditional cure for sciatica and lumbago is to carry a potato in your pocket.

The juice from a raw potato or the water in which potatoes have been boiled is said to relieve gout, rheumatism, lumbago, sprains and bruises.

Uncooked peeled and pounded potatoes are said to make a soothing plaster to scalds or burns when applied cold.

Potatoes contain little fat and provide more potassium *pro rata* than bananas, while the average potato contains as many calories as most apples or a glass of orange juice and can be eaten by those on a diet.

warning

Green potatoes contain the toxic alkaloid solanine, which can cause vomiting and stomach upset. Do not eat green potatoes. Be aware that the tomato-like fruits and leaves of the plant are also poisonous.

Harvesting and Storing

Harvest from mid-autumn. Lift as required; protect roots with a layer of straw, bracken or a similar material before severe frosts or snow. They can be lifted in autumn and stored in boxes of peat substitute, sand or sawdust, in a cool, frost-free garage, shed or cellar. Lift carefully with a garden fork; the roots "bleed" and snap easily.

If you begin lifting and find the crop misshapen, leave the roots buried in the ground and harvest the shoots and buds the following year. Next time, grow in sieved soil.

Harvest "chards" in early to mid-spring: scrape away the soil and cut the blanched shoots when they are 5–6 inches long. Or lift when 6 inches tall, without earthing up, though they are not as tender.

Pests and Diseases

Salsify is usually trouble-free but may suffer from white blister, which looks like glistening paint splashes and can distort plants. Spray with Bordeaux mixture and destroy any plants that are badly affected. Aster yellows cause deformed new growth and the leaf veins or whole leaf become yellow. Control the aster leaf hopper, which spreads the disease.

 ## container growing

Salsify can be grown in containers, but it is impractical to produce them in large quantities. However, if you are desperate, fill a large wooden box or plastic drum with sandy, free-draining soil or a loam-based compost with added sharp sand. Ensure there are sufficient drainage holes. Keep crops weed-free and water regularly.

 ## companion planting

Salsify grows well with mustard and, planted near carrots, discourages carrot fly.

 ## medicinal

Salsify is said to have an antibilious effect and to calm fevers. In folk medicine, it is used to treat gall bladder problems and jaundice.

 ## culinary

Salsify has a delicate oyster-like flavor and can be cooked in a variety of ways (there is bound to be a recipe that suits you). Peel after boiling until tender, "skimming" under cold running water as you would a hard-boiled egg.

Cut roots discolor, so drop them into water with a dash of lemon juice, then boil for 25 minutes in salted water with lemon juice and a tablespoon of flour. Drain and skin, toss with melted butter and chopped parsley and indulge.

Try them with a light mornay sauce, deep-fried or served *au gratin* with cheese and breadcrumbs. Perhaps sautéing them in butter and eating with brown sugar is more to your liking?

Roots can also be baked, puréed, creamed for soup or grated raw in salads. They stay fresh in the refrigerator for about a week.

"Chards" can be served raw in salads or lightly cooked. Young flowering shoots can be eaten pickled, raw or cooked and eaten cold like asparagus, with oil and lemon juice. The subtle flavor makes them an excellent hors d'oeuvre.

Pick flower buds just before they open, with about 3 inches of stem attached, lightly simmer and eat when they are cool.

Salsify in Batter
Serves 4

1½ pounds salsify, topped, tailed and cleaned
Vegetable oil, for frying
Lemon wedges, to serve

For the Batter:
1 cup all-purpose flour
1 teaspoon baking powder
1 egg

1 tablespoon olive oil
¼ teaspoon harissa
½ teaspoon ground cumin
¼ teaspoon dried thyme
Salt and freshly ground black pepper

Cut salsify roots in half and boil in salted water for 30 minutes. Rinse under cold water. Peel and cut into 3-inch pieces.

Make the batter: blend all the ingredients with ½ cup of water in a food processor for 30 seconds.

Heat the oil in a large frying pan. Dip the salsify in the batter and fry in oil until crisp and golden, turning. Keep warm while cooking the remainder. Serve hot with lemon wedges.

Salsify in Ham with Cheese Sauce
Serves 4

8 salsify, peeled and trimmed
8 slices cooked ham
2 tablespoons butter
2 tablespoons flour
1 teaspoon Dijon mustard
1¼ cups milk
4 tablespoons grated Gruyère cheese
Pinch nutmeg
Salt and freshly ground black pepper

Boil the salsify for 5 minutes and drain. Cut into roughly 4-inch lengths. When cool enough to handle, wrap each in a slice of ham and arrange in a greased baking dish.

Melt the butter in a heavy pan and stir in the flour to make a roux. Cook for a minute or two and stir in the mustard. Slowly add the milk, then the Gruyère, and cook until the cheese is melted.

Season with nutmeg, salt and pepper and pour over the salsify. Bake in a preheated oven at 400°F (200°C) for 20 minutes, until browned.

Salsify in Batter

Valerianella locusta. Valerianaceae

LAMB'S LETTUCE

Also known as Corn Salad, Mâche, Lamb's Tongues. Low-growing, extremely hardy annual grown for edible leaves. Value: good source of beta carotene, vitamin C and folic acid. Very few calories.

In spite of its delicate appearance, lamb's lettuce is an extremely hardy plant, particularly valued as a nutritious winter salad crop. Its attractive bright green, rounded leaves have a slightly nutty taste. Depending on the authority, it was named lamb's lettuce because sheep are partial to it, or because it appears during the lambing season. Another name, corn salad, comes from its regular appearance as a cornfield weed.

Gerard wrote: "We know the Lamb's Lettuce as loblollie; and it serves in winter as a salad herb among others none of the worst." He also noted that "foreigners using it in England led to its cultivation in our gardens." It has been popular for centuries in France, where it is known as *salade de prêtre* (as it is often eaten in Lent), *doucette* ("little soft one," referring to the velvety leaves), and *bourcette*, describing their shape. In England it declined in popularity in the 1700s and a 19th-century commentator noted: "…it is indeed a weed, and can be of no real use where lettuces are to be had." Before the appearance of winter lettuce varieties, lamb's lettuce was the main winter salad; it was at one time classified in the same genus.

varieties

There are two forms, the "large" or "broad-leaved" and the darker, more compact "green" type, which is popular in western Europe, but less productive.

'Cavallo'* has deep green leaves and crops heavily. **'Grote Noordhollandse'** is very hardy. **'Large Leaved'** is tender and prolific. **'Valeriana d'Orlanda'** is an Italian variety with larger leaves than **'Verte de Cambrai'**, which is a traditional French type with small leaves and good flavor. **'Verte d'Etampes'** has unusual, attractive savoyed leaves. **'Vit'** is very vigorous with a mild flavor.

cultivation

Propagation

Lamb's lettuce can be grown as single plants or "cut and come again" seedlings. Sow seeds successively from mid- to late spring for summer crops in drills 4–6 inches apart and ½ inch deep, thinning when seedlings have 3–4 seed leaves to about 4 inches apart. Sow winter crops successively from mid- to late summer. Seeds can also be sown in broad drills, broadcast, or in seed trays or modules for transplanting. Leave a few plants to bolt, and transplant seedlings into rows.

Growing

Lamb's lettuce flourishes in a sheltered position in full sun or light shade and needs a deep, fertile soil for rapid and continuous growth. It tolerates most soils, provided they are not waterlogged. Create a firm seedbed and rake in a slow-release general fertilizer at ¾–1½/sq ft before sowing in spring and summer. Overwintered crops growing on the same site should not need it.

Keep crops weed-free, particularly during the early stages, and water thoroughly to encourage soft growth.

Maintenance

Spring Sow successively.
Summer Continue sowing and harvesting; keep crops weed-free and water well.

Harvest before the plant starts flowering

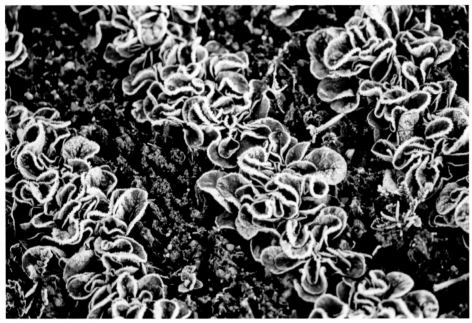

Productive even in winter

Autumn Sow crops under cover. Continue harvesting.
Winter When growth is slower, do not overpick.

Protected Cropping
Although it is extremely hardy, growing lamb's lettuce
under cloches, polyethylene tunnels or horticultural
fleece, or in an unheated greenhouse, encourages
better quality and higher productivity. Make the first
sowings in early autumn.

Harvesting and Storing
Harvest seedlings, pick leaves as required, or lift
whole plants when they are mature — about 3 months
after planting.

Do not weaken by removing too many leaves at one
picking. This is particularly important with outdoor
winter crops.

Leaves can be blanched for a few days before picking
by covering with a box or pot to remove any bitterness.
Young flowers can be eaten in salads.

Pests and Diseases
Some varieties are susceptible to mildew. Protect
seedlings from birds and slugs.

 companion planting

As plants take up very little space, lamb's lettuce is ideal
sown between taller crops.

 container growing

Can be grown in 10-inch pots of loam-based compost
with a low fertiliser content. Sow seeds thinly ½ inch
deep every 3 weeks from early spring to early summer
and again from early to mid-autumn, thinning to leave the
strongest seedlings at a final spacing of 4 inches apart.

Keep the compost moist when plants are growing
vigorously; reduce watering in cooler conditions.

 medicinal

With its high beta carotene, vitamin C and folic acid
content, it is regarded by many as a winter and early
spring tonic, and is useful when other nutritional
vegetables are scarce.

 culinary

Thinnings can be used in salads. Wash the
leaves thoroughly to remove soil. In 17th-century
Europe, lamb's lettuce was often served with cold
boiled beets or celery. The leaves are used as a
substitute for lettuce and combine well with it, also
complementing fried bacon or ham and beetroot.
Leaves can also be cooked like spinach.

Lamb's Lettuce and Shrimp Salad
Serves 4

*A bag of lamb's lettuce, or a mixture of winter
    salad leaves*
16–20 large fresh shrimp, peeled
Toasted sesame seeds

For the vinaigrette:
Lemon juice
Balsamic vinegar
Extra virgin olive oil
Mustard
Salt and freshly ground black pepper
*Chopped fresh herbs, such as sage, parsley
    and chives*

Wash the salad leaves and arrange on individual
plates. Season the shrimp with salt and pepper
and coat generously with sesame seeds. In a
heavy-bottomed frying pan, gently cook them,
turning after 3 minutes, when golden, to cook
the other side. Arrange on the salad. Make the
vinaigrette by mixing the ingredients to taste,
sprinkle over and serve.

Vicia faba. Papilionaceae
BROAD BEAN

Also known as Fava Bean, Horse Bean, Windsor. Annual grown for seeds, young leaf shoots and whole young pods. Value: low protein, good source of fiber, potassium, vitamins E and C.

They are thought to have originated around the Mediterranean, and the oldest remains of domesticated broad beans have been dated to 6800–6500 BCE. By the Iron Age, they had spread throughout Europe. The Greeks dedicated them to Apollo and thought that overindulgence dulled the senses; Dioscorides wrote that they are "flatulent, hard of digestion, causing troublesome dreams."

They may be the origin of the term "bean feast," being a major part of the annual meal given by employers for their staff. In the vernacular this has been changed to "beano." Great Britain has many folk sayings concerning the sowing date. Huntingdonshire country wisdom states: "On St. Valentine's Day, beans should be in clay," and it was generally accepted that four seeds were sown — "One for rook, one for crow, one to rot, one to grow." Flowers were considered to be an aphrodisiac — "there ent no lustier scent than a beanfield in bloom" — while the poet John Clare wrote: 'My love is as sweet as a bean field in blossom, beanfields misted wi' dew."

Hardy and prolific, they are the national dish of Egypt. An Arab saying goes, "Beans have satisfied even the pharaohs." How about you?

varieties

Broad beans are classified as "dwarf," with small, early-maturing pods that are excellent under cloches or in containers, "longpods," which are also hardy, and "windsors," with broad pods that usually mature later and have a better flavor. There are green- and white-seeded forms among the longpods and windsors.

'Aquadulce'* is a reliable hardy longpod for autumn and spring sowing. **'Aquadulce Claudia'*** is similar, with medium to long pods and white seeds, but less susceptible to blackfly; ideal for freezing. **'Bunyards' Exhibition'** is a reliable heavy cropper with a sweet subtle flavor and delicate texture. Good for freezing. **'Imperial Green Longpod'*** produces pods around 15 inches long with up to 9 large green beans. **'Masterpiece Green Longpod'*** is a good-quality, green-seeded bean that freezes well. **'Jubilee**

Hyson'* crops early with long pods of pale green beans; outstanding quality and flavor. **'Red Epicure'** has beautiful deep chestnut-crimson seeds. Some of the color is lost in cooking, but the flavor is superb. **'Sweet Lorane'** is a prolific, delicious small-seeded bean that is also cold-hardy. **'The Sutton'***, a prolific dwarf variety, grows to around 12 inches high, is ideal for small gardens and under cloches — excellent flavor. **'Witkiem Manita'*** is perfect for spring sowing, with sweet, succulent beans.

cultivation

Propagation
As they germinate well in cool conditions, broad beans can be sown from mid- to late autumn and overwintered outdoors for a mid-spring crop. Seedlings should be 1 inch high when colder weather arrives. "Aquadulce" cultivars are particularly suitable. When the soil is

workable, sow every 3 weeks from late winter to late spring for successional cropping.

Plant seeds 2 inches deep in rows or make individual holes with 12 inches in and between the rows. Or grow them in staggered double rows, with 9 inches in and between the rows or in blocks 36 inches square with 8–12 inches between plants. Tall plants should be 12–15 inches apart. Sow extra seeds at the end of rows, for later use as transplants.

Growing
Broad beans flourish in an open, sunny site but overwintering crops need more shelter. Soils should be deeply dug, moisture-retentive and well-drained, having been manured for the previous year's crop.

Alternatively, add well-rotted organic matter in late autumn before sowing. They need a pH of 6–7, so lime where necessary. Rotate with other legumes.

BROAD BEAN

Pods filled with flavor

Rake a granular general fertilizer into the seedbed 1 week before sowing. Mulch, hoe or hand weed regularly, especially at first.

Watering should be unnecessary except in drought, but for good-quality crops, plants need 60 gallons/sq ft per week from flower formation to harvest end.

Support taller plants with stakes. Planting several staggered rows allows plants to support one another. Dwarf types can be supported with brushwood.

Maintenance

Spring Sow early crops under glass, followed by later sowings until late spring.
Summer Harvest from late spring to late summer. Keep crops weed-free and water after flower formation.
Autumn Sow outdoor crops for overwintering.
Winter Protect outdoor crops in severe weather.

Protected Cropping

Where plants cannot be overwintered outdoors, sow under cover in pots or boxes from midwinter. Harden off and plant out in mid-spring. Remove cloches from protected early crops when the beans reach the glass.

Harvesting and Storing

Pick when the beans begin to show, before the pods are too large (and tough). Pull with a sharp downward twist or cut with scissors. Pods harvested at 2–3 inches long can be treated as snap peas and eaten whole, but picking at this stage reduces yields. Broad beans freeze well, especially green-seeded varieties. Wash, blanch for 3 minutes, and freeze in plastic bags or rigid containers.

Use within 12 months. Keep them in a plastic bag in the refrigerator for 1 week.

Pests and Diseases

Black bean aphid is the most common problem. Control by pinching off the top 3 inches of stem when the first beans start to form. This also encourages an earlier harvest.

Mice and Jays steal the seeds. Trap and tolerate.

 ## companion planting

Plant with summer savory to discourage black bean aphid and among gooseberries to discourage gooseberry sawfly. The flowers are very attractive to bees. Broad beans are a good "nurse" crop for developing maize and corn.

Interplant with brassicas, which benefit from the nitrogen-fixing roots. Dig in plant debris as a "green manure" to increase soil fertility. Seedling beans protect early potato shoots from wind and frost.

 ## container growing

Grow dwarf cultivars in containers of low-fertilizer loam-based compost at least 8–15 inches wide by 10 inches deep. Sow seeds 2 inches deep and 4–5 inches apart. Water regularly in warm weather, less at other times.

 ## culinary

Steam or lightly boil beans to eat with ham, pork and chicken. Eat with sautéed onions, mushrooms and bacon; dress with tomato sauce, warm sour cream or lemon butter and dill.

Broad Beans with Summer Savory
Serves 4

A dish that reflects the pure tastes of summer.

1 pound young broad beans, shelled weight
2 sprigs plus 2 tablespoons summer savory
2 tablespoons butter
Salt and freshly ground black pepper

Put the beans into a pan of boiling, salted water with the sprigs of summer savory and cook until just done, about 3–5 minutes. Drain and put the pan back on a gentle heat. Add the butter and toss well as it melts. Season with more summer savory and salt and pepper.

Bissara
Serves 4

An Algerian dish with subtle flavors, this is based on one from the late, great foodie, Arto der Haroturian.

1½ pounds young broad beans, shelled weight
1 small green chili, chopped

1 teaspoon paprika
1 teaspoon cumin seeds, crushed in a pestle and mortar
2 cloves garlic, peeled
8 tablespoons extra virgin olive oil
Juice of ½ a lemon
Salt and freshly ground black pepper
A little olive oil, lemon juice and paprika, to garnish

Boil the beans in lightly salted water until just tender. Drain and place in a food processor, together with the chili, paprika, cumin and garlic. Purée by slowly drizzling in the oil and lemon juice. Season and pour into a bowl.

Garnish with a little olive oil, lemon juice and paprika. Serve bissara with warm bread.

WASABI

Wasabia japonica. Cruciferae

Also known as Japanese Horseradish, Shan Kui. Hardy herbaceous perennial. Value: high in protein, potassium and moderate amounts of calcium and vitamin C.

This Japanese native, found in boggy ground by mountain streams, is highly prized for its horseradish-flavored roots, which are traditionally ground into a fine powder using a shark skin grater or *oroshi* before being turned into a paste. It has been cultivated in Japan since the 10th century CE; the highest prices are paid for natural water-grown *sawa* or semi-aquatic wasabi, the price and quality of field-grown or *oka* is correspondingly lower. At the time of writing, dried, field-grown wasabi rhizomes, cultivated on the U.S. Pacific coast, are retailing at about $40 per ounce. As demand outstrips supply beware of inferior products made of horseradish or Chinese mustard and food coloring — or grow your own.

A true vegetable delicacy

 varieties

Wasabia japonica grows up to 16 inches tall with glossy, almost heart-shaped leaves the size of small dinner plates, with coarsely-toothed margins and spikes of small white flowers in late spring.

 cultivation

Propagation
Repropagate plants every two years, as younger roots have a better flavor. Sow seeds in early spring in loam-based compost; transplant into individual pots when the "true" leaves are large enough to handle.

Grow them in the greenhouse for the first year, standing in trays of water so the compost stays constantly moist. Plant out in late spring or early summer of the second year after acclimatizing plants to outdoor conditions.

Alternatively, divide healthy plants in early spring as they start into growth, grow them on in an unheated greenhouse or cold frame and plant out in late spring the following year. Small offsets can also be detached from well-established plants in spring.

Growing
The plants will grow in boggy ground of any pH, or in fresh, pollution-free, running water, in sunshine or part shade, particularly in warmer climates. Cultivation techniques are similar to watercress (see page 191) and roots should be protected with bracken, straw or fleece over winter. The optimum water temperature is

WASABI

50–55°F (10–13°C) with air temperatures of 46–68°F (8–20°C), though plants still grow in less than perfect conditions.

Maintenance

Spring Sow seeds, divide or remove "offsets."
Summer Ensure plants remain moist. Harvest plants; retain divisions for replanting.
Autumn Remove leaves as they die down.
Winter Cover plants to protect from frost.

Harvesting and Storing

Lift rhizomes as needed and use immediately, for the finest flavor.

Worth their weight in gold

 container growing

Grow in large pots of loam-based compost kept constantly moist by standing in a bowl of water that is refreshed daily.

 medicinal

Wasabi is used to stimulate digestion, has antibacterial qualities, reduces mucus, and controls asthma and other congestive disorders. Isothiocyantates help detoxify the liver and gut; it is also a powerful antioxidant and has anticancer properties.

culinary

Use freshly dug rhizomes, as the flavor deteriorates rapidly once the root has been cut; it is similar but superior to horseradish and mid-green in color. Rhizomes harvested at 15–24 months old are considered to be the best. It is finely grated and turned into a paste and is the ideal complement to raw fish in *sashimi* or *sushi* dishes, added to soups or mixed with soy sauce to make dips. The leaves, flowers and leaf stems are also cooked and eaten. In Japan, the leaves and leaf stalks, flowers and rhizomes are soaked in salt water, mixed with sake lees and used to make a pickle called *wasabe-zuke*. Wasabi can also be bought in powdered form, in small cans. This recipe comes from *The Japanese Kitchen* by Kimiko Barber.

Wasabi and Avocado Dip

Serves 4

2 tablespoons wasabi powder
1 ripe avocado
2 tablespoons good mayonnaise
1 teaspoon light soy sauce
Salt (optional)

Mix the wasabi powder with 2 tablespoons water. Peel the avocado, remove the stone and roughly mash with a fork. Place the wasabi paste, mashed avocado mayonnaise and soy sauce into a food processor and blend until smooth and creamy. Have a taste and season with salt if necessary.

Zea mays. Graminae

CORN

Also known as Maize, Corn on the Cob, Indian Corn, Baby Maize, Sweet Corn. Annual grown for kernels of edible seeds. Half hardy. Value: high in carbohydrates and fiber, moderate protein and B vitamin content.

Wild plants of maize have never been found, but it is believed that the crop was first cultivated in Mexico around 7000 BCE. Primitive types, smaller than an ear of wheat, were found in caves at Tehuacan in southern Mexico dating from around 3500 BCE, yet they were bred by Mayan and Indan farmers almost to the size of modern varieties. Early American civilizations were based on maize, and life for the Aztecs revolved round the *milpa* or cornfield. Multicolored types with blue, scarlet, brown and almost black seeds predominated in South America. It became a staple crop in North America after 800 CE. The first types introduced to Europe in the 16th century from Central America were valued for both the cobs and the yellow meal. Corn flourished in Spain, France, Italy, the Balkans and Portugal.

Corn is a sweet form of maize, a starchy crop used for grain and fodder. The yellow-golden varieties are commonly cultivated for the kitchen, but those with multicolored seeds are extremely ornamental. Corn and maize are the third most important cereal in the world, after wheat and rice, and there are more than 500 different by-products. The seeds of corn also provide us with popcorn, with its exploding grains; starch extracted after milling has been used as laundry starch; the inner husks are used for making cigarette papers and the pith has been used for making explosives and packaging material. Best of all is delicious fresh corn eaten from the cob, dripping with butter; take the advice of Edward Bunyard: "The principle of the lathe is adopted in eating them."

 varieties

"Normal" varieties were the first selections and have the best seed vigor. "Supersweets" have very high sugar levels, a longer storage life than "normal" varieties but poorer germination. "Sugar Enhanced" are not as sweet as "Supersweet" but are better for storing and "Extra Tender Sweets" are sweeter and more tender. If you aim to grow "supersweet" varieties they should be at least 26 feet from ordinary varieties to prevent cross pollination. Alternatively, grow sugar enhanced types — if cross pollination occurs, the cobs will be more like traditional varieties.

Supersweet varieties
'Earlibird'* has good vigor and is a top-quality variety for cob size and flavor. **'Prelude'*** is vigorous and high yielding, with cobs up to 10 inches long. **'Ovation'*** is a mid-season variety with large tasty cobs up to 8 inches long. **'Northern Extra Sweet'*** is reliable and good in cooler climates — one of the earliest to mature and with top-quality kernels. Do not let it overripen.

Extra Tender Sweet varieties
'Swift'*, voted the best variety in independent trials, produces large cobs with exceptionally sweet, tender and succulent kernels. Does not need to be isolated from other varieties. **'Lark'*** has moderate vigor, very sweet cobs and performs well in colder soils.

Sugar Enhanced varieties
'Minipop' is a baby corn with sweet cobs. Plant in rows rather than blocks and harvest before they swell. Eat lightly steamed or with dips. **'Tuxedo'**, a tall variety, performs well under drier conditions and is exceptionally

drought resistant. **'Sweet Nugget'** grows to a moderate length, golden yellow cobs that taste very sweet. Ideal in cooler conditions.

Others

'Honey Bantam' grows exceptionally early, 7 inches long, with pretty yellow and white kernels that are very sweet indeed. **'Kelvedon Glory'** is an old variety with long, light golden cobs that are filled with flavor. **'Red Strawberry'** has tiny red kernels on compact cobs (only 2 inches long). Put them in the microwave and they explode into fluffy popcorn.

 ## cultivation

Propagation

Seeds do not germinate when soil temperatures are below 50°F (10°C). Better germination and earlier crops are achieved by sowing from mid-spring under cover in pots or modules. Plant 2–3 seeds 1 inch deep in pots of moist seed compost from mid- to late spring, at 55°F (13°C). After germination, thin to leave the strongest seedling. Corn is sensitive to root damage and disturbance, so thin with care, holding the strongest

Mini Pep

seedling while removing weaker ones. Harden off and plant out once there is no longer any danger of frost.

Plants should be 14 inches apart in and between the rows or spaced 10–12 inches apart in rows 24 inches apart.

To avoid erratic germination, seeds can be pregerminated. Put a few sheets of tissue paper or similar material in the bottom of a seedtray, moisten with water, place seeds evenly over the surface and cover with another layer of moist tissue. Put the tray in a loosely knotted plastic bag in an airing cupboard or warm room. When the seeds swell and tiny rootlets have formed, sow a single seed 1 inch deep in a 4-inch pot of seed compost or sow singly outdoors. Sow a few in pots to replace those that do not germinate outdoors.

Alternatively, sow *in situ* from late spring to early summer. When the soil is workable, make a block about 4–5 feet, comprising 4 ridges of soil about 12 inches high with 14 inches between the top of each ridge. "Station sow" 2–3 seeds in the furrow 14 inches apart each way and thin to leave the strongest seedling.

Cut a square of thin polyethylene or similar slightly larger than the block. Spread it over the furrows, dig a shallow trench round the edge and weigh the margins down with soil to hold the cover in place. As the seedlings emerge, cut crosses in the cover so they can grow through, or remove it and earth up around the stem bases when plants are 18 inches high. Alternatively, sow on a level seedbed and protect crops with fleece or cloches, which should be removed as soon as the plants become too large.

"Supersweet" varieties need slightly warmer conditions for germination; soils should be at a minimum of 55°F (12°C). Because corn is wind-pollinated, plants are sown in blocks for effective germination.

The male tassels (flowers) at the top of the plant shed clouds of pollen on to the female tassels or "silks" below. These are clusters of pale green strands on the ends of the cobs that become sticky before pollination and each strand is attached to a single grain. Each must be pollinated, and sowing in a block ensures effective pollination. On a calm day tap the stems to help pollination. Mini varieties can be sown in rows.

Seeds germinate in warm conditions

Growing

Corn needs a moisture-retentive, free-draining soil. Dig in plenty of organic matter several weeks before planting, or use ground manured for the previous year's crop. Ideally, the soil should be slightly acidic, with a pH of 5.5–7.0. Plants need a long, warm growing season to succeed, so grow fast-maturing, early cultivars in cooler areas. The site should be open, sunny, warm and sheltered from cold winds and frosts.

Rake in a slow-release general fertilizer after transplanting or when preparing the seedbed. Keep compost moist throughout the growing season. Watering is particularly beneficial when they begin to flower, and when the grains begin to swell. Apply 60 gallons/sq ft per week. Stake plants when growing on exposed sites.

Corn is shallow-rooted, so take care when hoeing to avoid damaging the roots. It is much better to mulch with a layer of organic matter to suppress weeds and retain moisture. Mulch with black polyethylene on level ground. Do not remove sideshoots (tillers). Earth up to make plants more stable.

Corn can easily be part of an ornamental garden

Maintenance
Spring Sow seed under cover or outdoors.
Summer Sow seeds; keep crops weed-free and water. Harvest.
Autumn Harvest.
Winter . Prepare the ground for next year's crop.

Protected Cropping
When soil temperatures are below 50°F (10°C), sow from mid-spring under cover in pots or modules at 55°F (13°C). Harden off and plant out once there is no danger of frost.

Harvesting and Storing
Each plant usually produces one or two cobs. Those sown *in situ* mature later than seed sown indoors. After pollination the silks begin to turn brown, an indication that the cob is maturing. Peel back the leaves and test for ripeness by pushing your thumbnail into a grain: if the liquid runs clear, it is unripe; if it is milky, it is ready to harvest; if it is thick, then it is overmature and unsuitable for eating. To pick, hold the main stem in one hand and twist off the cob with the other. Corn is ideal for instant eating. Have a pot of water boiling before you harvest!

Freeze within at least 24 hours of picking, before the sugars in the seeds convert to starch. Supersweet varieties hold their sugar levels longer.

To freeze, blanch cobs for 4–6 minutes, cool and drain, before wrapping singly in foil or cling film and placing in the freezer.

Cobs remain fresh for up to 3 days if they are stored in the refrigerator.

Pests and Diseases
Birds can pull up the seedlings and attack the developing cobs. Slugs attack seedlings. Smut appears as large galls on the cobs and stalks in hot dry weather. Cut off and burn the debris immediately after harvesting and do not grow corn on the site for at least 3 years. Frit fly larvae bore into the growing points of corn seedlings, which then develop twisted and ragged leaves. Growth is stunted and cobs are undersized. Use "dressed" seed and cultivate the ground thoroughly. Mice enjoy newly planted seeds, especially supersweet types. Trap, or buy a cat.

Enough to go around

Block planting results in good pollination

 ## companion planting

Grow corn with or after legumes. Runner beans can be allowed to grow over corn plants. Intercrop corn with sunflowers, allowing cucurbits to trail through them.

The shade they provide is useful to cucumbers, melons, squashes, zucchini, marrows and potatoes. Brussels sprouts, kale, Savoy cabbages, swedes and broccoli can be interplanted. Grow lettuce and other salads, French beans and zucchini between the crops.

 ## medicinal

Corn is said to reduce the risk of certain cancers, heart disease and dental cavities. Corn oil is reported to lower cholesterol levels more successfully than other polyunsaturated oils.

In parts of Mexico, corn is used to treat dysentery. It is also known in North American folk medicine as a diuretic and mild stimulant.

culinary

To serve whole, strip off outer leaves, leaving 2–3 inches of stalk on the ear. Pull off "silks." Boil in unsalted water, drain and eat hot with melted butter. Roasted corn is a favorite with most children — it tastes wonderfully succulent compared with the sogginess of canned corn.

Deep-fry spoonfuls of a mixture of mashed corn, salt, flour, milk and egg for 1–2 minutes or until golden brown to make corn fritters.

Seeds are ground, meal boiled or baked, cob can be roasted or boiled or fermented, maize meal is cooked with water to create a thick mash, or dough.

Tortillas are made by baking in flat cakes until they are crisp. Polenta is made from ground maize.

Dry-milling produces grits, from which most of the bran and germ are separated. Cornflakes are rolled, flavored seeds. Multicolored corn adds color and flavor to sweet dishes and drinks.

Baby corns are particularly decorative and the perfect size for oriental stir-fries, where they combine well with snow peas.

Barbecued Corn on the Cob

This is the way to really taste the flavor of corn. Take 1 ear of corn for each person. Boil them in salted water for 7–10 minutes and then drain.

Place each in the center of a piece of tinfoil. Use 1 tablespoon butter per ear and mix in 1 teaspoon fresh chopped herbs, sea salt and freshly ground black pepper; spread over the corn ears. Season well and then seal the foil.

Lay the cobs on a medium-hot barbecue or in a charcoal grill (in which case, keep it covered) and roast for 20 minutes, turning the cobs once, halfway through cooking.

Corn Maque Choux
Serves 4

Cajun cooking has become popular in recent years and this dish reveals the true taste of corn.

1 pound corn, cooked and stripped from the cob
1 tablespoon butter
1 large onion, coarsely chopped
1 green pepper, deseeded and diced
2 tomatoes, peeled, deseeded and diced
½ teaspoon Tabasco sauce
Salt and freshly ground black pepper

Heat the butter in a heavy pan and sauté the onion until softened. Add the pepper and continue cooking for 3–4 minutes. Toss in the corn and the remaining ingredients and, over a low heat, simmer for 10 minutes. Adjust the seasoning and serve.

Corn Maque Choux

Succotash
Serves 4

Native North Americans cooked succotash, and many recipes for it still exist. **'Silver Queen'** is a particularly good variety to use for this dish.

3 or 4 ears roasted corn
3–4 tablespoons unsalted butter
⅔ pound broad beans, cooked
½ pound French beans, topped and tailed
1 medium red onion, finely chopped
1¼ cups vegetable stock
½ red pepper, finely diced
1 beef tomato, peeled, deseeded and chopped
Salt and freshly ground black pepper

Melt the butter in a heavy frying pan and sweat the broad beans, corn, French beans and onion over medium heat for about 3 minutes.

Then add the stock and continue cooking for 5 minutes, before stirring in the remaining ingredients. Taste for seasoning, mix thoroughly and continue cooking for 5 minutes more. Serve hot.

Zingiber officinale. Zingiberaceae

GINGER

Also known as Stem Ginger, Canton Ginger. Herbaceous perennial grown for its aromatic rhizomes.

Ginger has been grown in tropical Asia for at least 3,000 years and was one of the first spices brought to Europe along the Silk Road from China. Arab merchants controlled the trade in ginger and other spices for centuries until explorers like Marco Polo reached the Indian Ocean. The Portuguese took ginger to their colonies and the Spaniards introduced it to the New World; in 1547 they exported over 1,000 tons of rhizomes to Jamaica and Mexico, and by the end of the century had a thriving trade with Europe. Fresh ginger is cultivated throughout the tropics and is freely available.

The creeping, branched rhizomes growing near the surface, with pale yellow flesh beneath a thin, buff-colored to dark brown skin, look like knobbly fingers and are often referred to as "hands." The stems can grow up to 4 feet tall, with narrow, lance-shaped leaves; the short-lived flowers are yellow-green and purple, marked with spots and stripes.

There are plenty of rhizomes below

 varieties

Each center of cultivation has its own forms. Several clones are found in India and three in Malaya. Two found in Jamaica are the high-quality white or yellow form and "flint ginger," with tougher, fibrous rhizomes.

 cultivation

Propagation

Propagate in late spring just before growth begins, using sections of rhizomes. Lift parent plants carefully to avoid rhizome damage, shake off the soil and break off sections about 2 inches long with at least one good bud. Dispose of older sections, keeping the young growth, and trim the ends with a sharp knife.

Plant, buds uppermost, 2–4 inches deep with 6 inches between rows. Water thoroughly with lukewarm water after planting.

Maintenance

Spring Plant rhizomes under cover.
Summer Water, feed and keep weed-free. Maintain high temperatures and humidity.
Autumn Lift rhizomes carefully.

Garden Cultivation

Ginger needs an annual rainfall of at least 60 inches, high temperatures and a short dry season for part of the year. The soil should be rich, moisture-retentive and free-draining; add well-rotted organic matter where necessary. It is essential that the ground is not

compacted and all debris is removed, otherwise the rhizomes become deformed.

Water plants thoroughly during dry periods and keep them weed-free throughout the growing season. In the humid tropics, ginger can be planted at any time.

Protected Cropping

Ginger can be grown under cover, but as it needs high temperatures and humidity, this is not normally practical, and for optimum productivity it is better planted outdoors.

As a "novelty crop" under cover, plant the rhizome just below the surface in peat-substitute-based compost in an 8-inch pot. Keep it constantly moist, and feed with a liquid general fertilizer every 3 weeks during the growing season.

Harvesting and Storing

Younger tender rhizomes are harvested for immediate use and for preserving; they become more fibrous and pungent with age.

A harvested root

The rhizomes need to be peeled before eating

Harvesting can begin from 7 months after planting. Rhizomes for drying should be lifted about 9–10 months after planting.

Fresh root can be stored in the refrigerator for several weeks wrapped in paper towels, foil or any container that allows it to "breathe." It can also be wrapped and frozen.

Pests and Diseases

Soft rot can appear as dark patches at the base of the shoots. To prevent, handle rhizomes with care and avoid waterlogging.

 culinary

Ginger is used throughout the world as a flavoring for sweet and savory dishes; it plays a starring role in foods like gingerbread, but is also an integral part of many spice mixes, appearing in cookies, cakes, soups, pickles, marinades, curry powder, stewed fruit, puddings, tea, beer, ale and wine.

It is the most important spice in Chinese cookery. In Japanese cookery it is used as a side dish called "gari" to accompany *sushi*. Besides being used fresh, dried and in powdered form, ginger is pickled, preserved in syrup, candied and crystallized. Rhizomes should be lightly scraped or peeled to remove the tough skin before use.

 medicinal

Ginger has been used for centuries in Chinese medicine. In the Orient fresh ginger is a remedy for vomiting, coughing, abdominal distension and fever. Many Africans drink ginger root as an aphrodisiac, while in New Guinea it is eaten dried as a contraceptive and in the Philippines it is chewed to expel evil spirits.

In the Middle Ages, it was believed to possess miraculous properties against cholera. Culpeper in his *Herball* of 1653 says: "It is profitable for old men; it heats the joints and is useful against gout; it expels wind." It can be rubbed on the face as a "rouge," stimulating circulation. Ginger is said to cleanse

the body and lower cholesterol; it can be chewed to alleviate sore throats, is a digestive, relieves dyspepsia, colic and diarrhea and prevents travel sickness.

PRACTICAL GARDENING

PLANNING YOUR VEGETABLE GARDEN

Several factors determine the planning and layout of a vegetable garden and the varieties that can be grown:

- the locality and climatic conditions
- the size and shape of the plot
- the number of people to be supplied with vegetables
- the duration of cropping
- the skill of the gardener, and the time available for maintaining the plot
- whether the vegetables are intended for use when fresh, stored or both

It is a good idea to list the vegetables you like then decide how and where they can be grown to achieve the best results. In large gardens a vast range and volume of tasty vegetables can be produced using crop rotation and protected cropping to extend the growing season. Smaller sites allow fewer opportunities for self-sufficiency, but it is still possible to grow a good selection of high-value crops like asparagus and try unusual varieties. Even the tiniest gardens, balconies or patios are suitable, particularly with the use of containers, while areas surrounded by buildings sometimes create favorable microclimates for tender vegetables and early crops. Protected cropping provides further opportunities to defy the cold weather.

Before preparing a planting plan it is important to be aware of the advantages and disadvantages of the site, considering everything from aspect and shelter to soil quality and drainage. Choose a design that suits your site and taste: traditionally, plots were planned in beds and rows, but you may prefer the potager (or "edible landscape") developed by the French, or the raised bed system, which is ideal for intensive small or large-scale cropping. It is essential to provide the best possible growing conditions for optimum production and the old saying, 'the answer lies in the soil', is particularly relevant to vegetable growing.

Accurate timing is also a prerequisite. A cropping timetable should make full use of the ground all year round, to the extent that it is possible. It is advisable to plan backwards from the intended harvesting date to work out when crops should be sown. The aim is to provide home-grown vegetables throughout the year, even if you have to rely on frozen or stored produce.

Kitchen garden (top)
Is there a more glorious site for a garden than the foot of the Alps? (bottom)

Site and Soil

Most vegetables are short-term crops, which are harvested before they reach maturity. To achieve the necessary rapid growth, the ideal site is warm and light with good air circulation. This is particularly important for the fertilization of wind-pollinated crops such as corn, and to discourage pests and diseases, which flourish in still conditions. However, it is worth noting that strong winds can reduce plant growth by up to 30%.

On a *gently sloping site* facing the sun, the soil warms faster in spring than in other aspects, making such an area perfect for early crops.

It is more difficult to work the soil on *steeper slopes*, especially if machinery is being used: crops should be planted across, rather than down the slope to reduce the risk of soil erosion during heavy rain. On *very steep slopes* the ground should be terraced.

A sloping site is ideal for early crops

There's plenty of cropping potential here

SOIL, SITES & PREPARATION

Soils and Preparation

Vegetables can be grown successfully on a range of soils by selecting varieties which flourish in the existing conditions or by improving the soil with the addition of organic matter or other materials. A slightly acidic soil, with moderate fertility and organic matter content is ideal, requiring only routine cultivation to produce a broad range of crops. Be aware of the compatibility between the selected vegetables and site, and choose the right plant for the right place for successful cropping: for example, don't grow asparagus on heavy clay. (See "Growing" under individual vegetable entries.)

If necessary, gradually improve the soil by planting a ground-breaking crop like potatoes or Jerusalem artichokes and enrich the soil quality by adding organic matter. Potatoes are often used for this as they require a number of cultivations to "earth up" and cover the tubers, so preventing weeds from becoming established. Potatoes also produce large leafy tops, blocking the light that is so essential for the germination of many weed species. Ensure that neglected, weed-infested sites are cleared thoroughly before planting, using translocated herbicides, cultivation and organic methods. It is better to start your garden clear from weeds than to tackle the problem halfway down the line.

Soil Structure

Light, free-draining, sandy soils are ideal for early crops, as they warm up quickly in the spring. However, as they are open and free-draining, moisture and nutrients are quickly lost. This can be redressed by irrigation and by the addition of fertilizer and copious amounts of well-rotted organic matter.

Heavier clay soils become waterlogged and sticky during torrential heavy rain, are slow to drain, take longer to warm up in spring and become cracked and unworkable (during prolonged drought). This makes the growing season shorter and cultivation extremely difficult. However, they retain water for longer periods and are usually very fertile; as a result they are suitable for hungry, leafy crops that require high nutrient levels. Incorporating well-rotted organic matter, sharp sand, horticultural grit and gypsum over several years gradually improves the soil structure.

A good soil structure call be easily damaged by cultivating when it is excessively wet or dry and by using heavy machinery — even walking on wet soil causes

Rotation is a system whereby groups of vegetables are grown on a different section of the plot each year, so maintaining the balance of soil nutrients for successive crops. Growing crops in this way avoids the buildup of pests and diseases, assists in weed control and prevents the soil from deteriorating.

For crop rotation to be effective, a large area of ground is required, particularly when controlling soil-borne pests and diseases. White rot (which attacks the onion family), clubroot (which damages members of the cabbage family) and potato cyst eelworm remain dormant in the soil for many years and can survive on any weeds that are relatives. This makes good husbandry just as vital as crop rotation.

Planning
Before planting, first list the vegetables you want to grow and group them together according to their botanical relationship. Draw a "map" of the garden plots to keep track of rotational plantings from year to year. Allocate each group to a plot, then compile a monthly cropping timetable for each space.

Rotational groups	Legumes	Onion family	Carrot and tomato families	Brassicas
	Broad bean	Bulb onion	Carrot	Cabbage
	French bean	Garlic	Celery	Cauliflower
	Pea	Leek	Pepper	Radish
	Runner bean	Salad onion	Parsnip	Swede
		Shallot	Potato	Turnip
			Tomato	

Next, allocate each rotation group to a plot of land ("plot A" etc.), and draw up a month-by-month timetable for each space.

Plot A	Year 1	Year 2	Year 3	Year 4
	Legumes	Onion family	Carrot and tomato families	Brassicas
	Broad bean	Bulb onion	Carrot	Cabbage
	French bean	Garlic	Celery	Cauliflower
	Pea	Leek	Pepper	Radish
	Runner bean	Salad onion	Parsnip	Swede
		Shallot	Potato	Turnip
			Tomato	

Plot B	Year 1	Year 2	Year 3	Year 4
	Onion family	Carrot and tomato families	Brassicas	Legumes
	Bulb onion	Carrot	Cabbage	Broad bean
	Garlic	Celery	Cauliflower	French bean
	Leek	Pepper	Radish	Pea
	Salad onion	Parsnip	Swede	Runner bean
	Shallot	Potato	Turnip	
		Tomato		

Plot C	Year 1	Year 2	Year 3	Year 4
	Carrot and tomato families	Brassicas	Legumes	Onion family
	Carrot	Cabbage	Broad bean	Bulb onion
	Celery	Cauliflower	French bean	Garlic
	Pepper	Radish	Pea	Leek
	Parsnip	Swede	Runner bean	Salad onion
	Potato	Turnip		Shallot
	Tomato			

Plot D	Year 1	Year 2	Year 3	Year 4
	Brassicas	Legumes	Onion family	Carrot and tomato families
	Cabbage	Broad bean	Bulb onion	Carrot
	Cauliflower	French bean	Garlic	Celery
	Radish	Pea	Leek	Pepper
	Swede	Runner bean	Salad onion	Parsnip
	Turnip		Shallot	Potato
				Tomato

This timetable fully utilizes the land and provides continuity of cropping. As space becomes available, plant the crops due to follow immediately. Crops may come from different groups, which means that rotation from one plot to another is a gradual process, rather than a wholesale changeover on a specific date.

GROWING SYSTEMS

Bed system, with paths separating them

Random Planting

Vegetables can be grown as "edible bedding plants" scattered among flowering plants and borders in the ornamental garden. Swiss chard, cabbage 'Ruby Ball', beet 'Bull's Blood', fennel and Brussels sprout 'Rubine' are particularly pleasing. (See also pages 255–57, "The Ornamental Vegetable Garden.")

The Potager

This is the French tradition of planting vegetables in formal beds; a practical and visually pleasing display.

Long-term Crops

Perennial vegetables such as asparagus are difficult to incorporate into a crop rotation program. For this reason, they are often grown on a separate, more permanent site for several years before being replaced.

What will I harvest today?

Rows

Traditionally, vegetables are grown in long straight rows, with plants close together within the rows, and paths to allow access. This has some drawbacks. Competition between plants for space in a row means that much of the plants' extension growth is into the pathways, causing leafy vegetables like cabbages, cauliflowers and lettuces to produce oval "hearts" rather than round ones.

Beds

These are effectively multirow systems, with equidistant spacing of plants in and between the rows. Plants may be set in staggered rows, creating a diagonal pattern. Major paths between beds should always be wide enough to accommodate a wheelbarrow; access paths can be narrower. Pathways between the beds are slightly wider than those on the row system, but closer plant spacing means that more plants are grown per square foot and their growth and shape are more uniform. Close spacing ensures that weed growth is suppressed in its later stages and the soil structure remains intact, because there is less soil compaction when pathways are further apart.

Raised beds should be about 3 feet wide so that it is easy to reach into the center without overbalancing. After initial double digging, and the addition of organic matter, they will not be trodden on, allowing a good soil structure to form. Layers of well-rotted compost added annually will be further incorporated by worm activity. Where natural populations are low, they can be bought from specialized suppliers. You can't have enough!

To ensure that plants are productive and the crops are of high quality, vegetables require careful nurturing and diligent husbandry. A neglected vegetable garden is neither productive nor ornamental and encourages pests, diseases and weeds, which are just an embarrassment to the gardener.

It is certainly worth remembering that whatever the effort required, laboring in the vegetable garden has its own delicious rewards. A little and often is the key.

Garden Hygiene

Crop hygiene is essential for healthy growth, particularly among young or weak plants that are more susceptible to pests and diseases. It is vital to keep the vegetable garden free from sources of infection. Always use clean, sterile containers and compost, particularly when propagating plants. The best time to sterilize pots and containers is just before they are to be used; if they are sterilized immediately after use and put into storage, fungal spores or insect eggs may contaminate the container, especially if they are stored outdoors. Wash pots with a scrubbing brush in a mild solution of disinfectant and rinse thoroughly; warm water is preferable, if only for the comfort of the pot washer!

Check plants daily, if possible, as pests and diseases are easier to control before they become established. Instant eradication is the most effective remedy: either remove the affected part or wipe off the pest or disease, as with aphids or scale. Where possible, plants showing signs of problems should be isolated immediately. If you have space, it is a good idea to put new plants into quarantine for a few weeks before introducing them to the greenhouse, so preventing new problems from being introduced.

Dispose of infected crop debris by recycling in your local authority "green waste" bin as high temperatures on large heaps kills spores. Persistent problems such as nematodes and clubroot should be put in the bin or burned as they cannot be destroyed by composting. Dig in or compost healthy remains before they become infected.

Greenhouses should be cleaned annually in winter: wash thoroughly with disinfectant to kill overwintering eggs and fungal spores. Winter is also the perfect time to disinfect plant supports, particularly bamboo canes, which are hollow and often split with age, creating cracks and crevices that form suitable sites for fungi and insect eggs to overwinter. These can be sprayed or dipped in disinfectant. Plastic supports do not cause this problem.

Observation

Examine plants regularly, taking precautionary measures or trapping pests when they emerge. Sowing broad beans in autumn or pinching out the growth tips helps to control black bean aphid and a dusk patrol to catch slugs as they feed can be very effective.

Organic vs. Synthetic

Organic gardeners avoid the use of artificial chemicals, relying on good management and natural predators to control pests and diseases while working to create an environment in which they are unlikely to occur. Synthetic chemicals are often general rather than specific in their action and can kill pollinating insects or predators further down the food chain.

While government legislation is reducing the number of harmful chemicals for garden use, there are now many methods of organic crop protection to help the gardener and the challenges of conservation have ensured that "organic" methods are now mainstream. Biological controls are available for a range of common problems from slugs to thrips and greenhouse red spider mite. A range of materials are being used as physical barriers, from copper bands against slugs, mesh and fleece preventing airborne access, to spray barriers based on garlic, while insecticidal sprays now contain fatty acids, plant and fish oil combinations and plant extracts. The number of biological controls using nematodes, insect predators at larval and adult stage is increasing rapidly and although they control rather than eradicate, gardeners are happy to make a contribution to conservation in return for chemical-free food, though some traditional treatments like sulfur and copper-based fungicides are still retained.

Other control methods include using resistant varieties, pheromone traps, encouraging natural predators into the garden by providing habitats like log piles or lacewing "hotels," growing companion plants to encourage beneficial insects into the garden and providing nesting sites for birds.

It is also important to keep plants healthy, a good soil is the basis for success, maintaining a compost heap or worm bin to recycle organic material, with regular feeding and watering, the use of soil and plant tonics and scrupulous hygiene are all beneficial in maintaining crop quality and ensuring bumper crops.

Cruciferous vegetable seedlings

Transplanting

Vegetables are usually transplanted after they have been germinated in a greenhouse and have reached a stage at which they can survive outdoors. The timing depends on the prevailing weather and soil conditions. All plants suffer a check in their growth rate after transplantation. This is caused by inevitable root disturbance and by the change in environment as they are usually moved on to somewhere cooler. Younger plants tend to recover rapidly, while older plants take longer. It is essential to reduce stress; ensure there is plenty of water available, transplant on an overcast day into moist soil and provide shelter from strong sunshine until plants become established.

Watering

It is vital to maintain rapid growth by watering regularly, otherwise plant tissues can harden and growth can be affected. Growth check in cauliflowers can cause young plants to prematurely form a small, poorly developed curd, while other plants will bolt. Seaweed is also beneficial.

Plant Supports

These should be positioned before they are required by the plants, preferably before sowing or transplanting. Plants growing tall without a support can be damaged or suffer a check in growth. Supports should be selected according to the plants being grown. Peas climb using tendrils, preferring to twine around thin supports such as chicken wire or thin spindly twigs, while runner beans hug poles or canes. Plants without climbing mechanisms should be tied to stakes using garden twine in a loose figure-eight loop, positioning the stake on the windward side of the plant.

WEED CONTROL

Any plant — even if it is ornamental — that grows in a place where it is not wanted is described as a weed, but the term is also used to refer to native plants that rapidly and successfully colonize gardens. These compete with crops for moisture, nutrients and light, acting as hosts to pests and diseases that can then spread to crops. Groundsel harbors rust, mildew and greenfly; chickweed hosts red spider mite and whitefly, while several species of nightshade in the potato family can carry viruses and eelworms, which cause severe damage to potatoes and peppers.

Types of Weed

Knowledge of a weed's life cycle enables the gardener to control weeds effectively.

Ephemeral weeds germinate, flower and seed rapidly, producing several generations each season and alarming quantities of seed.

Annual weeds germinate, flower and seed in one growing season; the parent dies after seed has been produced for the following generation.

Biennial weeds have a life cycle spanning two growing seasons; the parent dies after the seed has been produced in the second year.

Perennial weeds survive for several years, developing a perennating organ. They often spread through the soil as they grow, producing scores of new shoots and setting seed. New plants sprout from tiny fragments of root, rhizome or bulbils left in the soil, rapidly recolonizing the site.

Methods of Control

There are four main methods of weed control: manual, mechanical, mulching and chemical. Wherever possible, keep the garden weed-free and, if germination occurs, remove weeds immediately before they flower and produce seed. The old saying, "One year's seed is seven years' weed" is, unfortunately, scientifically proven. In some conditions, ephemeral weeds are capable of producing 60,000 viable seeds per square yard per year. The vast majority of weed seeds are found in the top 2 inches of soil, germinating only when exposed to sufficient light.

Thorough weed control is vital when preparing the soil for planting, particularly on new or neglected sites. Cover with carpet or similiar for several months and

Using a spade as a hoe, weeds get lifted from the soil

then fork through the area, removing weeds by hand, or spray with a systemic herbicide formulated for tough weeds. The latter may need to be undertaken several times before complete control is achieved.

Manual Weed Control

Digging, forking, hoeing and hand weeding are often the only practical ways to eradicate weeds in confined spaces where herbicides can harm nearby crops.

Digging cultivates the soil to a depth of at least 12 inches. Soil is turned over in a series of trenches, burying surface vegetation and annual weeds. Perennial weeds should be removed first; do not allow them to be buried among the surface vegetation. Trials have proved that the number of fat hen, cleavers and chickweed plants is considerably reduced when cultivation takes place at night, as many seeds are prompted to germinate after they receive a flash of light.

Forking cultivates the soil around perennial weeds before they are lifted by hand. If this is undertaken carefully, roots can be removed without breaking them into sections that form new plants.

Hoeing prevents weed seeds from germinating, reduces moisture loss and minimizes soil disturbance. An old gardener once told me: "If you hoe when there aren't any weeds, you won't get any." He was right. Hoeing is effective against all weeds except established perennials, severing the stem from the root just below the soil surface. Be warned: hoeing too deeply can damage the surface roots of crop plants; if in doubt, hand weed. The blade should penetrate no deeper than ½ inch. Hoeing is better undertaken in dry weather and, like all controls, before weeds flower.

Hand weed in dry weather when the soil is moist, so that weeds are easily loosened from the soil; always try to remove the whole plant. Remove weeds from the site to prevent them from rerooting.

Mechanical Weed Control

Machines with revolving rotary tines, blades or cultivator attachments are useful for preparing seedbeds and can also be used to control annual weeds between rows of vegetables. They should be employed carefully to avoid root damage. When clearing the ground of perennial weeds, the blades simply slice through their roots and rhizomes. While this increases their number initially, several sessions over a period of time should gradually exhaust and eventually kill the plants. This is only viable when there is plenty of time.

Biological Weed Control

Mulching is the practice of covering the soil around plants with a layer of organic or inorganic material to suppress weeds, reduce water loss and warm the soil. Traditional mulching materials were organic, such as straw or compost, and gardeners still use anything from newspaper and cardboard to old burlap-backed carpets. Choose your material carefully; straw harbors pests such as vine weevil and flea beetle and contains weed seeds, but is effective as an insulating layer over winter. It also draws nitrogen from the soil in the early stages of decay. Using partially rotted material like farmyard manure or spent hops avoids this problem or scatter high-nitrogen fertilizer before mulching.

Organic mulches are also limited where crops need to be earthed up — a process that disturbs the soil. Inorganic materials like plastic sheeting, though effective, are unattractive but can at least be hidden beneath a thin layer of organic mulch.

Inorganic Mulches:
• suppress weeds and prevent seeds from germinating.
• conserve soil moisture by slowing evaporation. If the soil remains moist, roots can continue to extract nutrients, which they are unable to do from dry soil. Plastic films are the most effective for this purpose, as many are nonporous.
• keep trailing crops such as bush tomato, squash or cucumber clean by preventing soil from splashing up on to leaves and ripening fruit. This helps to prevent disease, but may encourage slugs.
• *white plastic mulches* hasten growth and ripening by reflecting light onto leaves and fruit. This also keeps the soil cooler.
• *black plastic mulches* warm the soil in the spring, as they absorb the sun's heat.
• *sheet mulches* are most effective when applied before the crop is planted. Young vegetables are then planted through small holes made in the sheet.

Buried foliage rots down and feeds the soil

Organic Mulches:
• improve soil fertility and conserve its structure by protecting the surface from the splashing effects of heavy rain, cushioning the effects of treading on the soil, encouraging earthworm activity and by adding organic matter and nutrients to the soil.
• insulate the soil, keeping it cooler in summer and warmer in winter. Mulches can be packed around overwintering plants to reduce frost penetration into the soil, making root crops easier to harvest. Straw is ideal for this purpose.

Weeds that manage to push their way through are easily removed or spot-treated with a weedkiller. For effective weed control, organic mulches should be approximately 4 inches deep, to block out the light. Organic mulches are applied after planting.

In general, organic mulches have the advantage of improving soil fertility as they decay, while inorganic mulches are more effective against weeds because they form an impenetrable barrier.

Chemical Weed Control (Herbicides)
Choose and use herbicides with extreme care and ensure they are suitable for the weeds to be controlled. Follow the manufacturer's instructions carefully. Residual herbicides form a layer over the soil, killing germinating weeds and seedlings.

Contact herbicides only kill those parts of the plant that they touch. They are effective against annual weeds and weed seedlings but not against established perennials.

Systemic or translocated herbicides are absorbed by the foliage, traveling through the sap system to kill the whole plant, including the roots. Glyphosate is often the active ingredient. Individual weeds can be "spot-treated" using such herbicides in gel or liquid form.

Several chemical weed-control methods have been developed for use with vegetables. As many of the vegetables we grow have different tolerances to chemicals, no single chemical is suitable for all crops. This gives the grower three options: stock a range of chemicals and change the type regularly; use chemicals only as a last resort; or control weeds organically by cultivation, mulching or using wax-based sprays or a flame gun. I favor the latter!

Using and Storing Weedkillers Safely
Mixing
• Always wear adequate protective clothing, such as face mask, goggles, rubber gloves and old waterproof clothes when mixing weedkillers.
• Always dilute weedkillers according to the manufacturer's instructions.
• Never mix different chemicals together.
• Never dilute chemicals in a confined space, as they may give off toxic fumes.

Application
• Always wear the specified protective clothing, such as a face mask, rubber gloves and old waterproof clothes when applying weedkillers.
• Follow the manufacturer's instructions carefully and use only as recommended on the product label.
• Always apply weedkillers at the rate recommended on the manufacturer's label.
• Do not apply weedkillers in windy conditions; nearby plants may suffer serious damage.
• Do not apply weedkillers in very hot, still conditions when there is a high risk of spray traveling on warm air currents.
• If using a watering can to apply chemicals, ensure that it is labeled and at no times use it for any other purpose.

Storage
• Always keep chemicals in the original containers, making sure that the labels are well secured so that the contents can be positively identified.
• Mark the container with the date of purchase, so that you know how long it has been stored.
• Never store diluted weedkillers for future use.
• Always store out of the reach of children and animals, in a locked cabinet in a workshop or shed.
• Store in cool, frost-free, dark conditions.

After Use
• Always thoroughly wash protective clothing, sprayers, mixing vessels and utensils.
• Never use the same sprayer, mixing vessels and utensils for other types of chemical such as fungicides. The results could be disastrous!

Organic leaf mulch in a biodegradable jute sack

variety	resistant or tolerant to
Rutabaga	
Marian	clubroot
	powdery mildew
Magres	powdery mildew
Virtue	clubroot
	powdery mildew
Willemsburger	clubroot
Spinach	
Bergola	downy mildew
Fiorano	downy mildew
	powdery mildew
Galaxy	downy mildew
	powdery mildew
Mazarka	downy mildew
Palco	downy mildew
Senic	downy mildew
	powdery mildew
Space	downy mildew
Tetona	downy mildew
Tornado	downy mildew
Trinidad	downy mildew
Triton	downy mildew
Squash (Butternut)	
Metro	powdery mildew
Tomato	
Alexanovas	fusarium wilt
	tomato mosaic virus
Alicante	greenback
	powdery mildew
Amarel	blossom end rot
	tomato mosaic virus
Aviro	tomato mosaic virus
Cherry Wonder	fusarium wilt
	greenback
	leaf mold
	tomato mosaic virus
Craigella	greenback
Cristal	good disease resistance
Cumulus	fusarium wilt
	tomato mosaic virus
Cyclon	leaf mold
	tomato mosaic virus
	verticillium wilt
Delicate	good resistance
Dombito	tomato mosaic virus
Dona	fusarium wilt
	tomato mosaic virus
	verticillium wilt
Estrella	fusarium wilt
	greenback
	leaf mold
	tomato mosaic virus
	verticillium wilt
Eurocross	greenback
	leaf mold
Falcorosso	fusarium wilt

variety	resistant or tolerant to
	leaf mold
	tobacco mosaic virus
	verticillium wilt
Favorita	good disease resistance
Ferline	blight
	fusarium wilt
	verticillium
Golden Boy	alternaria stem canker
Golden Sweet	fusarium wilt
	rootknot nematode
Grenadier	fusarium wilt
	leaf mold
Herald	leaf mold
Husky Gold	fusarium wilt
	verticillium wilt
Ida	fusarium wilt
	leaf mold
	tomato mosaic virus
	verticillium wilt
Incas	blossom end rot
	fusarium wilt (high)
	verticillium wilt
Legend	blight
Libra	fusarium crown and root rot
Matador	greenback
Matina	greenback
Moravi	fusarium wilt
	leaf mold
	tobacco mosaic virus
	verticillium wilt
Nimbus	fusarium wilt
	tomato mosaic virus
	verticillium wilt
Olivade	good disease resistance
Piccolo	leaf mold
	tomato mosaic virus
Piranto	fusarium crown and root rot
Pixie	fusarium wilt
	tomato mosaic virus
	verticillium wilt
Primato	fusarium wilt
	leaf mold
	tomato mosaic virus
	verticillium wilt
Royal des Guineaux	good disease resistance
Sakura	fusarium wilt
	tomato mosaic virus
Seville Cross	leaf mold
Shirley	cladosporium
	fusarium wilt
	greenback
	tomato mosaic virus
Sonatine	fusarium wilt
	leaf mold
	tomato mosaic virus
Sungold	fusarium wilt
	tomato mosaic virus
Typhoon	fusarium wilt
	leaf mold

variety	resistant or tolerant to
	tomato mosaic virus
	verticillium
Turnip	
Oasis	turnip mosaic virus
Zucchini	
Afrodite	good disease resistance
Astia	powdery mildew
Defender	cucumber mosaic virus
Firenza	powdery mildew
Optima	cucumber mosaic virus
	powdery mildew
Pasqualine	cucumber mosaic virus
	powdery mildew
Supremo	cucumber mosaic virus
Sylvana	good disease resistance
Tarmino	cucumber mosaic virus
Zucchino	cucumber mosaic virus

CONTAINER CULTURE

The idea of growing vegetables in containers is not a new one: tomatoes and cucumbers have long been grown under glass in containers to prevent any contact with disease-infected soil. The main advantage is that the gardener gains almost total control over the contents and environment within the container. Portable containers give the flexibility to respond to weather conditions, moving plants outdoors once spring frosts end and putting them under shelter again at the onset of colder weather.

When room is limited, containers offer an alternative to ground space. They can be either functional or decorative. You can make good use of the patio, windowbox or even hanging basket: vegetables can be as ornamental as a conventional flower display, and even recycled plastic containers can be disguised within more attractive containers. It. is important to remember, though, that many vegetables are heavier feeders than the bedding plants that are usually grown in such ways. They also require regular and consistent watering to flourish and maintain growth.

selecting a suitable container

The chance of successful cropping is improved when large containers are used; they allow for a greater rooting depth, dry out slowly and provide adequate anchorage for crops that need staking. Composts should be moisture-retentive yet free-draining, reducing the likelihood of compaction due to heavy watering. Plastic containers (with drainage holes), while not always attractive, are more moisture-retentive than those made of wood or terracotta. To ensure good drainage, raise containers above the ground.

On the practical side, it is possible to grow early potatoes in garbage cans or growbags in which tomatoes, peppers or cucumbers were grown in the first year. For the potatoes, remove most of the plastic from the upper surface of the bag to expose a larger surface area of compost. Green onions, lettuces and radishes can also be grown in this way.

Zucchini growing in a pot

selecting crops

Vegetables most suited to container culture are either rapidly maturing crops such as mini beets, carrots, lettuces, radishes and green onions, or dwarf varieties of bush or climbing vegetables including eggplants, beans, cucumbers, peas, peppers and tomatoes, as these need little support. Deep-rooted vegetables like Brussels sprouts, maincrop carrots and parsnips can be grown in containers, providing they are at least 18 inches deep.

selecting a compost

Use a potting compost when growing vegetables in containers. Such compost has a good enough structure to encourage vigorous growth and contains the essential nutrients for healthy growth. Using garden soil is not recommended at all as most soils contain weed seeds, stones, pests and diseases and chemical residues. Their nutrient levels are also variable. Composts for containers are either loam-based or loamless:

Loam-based Composts
A formula for loam-based composts was developed at the John Innes Research Institute in the UK. They are not a brand but rather formulations that can be mixed to suit growing requirements. Those used for containers are numbered 1, 2 and 3, each with a different level of nutrients, with no. 3 being the strongest. Loam-based composts are much heavier, providing stability and support for the plants and better conditions for long-term crops. They release nutrients slowly, are free-draining and have a good structure. When using loam-based composts, place the container in its final position before filling with compost; once they are filled, the considerable weight makes them difficult to move.

John Innes compost mix
The basic John Innes soil-based mixture (by volume):
7 parts sterilized loam
3 parts sphagnum moss peat
2 parts sharp washed sand

John Innes base fertilizer (by weight)
2 parts bone meal
2 parts calcium phosphate
1 part potassium sulfate

John Innes no. 1
1.2 cubic feet John Innes compost mix
¼ pound John Innes base fertilizer
¾ ounce powdered chalk

John Innes no. 2
1.2 cubic feet John Innes compost mix
½ pound John Innes base fertilizer
1½ ounces powdered chalk

John Innes no. 3
1.2 cubic feet John Innes compost mix
¾ pound John Innes base fertilizer
2¼ ounces powdered chalk

Loamless Composts
These are traditionally based on peat with additional materials such as vermiculite, grit and shredded bark to improve drainage. With the ethical debate on peat, many compost manufacturers are using alternative materials such as coir or recycled organic waste. Loamless composts are generally lighter and cleaner to use than loam-based composts, they combine moisture retention with good aeration, and are long-lasting and cheaper. However, they are not as stable or moisture-retentive as loam-based composts and tend to decompose, reducing the volume in the container. They are also difficult to re-wet in drought conditions. Overall, loam-based composts are recommended, and organic matter can be added if required.

Watering
A regular and adequate supply of water is essential for plant growth. Stress due to drought, even for short periods, can greatly reduce the potential productivity of plants. When plants are actively growing, keep the compost moist but not waterlogged by watering thoroughly and regularly. It is best to water containers in the early morning or in the evening, particularly in the summer, as this reduces the amount lost through evaporation. Gardeners with a large number of containers should consider investing in irrigation systems to save time when watering and feeding.

Plenty of moisture is vital for success

PROTECTED CROPPING

Protected cropping extends the growing season in spring and autumn, accelerates growth and increases productivity. In cooler climates, crops sown earlier when external conditions are unfavorable will have grown considerably by the time the weather has improved, by which time they can be planted outdoors. This is particularly valuable when growing half-hardy vegetables like eggplant, sweet peppers and tomatoes. It also provides the option of growing crops of borderline hardiness under cover throughout the season; this makes cropping more reliable.

It is not only summer crops which benefit. Lettuce, spinach and other hardy winter salads produce more tender, better-quality crops when protected in an unheated greenhouse than those salads that remain outside.

Permanent Structures

These include greenhouses, either free-standing or lean-to, and allow almost total environmental control all year round if heat is provided.

Cold frames are ideal for raising seedlings or hardening off plants before transplanting outdoors. The lack of height limits the crops that can be grown in them. When covered with black polyethylene or layers of burlap, they provide a cheap and efficient method of forcing chicory and endive.

Semi-permanent Structures

Polyethylene tunnels are much cheaper to buy and easier to erect than greenhouses, but the plastic cover only lasts for about three years.
Cloches made of glass or plastic are easily moved to provide shelter to those individual plants or small groups that need it most.

Temporary Structures

Low polyethylene tunnels are like small cloches and are cheap, portable and versatile, but are of limited use because of their flimsiness and lack of height.

Crop covers and floating film were developed for commercial horticulture. These flexible covers can be laid immediately over the crop, or suspended on hoops as "floating mulches." As the plants grow, they are forced upward.

Fleece is lightweight, soft-textured spun polypropylene, which lasts for a year, provided it is kept clean, sometimes longer if well cared for. It is ideal for frost protection and for forcing early crops. Many vegetables can be grown under this, from sowing through to harvesting and it is an effective barrier against pests and diseases. More light and air can penetrate through this than plastic film.

Plastic film is usually perforated with minute slits or holes for ventilation, but even then the crop may overheat on sunny spring days. It is laid directly over the plants; as they grow, the flexible material is pushed upward, splitting open the minute slits and increasing ventilation. It is often used in the early stages of growth.

Plastic netting filters the wind and provides protection, but has little effect on raising temperature. It lasts for several seasons and is a useful pest barrier.

As many of these materials are manufactured in long, narrow rolls, the most effective way to use them is to grow crops in narrow strips. Greatest benefit can be derived from such materials when they are used in conjunction with free-draining, thoroughly prepared, weed-free soil. Insect-pollinated crops like zucchini, cucumbers, squash and tomatoes should have the protective covering removed or opened as the crop develops. This allows pollinatinginsects access to the flowers, or they can also be hand pollinated.

Protected Potatoes

Potatoes can be grown under polyethylene sheeting. Cultivate the soil deeply, cover it with black plastic, burying the margins and sides to stop it blowing away. Make cross cuts in the plastic, push a potato through the hole and about 6 inches into the soil. New tubers will form beneath the plastic, and are blanched without the need for earthing up. When the "haulm" turns yellow, the plastic can be removed and the tubers harvested.

Cabbage plants protected with garden netting

THE ORNAMENTAL VEGETABLE GARDEN

The sight of a neat, well-tended vegetable garden burgeoning with healthy crops is immensely satisfying. Conditioned to believe that vegetables are functional and flowers beautiful, many fail to appreciate the beauty and bounty of a vegetable garden with its contrasting colors, forms and textures, neatly framed by well-kept paths.

The traditional design for a vegetable garden is based on a system of rows. This gives ease of access and maintenance, enables crops to be rotated regularly and for maximum production while preventing the buildup of pests and diseases. Large kitchen gardens were formerly attached to a "great house," with the gardeners' task to cultivate a wide range of crops and supply the household with vegetables throughout the year.

By way of contrast, most gardeners now have smaller gardens, and the basis for what they grow and how they grow is more a matter of choice than necessity. This provides them with the opportunity to grow vegetables for their ornamental and culinary values so they can savor the flavor. For the same reasons, it may also be preferable to grow small quantities of a wider range of cultivars.

Color

Vegetables are not only eaten for their flavor and nutritional value but add welcome color to a meal. Consider the range of colors and tonal variation in a salad; it is generally greater than the range of flavors.

There are tones of green in lettuce, endive and cucumber, yellow in peppers, purple in beets and leaf lettuce and red in tomatoes and peppers. For centuries, only the French "potager" capitalized on this display of colors, but vegetables are at last more commonly used as design elements within ornamental planting schemes. The sight of vegetables dotted individually or grouped in the flower border has in recent years become a familiar sight. To the open mind and eye, all vegetables are ornamental, even if their attraction is more obvious in some than in others. The contrasting red and green foliage of ruby chard is sumptuous, as is beet 'Bull's Blood', while purple- or yellow-podded French beans and the mauve leaves of cabbage 'Red Drumhead' create their own exotic magic. Red-skinned onions like 'Red Barron' and the red-leaved lettuce 'Lollo Rosso' are equally stunning. Squashes impress with their bold shapes and color (think of 'Turk's Turban') while tomatoes like the golden 'Yellow Perfection' and striped 'Tigrella' delight the eye. Flowers, fruits and companion plants add other color accents.

Form

While you may not consider the shape of certain vegetables to be interesting (swedes or potatoes, for instance), a good many have appealing foliage or a distinctive habit. The bold architectural leaves and sculptured form of globe artichokes are prized by garden designers, a "wigwam" of bicolored runner beans or trailing cucurbits makes a dramatic focal point, while the compact growth of parsley and chives

Look closely and see a bud's true beauty

is a neat edging for borders. Members of the onion family, leeks, and chives have spiky, linear leaves, which contrast well with the rounded shapes of lettuce and the feathery, arching growth of carrot tops. Celery and Brussels sprouts naturally have a distinguished upright habit. Perhaps the most unusual of all, e.g., a purple Brussels sprout, 'Rubine', which is planted as a single specimen in a container, looks like an angular, alien sculpture.

Texture
Texture is rarely considered a design feature, yet the different colors and forms of vegetable foliage are underlined by their texture. Consider the solidity of a compact cabbage head, wreathed in glaucous, puckered leaves, or the soft billowing effect created by the dissected leaves of fennel or asparagus foliage. Exploiting such contrasts provides a foliage

display as interesting as a bedding scheme or herbaceous border. Even after harvest the impact remains; the tall dried stems of corn look wonderful when frosted on a winter's day and the rustling sound as the wind blows through their dead leaves brings life to a desolate garden.

Vegetables as Bedding Plants
Many vegetables are grown as annuals and, as each crop matures and is harvested, the appearance of the vegetable garden changes. Often, the only constant elements are the framework of paths and hedges and a few long-lived perennial crops.

Such intensively grown crops are easier to maintain when grown in a formal pattern as this provides the ideal opportunity to arrange crops in brightly colored, bold patterns or emphasise their subtle qualities. Brightly colored chard, lettuce or kale or the fernlike foliage of carrots can be used to provide a foliage display rivaling any bedding plant.

Vegetables which have run to seed look particularly spectacular; lettuces are upright and leafy, beets display their red veined leaves and bold flower spikes while onions and leeks produce symmetrical globes of flowers that are invaluable for attracting pollinating insects. Some gardeners allow a few plants to go to seed to enjoy such effects, but would you be daring enough to create a planting scheme with the specific purpose of featuring vegetables in their later stages?

One approach to creating a bedding scheme is to group together plants with a similar life span, for a long-term display. Alternatively, with skillful planning, it is possible to plant crops taking different times to reach maturity, filling any gaps with suitable vegetables after harvest, to retain the impact of the design. The time scale can vary considerably, with radishes taking a mere five weeks, and sprouting broccoli and winter cabbages remaining in the ground for several months. The rapid changeover of these crops means that colors and flavors are constantly changing within the scheme; there is a fine example at the Eden Project in Cornwall, UK.

Perennial vegetables such as asparagus, globe artichoke and rhubarb can be grown in separate beds or used as permanent feature plants within the design. In smaller or irregularly shaped gardens, crop rotation allows a wide range of annual design patterns and planting

arrangements. Growing vegetables purely for their ornamental value is an option that gardeners of such gardens should consider.

The "Potager"
Their love of food and appreciation of aesthetics motivated French gardeners to create the "potager," or ornamental vegetable garden, with a more obvious visual appeal than the average vegetable garden. Simple, formal, geometric shapes such as four square-shaped raised beds dissected by straight paths form a permanent structure, enlivened with a succession of vibrantly colored leafy crops chosen for their culinary and visual qualities. The main paths are wide enough for a wheelbarrow, but narrower ones, and stepping stones, allow access for maintenance and picking. Vegetables are placed according to their height and habit, larger vegetables forming centerpieces and smaller ones making up the rows. Climbing vegetables growing over ornamental tripods, arches or even canes provide height, and the whole area can be screened by trellis and can include vegetables in containers as additional features.

To maintain the symmetry, harvest plants with an eye to pattern: work evenly from both ends and from the center, or cut every other plant to keep the coverage balanced as far as possible. Make full use of successional cropping to ensure that the soil is always utilized and the pattern maintained.

Random Systems
Scattering vegetables individually or in groups among ornamental borders is becoming more popular. They should be planted according to their ultimate height with lower plants near the front of the border, using brightly colored vegetables strong enough to stand up to their brightly colored neighbors. Grow purple-pod climbing French beans through shrubs instead of clematis, runner bean 'Painted Lady' instead of sweet peas and purple-leaved cabbage alongside nasturtiums. Mini vegetables can be grown in window boxes or hanging baskets; try tomato 'Tumbler' or grow climbers as trailing plants.

The only requirement for successful growth of vegetables among ornamental plants is adequate soil or compost fertility, which can easily be maintained with well-prepared soil and careful feeding.

HARVESTING & STORING

Some vegetables, like lettuce, cannot be stored for long periods and must be harvested and eaten fresh. Traditional methods such as storing in clamps, pickling and salting have been joined by freezing, which has revolutionized the lives of gardeners and cooks — even corn, traditionally eaten immediately after harvest — can be enjoyed out of season.

While the majority of vegetables are not harvested until they reach maturity, others, like lettuce 'Salad Bowl' and arugula, are harvested while semi-mature or even juvenile. Seeds are sprouted too.

The methods of harvesting and storing vegetables depend on several factors, particularly on the individual plant's storage organ and the winter climate. Many leafy vegetables such as Brussels sprouts and broccoli are hardy, surviving outdoors in the ground in freezing conditions. The flavor of Brussels sprouts even improves immeasurably after they have been frosted.

Some root vegetables with a high moisture content are easily damaged in winter, even when protected by the soil. This is usually caused by rapid thawing after a period of cold weather. Carrots, parsnip and swede are exceptions to this rule; they are extremely hardy and can be left in free-draining soils until required. In wet soils these crops would suffer winter loss by slug damage and rotting.

Outdoor Storage

In colder areas, vegetables overwintering in the ground need additional protection. This can be provided by spreading a layer of loose straw or bracken over them to a depth of 8 inches and covering with soil. While this is labor saving, root crops stored in this way are less susceptible to attack by pests and diseases throughout the winter.

The traditional method for storing root vegetables is in a clamp or "pie." Low mounds of vegetables are laid on a bed of loose straw up to 8 inches thick. The top and sides of the mound are covered with a similar layer of straw, and then with a 6-inch layer of soil or sand. Clamps can be made outdoors on a well-drained site or under cover in a shed; for extra protection outdoors, they can be formed against a wall or hedge. If crops are to be stored for a long period, find a site that receives as little sunlight as possible during the winter. Although the storage conditions are very similar to those in the ground, harvesting from a clamp is much easier. However, losses from rodent damage and rotting can be high.

Longevity in Storage

The length of time that vegetables may be stored depends on the type and cultivar as well as the storage conditions. When traditional methods are used, the main cause of deterioration is moisture loss from plant tissue; for instance, beets and carrots desiccate very rapidly. Fungal infection of damaged tissue is common; onions and potatoes bruise very easily.

Vegetables for storage should be handled carefully; only store those which are in perfect condition, check them regularly and remove any showing signs of decay immediately. (See details under individual vegetables.)

Drying Vegetables

Peas and beans can be harvested when almost mature and dried slowly in a cool place. Either lift the whole plant and hang it up or pick off the pods and dry them on a tray or newspaper. Dried beans can be collected and stored in airtight jars until required. They will need soaking for 24 hours before use. Storage areas should be frost-free. Chilies, green peppers, garlic and onions can be hung indoors where there is good air

Harvest this one by lifting it with a fork

circulation. Peppers, tomatoes and mushrooms can be cut into sections and sun dried outdoors where conditions allow, otherwise in the gentle heat of an airing cupboard or above a radiator. Vegetables that can be dried include beans, chilies, garlic, onions and peas. (See details under individual vegetables.)

Freezing

Only the best-quality vegetables should be frozen, and should always be thoroughly cleaned and carefully packed. Vegetables should be fast frozen. Do not open the freezer door regularly or leave it open longer than necessary. (See details under individual vegetables.)

Vegetables Suitable for Freezing

Blanch	Shred, purée dice or slice	Freeze when young
Asparagus		
Beet		Beet
Broad bean		
Brussels sprout		
Cabbage	Cabbage	
Carrot		Carrot
Cauliflower	Cauliflower	
	Celery	
Corn		
Eggplant	Eggplant	
French bean		
Kale		
Kohlrabi	Kohlrabi	
Marrow	Marrow	
Parsnip		Parsnip
Pea		
Potato		
Runner bean		
Rutabaga	Rutabaga	
Spinach		
Spring onion		
Tomato		
Turnip	Turnip	Turnip
Zucchini		

GROWING SPROUTING
SEEDS & MICROGREENS

Onion sprouts

Sprouting seeds and microgreens are eaten in salads, sandwiches or as a garnish for other dishes. Containing high levels of minerals, protein, fiber and enzymes, they are not only delicious but also nutrient-rich. The difference between the two is that sprouted seeds are harvested when the seed leaves are present and microgreens when the first true leaves appear.

Suitable plants include: alfalfa, aduki beans, amaranthus, arugula, beet, basil, broad beans, broccoli, buckwheat, cabbage, carrot, chard, coriander, celery, clover, fennel, kale, leek, lovage, Mesembryanthemum chrystallinum, mizuna greens, mustard salad, onion, Oxalis, peas, radish, red mustard, salad cress, salad mixes, soy bean, wheatgrass.

sprouting seeds

Seed sowing
They can be sown in a "seed sprouter," a clear glass jar with a cheesecloth "lid" or a similar receptacle. Sterilize the equipment before use and after every 3 or 4 crops of seedlings by soaking for 10 minutes in a solution of 1 tablespoon of bleach or similar to a pint of water, before scrubbing and rinsing thoroughly.

To encourage germination, soak seeds for the time recommended on the seed packet at a 3:1 ratio of water to seed to start the germination process. Stir the seeds with a tablespoon or fork to ensure they are all moistened then place them in the sprouting container. Rinse the seeds thoroughly 2 to 3 times a day, using water under a high pressure and drain thoroughly to avoid disease problems. Keep the seedlings in a bright position, away from scorching sunlight and maintain the temperature between 55–70°F (13–21°C).

Harvesting and Storing
Harvest when the seedling leaves appear.

Ensure that sprouts are properly dry before storing in the refrigerator. Around 12 hours after their final watering, drain the seedlings thoroughly, using a salad spinner if possible and store them in a sealed plastic bag to prevent dessication. They will store for several days in the salad drawer of the fridge. When eating large quantities of sprouts, it is advisable to cook them first.

microgreens

At the time of writing, microgreens are very trendy and valued by top chefs for the subtle flavor of their stems. They are easy to grow and are the ideal way to make the most of half-used seed packages. Seedlings of a wide range of herbs and vegetables can be used as microgreens, particularly those whose leaves are traditionally eaten at maturity. Do not use seedlings from plants with poisonous leaves like tomato, potato and rhubarb.

Seed sowing
Sow successively from spring to autumn for a constant supply. Sow in seed trays in a 2-inch layer of compost. For larger volumes, make a wooden frame in a heated propagator in spring and fill it with compost to make a large seed bed. Sow seeds close together over the surface of the compost, but not so densely that they are too congested and prone to disease. Cover with a layer of compost or vermiculite or perlite to reduce moisture loss and keep the stems clean, and place the seed tray in a warm, bright place.

When growing seedlings on a windowsill, turn the trays every two or three days to maintain balanced growth and stop them from growing toward the light. Keep the compost moist but not waterlogged.

Harvesting and Storing
Harvest with a pair of scissors when the first true leaves appear, retaining as much of the stem as possible. Use new compost for each crop, adding used material to your compost heap. Large seeds like peas can be germinated on several layers of moist paper towel.

Water 24 hours before storing as they deteriorate rapidly if refrigerated when wet. Microgreens with soft stems are more vulnerable to damage through being wet when stored.

Small scale sprouting is still productive

GROWING MINI VEGETABLES

Miniature, or baby, vegetables are either varieties that are suitable for harvesting when young or those that have been specifically bred to be naturally small at maturity. Initially, mini vegetables were regarded as novelty crops, but they have now found a niche among small households where growing space is limited and are often grown for the pure virtue of being attractive. Many are ready to harvest in as little as 12 weeks and make a useful short-term crop.

Cultivation
Mini vegetables grow successfully in beds, pots, window boxes and hanging baskets but need at least 8 inch depth of compost or soil. The growing medium must be fertile and crops should be watered regularly and thoroughly to maintain rapid growth. Weekly feeding throughout the growing season is recommended.

Planning
Most miniature vegetables are grown from seed, with successional sowing every 2 or 3 weeks extending the harvesting period. Always have a supply of young plants or seedlings growing in pots or modules for transplanting when space becomes available.

Plant Density
By increasing the number of plants per square foot, competition between plants can be used to restrict the growth of larger cultivars. This is not true of all vegetables: lettuce do not form a good heart at close spacings unless naturally small cultivars are chosen.

Selecting Varieties
The planting distances for varieties sold as mini vegetables are indicated on the package. The spacing of larger varieties for harvesting when young can be gauged by experimenting.

Crops to Harvest Within Twelve Weeks of Sowing

Beet
This is one of the oldest crops grown as small vegetables, mainly for processing. Sow thickly, thinning to 1 inch apart with 6 inches between rows. Mini varieties include 'Pronto', 'Boro' and 'Pablo'.

Carrot
Amsterdam types can be grown for harvesting when small by sowing thickly and thinning to ½ inch apart in rows 6 inches apart. Varieties include 'Mini Finger' and 'Ideal'.

Kohlrabi
Harvest when the size of a golf ball for a milder flavor. Sow thickly, thinning to 1 inch apart with 6 inches between rows. The ultimate size is controlled by high-density sowing. 'Quickstar' and 'Logo' are mini varieties.

Onion
Bunching cultivars like 'Ishikura' and 'Hikari' are ideal as they do not form bulbs, and their erect foliage means they can be sown at higher density. For pickling onions try growing 'Paris Silverskin'.

Turnip
Sow thickly, thinning to 1 inch with 6 inches between rows for table-tennis ball sized roots. Grow 'Tokyo Cross' or 'Atlantic' for mini vegetables.

Zucchini
Most cultivars are suitable, especially F1 hybrids. Allow 24 inches between plants. Harvest several times a week to extend the cropping period. 'Black Forest' is a climber. 'Sunburst' and its relatives can be harvested when small.

Crops to Harvest Within Twenty Weeks of Sowing

Brussels Sprout
Growing tall, old cultivars such as 'Bedford' which are spaced 12 inches in and between the rows provides a continuous supply of sprouts throughout the autumn and winter. Due to their height, make sure that the rooting depth is at least 12 inches.

Cabbage
Try the small savoy 'Protovoy' and 'Primero' as mini vegetables. 'Protovoy' should be planted 6 inches apart in the rows with 2 inches between rows, 'Primero' at 6 inches square.

Cauliflower
Grown at 6-inch spacings, it is possible to produce small-headed cauliflowers about the size of a tennis ball. These take an average of 17 weeks from sowing until harvest. The mini variety 'Idol' is suitable for freezing.

Corn
These do not need to be grown in a block as they are harvested before pollination when the tassels begin to show. They should be spaced 12 x 12 inches apart. A good crop will depend on how sunny the summer is. Try the mini variety 'Minipop'.

Kale
Allow 6 inches square between each plant and harvest regularly to prevent the leaves from becoming stringy. Sow at 10-day intervals for successional cropping. 'Showbor' is a mini variety.

Leek
Spaced ½ inch apart in rows 6 inches apart, mini leeks have a mild flavor and can be steamed or eaten raw in salads. 'King Richard' is a good variety.

Parsnip
The narrow-rooted "bayonet" types are the best. Thin to 2 inches apart in rows 6 inches apart. Allow about 15 weeks from sowing. 'Lancer', a mini variety, is very resistant to canker.

Spinach
Sow every 2 weeks for continuous production. Protection may be needed for the early and late sowings. Choose cultivars with mildew resistance.

VEGETABLE DYES & OTHER USES

With vegetables being our primary food source, we often look no further than their use as food crops. However, many vegetables do have one (or more) other uses — as the basis for dyes, medicines, natural chemicals and even wines.

Dyes

Few vegetables contain plant juices with residual colors; all must be used with a mordant and the color varies according to the type used. Most vegetable dyes fade with time, and can only be used on natural fibers. The following are worth trying:

Beet: although notorious for staining the skin, extracted juices produce only drab brown or fawn when used for dying.

Onion bulbs are covered with several layers of dry, brown, papery skins. Large quantities are needed for dying and although the natural colors, ranging from pale yellow to a copper-brown, are bold, they tend to fade rapidly when exposed to light.

Leeks: the "flags" or foliage produce yellow and dull brown pigments.

Medicines

Food is considered by many as a potent medicine, providing the vitamins and minerals required for good health. It also contains pharmacological agents that act as medicines when ingested. The saying 'you are what you eat' is very true: a balanced diet promotes good health.

With the popularity of "fast food," vegetable intake has on average been reduced, thus creating an imbalanced diet. A good diet is one incorporating vegetables that ward off and relieve illness. Many vegetables, particularly "greens" and carrots, contain beta carotene, a precursor of vitamin A which is believed to prevent cancer; others, like garlic, reduce cholesterol. A diet rich in fiber can help prevent bowel cancer, and researchers have suggested that soya can help against breast cancer. Studies are currently underway to examine whether diet can explain differences in cancer rates between northern and southern Europe.

The nutritional value and medicinal uses of each vegetable are indicated under their individual entries. Vegetables are the ideal way to eat your way to health.

Wine

Many vegetable gardeners are also keen winemakers. A good-quality vegetable wine certainly makes an interesting topic of conversation over a meal. Beet, carrot, celery, parsnip and rhubarb are all excellent — but guests should be reminded to leave their cars at home as the alcohol content is usually high. Root vegetables with a high sugar content, such as parsnips, generally produce a wine that is very sweet.

Other Uses

Some vegetables make natural cosmetics, including face creams and packs. Cucumber and avocado are particularly good examples.

THE VEGETABLE GROWER'S DIARY

Planting seeds

This calendar assumes that the vegetable garden lies in northern Europe, the average date of the last major frost in spring being April 1 and an average date for the first frost being October 20. Gardeners with different frost dates can adjust this calendar accordingly. But, as any gardener knows, it is difficult to be precise — each year is different, likewise each garden. So use this calendar as a general guide, and see also page 272.

january
(Midwinter)

Prepare cropping plans and order seed. Lime autumn-dug plots if necessary. Place early seed potatoes in shallow boxes, with 'eyes' uppermost, and store in a light, frost-free place. Towards the end of the month, plant out shallots if soil is moist enough.

Protected cropping: sow radishes and carrots in growbags or in the borders of a cold greenhouse; sow lettuce for growing under cloches; and leeks.

february
(Late winter/early spring)

Sow broad beans, early peas and spinach. Sow early-maturing cabbage and cauliflowers in pots from the middle of the month onwards. "Chit" potatoes.

Protected cropping: sow cabbages, carrots, lettuces and radishes under cloches or in a polyethylene tunnel

march
(Early spring)

Plant onion sets in prepared ground. Sow beets, cabbage, carrots, parsnip, lettuce and maincrop peas.

Protected cropping: plant lettuce under cloches or in plastic tunnels, sow salad onions in growbags in an unheated greenhouse for early crops. Sow early cabbages and cauliflowers under glass for transplanting in mid-April and tomatoes from late March to early April.

Preparing the soil for seed sowing

april
(Mid-spring)

Dig plots occupied by winter greens and prepare for leeks; plant maincrop potatoes, cabbages and cauliflowers (sown under cover in March). Make further sowings of beets, radishes, spinach, carrots, cauliflower, maincrop peas, broad beans and parsnips. Sow Iceberg lettuce, salad onions and sea kale. From late April, sow winter cauliflower, Savoy cabbage, kale and broccoli into seedbeds. Transplant cabbages and cauliflowers sown in nursery beds in February. Pinch out the growing tips of flowering broad beans.

Protected cropping: tomatoes sown and "pricked out" in late March or early April should be transferred to a cold frame and hardened off. Sow marrows, squashes and corn at the end of the month. Prepare greenhouse borders or growbags for tomatoes, and plant towards the end of the month.

may
(Late spring)

Sow French and runner beans, carrots, zucchini, outdoor cucumbers, lettuce, turnips, spinach and parsley. Plant out celeriac, celery, corn and summer cabbage. Harvest asparagus, broad beans, cauliflowers, peas, radish and spinach. Earth up potatoes.

Protected cropping: transplant eggplant, outdoor cucumbers, tomatoes, peppers and corn.

june
(Early summer)

Sow French and runner beans, Chinese cabbage, carrots, zucchini, outdoor cucumbers, lettuce, turnips, spinach and parsley. Transplant celery, summer cabbage and tomatoes. Harvest asparagus, broad beans, broccoli, cauliflowers, peas, radish, spinach and turnips.

Protected cropping: transplant eggplant and corn; pollinate tomato plants.

july
(Midsummer)

Sow final crops of beets, carrots, lettuce, turnips, spinach and parsley. Sow salad onions, spring cabbage and sea kale for overwintering. Sow keeping onions in a seedbed for transplanting the following March. In colder areas, plant leeks sown in cold frames in January at the beginning of the month. Remove basal suckers from early celery, thoroughly water and earth up.

Protected cropping: harvest cucumbers and tomatoes regularly to encourage further fruiting, and pinch out the growing point when each stem contains about 5 or 6 trusses of fruit.

august
(Late summer)

Sow turnips for spring "greens" and Japanese onions for overwintering. Sow spring cabbage in nursery rows. To prevent windrock in autumn and winter, draw soil around the stems of winter greens, particularly Brussels sprouts, kale and broccoli. Earth up trench celery. Harvest maincrop onions, ensuring that the bulbs' outer skins are well ripened before storing.

Protected cropping: harvest cucumbers and tomatoes regularly, self-pollinate tomatoes.

A bell jar can be used to protect crops

september
(Early autumn)

Order seed catalogs for the following year. Plant out spring cabbages into permanent positions. Sow spinach for harvesting in April. Lift maincrop carrots, beets and potatoes, and store in a cool, dark place: later sowings may be left in the ground. Earth up celery before severe frosts. Lift tomato plants with fruits still attached and store; ripen on straw under cloches or in the greenhouse. Wrap green fruits in paper and store in the dark.

Protected cropping: plant thinnings from late-sown salads in frames or under cloches to provide crops during winter. Lettuces reaching maturity should be covered with cloches or frames; sow further crops in a cold frame. The autumn is a good time to lay drains through waterlogged sites.

october
(Mid-autumn)

Lift potatoes, beet and carrots for storing. Tie onions on to ropes when the skins have thoroughly ripened. Transplant lettuces sown in July to a well-drained, protected site to overwinter. Plant root cuttings of sea kale in pots of sand and leave them in a sheltered place until the spring. Cut down asparagus foliage as it turns yellow. Tidy the vegetable garden, removing all plant debris. Double-dig, adding organic matter, and lime if necessary.

Protected cropping: protect July-sown parsley with cloches for overwintering. Sow lettuce in greenhouse borders or growbags for cutting in the spring. Continue harvesting green tomatoes, storing in a dark frost-free place to ripen. Clear grow-bags used for cucumbers, peppers and tomatoes in the summer and replant with winter lettuce.

november
(Late autumn)

Sow broad beans, and round-seeded peas in the open; protect with cloches if necessary. Remove dying leaves from winter greens, allowing air to circulate between plants. Check stored vegetables regularly and remove any showing signs of decay. Use those which are slightly damaged immediately. Sow green manure.

Protected cropping: lift and store crowns of chicory as well as sea kale.

december
(Early winter)

Plan next year's rotation of vegetables, ordering seeds as soon as possible. Prepare a seed-sowing schedule. Lift and store swede and late-sown carrots. If heavy falls of snow or prolonged frosts are forecast, lift small quantities of vegetables such as celery, leeks and parsnips and store under cover in a cool, easily accessible place. Finish digging before the soil becomes waterlogged. On clay, spread sharp sand, old potting compost or well-rotted leaf mold on the surface and dig in as soon as conditions are favorable, allowing the frost to break down the soil. Sow green manure on sandy soils or cover with compost to reduce leaching.

GLOSSARY

Annual A plant completing its life cycle from germination to seed in one growing season.

Base dressing An application of organic matter or fertilizer, applied to the soil prior to planting or sowing.

Bed system A method of planting vegetables in close blocks or multiple rows.

Beta carotene The orange-yellow plant pigment and precursor of vitamin A that protects against certain cancers and heart disease.

Biennial A plant completing its life cycle in a two-year period.

Blanch To exclude light from leaves and stems and prevent development of green coloration. In the culinary sense, to immerse in boiling water for the removal of skin or color, often as a preparation for freezing.

Bolt To flower and produce seed prematurely.

Brassica Member of the cabbage family (*Brassicaceae*).

Broadcast To scatter granular substances such as seeds, fertilizer or pesticide evenly over an area of ground.

Bulb A modified plant stem, with swollen leaves acting as a storage organ.

Capping A crust forming on the surface of soil damaged by compaction, heavy rain or watering.

Catch-crop A rapidly maturing crop sown among slow-growing vegetables to make maximum use of the ground.

Chitting Pregermination of seeds before sowing. The same term is used for sprouting potatoes.

Clamp A structure made of earth for storing root vegetables outdoors.

Climber A plant that naturally grows upwards covering supports or other plants.

Cloche A small portable structure, often made of plastic or glass, used to protect early crops grown outdoors.

Cold frame A low-lying square or rectangular unheated structure, with a glass or plastic lid.

Compost Decomposed organic material used as soil conditioner, mulch, potting or seed-sowing medium.

Crop rotation A system where crops are grown in different plots on a three- or four-year cycle, limiting the buildup of pests and diseases and making the best use of soil nutrients.

Cultivar A contraction of "cultivated variety," a group of cultivated plants that retain desirable characteristics when propagated.

Cultivate The practice of growing plants in soil or compost. Can also be used to describe methods of soil preparation.

Cut and come again crops Seedlings, mature or semi-mature varieties, where several harvests can be taken from one crop.

Deciduous Plants that lose leaves at the end of the growing season and redevelop them the following year.

Dormancy Temporary cessation of growth during the dormant season.

Double digging A cultivation technique that penetrates to two spades' depth, also known as trench digging or bastard trenching.

Earth up To draw the soil around the base for support or to cover a plant for the purpose of blanching.

Evergreen Plants retaining their leaves throughout the year.

F1 Hybrid First-generation plants obtained by crossing two selected pure-breeding parents to produce uniform vigorous offspring.

Fanging A term used to describe the forking of a root vegetable.

Fertilizer A chemical or group of chemicals applied to the soil or plants to provide nutrition.

Fleece Lightweight, woven polypropylene cover used for crop protection.

Floating mulch (floating cloche) Sheets of flexible lightweight material placed over plants to provide protection.

Fluid sow A method for sowing germinated seeds into the soil using a carrier gel.

Folic acid Part of the vitamin B complex, found in leafy vegetables. Deficiency of folic acid causes anemia.

Friable Used to describe soil with a crumbly, workable texture, capable of forming a tilth.

Fungicide Chemical used for the control and eradication of fungi.

Genus A taxonomic classification used to describe plants with several similar characteristics.

Germination The chemical and physical changes that take place as a seed starts to grow.

Green manure A rapidly maturing, leafy crop grown for incorporation into the soil to improve its structure and nutrient levels.

Growbag A bag of compost used as a growing medium.

Half hardy Plants that tolerate low temperatures but not frost.

Harden off To acclimatize plants gradually, enabling them to withstand cooler conditions.

Hardy Plants that can withstand frost without protection.

Haulm The foliage of plants such as potatoes.

Heart up The stage at which leafy vegetables, like cabbage and lettuce, swell to form a dense cluster of central leaves.

Heavy soil A soil with a high proportion of clay particles, prone to waterlogging in winter and drying in summer.

Herbicide A chemical used to control and eradicate weeds.

Humus The organic decayed remains of plant material in soils.

Hybrid A variety of plant resulting from the crossing of two distinct species or genera.

Inorganic Term used to describe fertilizers made from refined naturally-occurring chemicals, or artificial fertilizers.

Insecticide Chemical used to eradicate insects.

Intercropping The practice of planting fast-growing vegetable crops between slower-growing varieties (see *Catch-crop*).

Inulin An easily digestible form of carbohydrate.

John Innes compost Loam-based growing medium made to standardized formulas.

Leaching The downward washing and loss of soluble nutrients from topsoil.

Leaf A plant organ containing chlorophyll essential for photosynthesis.

Leafmold Decaying leaves.

Legume A single-celled fruit containing several seeds that splits on maturity, e.g., beans and peas.

Lime Calcium compounds used to raise the pH of the soil.

Loam The term used for a soil of medium texture.

Maincrop The largest crop produced throughout the main growing season. Also used to describe the cultivars used.

Module A generic term describing the containers used for propagating and growing young plants.

Mulch A layer of organic or inorganic material laid over the ground that controls weeds, protects the soil surface and conserves moisture.

Nematacide Chemical used for the control and eradication of nematodes (eelworms).

Neutral Soil or compost with a pH value of 7, which is neither acid nor alkaline (see pH).

Nutrients Minerals that are essential for plant growth.

Organic Term used to describe substances that are derived from natural materials. Also used to denote gardening without the use of synthetic chemicals and composts, mulches and associated material.

Pan A layer of compacted soil that is impermeable to water and oxygen, and impedes root development and drainage.

Perennial Non-woody plants that die back and become dormant during winter, regrowing the following spring.

pH A measure of acidity or alkalinity. The scale ranges from 0 to 14, and is an indicator of the soluble calcium within a soil or growing medium. A pH below 7 is acid and above, alkaline.

Pinch out To remove the growing tip of a plant to induce branching.

Potager An ornamental vegetable garden.

Pot on To move a plant in to a larger pot.

Prick out To transfer seedlings, from a seedbed or tray, to a further pot, tray or seedbed.

Propagation The increase of plant numbers by seed or vegetative means.

Radicle A seedling root.

Rhizome A fleshy underground stem that acts as a storage organ.

Root The part of the plant that is responsible for absorbing water and nutrients and for anchoring the plant into the growing medium.

Root crops Vegetables grown for their edible roots, e.g., carrot and parsnip.

Seed A ripened plant ovule containing a dormant embryo, that is capable of forming a new plant.

Seed leaves or cotyledons The first leaf or leaves formed by a seed after germination.

Seedling A young plant grown from seed.

Sets Small onions, shallots or potatoes used for planting.

Shoot A branch, stem or twig of a plant.

Shrub A plant with woody stems, branching at or near the base.

Sideshoot A branch, stem or twig growing from a main stem of a plant.

Single digging A cultivation technique that penetrates to one spade's depth.

Species A taxonomic classification of similar closely related plants.

Spore The reproductive body of a nonflowering plant.

Stale seedbed method A cultivation technique whereby the seedbed is created and subsequent weed growth is removed before crops are sown or planted.

Thinning out seedlings

Stem The main axis of a plant, from which lateral branches appear.

Subsoil Layers of less fertile soil immediately below the topsoil.

Sucker A stem originating below soil level, usually from the plant's roots or underground stem.

Systemic or translocated A term used to describe a chemical that is absorbed by a plant at one point and then circulated through its sap system.

Tap root The primary anchoring root of a plant, usually growing straight down into the soil. In vegetables this is often used for food storage.

Tender Plant material that is intolerant of cool conditions.

Thinning The removal of seedlings or shoots to improve tle quality of those that remain.

Tilth The surface layer of soil produced by cultivation and soil improvement.

Top-dressing The application of fertilizers or bulky organic matter to the soil surface, while the plants are in situ.

Topsoil The upper, usually most fertile layer of soil.

Transpiration The loss by evaporation of moisture from plant leaves and stems.

Transplant To move a plant from one growing position to another.

Tuber A swollen underground stem used to store moisture and nutrients.

Variety Used in the vernacular to describe different kinds of plants. Also used in botanical classification to describe a naturally occurring variant (varietas) of a plant.

Vegetative Used to describe parts of a plant that are capable of growth.

Weathering Using the effect of climatic conditions to break down large lumps of soil into small particles.

Wet down To wet the floors and benches in a greenhouse in order to increase humidity and lower high temperatures.

Wind-rock Destabilizing of plant roots by wind action.

ROYAL HORTICULTURAL SOCIETY AWARDS

After cultural trials, the RHS grants an Award of Garden Merit (AGM) to plants of outstanding excellence. Some plants are judged Highly Commended (HC). An asterisk (*) beside a variety name in the A–Z indicates a vegetable that has received an RHS award. the following list includes all RHS awards made up until the end of 2007. For current information visit www.rhs.org.

In the United States All-American Selections, a national network of trial grounds, AAS awards medals annually to the best new bedding plants and vegetable and fruit varieties, and to plants that are proven to be consistently superior performers. For a list of the AAS Vegetable Award winners from 1933 onward, go to www.all-americaselections.org.

Allium cepa (Onion)
Salad type (non bulbing with strong flavor — A. fistulosum and hybrids): 'Beltsville Bunching', 'Emerald Isle', 'Emerald Star', 'Feast', 'Guardsman', 'Isiko', 'Isikura', 'Laser', 'Long White Koshigaya', 'Parade', 'Photon', 'Savel', 'Summer Isle', 'White Spear'
Salad type (traditional): 'Deep Purple', 'Elody', 'Lilia', 'Ramrod', 'White Lisbon', 'Winter Over', 'Winter White Bunching'
Maincrop bulb type: 'Golden Bear', 'Goldito', 'Hygro', 'Hyton', 'Marco', 'Rijnsburger 5 Balstora', 'Unwins Exhibition'
Overwintered bulb type, grown from seed: 'Buffalo', 'Imai Early Yellow'
Bulb type grown from sets: 'Autumn Gold Improved', 'Centurion', 'Hercules', 'Jagro', 'Jetset', Setton', 'Sturon', 'Turbo'
Red, from seed or sets: 'Red Baron', 'Red Spark'

Allium cepa Aggregatum Group (Shallot)
'Atlantic', 'Delvad', 'Giant Yellow Improved', 'Golden Gourmet', 'Jermor', 'Longor', 'Matador', 'Pikant', 'Santé', 'Success'

Allium porrum (Leek)
Early maturing type: 'Autumn Giant — Porvite', 'Autumn Mammoth 3 — Firena', 'Brecon', 'Carlton', 'King Richard', 'Mammoth Blanch', 'Pancho', 'Swiss Giant — Prelina', 'Swiss Giant — Tilina', 'Upton'
Maincrop type: 'Apollo', 'Autumn Mammoth 3 — Cobra', 'Autumn Mammoth' — Enak', 'Blauwgroene Herfst — Profina', 'Blauwgroene Herfst — Verina', 'Blue Green Autumn — Conora', 'Blue Green Autumn — Poristo', 'Blue Green Winter — Laura', 'Giant Winter — Catalina', 'Kajak', 'Longbow', 'Mammoth Pot', 'Oarsman', 'Swiss Giant — Jolant', 'Toledo', 'Winterreuzen — Granada'

Allium sativum (Garlic)
'Arno', 'Cristo', 'Early Wight', 'Eco', 'Germidour', 'Ivory', 'Long Keeper', 'Solent White', 'Spring Wight', 'Wight Cristo'

Apium graveolens var. dulce (Celery)
'Celebrity', 'Crystal', 'Giant Pink — Mammoth Pink', 'Granada', 'Ivory Tower', 'Lathom Self Blanching Galaxy', 'Lathhom Self Blanching', 'Loret', 'Loretta', 'Moonbeam', 'Octavius', 'Tango', 'Victoria'

Apium graveolens var. rapaceum (Celeriac)
'Diamant', 'Kojak', 'Monarch', 'Prinz'

Asparagus officinalis (Asparagus)
'Backlim', 'Connover's Colossal', 'Gijnlim', 'Lucullus'

Beta vulgaris subsp. vulgaris (Beet)
'Cheltenam Green Top', 'Forono', 'Action', 'Alto', 'Bikores', 'Boltardy', 'Bonel', 'Boro', 'Monodet', 'Monogram', 'Pablo', 'Pronto', 'Red Ace', 'Regala', 'Rubidus', 'Solo', 'Wodan'

Beta vulgaris subsp. cicula var. flavescens (Chard)
'Bright Lights', 'Bright Yellow', 'Charlotte', 'Fordhook Giant', 'Lucullus', 'Rhubarb Chard'

Beta vulgaris subsp. cicula var. cicula (Spinach Beet)
'Perpetual Spinach'

Brassica napus Napobrassica Group (Rutabaga)
'Brora', 'Magres', 'Ruby', 'Wilhelmsburger'

Brassica oleracea Acephala Group (Kale)
'Afro', 'Bornick', 'Fribor', 'Redbor', 'Reflex', 'Winterbor'

Brassica oleracea Botrytis Group (Cauliflower)
Winter type for spring heading (maturing from March to May): 'Admirable', 'Aalsmeer', 'Christingle', 'Colombo', 'Evita', 'Galleon', 'Jerome', 'Martian', 'Mayfair', 'Nomad', 'Patriot', 'Prestige', 'Walcheren Winter — Armado', 'Walcheren Winter — Armado May'
Summer heading type (season June to mid-July): 'Amsterdam', 'Andes', 'Asterix', 'Aubade', 'Avalanche', 'Aviron', 'Barcelona', 'Beauty', 'Fargo', 'Fastman', 'Flamenco', 'Gypsy', 'Mayflower', 'Nautilus', 'Perfection', 'Plana', 'Predominant', 'White Rock'
Autumn heading type (season September to November): 'Autumn Glory', 'Aviso', 'Belot', 'Castlegrant', 'Kestel', 'Lindon', 'Minneapolis', 'Moby Dick', 'Pavilion', 'Regata', 'Skywalker', 'Talbot', 'Valtos', 'Vidoke', 'White Excel'
Coloured and romanesco type: 'Alverda', 'Cheddar',

'Emeraude', 'Esmeraldo', 'Graffiti', 'Marmalade', 'Minaret', 'Red Lion', 'Veronica', 'Violet Queen', 'Violetta Italia'

Brassica oleracea Capitata Group (Cabbage)
Spring type: 'Dorado', 'Duncan', 'Durham Elf', 'First Early Market — Early Market', 'First Early Market — Mastercut', 'First Early Market', 'Jason', 'Offenham Myatt's Offenham Compacta', 'Offenham — Mastergreen', 'Pixie', 'Pyramid', 'Sparkel'
Summer type (season June to August): 'Augustor', 'Candissa', 'Cape Horn', 'Charmant', 'Derby Day', 'Elisa', 'Excel', 'First of June', 'Golden Cross', 'Gonzales', 'Green Express', 'Grenadier', 'Greyhound', 'Hermes', 'Hispi', 'Hotspur', 'Independence', 'Marshall's Kingspi', 'Metino', 'Nordri', 'Patron', 'Puma', 'Pyramid', 'Redsky', 'Shelta', 'Spitfire', 'Stonehead'
Savoy type (season September to March): 'Alaska', 'Clarissa', 'Denver', 'Endeavour', 'Famosa', 'Julius', 'Midvoy', 'Primavoy', 'Protovoy', 'Taler', 'Tarvoy', 'Tundra', 'Wintessa', 'Wivoy'
Early red type (non-storing; season September to October): 'Langedijker Red Early', 'Rodeo', 'Rondy', 'Rookie', 'Ruby Ball'
Winter hybrid type (season November to March): 'Beretta', 'Celtic', 'Colt', 'Embassy', 'Renton', 'Roulette', 'Winchester'
January King Type (season November to March): 'Flagship', 'Holly', 'Marabel', 'Robin'
Winter white type (for storage): 'Marathon'

Brassica oleracea Gemmifera Group (Brussels Sprout)
'Abacus', 'Bosworth', 'Braveheart', 'Cascade', 'Cavalier', 'Clodius', 'Diablo', 'Eclipsus', 'Genius', 'Icarus', 'Igor', 'Lunet', 'Maximus', 'Montgomery', 'Nelson', 'Oliver', 'Patent', 'Revenge', 'Roger', 'Romulus', 'Silverline', 'Wellington'

Brassica oleracea Gongylodes Group (Kohlrabi)
'Adriana', 'Domino', 'Erko', 'Kolibri', 'Kongo', 'Korist', 'Lanro', 'Olivia', 'Quickstar', 'Rapidstar'

Brassica oleracea Italica Group (Broccoli, Sprouting)
Purple sprouting broccoli: 'Bordeaux', 'Claret', 'Early Purple Sprouting Improved', 'Late Purple Sprouting', 'Purple Sprouting Improved', 'Red Arrow', 'Red Spear', 'Redhead'
White sprouting broccoli: 'White Eye', 'White Star'

Brassica oleracea Italica Group (Broccoli)
'Arcadia', 'Belstar', 'Corvet', 'Fiesta', 'Flash', 'Griffen', 'Hydra', 'Kabuki', 'Lord', 'Mistral', 'Skiff', 'Tiara', 'Trixie', 'Viking'

SELECTED BIBLIOGRAPHY & OTHER USEFUL BOOKS

The Allotment Book
Andi Clevely
(Collins, 2008)

The Allotment Book: Seasonal Planner and Cookbook
Andi Clevely
(Collins, 2008)

Biodynamic Gardening
John Soper
(Souvenir Press, 1983)

Bob Flowerdew's Complete Book of Companion Gardening (New Edition)
Bob Flowerdew
(Kyle Cathie 2004)

Collins Guide to the Pests, Diseases and Disorders of Garden Plants
Stefan Buczacki & K. M. Harris
(Harper Collins, 1994)

The Complete Know and Grow Vegetables
J.K.A. Bleasdale & P.J. Salter
(Oxford Paperbacks, 1991)

Control Pests
Richard Jones
(Impact Publishing, 2007)

Create Compost
Pauline Pears
(Impact Publishing, 2007)

Creative Vegetable Gardening
Joy Larcom
(Mitchell Beazley, 2008)

Crops in Pots: 50 Great Container Projects Using Vegetables, Fruit and Herbs
Bob Purnell
(Hamlyn, 2007)

Domestication of Plants in the Old World
Daniel Zohary & Maria Hopf
(Oxford Science Publications, 1994)

Dye Plants and Dyeing
John & Margaret Cannon
(Herbert Press, 1994)

Encyclopedia of Gardening (RHS) (Revised Edition)
Christopher Brickell
(Dorling Kindersley, 2007)

The English Gardener
William Cobbett
(Cobbett, 1833)

Gardening and Planting by the Moon 2008
Nick Kollerstrom
(Quantum/Foulsham; published yearly)

Growing Fruit and Vegetables on a Bed System the Organic Way (new edition)
Pauline Pears
(Search Press Ltd, 2004)

The Half-hour Allotment (RHS)
Lia Leendertz
(Frances Lincoln, 2006)

HDRA: Encyclopedia of Organic Gardening (Henry Doubleday Research Association)
Pauline Pears
(Dorling Kindersley, 2005)

Jane Grigson's Vegetable Book
Jane Grigson
(Penguin, 1988)

The Gardeners and Florists Dictionary or a Complete System of Horticulture: Volumes 1 & 2
Phillip Miller
(Charles Rivington, 1724)

Gourmet Gardener (New Edition)
Bob Flowerdew
(Kyle Cathie, 2007)

Grow Your Own Veg (RHS)
Carol Klein & Royal Horticultural Society
(Mitchell Beazley, 2007)

The History and Social Influence of the Potato
Redcliffe Salaman
(Cambridge University Press, 1984)

The Kitchen Garden: a Historical Guide to Traditional Crops
David Stuart
(Hale, 1984)

Maison Rustique, or the Countrie Farme
Charles Estienne & Richard Surflet
(1600)

Organic Gardening: The Natural No-dig Way
Charles Dowding
(Green Books, 2007)

The Organic Salad Garden (New Edition)
Joy Larkcom & Roger Phillips
(Frances Lincoln, 2003)

Oriental Vegetables
Joy Larkcom
(Frances Lincoln, 2007)

The Ornamental Kitchen Garden
Geoff Hamilton
(BBC Books, 1990)

Queer Gear; How to Buy and Cook Exotic Fruits and Vegetables
Michael Allsop & Carolyn Heal
(Century Hutchinson, 1986)

RHS Pests and Diseases
Pippa Greenwood & Andrew Halstead
(Dorling Kindersley, 2007)

Tropical Planting and Gardening
H.F. MacMillan
(Malayan Nature Society, 1991)

The Vegetable Garden Displayed
Joy Larkcom
(RHS, 1992)

Vegetables
Roger Phillips & Martyn Rix
(Pan Macmillan, 1993)

Vegetables of South East Asia
G.A.C. Herklots
(Allen & Unwin, 1973)

The Yellow Book: NGS Gardens Open for Charity (Revised Edition)
Stephen Anderton, Tim Wonnacott & Zac Goldsmith
(The National Gardens Scheme, 2008)